Modern Astrologers

THE LIVES OF ALAN & BESSIE LEO

Copyright © 2018 by Kim Farnell

The right of Kim Farnell to be identified as the Author of the Work has been asserted by her in accordance with the Copyright, Designs and Patents Act 1988.

All rights reserved. No part of this book may be reproduced, stored in or introduced into a retrieval system, or transmitted, in any form, or by any means (electronic, mechanical, photocopying, recording or otherwise) without the prior written permission of the publisher, except in the case of brief quotations embodied in critical articles or reviews.

Published by Kim Farnell.

A catalogue record for this book is available on request from the British Library.

Cover design by Kim Farnell
Interior design by Kim Farnell

ISBN: 978-1-9993544-0-4
First Edition: January 2019

ACKNOWLEDGEMENTS

This book came into being after a discussion with Janet Lee who I thank for insisting that I got on with it.

On the theosophical front I am exceedingly grateful to Leslie Price for his feedback, assistance and remarkable networking skills. I also wish to thank Debbie Elliot and Kurt Leland (especially for their help with tracing membership records), Damon Scothern and Barry Thompson.

The Hermes Lodge were extremely helpful in supplying details of early meetings of the Lodge and background information about its formation. In particular, I thank Patricia Harris.

Thanks are due to Frederick Lacey's descendants for information about his life. I am grateful to Caroline Bonham and to John Halsey for sharing his research.

I am grateful to Lucya Szachnowski who kindly allowed me to see a copy of the horoscope Alan did for her grandmother, May Robbins, along with a full set of lessons from Alan's correspondence course.

Nicholas Campion kindly lent me the horoscope Alan prepared for David McCarthy.

Philip Graves was helpful in tracking down sources and references as well as dealing with numerous nitpicking queries while the book was in process.

Bernard Eccles supplied much appreciated feedback of early drafts of the text and I am grateful to Derek Norcott for proofreading it. Also my thanks to Nash Ventress for last minute assistance with deciphering Alan's handwriting.

Thanks to Geraldine Beskin and Kevin Tingay for discussions about Alan's occult and masonic life.

Thanks are also due to the as yet unmentioned members of the Alan Leo Facebook group who offered support, feedback and assistance while the book was being written: Israel Ajose; Catherine Blackledge; Frances Clynes; Adelais Farnell Sharp; Stevi Gaydon; Erica Georgiades; Geraldine Heil; Muriel Pécastaing-Boissière; Izabela Podlaska-Konkel and Geraldine Williams.

During the last two years, I have had innumerable discussions with a wide range of people about Alan's work and received valuable feedback. I apologise if I have forgotten to mention you here. That is my failing and doesn't mean your help is any the less appreciated.

CONTENTS

1: Was it not Curious?   1

2: Chiefly to Please Him   17

3: Forms the Most Hideous   27

4: Phrenologists Advancing   43

5: Flapdoodle Astrologers   55

6: Impulsive Souls   65

7: Count on my Support   79

8: Mrs Gaskell's Costume   91

9: Golden Chariot   99

10: All Kinds of Pretenders   111

11: No Trouble and Annoyance   127

12: Magnetic and Electric   133

13: To this High End   153

14: Torchbearer of Truth   163

15: Reverence and Obedience   183

16: All is Just a Vibration   197

17: Kind and Dear Souls   207

18: Dreaming Wonderful Dreams   213

19: Early Mimosa in the Garden	223
20: A Bomb More Cruel	233
21: Reaching Modernity	243
A Chart by Alan	249
Pseudonyms	257
Alan's family tree	259
Bessie's family tree	261
Works by Alan Leo	264
Images	266
Endnotes	267
Bibliography	279
Index	301

Nay, seer, I do not doubt thy mystic lore,
Nor question that the tenor of my life,
Past, present and the future, is revealed
There in my horoscope.

There is no puny planet, Sun or Moon,
Or zodiacal sign which can control
The God in us! If we bring that to bear
Upon events, we mould them to our wish:
'Tis when the infinite 'neath the finite gropes
That men are governed by their horoscopes.

To an Astrologer: Ella Wilcox Wheeler

A brief note on currency

Until 1971 British currency comprised pounds, shillings and pence. There were 12 pennies to the shilling and 20 shillings to the pound. A guinea was 1 pound and 1 shilling (21 shillings) and was used in auctions and legal contexts, although it was falling out of general use.

Prices could be expressed in a variety of ways. For example, 5 pounds and 3 shillings could be written £5/3, £5-3 or £5 5s. Shillings and pence would usually be written 3/6 (3 shillings and 6 pence). A dash was often used after the pound to indicate no pence 3/- (3 shillings).

Monetary amounts given in quotes have been left in their original form.

CHAPTER ONE

WAS IT NOT CURIOUS?

*I*N 1885 WILLIAM ALLAN SAT in a crowded waiting room. He'd never had much faith in doctors — they were expensive and he didn't like the idea of taking prescribed drugs. And a few years earlier his jaundice had been resolved by the simple expedient of ingesting rosemary. However, it was comforting to listen to chatter about how clever the doctor was.

Finally, it was his turn. 'How old are you?' asked Dr Richardson without preamble. 'Give me the place, time, and date of your birth.'[1]

William waited while Dr Richardson consulted his books and then drew a map with figures on it. 'You are suffering from kidney trouble, but will be quite well in about three weeks,' the doctor said, handing William a herbal prescription. 'Come back in a week.'[2]

It wasn't until William's third visit that he summoned up enough courage to ask what his birth details had to do with his illness.

'As I see by your map you can be trusted,' said the doctor, 'I will tell you. I study astrology.'[3] And he went on to explain what this meant, and how he found out by this means the treatment his patients required.

Fascinated, William listened closely. He was so absorbed that Dr Richardson asked him to come to tea on the following Sunday when he would show him how to cast a horoscope.

'Was it not curious ... that directly I heard the word "Astrology,"' said William later, 'I knew it, and knew that all I heard was true.'[4]

Indeed, it was curious. Especially as William later claimed to have begun his astrological studies about ten years earlier.[5] Perhaps it isn't important; at least, not as important as the fact that Robert Francke Richardson[i] became William's friend and taught him astrology.

Richardson operated his practice on Drury Hill, Nottingham, close to where he'd been born. He'd trained in medicine in Maine, USA from about 1870 and then lived in Cincinnati, Ohio. By 1877 he'd returned to Nottingham and married Eliza Radford, although Richardson was never registered as a doctor in Britain—he also doesn't appear to have graduated until 1887, which is when his advertisements begin to appear in the press.[ii]

HERBAL REMEDIES.—Quickest Cures; advice free.—Consult Dr. Richardson. (American Physician.)[6]

It was a competitive market. Drury Hill alone held four herbalists, and Nottingham was the home of Boot's chemist's. But you couldn't ask for a more picturesque location. Absurdly steep, the medieval Drury Hill was so narrow it was said that at its narrowest people from the two adjacent buildings could reach over and join hands.[iii] Following the cobbled pavements to the top, you reached two Regency town houses that sat over huge stone caves, one of which was circular with a carved central pillar and carved seating around the wall.

For the next two years William busied himself studying astrology. But there also were other things on his mind. Maybe it was due to his short temper. Perhaps he'd simply experienced a run of bad luck. Whatever the reason, when William moved to London in 1887, he was alone, unemployed and without a penny to his name. It wasn't the first time he'd been in this situation.

Three times he'd signed up as an apprentice, and three times it had gone wrong. He'd lasted three months as a draper's apprentice, six in a chemist's and two years in a grocer's shop—although that time he wasn't actually sacked. At sixteen he'd slept on the streets of Liverpool until he'd managed to find work. Two years later he was broke again, but things

---

i Sometimes given as 'Franks'. Born in Newark, Nottingham (1854–1917).
ii In later years, Richardson would claim telepathic powers (which greatly excited the *Daily Express*), Despite the support of the journalist W T Stead, who allowed the initial tests to take place at the *Review of Reviews* office, subsequent testing by the Society for Psychical Research resulted in abject failure, although the Society appeared to think he was a nice chap.
iii It narrowed to 4 foot 10 inches. Drury Hill was demolished in 1971 to make way for the entrance to the Broad Marsh Shopping Centre.

looked good for a while—until he was 'ruined by the dishonesty of his master who had robbed him to the utmost limit'.[7]

What he *didn't* do is work with the poor in the slums of London as he later claimed. However, he found work as a travelling salesman, selling automatic sweet machines. Who knew how long that would last?

London was the city of William's birth, and he knew the poor of the slums well—he'd started life as one of them, born 7 August 1860 at 20 Bowling Street, near Westminster Abbey. The street ceased to exist in 1869 as it was merged with Tufton Street,[iv] which it originally led to from Dean's Yard. Cheap and over-crowded lodging houses were filled with the poor and unfortunate, desperate to make a living however they could. Street musicians dressed in kilts wandered as they played bagpipes, pickpockets roamed on constant alert, and filthy and naked children swarmed, demonstrating their talents of language fit to burn the ears of the more genteel, while prostitutes touted for business in the multitude of pubs in the area. It was one of the worst areas of London, dubbed *The Devil's Acre* by Charles Dickens in the 1850s.[8]

Thomas Beames in his *Rookeries of London* makes it clear that Westminster in the mid-nineteenth century was nothing like the Westminster of today:

> The shelter and resort of lawless characters, who find a fitting home in the dirty, narrow, uncleansed streets,—its miserable, undrained, dilapidated courts and alleys, reproduced and rebuilt time after time with the determinate purpose of receiving only the degraded and outcast of the population. The accumulations of filth in the courts without an outlet—the absence of water—the crowding of people—the contamination of vice and idleness—the filthy stenches—the boarded rooms not weatherproof—the despair of improvement and better situation—and the facilities offered for sinking yet lower, by low and numberless beer-shops and pawnbrokers ... Added to these causes of wretchedness is the natural lowness of the ground, which requires the utmost resources of science to obviate its inevitable results; flooding cellars, densely peopled, with loathsome streams accumulating in the gutters and kennel-stagnant refuse waters emitting abominable smells—and noxious vapours increased by heaps of garbage by the road-side.[9]

---

iv Originally, Bowling Street was a continuation of Tufton Street northwards beyond Little Peter Street/Wood Street. When the streets were merged, a number of properties were renumbered.

Devils Acre by Gustav Doré

Unlike many local couples, William's parents were actually married. Caroline Beresford was living in Clerkenwell with her parents and five siblings when she met William Allan in a Methodist chapel. Born in Barnet in 1838, although her family originated from Lincolnshire, Caroline was one of six children. She'd become a Christian at the age of eleven and by adulthood was a member of the Plymouth Brethren.[v] The Brethren was one of many strict Christian sects that had sprung up early in the nineteenth century due to dissatisfaction with the Anglican Church. Brethren see themselves as a network of like-minded Christians, rather than a church, and rely on the Bible as the supreme authority.

William Allan (the elder), born in 1825, hailed from Edinburgh and was a hall porter in the dispensary of the nearby Westminster hospital. On 27 March 1845, at the age of eighteen, he'd joined the 78th Regiment of Highlanders as a private. The 78th was in India in May 1857 to help suppress the Indian Rebellion and took part in the recapture of Cawnpore and then the reinforcement of Lucknow. Allan had been present at the

---

[v] The occultist Aleister Crowley's family were Brethren as was that of Sir Robert Anderson the Scotland Yard detective, known for his involvement in the Jack the Ripper case.

Siege of Lucknow. He'd also spent twelve years in the East Indies, once being court-martialled for falling asleep at his post but also gaining two good conduct records. He was shot in the leg in 1857 by a musket ball while on duty and discharged 5 October 1858 due to his injury, which was to leave him lame for the rest of his life.

Caroline and Allan quickly became friends, marrying in 1859. A hastily compiled biography published after William's death detailed his unhappy childhood.

> [William] was born nearly seven years after his parents' marriage, and according to his mother's account was small for his age. As their income was a very limited one, his mother had not much time to nurse him; and, so she told me, he would play by himself in his cot or his high chair for hours, rarely cried, and was most patient and quiet. She described him as being a very solemn child! When quite a tiny tot he loved pictures, and would sit for hours absorbed in a rag picture book; a solemn, brown-eyed baby, who had to find his own amusements because two more children followed him quickly, a girl and a boy, born in rapid succession … was a young domestic drudge and always had a baby to look after, nurse, and amuse; and with a white apron folded about his small person he would often be made to wash up cups and saucers and lay the cloth; this at the early age of five or six.[10]

Which sounds sad, but couldn't have happened—at least, not in the way described. William's younger brother George wasn't born until 1867 when William was six, and by the time his other siblings arrived, William was already attending school.

According to the above-mentioned biography, Caroline and Allan had a stormy marriage—'she wanted to dominate him'[11]—and after a huge argument Caroline stormed off to Edinburgh around 1869 to stay with members of Allan's family while Allan went abroad, never revealing where he was but sending money for his children's maintenance. Reuben was born in Edinburgh 27 October 1869 followed by Caroline in 1871. Storming off to Edinburgh with a young child while pregnant was an odd thing to do for someone who had family a few streets away. Which is probably why it didn't happen.

Maybe it was a family trait, but Allan the elder also found it hard to hold down a job—he was unemployed in 1871, for example, although he soon found work as a hospital porter. However, he never disappeared abroad or anywhere else. And the family weren't penniless during the difficult times as he received a small pension. Plus, Caroline, the daughter of a master tailor, made money from her needlework. The family stayed in Edinburgh, living at the tenements in Wright's Houses, until at least 1872, moved to Dudley in Staffordshire, where David was born in 1875, and by 1881 they were living in Milton Terrace (later Pitt Street) Prestwich, Lancashire. By now, William had left home and lived in Manchester at 27 Collyhurst Street where he lodged with Amelia Simister.[vi] He's recorded as a 'provision shopman' on the 1881 census, although he clearly worked as a travelling salesman by this point as he also appears on the 1881 census in Stoke-on-Trent where he was staying with Phillip and Rebecca Burski, and is recorded as a 'fancy goods hawker'.[vii]

It's also unlikely William had grandparents straight out of a picture book:

> His only periods of joy being visits to his grandparents who lived in a pretty cottage at Wells. He described with gratitude the tenderness of the old couple to him, for Mr and Mrs Beresford loved their eldest grandchild and tried to make his visits happy ones. The old china tea cups, beautiful silver tea-pot, and thin bread and butter, served at 5 o'clock, remained in his memory. Especially did he remember the old-world garden and the flowers; but usually after a month's visit his mother would arrive on the scene, say she could not spare him any longer, and take him back to hard work.[12]

Neither side of the family appears to have had a connection to Wells, country cottages or flower-filled gardens (or even a connection to someone who could afford to buy a silver teapot), and the Beresfords stayed firmly in Clerkenwell throughout William's childhood. And, as we've already seen, William was never a 'domestic drudge'.

However, he and Caroline didn't get on. From his point of view, Caroline was obsessed with religion and reading *Foxe's Book of Martyrs*, a book that outlines the suffering of Protestants under the Catholic Church. He later complained she rose at five every morning and started

---

vi Widowed Amelia (1844–unknown) lived with her sons William (born 1868) and Frank (born 1877). Also lodging at the house was William Thompson (born 1860), a 'grocer shopman'.

vii Census enumerators distributed their schedules some days before they needed to be returned, advising households to include anyone who was out travelling or working and was not enumerated elsewhere. This led to a number of people appearing twice on a census, especially people who were on the move at census time.

the day with two hours of prayer. Perhaps that was when William was required to help around the house, something he resented as much as all young boys. 'I was made to take life seriously ... and Sunday was just a dreadful day in our home,' he said sulkily.[13]

In about 1876, William left home and began his blighted career. He slept at his workplace and rarely saw his family from this date.[viii] He was twenty-one when his employer died and his employer's brother offered him work in Manchester, working in, and later running, one of his two grocer's shops—at least that's how he described being a hawker.

Later, he ended up working as a clerk in a sewing machine factory, and after two years was promoted to a travelling salesman. As part of his job, William visited factories to superintend the fitting of machinery, hence finding himself in Nottingham in 1885 where he worked in a lace factory. This job was hard to handle as many of the men he had to supervise were much older than William. Then in 1887 his employer died, and he decided to return to the city of his birth to look for work.

He hadn't been in London long when he managed to land a job at Ebenezer Roberts's confectionery firm. The company, formed in 1852, owned a huge factory on Camberwell Road. The main premises was an old manor house surrounded by numerous workshops. It was so large that Roberts had made a private road running between the factory buildings and the counting houses, which gave access to two main roads, saving his employees a long journey, although this short-cut was also often used by locals. In addition to selling automatic sweet machines, Roberts sold his Patent Imperial Freezers and ice-cream powder, which were hugely popular and were later patented in the USA, Canada and India as well as in the UK. Part of the firm's success was due to the fact it was one of very few at the time to advertise based on testimonials. This was true modernity![ix]

Now in a better financial situation, in January 1890 William sought a house to rent. When he came across 12 Lugard Road in Peckham, near his work, he signed the lease and moved in the same day.

The area was made up of small back-to-back terraced houses, many of which were divided up into rooms that were rented as furnished apartments and filled with artisans and clerical staff travelling into the

---

viii William's father died in 1887 and Caroline died in Liverpool in 1901 after supporting herself through her sewing.
ix The ice-cream maker, which could apparently make twenty ices for less than a shilling, held ice-cream powder mixed with milk in an inner drum while the outer drum was filled with broken ice and salt. You simply turned a handle to create the ice-cream.

city and to the docks, as well as those working locally. A typical street, it hosted a pub, the Lugard Tavern, the Lugard Palace hotel, a masonic hall and numerous shops. It was also at the centre of a transport hub. In 1851 Thomas Tilling had started an innovative omnibus service from Peckham to London, the first to use pre-arranged bus stops which helped them run to a reliable timetable. Tilling's horse-drawn buses used the 'knifeboard' design which had extra seating on the roof on which passengers sat back to back, allowing extra passengers to be squeezed in, and his main depot was on Rye Lane in Peckham.

The nearby Queen's Road railway station had opened in 1866, a year after Peckham Rye station, and numerous lines converged in Peckham, allowing easy travel. Horse tram lines used two horses to pull a sixty-person car, offering a cheaper option than an omnibus or Hackney carriage.[x] Lugard Road itself was the location of a passing station for trams, allowing for easy changes, with numerous other passing stations within a few minutes' walk.

So it was easy for William to meet the first friend he made in London, Frederick William Lacey, with whom he could discuss astrology. Lacey obligingly describes William for us:

> The hair is dark, forehead high, eyes moderate in size, bright hazel in colour. The complexion is sanguine (dark), the appearance of the face thoughtful ... is fleshy, strong and in height about five feet seven inches, bones rather large, what many would call a 'well-made man'.[14]

In comparison, Lacey was:

> 5-ft. 8-in. in height, slim, black hair, on the head thin in texture, not the slightest tendency to curl or wave, beard thick in texture, very prolific, of black, light and dark brown shades. The head is long, the face oval, the complexion clear, more dark than fair, the eyes hazel in colour and very bright, the neck neither short nor long, arms long and slender, not fleshy, very hairy, very little muscular strength, but a very strong wiry constitution.[15][xi]

---

x Although mechanically propelled omnibuses had appeared on the streets of London in 1833, from 1861, legislation—including speed limits of five miles per hour—virtually eliminated them from British roads for thirty years.

xi Born 26 March 1854 in Berkhamsted, Hertfordshire to Frances Lacey, the identity of his father is unknown (although his birth certificate stated his father was William Lacey, this entry was deleted by the registrar when the birth was registered). There was an unsubstantiated family legend that Frederick was the illegitimate son of Lord Carrington

Lacey took on a dizzying array of jobs. At different times, he worked as a travelling salesman, music teacher, clerk, and company secretary. And as if in fear of having any spare time, he played the organ on Sundays, performed at Sadler's Wells and locally throughout the 1880s, and conducted choirs. He was also a songwriter, and wrote the music for a number of songs published in the 1880s, with the lyrics mainly supplied by George Claxson (not a typo) Bellamy.[xii][xiii]

In 1884, Lacey married Florence Marshall and they rapidly produced two children. By the time William and Lacey met, the Laceys were living with Florence's mother Emma and her two sisters, Emma and Helena, in Brixton.[xiv]

It's hard to see when Lacey had time to fit astrology into his schedule, but somehow he managed it. Although he'd long been interested in the occult, he'd never come across astrology before and was intrigued by a column he read in the *Society Times* in 1887. Edited by R H Penny under the pseudonym 'Neptune', it was an astrological problem page. Readers sent their questions to the *Times* along with a small fee, and Penny used their birth details to supply answers.

Born in 1838,[xv] Richard Penny had served in the Crimea and in China when in the navy and had taken up astrology after being discharged in 1868. In 1880 he'd gone to New York and became an assistant to Dr J W Monk who practised as the 'American rubber'. While with him he assumed the name of 'Neptune'. He returned to London in 1882.

---

who lived in the family seat at the Abbey, Great Missenden near Berkhamsted. By the time Frederick was seven, Frances had moved to Islington with her mother, also called Frances. In 1871 Lacey was working as a solicitor's clerk and in 1881 he lived with his uncle William and his mother (now a widow—she married John Smith in 1865 in Islington) at 32 Aden Grove, Stoke Newington and worked as a piano tuner. Another family legend that he was educated at Balliol College, Oxford appears to have no grounds in reality.

xii These included 'A Gavotte' 1880; 'Song Bird of the Wilderness' 1880; 'St Ronan's Eve—When the Evening Twilight Falls' 1881; 'Bid Her, Remember' 1882; 'The Gladiators' 1882; 'Hand in Hand' 1882; 'The Village Fete' 1882; 'Three Little Maids,'1883; 'The Rovers of the Sea' 1884; and 'Ye Olde Sundial' 1890.

xiii George Claxson Bellamy (1856–1914) made a living as an insurance clerk. His son Howard bigamously married Anna Kingsford's daughter Eadith in 1915. He'd married Cissie Ethel Harris by licence the year before.

xiv On 15 March 1884, Lacey married Florence Regina Marshall at Christ Church, Hoxton in Shoreditch and claimed to be the son of Frederick Lacey, a deceased stockbroker. When William and Lacey met, the Laceys were living at 14 Knowles Road, Brixton. The Lacey's children were Charles Frederick (13 April 1885); Harold Ernest (11 January 1887); Dora Lilian (1892); Gordon Herbert (1893); Wilfred Eric (1896)and Mary Florence (1900).

xv 17 July 1838, Margate 8:11. His father, Eddell Penny, was a solicitor's managing clerk and a Wesleyan 'lecturer'. Penny took care of his mother, Eliza, until at least 1891.

Alan Leo

Frederick Lacey

R H Penny

Walter Old

'This gentleman is the only astrologer I have seen who looks his profession,' exclaimed Lacey at a later date. 'He at once reminds me of the idea I have always had of the ancient Egyptians, a re-incarnation of whom he may be for all I know.'[16]

Lacey wrote to Penny and: 'In due time the reply to my queries came, and were a revelation to me then. I thought there was something in it worth investigation, so I sent a fee and had my horoscope cast, and in reply to a query of mine as to a suitable book for a beginner to study, I was advised to obtain A J Pearce's *Text Book of Astrology*; I procured this book but, not being a mathematician, I made very little progress. I therefore wrote again and told the Editor it was too involved for me, and enquired whether he could recommend a simpler work.'[17]

By the time this letter the *Society Times*, Penny was no longer writing his column as he'd been arrested and charged with fortune-telling under the Vagrancy Act and fined £5. Seriously put out by the whole affair, he threatened to leave for California, assuming his solicitor, Charles Carlton Massey[xvi] could raise enough money for him (he couldn't) where, amongst other things, the mail service was unlikely to target him.

> The Post Office ... have been returning all my letters addressed to me in my professional name ... Why they should take the matter up in such a manner, adding insult to injury, passes my comprehension, when they know full well I am still here.[18]

Unfortunately, the Post Office was relentless, and a year later Penny repeated his complaint. Still unsuccessful, at this point Penny gave up. Dealing with the courts is one thing, but the Post Office presented a challenge too many.[xvii]

He resigned from his post and was replaced by the up-and-coming astrologer Walter Old, who wrote under the name of Sepharial, about whom Ralph Shirley, the editor of the *Occult Review*, said with glee, 'My friend Sepharial is, I am afraid, a terrible iconoclast ... I plainly foresee that we shall have the whole astrological edifice about our ears directly. Nothing is sacred.'[19]

Lacey was less impressed: '"Sepharial" has a thick crop of dark, curly, unruly hair. He is tall and thin.'[20]

---

xvi Charles Carlton Massey (1838–1905) had given up his call to the bar for a life of travelling, translating, lecturing and devotion to spiritualism and theosophy and defended a number of spiritualists and astrologers.
xvii Penny continued to work as an astrologer and was again convicted in 1903.

Old[xviii] was from Birmingham and had been briefly apprenticed to a chemist. In 1886 he was engaged to be married. When his fiancée broke off the engagement, Old spent his time haunting bookshops for mystical texts and more or less gave up sleep. He then had a mystical experience followed by a breakdown. A doctor prescribed complete bed rest and for two weeks Old wept, slept, could only see clearly in the dark and then suddenly recovered. 'I had discovered the secret which I was in search of, myself, my misremembered self. I have found that happiness does not lie in the memory of the past, but in the life which now is, with all its golden possibilities in our very hands.'[21] That, to Old, meant he should become an astrologer.

After taking over Penny's column, he wrote to Lacey, advising him to read Raphael's *Guide to Astrology*. According to Lacey, full of enthusiasm Old further, 'Very kindly said that if he could assist me in making headway, smoothing the course of astrological study he would be very pleased to do so.'[22]

Old and Lacey began to correspond, but it soon became clear that what Lacey really needed was to meet other astrologers, to discuss astrology with them and gain guidance for his studies. He sent a letter to one of the few astrological publications, *Astrologer* magazine published by Philip Powley[xix] in Hull, asking those interested to contact him.

'I occasionally asked questions and wrote letters to the periodical,' said Lacey, 'and in one I stated that a student living in the south of London would be pleased to correspond with or meet other astrological students for mutual improvement.'[23]

A letter also appeared in *Astrologer* from Henry Perhouse[xx] suggesting astrologers should wear a pin to aid recognition. (This was to become a recurring theme.) They needed a subtle way of finding each other—to

---

xviii Born 20 March 1864. (Originally, the time given was 13:30, later amended to 1:30 with the claim that he had been muddled with a younger brother. Later the time was rectified to 2:03. As a theosophist, Old was Vice President of the Blavatsky Lodge, General Secretary of the British Section, and Librarian. He was present when Blavatsky died in 1891. In 1894 Old was involved in a theosophical scandal regarding WQ Judge's claim to have received precipitated letters from the Mahatmas confirming his claim to the presidency of the Theosophical Society. Old wrote at least 58 books, edited a number of magazines and wrote for innumerable publications. In 1929 he joined the Elim Church, and died on 23 December that year.

xix Born in Norfolk in June 1839, Powley lived in Kingston-upon-Hull and worked as a skin dyer. By 1891 he was working as a herbalist in Aston, Warwickshire, with his son, William, as his assistant. He died July 1897.

xx Born Gravesend 1860–1906.

describe astrology as a niche interest would be drastically understating the situation.

However, although astrology had disappeared from academic and intellectual circles, it had a strong hold on the general public who soaked up almanacs. The astrologer Raphael's publications sold up to 120,000 copies apiece and Zadkiel's sold 40–50,000 copies in the mid-nineteenth century. And astrology survived in the public consciousness. In January 1888, chaos broke out in Birmingham after the prediction that 'fiery, violent Mars' conjoined with 'evil Uranus' and making an evil aspect to Mercury would lead to deaths, accidents, murder, explosions, wars, earthquakes and all manner of other calamities. Darkness fell early that day, and the sales of Bibles sky-rocketed. Children were kept away from school, young women lay in bed waiting for the end, and the baffled police force fended off panicked locals.[24]

A sense of panic often went hand-in-hand with astrology, especially when considering its dubious legality. In 1871 the police attended an astrological lecture where: 'No sooner had an officer announced his errand and requested the names and addresses of the forty fair ones, then with one universal shriek, the whole female train ... dashed at the door, overturned an unfortunate detective ... hopping over his prostate body [and] made good their escape.'[25]

Despite having to keep one eye on the door when it came to public engagements, astrologers continued their everyday work as they offered advice about illness, love, lost property, and money to their clientele, many of whom were found from advertisements in the provincial press.

William also bought a copy of the *Astrologer* and came across Lacey's letter. Perhaps as an attempt at bonding, William added Frederick to his name when he responded—wasn't that a coincidence? They had the same name![xxi] One of the first things he did on meeting Lacey was borrow some money to tide him over—his job at Roberts's started shortly after they first met.

Four other people had responded to Lacey's letter: James Green, born in 1855, a printer's compositor who lived in Kew; Charles Baddeley, born 1855, from Birmingham who lived in Hanover Square—he was clearly of a different class to the others and described himself as an inventor, the son of a medical botanist; a Mr Smarry and a man whose name Lacey could not later recall. It isn't clear precisely who Smarry and the nameless man were, but according to Lacey one of them was American (or at least

---

xxi 'Frederick' doesn't appear on Allan's birth certificate.

had spent much of his life in America) and had succeeded in gaining patents for many of his inventions. He returned to America a few years later.

After an exchange of correspondence, they decided to meet at Lacey's house in Brixton on Friday evenings. William, Lacey and Green also met for lunch every Wednesday.

William's interest in astrology had saved his sanity. He knew his previous trials had been due to the planet Uranus creating ups and downs at the drop of a hat. But he found work depressing as 'a practical, keen, observant, business man, with astrological ability above the average; somewhat reticent; one reliable and trustworthy; sincere in friendship; a lover of truth; firm, determined, and persevering, yet not bigoted; broad in his views, and tolerant of others opinions, and, in his disposition, reflective.'[26]

He was surely meant for better things than selling ice-cream makers. In fact, he was too good a salesman; he managed to sell so much that his firm had problems keeping up with the orders. And when customers were let down, they wrote to William to air their complaints. He needed something else to sell. And a salesman was one thing astrology didn't have.

But there was a problem: most astrologers of the period adopted pseudonyms—often with mystical overtones. Their audiences expected it, and they didn't want to risk their day jobs (not a problem for William—Roberts was one of his earliest clients) or attract police attention. 'William Allan' simply didn't cut it. Plus, William's birth chart showed he'd been born with Virgo rising. Lacey wasn't impressed; the sign of the servant didn't suit William. They tweaked and twiddled his horoscope, taking advice from Old, who was hot at this sort of stuff. If William had been born a few minutes earlier, his rising sign would have been Leo, the same as his Sun sign.[xxii] He might have been; Caroline wouldn't have realised the importance when she told him his birth time.

He was clearly a Leo, the sign much more suited to the king[xxiii] of astrologers—which is what he planned to become. After all, he played his sunny side up to the hilt, as Henry Selby Green later pointed out:

---

xxii Mercury, Jupiter and Saturn were also in the sign of Leo in his horoscope. Alan Leo was born 7 August 1860 in Westminster, London (51N30 00W09). The varying times given for his birth are: 6:10 am, *The Astrologer*, February 1890; 'about 6 am' *The Life and Works of Alan Leo*; 5:51:28, Sepharial's rectification; 5:49 am, *Esoteric Astrology* and *The Progressed Horoscope* 'approximately'.

xxiii Leo is, as astrologers know, the sign of the king.

'One of his most prominent characteristics was his extreme cheerfulness, accompanied by an exuberant vitality. When visiting him at his office on a dull winter day, he told me that to him the room appeared as if flooded with sunlight, so much so that he found it difficult to realise that the Sun was not actually shining.'[27]

This gave the clue to his new name.

Alan Leo was born and he was going to sell astrology.

Bessie Burch

CHAPTER TWO

CHIEFLY TO PLEASE HIM

MEANWHILE, BESSIE BURCH SPENT most of her time at home, watching life pass her by. She lived with her elderly father, Michael Phillips, and resented every minute of his presence:

> My father completely dominated my life, and when occasionally I used to remonstrate with him, he said he would break my spirit or break my heart, and he had such furious fits of passion that he did not hesitate to strike me if I in any way annoyed him ...[1] He was the most selfish being I ever met ... Constant disharmony, jangle and jar—my faults all recited to visiting friends ... continual fault finding, grumbling and upbraiding.[2]

They'd moved to Southampton[i] in about 1874, when, to her horror, Bessie discovered she was expected to run the house at the age of sixteen. And she had no idea what she was doing. 'He was very unreasonable as he expected me entirely without training to be an experienced housewife and manager ... I had never been trained in any method of domestication, so a war of words ensued, tears and recrimination became the order of the day.'[3]

Every evening, Bessie played the piano and read to her father before turning the lights out and going to bed at nine o'clock. She'd made a few

---

i To 83 Marland Place. Also known as 'Above Bar Street'.

friends but was rarely allowed to invite them into the house and had to sneak out to see them.

Even worse, Bessie was aware that Phillips had plenty of money but he refused to spend it. 'My father was a man of strong will and most selfish disposition ... could have lived on £5,000 but lived on £200 ... he loved money better than anything in the world.'[4] He was happy to buy Bessie clothes and whatever else she needed, but Phillips baulked at the idea of handing over hard cash. Apart from anything else, he knew Bessie's mother occasionally sent her money—plus she was rarely out of the house. What could she spend it on, anyway?

Every so often, Bessie decided she'd had enough and rushed back to Salisbury where her mother, Murray, still lived. And each time, after a few days of tea and sympathy, she was unceremoniously sent home.

They did try to get along. In 1879, Phillips took Bessie to the US for two months.[ii] And what better way to please him than adopting his religion? Phillips was Jewish but Bessie's mother wasn't, and after their trip overseas, Bessie decided to convert to Judaism, although in a half-hearted fashion. 'Some of the inner teachings of Judaism, particularly the belief in the One life ... greatly attracted me ... I thought it would do as well as any other religion, for at that time I had no religion at all.'[5]

There'd been no synagogue to attend in Salisbury, but there was one (although it wasn't that busy) in Southampton.[iii] After taking classes, Bessie was given a certificate to say she was a Jew and added 'Rachel' to her name, although she only used it when attending synagogue. She was smugly pleased that Phillips had to spend £100 to facilitate the process, showing he valued her effort. 'My father's mind somewhat dominated mine and I did it chiefly to please him,' she said.[6]

Things changed in 1883 when Bessie received the news that Murray was ill after a fall she'd had while out walking. Although Bessie rushed to her side, with Phillips shortly behind her, a week later Murray died of brain damage. 'At her death I had a curious psychic vision, I saw her standing all in white near the door, and heard her voice faintly declare it was well with her and beg me not to grieve.'[7]

Phillips promptly changed his will so Bessie would have a life interest in his property, then worth about £80,000—around £8,000,000 in today's terms. In 1887, Phillips again changed his will, leaving everything to

---

ii Part of Phillips' family settled in New York.
iii Erected in Albion Place, 1865.

Bessie. All she had to do was wait. Phillips was old and surely wouldn't live long?

It may have rankled that Phillips insisted on describing Bessie as his 'adopted' daughter—but that was probably to save face. After all, her background could hardly be described as conventional.

Phillips was born in Alexandrova, Prussia (now Poland) in about 1808. He appears to have been the son of Philip Schönlanker from Posen. Although a number of laws requiring Jews to adopt permanent surnames were passed at various times by different countries, many didn't do so until it became essential. Even then, names were flexible, and Phillips was the most popular English name chosen by Jews entering Britain during this period. He'd arrived as part of the Great Emigration following the failure of the November Uprising of 1830-1, the rebellion of the Poles against the Russian Empire. The Act of Dethronisation of Tsar Nicholas I in January 1831 amounted to a declaration of war on Russia and fighting had begun almost immediately. Despite the lack of governmental support for the Poles from the French and British, many people supported their cause and England's open door policy made it a popular destination for the thousands who fled from repression, persecution and deportation, especially Jews like Phillips who sought emancipation. From 1823 throughout the nineteenth century, Britain didn't expel a single refugee or turn one away. And of those refugees, the Poles were the most numerous and the most permanent.[iv]

Apparently, Michael Phillips arrived in London in May 1831 with a box of pencils and three words of English: *Will you buy?* [8]

It was rumoured you could sell anything at the Royal Exchange.

> The royal exchange may be considered as the emporium of the world; and rising in all the majesty of commerce, presents and objects which must fill the mind of every Englishman with delight and pride, as a principal support of that greatness which is unrivalled among the nations of the world.[9]

Firmly dominating the heart of the City, the Exchange thrived with merchants and brokers. There were no longer shops in the Exchange itself, but creeping towards it were lottery offices, newspaper offices, watchmakers, notaries, stockbrokers, coffee houses …

The grand open court was surrounded by porticoes, archways, towers. Statues of kings and queens watched from niches, emblems of

---

iv However, between 1831 and 1833 no more than fifty Poles came to England, many of whom left the country soon after their arrival. The Jewish population was also small.

commerce, heralds, griffins and other mythical creatures adorned the stonework. Dragons peered down alongside giant grasshoppers.

But there was no need to go inside to hear the four-dialled clock strike, which it did four times daily—at three, six, nine, and twelve o'clock—a different tune each day, on Wednesdays the well-known 'There's nae Luck aboot the Hoose' and on Thursdays 'See the Conquering Hero Comes'.

The arcade within this temple to commerce housed foreign and domestic merchants, all of whom it might be assumed would make good use of a pencil or two. Apparently not. Phillips tried for three days before he gave up.

As a child, Phillips had watched Napoleon's army retiring from Moscow in 1812. The Cossacks had burned villages, towns and crops and starvation had set in amongst the French. Almost all of the horses had died or were killed for food. Cavalrymen had to march on foot, cannons and wagons were abandoned, and deserters were taken prisoner or killed by Russian peasants. Many, overcome by the cold, fell to the ground, too weak or too numb to stand. And once they surrendered to sleep, they died. The road was littered with corpses.

But this was a different world. One in which pencils didn't sell well.

Phillips barely understood English, although he did speak German and Russian (probably French as well) in addition to Polish, and he soon got chatting to other hawkers. And one of them told him about an opportunity. A jeweller in Salisbury needed someone to carry a box of his wares from door to door. There was a long history of Jews working as door-to-door salesmen in the south-west, especially those from Germany and Poland. Immediately, Phillips set off.

He got the job. For the next six years he carried his box of trinkets and made enough sales to save a few pounds. Actually, a lot more than a few pounds. And when he heard that Abraham Rozenbaom who had run the Salisbury Bazaar in Catherine Street was going bankrupt in 1837,[10] Phillips saw his chance and bought the entire contents of his shop.

The following year he announced the re-opening of the Bazaar and that, as Rozenboam's successor, he'd just arrived from the continent with French, Swiss, German and Italian goods, kept a jeweller and watchmaker to hand and would sell toys.[11] However, although Phillips offered a dizzyingly wide-ranging amount of goods, and even sold cigars and tobacco on the side, he never reached the dizzy heights of Rozenbaom's efforts—he used to offer an Indian juggler's show with music and magic tricks to liven the place up.[12]

Catherine Street was a busy high street, filled with shops with flats above. Many of its buildings were relatively new at the time, and they were filled with the shops you might expect to find on a busy high street—photographers, jewellers, tobacconists ... it was an ideal location for a fancy goods shop.

However, Phillips didn't rely on his shop-keeping abilities alone. By chance he was introduced to a spendthrift aristocrat who had been in the habit of going to London to borrow money and he was asked to discount a bill. Phillips agreed and then found out how to do it. It wasn't long before he'd gained a reputation as a money lender and was able to plough the money he'd made into shares that brought in a respectable income each month, although he also lost money on some of his wilder speculations.

He was extremely busy (until 1851 he also ran a drapery shop on the canal) and couldn't manage everything alone, so in 1838 Phillips hired twenty-two year old Murray Lake[v] to work as his assistant. Although born in Weymouth, Murray had family in Salisbury, and her father and uncle owned property in the city. She began running the shop single-handedly almost immediately. And she also moved in with Phillips in the rooms above.

By now, Phillips described himself as a 'retired jeweller', despite being neither retired nor a jeweller. He had aspirations to become a gentleman, even to the extent of riding in the local hunt, although, 'If rumour had it correctly, he hardly rode like a centaur.'[13] He was also a property owner and was determined to avail himself of his right to vote. The problem was it took more than money to achieve the status he wanted. He looked and sounded like a foreigner.

> We were deprived of some amusement by the unexpected illness of Mr Michael Phillips which cast quite a gloom over the whole court. Mr Phillips was objected to as being an alien, and last year his accent and appearances convinced the Barrister of the truth of the objection. This year Mr Phillips was objected to on the Burgess List but knowing how much his looks belied him, he prudently sent a medical certificate with his shopwoman who was examined in proof of his qualification. The Mayor, however, stated he should reject the vote in the event of the party himself

---

v Ann Elizabeth Murray Lake from Weymouth, Dorset. According to Bessie in *Esoteric Astrology*, Murray was forty-two in 1858, suggesting she was born in 1816. She used 'Murray' as her given name, although this is mistranscribed in the 1851 census as 'Mary'. In the late 1850s she also went by the name 'Ann'.

failing to appear, and Mr Phillips was so far recovered on the following evening to come to the court and confirm by the rule of contrary, every word he had stated the year before. The trick of the medical certificate was tried again before the Barrister, but Mr Slade is the wrong man to be caught in such a snare, and he again insulted Mr Phillips's patriotic feelings by expunging his name from the Register.[14]

Michael Phillips

Phillips didn't give up easily, and in 1846 he was naturalised as a British subject, with local shopkeepers (Thomas Maylam Walker, a tailor; Thomas and John Meatyard, butchers; and William Hemin, currier and builder) vouching for him. Finally, he had the right to vote.

Although there weren't many Jews in England then, Phillips wasn't alone. He was simply the first of his family to arrive. In 1851 his three brothers Solomon, Henry and Joseph visited him, staying at the Plume of Feathers inn at 15 Queen Street at the end of Catherine Street, all describing themselves as travellers in jewellery. The huge inn might be better described as a hotel. Originating as a fourteenth-century merchant's house, it had been converted to an inn in the seventeenth century and comprised seven buildings of several storeys surrounding a narrow yard entered from Market Place.[vi]

---

vi It's now a listed building and part of Cross Keys Arcade. Some of its original features, including an unusual open Jacobean staircase, still exist.

First settling in Portsmouth, perhaps in one of the properties Michael Phillips owned, Henry and Solomon later (before 1861) set up home together at 7 Charlotte Street in Salisbury, less than a mile away from Phillips. Joseph moved to Dorchester where he worked as a grocer and lived with his wife Elizabeth and father-in-law Robert Collins.

In 1855 Phillips decided to 'officially' retire and Murray took over the shop in her name. In general terms, life was good. At least, it would have been had Phillips had a better hold on his temper. In 1857 he was out walking when Charles Miller grabbed him by his coat and demanded to know who was the biggest rogue of the two. Miller—who Phillips claimed not to know—was bound over to keep the peace, and Phillips commented that he was frequently insulted in the street by people he didn't know at the instigation of others.[15]

More than one person said in annoyance, 'I have heard that Mr Phillips is a man very fond of money.'[16] It might have helped if Phillips hadn't spent so much of his time in court. He was constantly chasing debts relating to his mortgages, and often gave evidence in other cases— at least two assault cases and more than one case of forgery. He called the police when people attempted to pass him stolen goods, and forced customers into bankruptcy, attempting to get made the assignee so he could end up with their property. This often worked. And he continued to expand his investments. Phillips lent money on shops and land (in 1860 he held mortgages on nine cottages and bought shares in up-and-coming companies; in 1846 he advertised asking if anyone wanted to sell shares in the Manchester and Southampton railway), ended up owning the Goat Inn in Milford Street in 1853, and bought shares in several mines throughout the 1860s. And he wasn't averse to suing simply because he felt insulted. In 1860 Henry Mullins, another local broker, was summonsed for using threatening language against Phillips, two years after losing a court case against him. When asked, he refused to stop annoying Phillips and so was bound over to keep the peace. William Webber was also summonsed for using threats towards Phillips in 1861, and the same year a Mr Simmonds, a jeweller he was dealing with, was affronted at being called a thief:

> The defendant was in the shop of Mr Carter, at Salisbury, relating the transaction, when the plaintiff came in. According to Simmonds, the defendant said, 'Here comes the greatest thief a going,' but according Mr Carter the words were, 'He has acted like the greatest thief in England.' Plaintiff said, 'Who do you mean?' and defendant replied, 'Why you.' Plaintiff said, 'I shan't quarrel

with such a monkey looking fellow as you,' and left the shop, returned to Bath and consulted his solicitor, who commenced an action without writing to the defendant to know what he meant, or even to demand an apology.'[17]

It's safe to say Phillips could be difficult. However, Murray stuck with him. And then, at the age of forty-one, she fell pregnant. Considering their long relationship, it wouldn't have been surprising for the couple to have hurriedly married. Instead, and probably in a state of astonishment, Murray married Samuel Burch on 24 December 1857, when she was six months pregnant.

It's because of one of Phillips' court cases that we know he employed Burch as a builder. He stated as much in 1852 when he was accused of refusing to pay a bill for carpentry work done at the Goat Inn, which he owned. Phillips was losing the case when he said in a fit of pique, 'As your Honour seems determined to go against me, I will pay the money and save the trouble of a decision.'[18] The judge was equally frustrated and said he wouldn't add what he thought of the defendant's testimony. Which was probably for the best.

Samuel Burch came from a family of builders based in Milford Street, close to Catherine Street and the Goat Inn. (Given the number of properties Phillips worked on at any one time, he probably provided Burch with regular business.) Why he and Murray agreed to marry is unclear (money may have been involved; Burch later owned a number of properties), but marry they did, and Ada Elizabeth Murray Burch was born 5 April 1858.[vii]

Despite what it said on her birth certificate, it was an open secret that Phillips was Bessie's (as she was known) father. Murray and Phillips brought up Bessie together, to the extent of Phillips walking Bessie to school while Murray was working. And despite Murray marrying Burch, they still lived together with Phillips occupying the rooms on the upper level and Murray and Burch on the floor below. In Bessie's own account of her childhood, she wipes Burch from existence.

> My parents were passionately attached to me, for I was their own child and my mother's age precluded her having any more ... My mother loved me dearly ... and spent hours curling my hair, which fell to my waist, and designing beautiful dresses for me; but my body and soul were alien to her perception. I was like

---

vii 5 April 1958, Salisbury 6:47:12 as rectified by Alan Leo.

none of her family, such a curious child, almost like a changeling ... I was a queer, weird child; I had practically no physical plane playfellows, but used to construct dream children and play with them, and was always trying to fly ... [I was] obsessed by books and always looking for fairies and frightened of goblins ... did I not see real children flit about me and sit on the chairs I placed for them?[19]

Bessie had a multitude of cousins living up the road, so it seems odd to claim she had a lonely childhood. However, in about 1867 Henry and Solomon Phillips moved their families to London.

Henry's daughter Amelia married cabinet maker Harris Levy in 1873 and, unable to have children, took it upon herself to rescue young Jewish women. Amelia deserves a book of her own and we shall meet her again later. In 1881 she moved to Manchester after her husband was offered a job, where she became a district visitor. She stayed in contact with Bessie and they wrote to each other regularly.

Much of Bessie's parents' time was taken up with their business interests. Burch ran the bazaar for a short while after Bessie was born, but by the following year Murray was back at work. By now Phillips owned a pub in Southampton that he later sold for £500 and he bought a small estate near Netton and Woodford, Salisbury, plus a farm he later sold for over £2,000. At one point he was estimated to be worth over £100,000 (about £87,000,000 in modern terms).

One advantage of Murray running a shop that sold toys (as it primarily did by then) was that Bessie was never short of playthings. She proudly kept a collection of twenty dolls, until she was twelve and her attention turned to books. 'I learnt to read very readily, practically taught myself, and at seven years of age could read and write well; indeed, my mother's sisters, maiden aunts, thought my letters wonderful for so young a child; they sent me a bright new sovereign in a little box for each, which my mother immediately banked for me, much to my childish sorrow, as I liked to play with shining things.'[20]

Bessie studied at an art school and took piano lessons, and said that when she was ten the family moved to a nice house with a garden. The census says otherwise. She was sent to a boarding school in Kilburn at twelve but hated it so much that she threatened to run away, so Murray brought her back home. She was later sent to another less demanding school, somewhere in the countryside, where she stayed until she was fifteen when she returned to study music and drawing at home.

And shortly after she'd returned (presumably, it wasn't related), Murray and Phillips' relationship collapsed and they parted company. Murray and Burch stayed at Catherine Street until 1876 when they stopped trading and the chemist next door took over the building to extend his own shop. By then Burch was running his own successful business, employing eleven men, and they moved to Milford, Alderbury. After Murray's death, Burch met Charlotte Law, the daughter of a local surveyor, and they married the following year. He died in 1894.

Bessie was alone with her father and needed something in her life.

That something turned out to be phrenology.

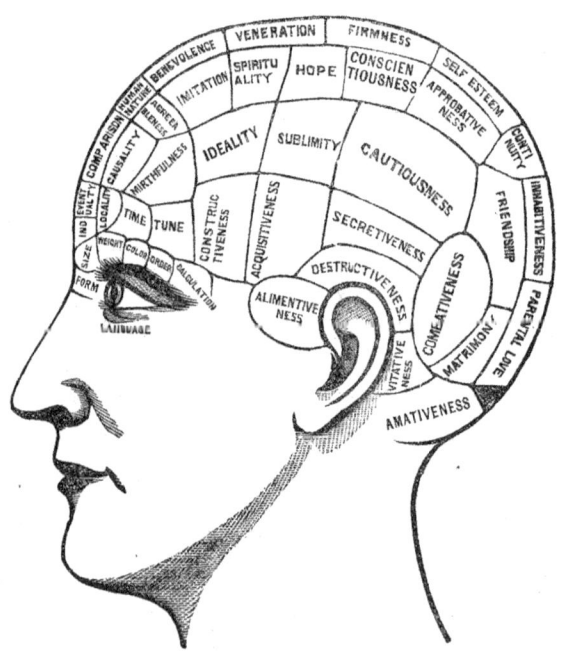

CHAPTER THREE

FORMS THE MOST HIDEOUS

*T*HE DEMAND FOR SWEET and ice-cream machines kept Alan on the road from Monday morning until midday Friday. From time to time, he ended up in a town where he could visit someone he'd corresponded with through magazines—and he always availed himself of this opportunity. Late in 1889 he called on John Thomas, better known as Charubel, in Chorlton near Manchester.

Born in 1826,[i] by his early twenties Thomas had studied Calvinistic Methodism (a distinctly Welsh denomination that became the Presbyterian Church of Wales) under the Reverend Lewis Edwards at Bala Theological College. He never became a preacher but instead dedicated himself to studying the laws of nature and of life, claiming to be gifted with second sight or precognition and a sixth sense for seeing frightening and horrifying forms, described as *submundanes* or elementals.

'Whenever I was alone,' he said, 'I would be visited by forms the most hideous, such as dogs grinning and serpents hissing at me and being part human and part brute jabbering some kind of sounds.'[1]

More usefully, he was renowned for his healing skills, specialising in the treatment of rheumatism, and also practising as a herbalist and mesmerist. He often relied on precipitated letters from the spirit world for his methods of treatment, and prepared hundreds of horoscopes in his time, taking the trouble to draw them in parchment. He also did a roaring

---

i Born 7 am on 9 November 1826 at Cwmbau, Castellcaer-Einion, Montgomeryshire.

trade in talismans. Thomas claimed money wasn't of great interest to him (which was fortunate as he rarely had any), although he advertised in the press as 'Julius Balsamo'[ii] promising clairvoyant advice through the post.

Alan certainly had faith in him, as Henry Selby Green later commented: 'After seeing him Alan told me he was undoubtedly a genuine "Seer" and highly gifted; he thought Charubel far above other such men he had previously met.'[2]

Thomas published a monthly magazine called *The Occultist*, to which Alan and Lacey subscribed. *The Occultist* had originally appeared under the name of *The Seer and Celestial Reformer* in July 1884and had been renamed in January 1885 when Peter Davidson and Thomas Burgoyne of the Hermetic Brotherhood of Luxor offered to support the magazine in exchange for space to promote their society within its pages.

'Of course' said Thomas, 'we were duly informed that these kind offers were being made disinterestedly. That it was purely out of kindness to us, as proprietor, that so liberal an offer was made, and that no ulterior or selfish ends were concerned. O dear, no, they were far above that sphere, of course. But, and at the same time, we would have to pay the Printer, they were not so low as to be capable of descending to matters of that kind.'[3]

Suspicious he was being taken for a ride, Thomas asserted his copyright to the title. After a frank exchange of views, Davidson and Burgoyne launched the opposing *Occult Magazine*, but couldn't resist stabbing Thomas in the back.

'A secret current of private slander was put into circulation, we were most cruelly treated by false representation,' said Thomas. 'The few friends we once had become alienated from us, and forbidden to correspond with us. Our main support, on which we relied for our bread was broken. The fact is, we were "Boycotted" as a "Black Magician" and branded as a "Hypocrite".'[4]

Davison and Burgoyne's society, the *Hermetic Brotherhood of Luxor*, had first appeared in 1884 when an advertisement in the book *The Divine*

---

ii A reference to Count Alessandro di Cagliostro (1743–1795), the alias of occultist Giuseppe Balsamo. Associated with the royal courts of Europe, Cagliostro pursued various occult arts, and established a reputation that lingered after his death, although he was later regarded as a charlatan. He was involved in the Affair of the Diamond Necklace in 1785 at the court of King Louis XVI of France involving his wife, Queen Marie Antoinette. The Queen had been accused of defrauding the crown jewellers of the cost of a diamond necklace. The Affair is one of the events that led to disillusionment with the monarchy and the French Revolution.

John Thomas

Pymander of Hermes Mercurius Trismegistus invited enquirers to send a photograph and natal chart to see if they were suited for occultism (for a small fee, you could have your horoscope calculated). Those who made it into the Brotherhood received mail order lessons and were allocated a mentor. According to its own account, the HBoL began in Egypt in 1870 (although it dated its roots back to the ancient Egyptian city of Luxor).

The Brotherhood had been formed by Max Theon[iii] who had initiated Davidson into the Order and charged him with establishing the Exterior Circle of the HBoL. Davidson[iv] was a violin maker and herbalist born near Findhorn, Scotland who had written a handbook about violins which he'd stuffed with occult lore. By the 1870s he was interested in contacting guardian spirits with magic mirrors and claimed to be in touch with a Tibetan adept. The Brotherhood's secretary Burgoyne was also Scottish and claimed that as a child he'd made contact with the Hermetic Brotherhood of Light, a group of discarnate, advanced beings.

At this time, societies with spiritualist and occult agendas were sprouting up at an alarming rate, and there was no reason to suppose one would be more influential than any other.

The Hermetic Brotherhood of Luxor soon became the chief rival of the Theosophical Society, although many people were members of both. Matters came to a head when in 1886 it was announced that Burgoyne was in fact Thomas Dalton (or D'Alton) who had been convicted of mail fraud in Leeds in 1883 and sentenced to seven months.

> John Thomas Prince (23), mason, and Thomas Henry Dalton (27), grocer ... were charged with having conspired to obtain by false pretences ... on October 19th the following advertisement appeared in the Leeds Mercury—"Grocer's Assistant Wanted; permanent situation; good salary given to a steady and energetic young man ...' Letters were found upon one of the prisoners after his arrest which showed that the advertisement was a fraud. The practice pursued by the prisoners was to write a letter to each applicant informing him that he had been selected for a situation and stating that a further remittance of 2s 5d. was required. About October 21st the prisoner Prince called at the Mercury office ... and was handed a number of letters ... Outside the office Prince was joined by the other prisoner. A day or two afterwards when

---

iii Maximilian Louis Bimstein, the son of a Warsaw rabbi, Born 1850.
iv Davidson (1837-1915) wrote under the pen name 'Mejnor', Zanoni's spiritual mentor in Bulwer Lytton's novel *Zanoni*.

Prince received more letters, a detective officer followed him to his lodgings ... and there arrested him ... In reply he stated that a man named Seymour had been living there but had gone away to Pickering and he was about to send the letters to him. He added that he had met this man at a railway station, but knew nothing about him. The prisoner Dalton ... informed the officer who took him into custody that Prince was his brother-in-law, and that they would not have done it if they had not been hard-up ... the prisoners were sentenced to seven months imprisonment.[5]

A photograph of Burgoyne in his prison uniform was circulated among American Theosophists and Burgoyne fled to the United States to escape the scandal of his arrest.[v]

The Theosophical Society had been founded in New York on 11 November 1875 by Helena Blavatsky, William Quan Judge[vi] and Henry Steel Olcott.[vii]

Born 12 August 1831 (NS), Ekaterinslav, Russia (now the Ukraine)[viii] of an aristocratic family, Blavatsky ran away from her first husband, Nikifor Vassilievitch Blavatsky, after three unhappy months. She reputedly travelled the world, spending time in Tibet studying with men she called the 'Brothers'. In 1858, she returned to Russia, later to leave with Italian opera singer Agardi Metrovich, by whom it's rumoured she had a son. After spending some time in Cairo, where she formed the occult Société Spirite, Blavatsky emigrated to New York City in 1873 where she soon established a reputation for her psychic abilities, performing levitation, clairvoyance, out-of-body projection, telepathy, materialisation, and clairaudience.

In 1874, she met Henry Steel Olcott, a lawyer, agricultural expert, and journalist who covered spiritualist phenomena. Olcott later became

---

v Dalton (1855–1894) married in the early 1880s and fathered two children, a boy and a girl. He left his family behind when he went to the US to found the HBoL colony with Peter Davidson, although they moved to the US in the early 1920s. Dalton later published the teachings of the HBoL in 1889 as *The Light of Egypt* under his pen name, 'Zanoni'. He may have adopted the alias of Norman Astley and married Genevieve Stebbins.

vi Judge (13 April 1851, Dublin, 5:07–21 March 1896) later became General Secretary of the Theosophical Society's American Section and Vice President of the international Society. An argument within the Society, relating to whether or not Judge had genuinely received letters from the Masters, led to the secession of the American Section of the Theosophical Society in 1895.

vii Born 2 August 1832, Orange, New Jersey, 11:15.

viii At about 1:42.

known as the first prominent person of Western descent to make a formal conversion to Buddhism.

The third of the trio primarily responsible for the early TS, William Quan Judge, was born in Dublin in 1851. His family had emigrated to New York in 1864 where he became a commercial lawyer.

In 1875 Blavatsky had claimed to be in communication with an Egyptian Lodge, called the *Brotherhood of Luxor*, composed of 'Adepts' or 'Brothers'. She persuaded Olcott that one or more of these Brothers—the Masters Tuitit and Serapis—had accepted him as a pupil, and he received communications from them through her.

The similarity of names led to questions whether the HBoL was the same group under a modified name, but no evidence of the Brotherhood of Luxor's existence has ever surfaced.

Thomas certainly recognised the existence of the 'Brothers', as he called them. When the time arrived for their appearance (he'd been expecting them), he told his friends that a great manifestation of the Brothers was to take place in his own room and so he confined himself there for three days. He was subsequently found lying unconscious on the floor and it was never clear what had happened.

As far as Thomas was concerned, the Brothers were behind the society he set up, and he was acting on their behalf, saying, 'I am the agent, the instrument of a Brotherhood among whom exists a wisdom long since lost to the men of this earth. I know I am in daily communion with Men who have conquered death and live on through the ages and changes, who passed a change, the change that transforms the mortal into the immortal. There are 10,000 of these, awaiting their day! These are the executants of the Divine decrees!'[6]

Alan contributed brief articles on astrology to *The Occultist*. For example, in August 1888 he wrote an analysis of Thomas's birth chart, concluding, 'The whole nativity shows a very complex character and great powers, but principally tending in an inward, intellectual, psychical or transcendental direction.'[7]

Given the revelations he had to share, Thomas felt compelled to set up a society. Not that he'd accept just anyone as a member. 'First the person must be a man of good character—second a man who can keep a secret—third a man who will pledge never to recopy the work for any other person—and lastly I must have £5.0.0. for my labour, and as some recompense for what I have undergone.'[8]

In July 1884 the *British and Foreign Society of Occultists* was announced in *The Seer and Celestial Reformer* with the aim of, 'Peace on earth and good will towards men, and Glory to God in the Highest ... The teachings of this fraternity are of two kinds: Esoteric or secret, and Exoteric or what is for publicity.'[9]

The *Celestial Brotherhood*, or as it was known to the public, The British and Foreign Society of Occultists, was a short-lived organisation. It did, claimed Thomas, offer the opportunity to meet the Brothers: 'There is a higher grade of Celestial Brother in the order. These appear in the bodily form. I never had the privilege of seeing these with the fleshly eyes but on one occasion when there were about 12 of us together in my old neighbourhood of Kingsley, when two appeared. The room was at the time in darkness but where they were was a flow of light like the rising sun ... The one walked up towards me, and stood within a yard of me. He made several symbols with his hand, then held both hands towards heaven and drew them down towards me, blessing me . . . These were the chief adepts of the order.'[10]

To Alan, the Society was irresistible. Secret Chiefs who appear to the chosen few; secret signs and names, and the opportunity to dress up in robes when performing rituals—if they ever met up. Most members didn't. The BFSO was very much a mail-order society.

Members received a certificate of membership with an occult name (derived psychically by Thomas from astrological significators, numerology and geometry) and a seal, plus an explanation of their name and instructions on how to draw the seal. Each name ended with 'el' to signify divinity, or belonging to the *Elohim*.[ix] Or as Thomas said, 'In each seal the higher order of Intelligences can read the whole life & destiny of a person, this is the language of the angels. Further each seal is in itself a lasting invocation on the part of the being it represents.'[11]

On joining, Alan became *Agorel*[x] and Lacey *Aphorel*, the name he would use for his astrological writing in the future.[xi] Alan, however never used his name as Green explained, 'I remember that he said he wished the word had ended with the termination -id as did the names of one or

---

ix One of the most frequently used names for God in the Old Testament. It is a plural form and therefore allows for plurality within the Godhead. It is often shortened to *El* and used as part of a longer name. Elohim is also used to designate angels and powerful humans and in occultism means 'planetary spirits'. It is also associated with pi and the circle, and therefore the celestial spheres, the planets and the zodiac.

x *Agor* is to open or expand in Welsh.

xi Other renowned members (although their membership dates from later, July 1890) included the renowned freemason and occultist John Yarker (1833–1913), known as *Arokiel* and the freemason and occultist Francis George Irwin (1828–1893), known as *Morathiel*.

two other persons whom we knew, because it sounded more musical in that form, but he had no power to alter it.'[12]

The Occultist ceased publication in summer 1889 and Thomas needed new ways to attract members. Most of the members were or had been freemasons. Unfortunately, many turned out to be nasty people who gave Thomas a hard time. Brother John Hawkins of Fallowfield, Manchester was 'very honest but he has a weakness Drink' and 'Then there are a lot in Yorkshire who are renegades—also in my own neighbourhood—renegades'. Pattinson and Thomas Holms, of Boulden near Leeds 'are now my foes' and the Reverend W A Ayton[xii] 'grew cool for the want of an organising power at work.'[13]

For a while, Thomas had sought to become a mason—he certainly thought that those on the esoteric fringes of masonry would support his society—but he was rebuffed, and when told by a clergyman friend it cost him fifty pounds a year, Thomas knew he simply couldn't afford it. So he instantly developed a disdain for freemasonry.

The Celestial Brotherhood had a ritual. The Order of Opening of a meeting of a lodge was:

1. Incense is ignited and placed in the centre of the room on a round table.

2. When well kindled and the fine aroma is ascending, we all arise & with faces to the East, right hands up with palms towards the East we go over the sentences I have marked.

3. Then whilst in the same position we sing the hymn marked B, at the end of the singing we all repeat the Invocations marked C. When we come to the Amen we each make the five pointed Star or pentagram, ending where we began. This is made by the motion of the hand, each does the same & at the same time, we are all in earnest and we are all alive to the great fact, that some of the C[elestial] B[rotherhood] is superintending and watching over us and that sometimes very suddenly they will make themselves known in our midst as one of us, and give us the highest Instructions.[14] [xiii]

Whether any practical work was carried out seems unlikely as no meetings are recorded. Maybe this is why Alan sought another society.

---

xii William Alexander Ayton (28 April 1816–1 January 1909), an Anglican clergyman with an interest in alchemy who became a member of the Golden Dawn.
xiii Identical to one of the banishing Pentagram rituals (of fire) of the Golden Dawn.

Like many others of the period, Thomas was also a theosophist. Although Charles Carlton Massey had opened the first European branch of the Theosophical Society in London in 1878[xiv] and became first president of the British Theosophical Society, he'd resigned in 1884 after finding that his discovery of what he thought to be a precipitated letter had been staged.[xv] Theosophy taking off in England was due to the efforts of Alfred Percy Sinnett.[xvi]

Alfred Percy Sinnett

Sinnett was a journalist who had worked on *The Pioneer*, the leading English-language daily of India, in Allahabad from 1872. He'd met Blavatsky in 1879 and was soon[xvii] receiving precipitated letters from the Masters with almost monotonous regularity. These letters, which appeared to fall from the ceiling or materialise in a special cabinet owned by Blavatsky, were later expanded upon by Blavatsky in the *Secret Doctrine*, superseding the explanations in Sinnett's books.

Sinnett's enthusiastic campaigning for theosophy lost him his job in India and he returned to England in April 1883 where he quickly made himself and his home a centre of theosophical activity in London. Only a

---

xiv He was also one of the founders of the Society for Psychical Research in 1882.
xv The second president, George Wyld, also abandoned theosophy in its early years.
xvi 1840–1921.
xvii Along with fellow early theosophist Allan Octavian Hume (1829–1912) a British civil servant, political reformer, and one of the founders of the Indian National Congress.

year later, he manoeuvred Anna Kingsford out of office as president of the Theosophical Society, and to most intents and purposes was theosophy in England.

Although during February 1884 the Theosophical Society was under attack at their headquarters in Adyar, Madras when Blavatsky was charged with fraud, in London theosophy was as strong as ever. On Tuesday afternoons the Sinnetts were 'at home' to visitors as A E Waite[xviii] later recalled: 'I remember very well the strange crew that filled Sinnett's drawing room at the gatherings, the astrologers, the mesmerists, the readers of hands and a few, very few only, of the motley spiritualist groups.'[15]

The doctrinal core of theosophy was derived from Blavatsky's books *Isis Unveiled* (1877) and *The Secret Doctrine* (1888). Theosophists believed that the world's religions were underpinned by divine wisdom passed down from the ancients, and their teachings borrowed from Buddhism, Hinduism, and Western esoteric thought. They believed that nothing in nature occurs through chance: every event happens because of laws that are part of a universal paradigm and everything is impregnated with consciousness. And the theory of reincarnation is a fundamental part of theosophy.

When Blavatsky moved to England in May 1887, she quickly opened her own 'Blavatsky Lodge' at 17 Landsdowne Road in Notting Hill[xix] which instantly became popular and met on Thursday evenings. Sinnett was furious and announced that anyone who wished to be part of the new lodge was no longer welcome at his. Half of his membership immediately defected and fourteen theosophists joined the new lodge.

Blavatsky held 'at homes' on Saturdays when there would be a succession of guests, and during the week the dinner table was often set for twenty. Non-members were admitted strictly by invitation—and the cards of entry were in constant demand. Theosophy was highly fashionable; scores of people poured into the new headquarters to meet the famous Madame. *Pall Mall Gazette* editor W T Stead,[xx] William Butler

---

xviii American-born Arthur Edward Waite (2 October 1857–19 May 1942) wrote extensively on occult and esoteric matters, and was the co-creator of the Rider-Waite tarot deck. Waite joined the Hermetic Order of the Golden Dawn in 1891 and the Societas Rosicruciana in Anglia in 1902.
xix The house belonged to the theosophist Bertram Keightley.
xx William Thomas Stead (5 July 1849–15 April 1912) was editor of the *Pall Mall Gazette* from 1883, and is best known for his 1885 series of articles 'The Maiden Tribute of Modern Babylon', written in support of a bill to raise the age of consent from thirteen to sixteen. To back up his assertions, Stead arranged the 'purchase' of Eliza Armstrong,

Yeats and George W Russell[xxi] (AE) were amongst the visitors. George RS Mead[xxii] became a member of the household as Blavatsky's private secretary and the Wilde family drifted in and out of the theosophical world with Oscar Wilde's wife Constance joining the society. [xxiii]

One of those visitors was Walter Old. Theosophy was a family affair for the Olds; Walter's brother Sydney was secretary of the Birmingham Lodge and his brother Bernard was also an active theosophist. Old soon began a lengthy correspondence with Blavatsky. In fact, he was soon writing to one theosophist or another on a daily basis, and then, 'A letter from a London friend informed me that he had arranged for a few friends to meet at his house ... and if I would go up to town that evening, he would take me round to see "H.P.B" on the morrow.'[16]

After a long chat and some shared cigarettes, Old left 'the most interesting person I have ever seen'[17] and decided to throw himself into becoming a theosophist. In April 1888 he moved into headquarters. Old was part of the Esoteric Section and by 1889 was Vice President of the Blavatsky Lodge and had begun using the name 'Sepharial'.[xxiv]

---

the thirteen-year-old daughter of a chimney sweep. His first instalment was trailed with a warning guaranteed to make the *Pall Mall Gazette* sell out. Copies changed hands for twenty times their original value and the office was besieged by 10,000 members of the public. This led to his conviction for abduction and a three-month prison term. Stead also changed journalism through innovations such as incorporating maps and diagrams into a newspaper for the first time, breaking up longer articles with eye-catching subheadings, and blending his own opinions with those of the people he interviewed. He conducted numerous successful campaigns against the government. He resigned his editorship in 1889 to found the *Review of Reviews*. In the 1890s, Stead became increasingly interested in spiritualism and founded the journal *Borderland* in 1893. In 1912 Stead was asked to speak at an international conference on world peace in New York. He decided to travel to America on the Titanic. It was later reported that he made no attempt to get into the final lifeboats and was last seen standing upright on the deck in prayer.

xxi Known primarily as a poet and artist, Russell, (1867–1935), was a lifelong theosophist who belonged to the Dublin group. Russell maintained the Hermetic Society in Dublin until 1933 and was a frequent visitor to London headquarters. Today he is remembered as a major figure in the revival of Irish literature.

xxii George Robert Stowe Mead (22 March 1863–28 September 1933) joined the Theosophical Society in 1884. In August 1889 he became Blavatsky's private secretary and remained so until her death in 1891. Mead was appointed General Secretary of the European division of the Society in 1890 and edited the Theosophical Review from 1898 to 1909. He resigned from the TS in 1909 in protest after Annie Besant brought C W Leadbeater back into the Society. He was offered the presidency following Olcott's death, but turned it down. In 1909 he founded the Quest Society with A E Waite. He is remembered for his scholarly translations of Gnostic and Hermetic works.

xxiii She later became a member of the Golden Dawn.

xxiv First appears in a letter in *Lucifer*, February 1889.

Walter Old

But whilst members of the Theosophical Society had to rely on Blavatsky and her invisible Masters for their miracles and communications, the Hermetic Brotherhood of Luxor offered practical lessons in achieving access to such wisdom. The HBoL believed Blavatsky had fallen under the spell of Buddhist masters, initiates of a lower order of enlightenment. The theosophists thought the HBoL was a sinister order of low-grade occultism, newly invented as a mockery of the 'real' Brotherhood of Luxor which had inspired the beginnings of the TS.

Another threat was the creation of the *Hermetic Order of the Golden Dawn*, a quasi-masonic, occult organisation that taught the secrets of Hermeticism through progressive initiations. Founded by William Robert Woodman,[xxv] William Wynn Westcott,[xxvi] and Samuel Liddell MacGregor Mathers,[xxvii] all prominent British occultists and members of fringe masonic groups, the Golden Dawn drew hundreds in search of occult knowledge, many from the Theosophical Society.

Blavatsky's response was to found an esoteric school within the TS in 1888, although as she was opposed to teaching practical occultism, it didn't last long. Members of the section were not taught practical occultism or how to perform psychic phenomena. But as all its activities were carried out under a strict pledge of secrecy, it is unclear how many were taught. Blavatsky's intention was to stop would-be practical occultists from defecting to other groups. Members who joined the esoteric section weren't allowed to join any other occult order. The teachings Blavatsky offered were far from practical. Instead, the students attending meetings asked questions and Blavatsky supplied answers.

Another major change within the TS was heralded in 1889 when Blavatsky met Annie Besant[xxviii] for the first time. Besant was friendly with

---

[xxv] Woodman (1828–20 December 1891) was a doctor who had volunteered as a surgeon during Napoleon III's coup d'etat. He had a practice in Stoke Newington.

[xxvi] William Wynn Westcott (17 December 1848–30 July 1925) was a doctor and coroner.

[xxvii] Samuel Liddell (or Liddel) MacGregor Mathers (8 or 11 January 1854–5 or 20 November 1918) knew a wide range of languages and made a number of translations, making what had previously been inaccessible material widely available to the non-academic English speaking world.

[xxviii] Annie Besant, née Wood (1 October 1847–20 September 1933) married clergyman Frank Besant in 1867 and they had two children, but Annie's increasingly anti-religious views led to a legal separation in 1873. Besant had been a prominent speaker for the National Secular Society and involved with union actions including the Bloody Sunday demonstration and the London matchgirls strike of 1888. She was a leading speaker for the Fabian Society and the Marxist Social Democratic Federation (SDF). She was elected to the London School Board for Tower Hamlets, topping the poll even though few women were qualified to vote at that time.

W T Stead and he'd asked her to review *The Secret Doctrine* for the *Pall Mall Gazette*. Besant asked Stead for a letter of introduction to Blavatsky which she forwarded with a note asking for permission to call. On 15 March 1889 Blavatsky wrote back enthusiastically asking Besant to call as and when she wished—and to bring anyone she wanted with her.

Besant was already known as an agitator in radical political circles, a champion of science, an atheist, feminist, social and educational reformer, author and the first prominent woman to wage war on behalf of birth control. Feeling disillusioned, Besant had recently begun to take an interest in psychology, hypnotism and spiritualism and was poised for change.

At the final moment of her visit, as Besant and her friend Herbert Burrows turned to leave, Blavatsky cried, 'Oh, my dear Mrs Besant, if only you would come among us!'[18] Although Besant was transfixed she didn't call again until the end of April. On 10 May 1888 Besant visited the office of the Theosophical Publishing House, asked Constance Wachtmeister for an application form, filled it in and hurried to Lansdowne Road. She knelt at Blavatsky's knee saying, 'Will you accept me as your pupil, and give me the honour of proclaiming you my teacher in the face of the world?'[19]

With Besant publically joining the TS, being associated with it became even more of an attractive proposition. And in the summer of 1889, Lacey said, 'He [Old] invited Alan and me to … the headquarters of the Society. I might remark that we both had already subscribed to *Theosophical Siftings,* and other books published by the Society. On a certain evening we went, the first of many visits, and were introduced to Madame H. P. Blavatsky, and in time we met Col. H. S. Olcott and Mr W. Q. Judge there.'[20]

On 5 April 1890, sponsored by Old and Herbert Coryn, Alan applied to join the TS and gained his diploma on 14 April. Lacey joined at the same time. In May 1890, the Philalethian Lodge was founded in Brixton by Herbert Coryn. Theosophists had been active in Brixton for some months—a theosophical lending library had been established there in April 1890 at Herbert Coryn's house. (Lacey later claimed that he and Alan were amongst its founder members, but that seems a little unlikely unless he simply meant they were among the first members.) They met fortnightly on Fridays near where Lacey lived in Acre Lane.

A doctor himself, Coryn[xxix] was the son of a physician and had studied medicine and became a member of the Royal College of Surgeons of

---

xxix Coryn (1863-1927) later moved to the USA and worked with W Q Judge in New York. In 1895 he published *The Pageant of the Fifth Act. A Study of Mrs. Besant*. In 1900 he joined Katherine Tingley at Point Loma. He was editor of *The New Way*, a magazine

London in 1889. He was associated with his father in a medical practice for many years. Along with his sister Frances (they both lived at 159 Acre Lane) he applied to join the TS on 16 March 1889.

The opening night of the Philalethian featured a lecture by G R S Mead who had joined the TS in 1884 whilst reading classics at Cambridge and decided to devote his life to the cause. Alan was singularly unimpressed with his offering, saying simply, 'Doesn't Mead like long words.'[21]

A taste of what was offered at many TS meetings was satirised by Mabel Collins in her novel *The Mahatma*.

> She was asked by the old lady to read Mr Waters writing aloud ... she did so, in a high-pitched, monotonous voice, and with elaborate emphasis:
>
> In the beginning of all things, there was nothing.
>
> There was less than nothing, for there was no mind to realise the nothingness.
>
> In the beginning, there was not chaos, for there was no consciousness with which to know there was chaos.
>
> In the beginning there was neither light nor dark nor cold nor shape nor form.
>
> Nor yet was there any knowledge that these things were not.
>
> In the beginning there was not the spirit of the world, which has created and built it up.
>
> Nor was there any fire, nor anything of which chaos could be made.
>
> In the beginning there was neither movement nor stillness.
>
> Nor was there anything which could move or be silent.[22]

Alan and Lacey had remained in contact with Thomas who by 1890 was in dire financial straits:

> He has come entirely to grief and is sending begging letters to every one. He was a Medium in 2 with the Colour Spirits with whom he appears to have had a Pact, but on two occasions nearly lost his life thro' them. The most apparently peaceable Elementals, if a storm happens to come on, will become very violent and uncontrollable. The conflict of the elements seems to excite them to fury, and woe to the mortal, not being an Adept, who encounters them. Thomas has gone the way of all Mediums.[23]

---

founded by Tingley in 1911. Coryn was also a freemason, and a member of the Bon Accord Mark Masonry Lodge with Archibald Keightley and Basil Crump. He never married.

His health had also begun to fail. It looked like the beginning of the end for Thomas, but despite this in July 1893 he began to write, print and publish a new occult journal, the *Psychic Mirror*, which ran for seven volumes and seventy-five numbers until 1900.

Thomas's first wife (he'd married in 1852) had died and to everyone's surprise, and at the grand age of seventy-two, on 10 December 1898 he married thirty year old Elizabeth Adams (Lilly) after having boarded with her and her mother for some years, and after having been accused of living with her in an adulterous relationship.

In 1906 Thomas persuaded his friend, the moneylender and debt collector Robert Welch, to publish his articles from the *Psychic Mirror* in the form of a book he entitled *The Psychology of Botany*, leaving Welch the rights to his work. He died in Manchester on 11 November 1908[xxx] after having had two strokes and being confined to his bed since the beginning of the year.

Through Thomas, Alan had learned about two planets he claimed to have discovered (although unacknowledged by astronomers),[xxxi] the dark moon, theories regarding the structure of the Earth, the planets, stars and their inhabitants, and that plants, like people, have individual characteristics which reveal themselves to the receptive mind through the aura surrounding the plant.

In the then distant future, after Alan's death, a psychic had a vision that Alan and Thomas had met on the astral plane, and Alan 'was evolving towards the status of a king and would actually be born a king in the course of a few more incarnations.'[24]

Alan's interest was focused on achieving kingly status in his current incarnation.

---

xxx At 11.40 p.m.

xxxi Undiscovered planets were a popular subject of discussion. Sinnett claimed there were planets within the orbit of Mercury and two beyond Neptune, and an inter-mercurial planet was postulated by Thomas Lake Harris in 1884.

CHAPTER FOUR

PHRENOLOGISTS ADVANCING

'I MET BY CHANCE A book on phrenology, and this I studied hard for several months,' said Bessie, 'and then I found another dealing with physiognomy and later on one on palmistry and graphology ... The study of human nature I loved and required no compulsion to drive me towards it; for three years I studied these subjects thoroughly, getting every book on the subject I could procure.'[1]

She wasn't alone. Britain was obsessed with head size and shape, to the extent that numerous phrenological expressions have passed into the English language. If you've ever said something is 'highbrow' or described someone as 'well rounded,' you're talking phrenology. If you've said someone needs to 'get their head examined' or see a 'shrink,' you've been talking phrenology.

Dating back to the late eighteenth century, phrenology was based on Franz Joseph Gall's[i] theories that each part of the mind has a separate seat (organ) in the brain and its size is a measure of its power and affects the shape of the brain. As the skull takes its shape from the brain, the surface of the skull can indicate psychological aptitudes and tendencies. In other words, by examining the shape and unevenness of a head or skull, a phrenologist could discover the development of the organs responsible for different character traits. For example, a protuberance

---

i 1758–1828.

in the forehead at the position attributed to the organ of benevolence shows you're a kind and considerate person.

It's also worth remembering that phrenology, although now discredited, wasn't totally wrong in its assumptions. The brain is compartmentalised, with each piece serving a specific function, and the brain does change with use (a property called plasticity), although only on a microscopic level. There were some, notably Pierre-Paul Broca, who used cranial anthropometry (using callipers to measure the dimensions and angles of a skull) to support their belief that Europeans were superior to other humans, but such theories were derived from phrenology and not part of it.

Enthusiasm for phrenology had ebbed in the 1860s, but it was revived in the US (and later the UK) by the Fowlers, who generated a wealth of self-improvement literature. Lorenzo Niles Fowler[ii] and his brother Orson Squire Fowler[iii] became converts to phrenology when students in New York. They were soon reading heads and performing lectures, assisted by their sister Charlotte. In 1836 Lorenzo set up a phrenological establishment in New York and in 1838 Orson set up another in Philadelphia. They also founded the *American Phrenological Journal and Miscellany*, which continued until 1911. Expanding into publishing reprints of the phrenological greats as well as their own works, by the 1840s they had one of the largest publishing concerns in New York.

Lorenzo travelled to England in 1860 with his wife Lydia, daughter Jessie, and his partner Samuel Wells.[iv] Fowler lectured widely in Britain and his tours resulted in the birth of numerous new phrenological societies. In 1862 Fowler emigrated to Britain and the following year he established the *Fowler Institute* at Imperial Buildings, Ludgate Circus in London. The *British Phrenological Association*, which was established in 1886, survived until 1967—and attracted plenty of press attention. After all, phrenologists were going to change the world.

Phrenologists Say They are Advancing

The opening meeting of the autumn session of the British Phrenological Association was held at the Memorial Hall, Farringdon-street, on Tuesday evening, when a paper was read by the honorary secretary on 'The Present Position and Future Prospects of Phrenology.'

---

ii 1811–1896.
iii 1809–1887.
iv 1820–75.

The writer of the paper said phrenology was making rapid progress among the masses. It was gradually taking the place of vague and abstract philosophies. The only opponents of phrenology were scientific men, who, whenever they referred to the subject, showed that they had not taken the trouble to make themselves even moderately acquainted with its teachings.[2]

When Bessie took it up, a phrenologist provided character analyses as well as speculating on the interactions between the faculties. Most phrenologists ran their bare fingertips over a head to distinguish any elevations or indentations. Sometimes callipers, measuring tapes or other instruments were used. A skilled phrenologist knew not only the cartographic layout of the head according to their phrenological chart but also the details of the organs and their relationships. Interpretations relied on temperament and humour, based on the four elements of fire, earth, air and water, and the qualities of hot, cold, moist and dry plus the four essential fluids of blood, phlegm, yellow bile and black bile. In other words, phrenology used the same conceptual basis as astrology. In fact, a phrenological interpretation reads very much like an astrological analysis. For example, a 1912 reading by William Hatfield for a Miss Percival says:

> She has a large brain, combined with a good share of vitality, and Nature has furnished all the elements necessary for the development of distinct ability, and strength of purpose. She inherits her qualities from the father's side, and during her youth will be quite a 'tomboy'. She is sensitive, and extremely susceptible to mental and social influences. She is well balanced yet precocious. She has a high degree of nervous activity. As she grows up, let her amuse herself with boys, picture books and play with children her own age. Do not think of sending her to school, till she is at least seven.
>
> Her head is full at the sides, giving courage, energy, and executive power, hence she will quickly translate her thoughts into actions, and be known as a brave and fearless character. She will be industrious, and show an aptitude for business, money making, and never remain poor. She has natural sagacity, reserve, tact, and forethought, and though she is forcible and determined, yet she will be watchfull [sic] and equal to an emergency.
>
> In reference to a vocation, she will be in her element as a lady doctor or science teacher.[3]

But many accounts of the later stages of phrenology miss the point. It didn't just involve reading bumps on the head. For most people, phrenology was primarily a form of entertainment. Phrenologists often appeared on bills with musicians, singers and other entertainers. Despite demands to be taken seriously, they were under no illusion as to what their audiences thought of them. 'The phrenologist's work is not one of idly entertaining people or catering to their sense of the ridiculous and making them laugh,'[4] John Thompson said defensively in about 1890.

It often was.

What had started out as cutting-edge science had morphed into a practical and straightforward means of character analysis, a new type of popular psychology, and a way of transmitting medical advice—especially in terms of birth control and women's health issues. Indeed, many talks were delivered solely to women for this reason. (Lydia Fowler was only the second woman in the US to receive a medical degree and she used phrenology as part of her medical practice.)

And its followers weren't limited to the ignorant and gullible. For example, in 1850 Karl Marx conducted a phrenological examination as part of his interview of Wilhelm Liebknecht when he arrived in London to become a member of the *German Workers' Education Society*.

Phrenology also had a spiritual component for many who saw in the organs *Veneration* and *Wonder* additional evidence for the design of a Creator. However, phrenology gradually became associated with social activists, providing a scientific justification for establishing the type of social order they craved. It was applied to education reform and the treatment of the insane and criminal, as well as to the hiring of servants. Phrenologists often provided character references to ensure a prospective employee was honest and hard-working.

It sounds marvellously respectable and Victorian. Phrenology had become a movement based on self-improvement through self-knowledge. And what its audiences wanted to improve their self-knowledge on was their sex life—how to do it, when to do it, who to do it with, and what would become of you if you did it alone.

In 1877 Annie Besant and Charles Bradlaugh had been convicted of obscene libel for publishing Charles Knowton's *Fruits of Philosophy*, a treatise on contraception. The sentence was overturned on appeal and Besant published her own book advocating birth control, *The Laws of Population*. The idea of a woman advocating birth control received widespread publicity. Newspapers like *The Times* accused Besant of writing 'an indecent, lewd, filthy, bawdy and obscene book'.[5]

In such an atmosphere, reliable information could be hard to find. But the phrenologists, the physiogonomists (face readers), and other related 'ists' not only discussed sex (and subjects such as masturbation, abortion and menstruation) openly, they did so in an entertaining way. And they produced book after book expanding on their views. For example, John Thompson said in *Man and his Sexual Relations: Embracing the Evils and Remedies of a Misguided Youth, Manhood, and Married Life* (a title that promised to be pleasingly comprehensive)[v] in 1883 said:

> Seduction is a crime that may be worse than murder, and is a thousand times worse than any other. It is without a parallel! Nothing in the world is so inhuman, so villainous, so damnable, as this crime! Those who commit it should be submitted to the uttermost bodily torture that human skill can contrive, and should afterwards be rendered incapable of repeating the offense.[6]

John Thompson

Thompson also pointed out: 'Every man has the power to regulate the number of his own offspring.'[7] He excitedly ascribed insanity, criminal tendencies, and suicide to childhood self-abuse. Everything wrong with society was due to sex. 'I know of nothing so perverted as man's sexual nature. Society is rotten—rotten to its very core!'[8]

---

v Thompson was also the author of *Phrenology and its Uses* (1880); *Body, Brain, and Mind; Facts About Tobacco* (1890); *How to Remember: or, The Art of Never Forgetting; Love and Matrimony* and *Fashion and Folly: a dissertation on dress reform, embracing tight-lacing and other fallacies* (1890).

It was obviously a good idea to have a phrenologist check out your amativeness organ, which amongst other things indicated your desire to caress, kiss and fondle, something Bessie had no desire for at all. She'd told Murray she was going to lead a celibate life and wanted to marry someone who thought the same as her, with whom she could live for companionship alone. Murray said such a thing wasn't possible for men and women. Phillips simply told her she was crazy.

Although sex scandals permeated the occult scene, and numerous people practiced forms of sex magic (although often only between married couples), there were many who insisted celibacy was the key to enlightenment, as described earlier—a number of theosophists amongst them. Blavatsky claimed to be a virgin, although many of her biographers dispute this, pointing out she married twice and probably bore a son. 'For morality to exist between men and women in their daily life, they must make perfect chastity their law,'[9] she insisted. 'The use of liquors, of beef, and certain other meats and certain vegetables, and the relations of marriage prevent spiritual development.'[10]

Olcott advocated strict celibacy, despite having married and fathered children. Judge was a little more restrained saying, 'Sexual intercourse is a right and proper thing when used for its right object as intended by nature, i.e., the propagation of children. But, if indulged in simply for personal and sensual gratification, it becomes like any other passion, and as regards this you can decide for yourself.'[11]

People did decide for themselves. Celibacy was never a theosophical rule, although many theosophists recommended abstinence. Taking up phrenology did more for Bessie, however, than simply supply her with a rationale for her views on sex—money was a major consideration. Phillips complained that Bessie had never made a penny and wouldn't be able to manage without him. 'I can make a good living as a phrenologist,' said Bessie, ' and can be quite independent of you if you will only let me do it.'[12]

Phillips laughed at her—he did this a lot—but Bessie was determined. She took classes from the Fowler Institute and was examined by a lady from Hastings who travelled to Southampton to assess candidates. Bessie was then granted a diploma in phrenology and placed a brass plate on her front door, which stated:

Miss Birch[vi] Professor of Phrenology, Graphology and Palmistry[13]

And she gained clients almost immediately.

---

vi Bessie used the spellings 'Birch' and 'Burch' interchangeably.

> The lady has a decided gift for palmistry and, I believe, for psychometry as well. I know quite a number of persons who have been astonished at her power to trace out the varying incidents of their lives in the lines of their hands.[14]

At first, Bessie charged five shillings a reading, but she was soon able to charge a guinea for a full reading—for a written one, two guineas. When she had saved £40, she took it into the dining room and poured it onto the table saying, 'There, that is my money, I have made it.'[15] At last Bessie had her father's respect.

And from about 1888, Bessie joined the lecture circuit. Any reservations Phillips might have had disappeared when she was paid five guineas for a lecture one evening. Bessie travelled widely giving talks and performing readings. She also had an office at home where she saw clients and wrote up her analyses. Many of Bessie's talks took place at charitable events, and for at least some of these she donated her fee.

> Miss Burch gave phrenological delineations, and her efforts on behalf of the good cause were much appreciated.[16]

But her talks with titles such as *Love, Courtship, Marriage* served to highlight the fact she was still unmarried. This bothered Phillips more than Bessie. She'd had several Jewish suitors, and Phillips told her that if she married one who was particularly wealthy, he'd give her £10,000 on her wedding day.[17] Bessie refused and Phillips later joked she'd saved him money. And she may have stayed unmarried if it hadn't been for a pesky holiday romance.

At some point on her phrenological travels, Bessie met Hannah Thompson,[vii] a fellow phrenologist, and they became close friends. Hannah was married to John Thompson[viii]—the man who was so excited about seduction above. Thompson was from a family of miners. Indeed, he'd started his working life as a miner himself, and he wasn't the only member of his family to adopt a change in career. His brother William also became a phrenologist along with his wife Martha Ann,[ix] and Thompson's sister Elizabeth[x] was an astrologer who married the phrenologist John Barton Keswick[xi] from Wigton

---

vii 1866–unknown.
viii Thompson (1858–1921) became bankrupt in Harrogate in 1905, complaining that people insisted on going to the theatre or football matches rather than have their heads examined.
ix 1863–unknown.
x 1866–1935.
xi 1856–1935.

in 1883—hurriedly, as she was heavily pregnant at the time.

The Thompsons lived with their two children, Florence and John, Hannah's father Joseph, a retired boot manufacturer, Hannah's sister Annie, and her brother John Joseph Spark[xii]—also a phrenologist—in Broughton House, Scarborough.[xiii]

The three families formed a phrenological powerhouse. They toured the country, especially the north-west of England and Wales, to give lectures and readings, published each other's books and from at least 1888 ran a hydropathic hotel in Scarborough—in the past, Joseph Spark had run a temperance hotel, so he knew what he was doing.[xiv] It was a risk considering that a few years before Robert Blackley Wells,[xv] an American phrenologist living in Scarborough, had extended his home at Observatory Villa, West Bank to turn it into the Scarborough Hydropathic Establishment.

Following Keswick's twenty-seven rules for administering water treatment, Broughton House offered covering of the whole body in a wet blanket, wet girdles or an oil inunction. Perhaps you'd prefer a magnetic rubbing performed by a 'highly magnetic person', a douche or enema? Or you could take an electric bath, which involves placing a negative pole in the bath and applying the positive to the nape of the neck through a sponge—something Keswick recommended was best done by a skilled operator.

And in the evenings, you could have your head read.

This was where Bessie took her summer holidays. Spark was smitten with Bessie and asked her to marry him. 'But I refused, partly because I did not love him, and partly because I knew my father would never permit the union.'[18]

Although he was based in Bournemouth,[xvi] for much of 1890 and 1891 Spark spent his time in Cardiff where he'd hired a shop in the

---

xii 1863–1918.

xiii The Sparks were originally from Bishop Auckland, Durham. The Keswicks were still at Broughton House until at least 1896. At some point the hotel was sold and the new owners went bankrupt in 1907.

xiv Phrenologists were in general fond of hydropathy. Lorenzo Fowler had co-founded, and was for a time vice-president of, the American Hydropathic Association and John Barton Keswick wrote *Baths: Or, The Water Cure Made Easy* in 1887, which was published by John Thompson.

xv Died 1903. Wells was convicted of indecency and obscene libel in 1900 and imprisoned for twelve months. Closed in 1904, his hydropathic hotel was renamed the Green Gables Hotel in 1923 and still exists as a hotel at the time of writing, although its days appear numbered.

xvi Living at 109 Christchurch Road.

highly fashionable Queen's Arcade[xvii] to read heads as 'Professor Spark' on weekday evenings and Saturday mornings, charging one shilling a reading. He also offered delineations from photographs, for which he charged more and promised to teach clients 'the secret of success in life, how to marry suitably, to understand each other, to train peculiar children, the Art of Self-improvement, etc.'[19] When Spark first started working in Cardiff, John and Hannah Thompson were down the road in Newport, offering a three-week course in phrenology. In his free time, Spark preached for the Wesleyan church.[20]

Spark proudly displayed the letters F S Sc after his name. Unfortunately, the *Society of Science, Letters and Art*, which flourished between 1882 and 1902 was a bit on the dodgy side and was exposed in 1892, when it had 1,500 members, by the journal *Truth*. It sold fellowships and a nice badge so people who hadn't got any real academic kudos could look interesting. John Yarker and his cohorts were also members; in fact, the Society was packed with freemasons. The Society's dodgiest move was selling exam papers to schools—which they did a roaring trade in—this wasn't so bad until they refused to mark them. Nonetheless, the Society continued to be popular and hosted monthly talks, many of which Spark gave.

Like other phrenologists, Spark offered consultations which dealt with the nitty-gritty of life—life and death, sex and family, which he described in 1891:

> In the course of his ordinary duties he [the phrenologist] must, as a priest, give advice on health, as a judge with acuteness decide between contending parties ... he is often a mesmerist, a medical electrician, a hydropathist, a psychologist, and an astrologist. The sanctum, or consultation-room, of the phrenologist may well be regarded as a hallowed place. There is a veil of mystery overhanging it, which lends its charms to the minds of thousands ... Curiosity prompts us to push the veil aside, and commune with the phrenologist ... Having entered, we may find the stock-in-

---

xvii Cardiff's first arcade was built in 1835 on Church Street. Encouraged by its success, and as part of the Cardiff Arcade Company's attempts to improve the area, further arcades were built hosting a staggeringly wide variety of trades. Opened in 1875, Queen Street Arcade went from Queen Street to Working Street and looked down on the Glamorganshire Canal which passed under Queen Street to the east. It comprised pierced pinnacles, trefoiled decorations and balconied windows, and bustled with offices, tailors, wine merchants, jewellers, architects and artists. At the time Spark was working there, it was prime shopping space. In 1992 it was demolished along with Alder's department store which stood next to it on Queen Street to be replaced by Queens Arcade in 1994.

John Joseph Spark

trade ... It may consist of a few folding chairs and a table ... a few charts hung up on the wall, a number of registers on the table, pen, ink, blotting paper, etc., or we may find ourselves ushered into a magnificent gallery of oil paintings representing all the most notable characters, with here and there a statue, true to life, and on the bookstands volumes of mind lore, such as the ancient seers sighed for in vein, without which philosophers were drowned in the sea of their own speculations on mental science, and which were the dream of poets ...[21]

Obviously, some phrenologists offered better advice than others. Robert Blackley Wells came up with gems like, 'Some ladies are hard to please in the selection of a pattern for a new dress'[22] and 'Excessive tea drinking tends to produce irritability of temper and consequent scolding.'[23]

Spark hadn't given up with Bessie. They collaborated in writing a book entitled *The Right Girl, The Right Place* which discussed ways of locating the right servants and was published in 1891. The same year, they also produced another book entitled *Marriage a Success. Choice in Wedlock, Embracing Love, Courtship, etc.* describing Bessie's (and what she believed were Spark's) views on love and sex.[xviii]

Physical love is like fire, a good servant when held in subjection, but a dreadful master; those ladies know this, to their sorrow, who have sensual husbands. Thousands have married for what they thought was true love, but which they soon found out was merely mock love. In choosing a sweetheart allow judgment to be satisfied first; then love freely, and you will love well and long. Though spiritual love is the most important, we must not underrate the value of physical love. Amativeness, another name for physical love, helps to form the basis of choice in the selection of a partner.

Perverted love, i.e. lust, is the biggest of hypocrites, commonly going under the name of love, traducing the honour and blighting the well-being of hundreds and thousands, in so much that they long for death to put an end to their pain. Perverted love gives rise to wranglings, jealousies, bitter hatred, open fights, murders, revolutions, and wars between nations. In its various forms it has caused inestimable ill. Often crawling in serpent fashion it fixes its seductive glance upon its poor victim, strikes its deadly fangs

---

xviii Spark also wrote *The Human Face Divine and How to Read It* (1891), which he dedicated to Bessie in thanks for her revisions and corrections.

into it, then flings its coils around it in its deadly embrace; or, as a ravenous beast, preying upon our loved ones—mothers, sisters, daughters—devouring their honour, beauty, happiness, health, and life. This passion, when uncontrolled, is the world's vampire.[24]

Again, Spark suggested they married. 'I told him I had never yet cared for any man in that way,' said Bessie, 'and … that my marriage to a Christian was impossible.'[25]

To Bessie's surprise, Spark offered to convert to Judaism. 'I will become a member of the Hebrew faith for your sake, and shall call on your father and tell him so.'[26]

'I tried to point out the physical danger he would incur and that it would be a great ordeal,'[27] Bessie said, but Spark was insistent.

Bessie pointed out, yet again, that she planned a celibate life. Spark said this was fine by him as it was what he wanted too. And as part of this companionable life, they could work together as phrenologists. Spark said that although he had no money, he was a hard worker and between them they would do well. 'It never once occurred to me that as my father was then a very wealthy man I should be considered a good match from that viewpoint,'[28] Bessie later said, unconvincingly.

Finally, Bessie asked for six months to think it over. She spent much of the summer of 1892 in Bournemouth with Spark, helping him with his business. In June 1892, she was staying in Weston-Super-Mare while the Keswicks were working twenty miles away in Wells—it's likely they spent time together.

Bessie returned to Southampton in August. However, she soon went back to Spark, returning for the second time in October. Finally, she accepted Spark's proposal and Spark went to see Phillips—who instantly decided he liked him, describing him as 'clever and unselfish,'[29] not least because he was willing to become a Jew, although he said it was Bessie's problem if she chose a poor man—and he wasn't giving her any money. A month later, Spark had converted to Judaism and wedding plans were underway. Bessie wrote to her cousin Amelia in excitement:

> Dear Amelia, No, I have not forgotten you but am professional now, with a brass plate on the door and heaps to do. I get no time for correspondence. Still I should have written you shortly to tell you some news. I am going to be married soon to a gentleman who has become a Jew for my sake. I have known him several years. He is a professional man, but not rich. That I do not mind. He is clever, well behaved, a good man, and unselfish. It makes or mars a woman's life into what man's hands she falls.[30]

CHAPTER FIVE

FLAPDOODLE ASTROLOGERS

THE SALES OF POWLEY'S *ASTROLOGER* MAGAZINE had begun to wane, along with his enthusiasm. It appeared less regularly and, as a last attempt to attract readers, Powley alienated the few serious astrologers who still read it by including material on horse racing—the horror!

Powley wrote regularly to Lacey, and he mentioned the end was nigh for the *Astrologer*. That gave Lacey an idea. He wrote to Alan and asked him to call to discuss a proposition. 'He came and I suggested that it was evident the *Astrologer* would not last much longer, and we might start a new magazine devoted solely to "Astrology," with no horse-racing introduced.'[1]

They talked it over at length and decided to discuss the suggestion with everyone else at the next meeting of their astrology group at Lacey's house. Lacey said, 'We accordingly did so, and asked if they would be disposed to take a part financially and astrologically in the suggested undertaking.'[2]

Everyone thought the idea was good, but investing money in it was a different matter entirely. After all, no astrology magazine lasted long. Although Lacey and Alan argued that former periodicals had been heavy reading and on the dull side, and all they needed to do was produce more interesting copy, no-one was convinced. In the end, they decided to revisit the matter at a later meeting.

It made no difference. After the meeting was over, Lacey walked Alan to the station and told him that if he was, 'Prepared to put down a certain sum, which I named, I would do likewise, and that the Magazine should be run on business lines for twelve months, and that if during that period it was a success we would jointly continue it.'³ He told Alan to think it over and let him know the next week.

Alan did so, and he agreed. They were going to produce a magazine, despite neither of them having any idea of what it entailed. As astrologers, they did the obvious and set up a chart for that date—21 November 1889—and saw, as Lacey said, 'The testimonies for success were exceptionally good.'⁴

Although Alan and Lacey had no experience in publishing magazines, they did have experience in what astrologers wanted to read. For one, Powley's decision to include correspondence from readers was a first in astrological literature and they recognised the importance of this. And Alan at least had big ideas, as Lacey pointed out:

> Alan's ideals were always lofty; he always wanted the best. His idea was to have a very attractive cover, but when the estimate of the cost of the one he would have liked came before us, the price was too high so he reluctantly abandoned the idea for the time and suggested that I should design some kind of border having the signs of the Zodiac and the planets thereon. I made two or three sketches, and we adopted one, which he had photo-lithoed, the cost being comparatively low.⁵

It took a while to decide on the title, but they eventually settled on the dull but to the point the *Astrologers' Magazine*, and decided to charge 4d per copy and base its size on the popular *Strand* magazine.ⁱ However, on consulting the stars, Alan and Lacey discovered there wouldn't be a good date for its launch until 20 July 1890—at least they had plenty of time to get organised.

Powley was happy to advertise the forthcoming magazine in the Astrologer and Lacey and Alan discussed their project at length with friends, at one point telling Walter Old their plans. He wished them success and promptly launched his own magazine, *Fate and Fortune*, in June 1890—the same month that the *Astrologer* folded.ⁱⁱ

It wasn't as if Old could pretend he hadn't realised, so in the first issue of *Fate and Fortune* he said, 'We understand that a new magazine on

---

i The first copy went on sale late 1890 and sold nearly 300,000 copies. It lasted until the 1930s.
ii It was briefly replaced by the *Attractor* of which only one issue appeared.

Alan Leo

astrology is to follow close on our heels. The *Astrologers' Magazine* is to be devoted solely to astrology, and promises to be a good thing from the notice we have elsewhere read.'[6]

'We foresaw uphill work in consequence of this competition, but we would not alter the date of our publishing, nor did we,' said Lacey determinedly.[7]

They had to think, and fast. Much of the content had already been decided—beginners' lessons, a letters page, a notable horoscope and extracts from the works of renowned astrologers of the past, all to be written by their contacts, including 'Edwin Casael', 'Asthomel', 'Athomiel' (presumably from the Celestial Brotherhood), the American astrologer Charles Hatfield and N Chidambaram Iyer, a fellow theosophist and an expert in Hindu astrology as well as palmistry.

Their finances were helped along by Ebenezer Roberts agreeing to take out advertising space in the magazine. Alan had been supplying Roberts with astrological reports from the start of his employment. His reputation (although not Roberts' cash flow) was enhanced when he warned Roberts against making an investment in a company suggested by his sons. Roberts ignored him and subsequently lost £3,000.

Alan and Lacey needed something more, something to persuade potential readers that their magazine was the one to buy. And they needed subscribers. 'We decided to give horoscopes free of charge with a short delineation to annual subscribers who remitted their subscriptions direct to us,' said Lacey, 'and with this object in view we arranged to insert a loose coupon in every number issued.'[8]

Lacey refused point blank to do the required calculations, saying he had enough of figures in his day job. So the calculation was left to Alan with Lacey writing the interpretations. Alan wasn't much of a writer anyway, so Lacey agreed to write the astrology lessons as well as deal with any correspondence. In short, Lacey agreed to produce most of the magazine, while Alan dealt with the business end of arranging printing and distribution.

Nervously, they went ahead as planned, although they were only assured of twelve subscribers for the first issue. As it worked out, they sold fifty copies.

Alan was away for most of the week and Lacey worked until six o'clock—plus he played the organ for much of Sunday. When the coupons for free charts started to come in, Alan calculated the charts on Friday evenings and took them to Lacey to delineate. Once the number increased, Alan spent most of Saturday and Sunday, working until the early hours of the morning, calculating horoscopes and posting them to Lacey on Sunday night who wrote out the judgments piecemeal during the week. (Occasionally, when the workload was particularly high, Alan did a few of the delineations.) During the first year, they sent out 1,500 free horoscopes. By the time the free horoscopes ended, about 4,000 had been sent out.

But that came later. Lacey and Alan waited with bated breath for feedback from their first issue. The astrologer Raphael[iii]—one of the biggest names on the astrological scene at the time (which wasn't much of an achievement; it was a small scene) made encouraging comments in his almanac, which was nice, but more helpfully the *Daily News*[9] printed a column under the heading 'Cheap Astrology'. Never has 'all publicity is good publicity' been more true. Not only did it drastically increase the magazine's circulation, it offered advertising far beyond what Lacey and Alan could have afforded to pay for.

In September 1890, Old admitted defeat. Alan promptly went to see him and engaged his services, later announcing, 'It having been found that two periodicals on Astrology must be somewhat antagonistic … we decided after mature consideration that the interests of the science would be best served by only one periodical continuing.'[10]

Old's version was slightly different: 'Owing to the great demand made upon our time by the publication of *Fate and Fortune*, added to the fact that it has always been an expense to us, which we do not feel justified in meeting any longer, we beg to announce that we have transferred our copyrights and interest, without reserve, to the proprietors of the *Astrologers' Magazine* … It is respectfully suggested that our subscribers should consent to receive copies of the *Astrologers' Magazine*.'[11]

From the November 1890 issue, Old was listed as joint editor of the *Astrologers' Magazine*, and now almost every astrologer wanted to write for it. They even persuaded John Thomas to offer his 'Symbols of the Degrees of the Zodiac'—after testing its content and deciding it was 'satisfactory.'[iv] Alan called to visit Thomas again and the series continued

---

iii Robert (born Frederick) Thomas Cross (15 May 1850, Worstead at 2:35–26 February 1832) began his astrological studies in 1862 and moved to London at the age of fifteen to work in an engineer's office. Editor of the *Prophetic Messenger*, Cross obtained the copyright to *Raphael's Ephemeris* in 1874. Cross was convinced he was able to mesmerise both animals and vegetables and in 1885, he returned to his home town to grow and sell exotic plants (especially orchids). In 1893 Cross's almanac sold 200,000 copies. He joined the Theosophical Society 12 January 1891.

iv No-one understood why Thomas believed the zodiac began at 25 degrees of Libra. The degree descriptions were obtained psychically to help rectify horoscopes. They gained the

for three years. George Wilde, who had written for Powley's *Astrologer* under the name of 'Mars and the Goat (♂ in ♑), offered to supply some material, although grudgingly. As he later said, 'I am no flapdoodle astrologer'.[12]

Alan was still travelling around the country, increasing his circle rapidly. At the start of 1891, he announced he would be visiting Leamington Spa, Liverpool, Burnley, Manchester, Bristol, and Gloucester in February, and would give free lectures on astrology. Whether or not people wanted a lecture from Alan, they were going to get one. At least one, as Lacey explained:

> He arranged and delivered these lectures on his journeys in response to invitations from students in those towns, and the result encouraged him. This was the start of his career as a lecturer on Astrology ... He would give lectures in series; one introductory lecture on the general principles of Astrology at his first visit, and other lectures on the various details of signs, planets, houses, and so on at subsequent visits.'[13]

At Lacey's suggestion, Alan called on Henry Selby Green in Bournemouth. Green, who was to become Alan's lifelong friend, was originally from Norfolk and had been a spiritualist since at least 1879, when a letter appears from him in the *Medium and Daybreak*. Green had moved to Christchurch where he ran a chemist's shop on the high street and was 'a vegetarian, teetotaller and a confirmed bachelor, and he suggestively says he shall remain so.'[14] He was soon to write under the name of 'Leo' or 'H. S. G.' in the *Astrologers' Magazine*.[v]

When they first met, Green didn't find Alan to be much fun, 'There were times when the seriousness of Saturn showed itself markedly in his demeanour and ... Alan was somewhat reticent and even melancholy at times.'[15] (Fortunately, in the long term Green thought Alan became 'a very happy man, smiling and light-hearted.'[16])

A more local recipient of Alan's visits was Yorkshire born Thomas Wilson[vi] who was friendly with R H Penny and lived with his wife Matilda in Caledonian Road, London. Wilson was a spiritualist and described

---

attention of Marc Edmond Jones, who decided he wanted to create a more universal set of symbols, which led to the creation of the Sabian Symbols with Elsie Wheeler in 1925.
v From about June 1891, Green's articles appeared in almost every issue. He was later Secretary of the Bournemouth Theosophical Lodge, His business was highly successful and by 1911 he had retired to live alone with his cook, housemaids, chauffeur and footman.
vi He died early 1895.

himself as a 'medical galvanist' in 1891. In 1880 Wilson was charged at Clerkenwell with unlawfully pretending to tell fortunes, despite having worked as an astrologer for fifty years.

Although Alan would descend upon people at the drop of a hat, that didn't mean his visits were unwelcome. On the contrary, a number of subscribers wrote and suggested Alan—and Lacey—should call to see them. Usually, they politely refused such requests. However, one lady in Yorkshire refused to give up. While she was waiting for a positive response, she asked if Alan or Lacey could do a horoscope for a ship. Alan was ready to refuse, but Lacey decided it was worth a go and sent his delineation. Considering she'd sent them a number of subscribers, Alan made sure to visit when he was in the area and spent the day with her, declaring her to be 'a very talented lady, extremely fond of the occult'.[17]

This unnamed lady suggested Alan returned, this time with Lacey. They decided to spend the weekend with her and travelled overnight to arrive on the Saturday morning. The next day, their hostess had invited twenty-five locals to meet Alan and Lacey. It was the first time Lacey had heard Alan speak, and he listened to him patiently for an hour. When Lacey was asked if he'd speak, he demurred. And then one of the men mentioned he was the owner of the ship Lacey had cast a horoscope for.

He stood up and said, 'If the data supplied were correct, whatever I stated in my remarks on the subject I adhere to. In my opinion, the same astrological rules should apply to a ship as to a child. I should be very glad to hear whether the submitted delineation was borne out by facts.'[18]

The man responded that he was astounded to receive the delineation and asked, 'Have you been in this part of England before?'

'No,' said Lacey, 'this is my first visit.'

The man went on to say that apart from one or two minor points, the delineation was accurate, to the extent that it was wrecked at the time Lacey had suggested. Everyone was delighted with the outcome and suitably impressed—apart from Lacey who fretted he hadn't had the sense to keep a copy of the chart so he could publish it.

In June, 1891, Alan prepared a balance sheet. They were able to recoup their investment and so decided to continue. To make a little extra money, they had their back issues bound in volumes. And the free charts continued. Anyone renewing their subscription could receive a year's prediction; new subscribers a short horoscope as before.

There was one astrologer who was less than appreciative of their work—Alfred John Pearce, or as he was better known, *Zadkiel*.

Pearce[viii] was the son of a homeopathic physician and had ceased his medical studies due to a lack of funds, although he did work as an assistant to physicians for a while. He had studied astrology with Richard James Morrison (the first Zadkiel) and in 1875 he was offered the editorship of *Zadkiel's Almanac*. Pearce regarded astrology as a science, favouring weather prediction and political astrology over the character reading astrology Alan was so fond of. He also rejoiced in pointing out other people's mistakes and drove Lacey into a state of apoplectic fury. It came to a head when he revealed a number of the *Astrologers' Magazine's* contributors' true names in his magazine *The Future*. Not only was this the height of bad manners, it also put people at risk of losing their jobs and having legal action taken against them. Also, he persisted in pointing out calculation errors, blaming Lacey for them. Although any calculation was normally left to Alan, Lacey was forced to defend himself.

It would be tedious to go into the details of their arguments, although it's delightful to read later that things were stirred up by one who was 'Wilde by name and wild by nature'.[ix] [19] As Lacey said, 'These silly attacks of our contemporary are in reality beneath my notice.' Unfortunately, Lacey continued to poke at Pearce, writing an article entitled 'False prophets and teachers' after which Pearce expanded his attack to include other contributors to the *Astrologers' Magazine*. And it didn't help when Pearce declared theosophy was 'nauseating'.[20]

By July 1894, Lacey had had enough.[x] He decided to give up his role as editor, although he still occasionally contributed articles to the

---

viii Zadkiel III's father, Charles Thomas Pearce (1815–1883), an homeopath, was tried for manslaughter in 1849 after his brother died following homeopathic treatment. Pearce was acquitted and he and his son went on to work together in medicine. Alfred John Pearce was born at 9:20 am on 10 November 1840 in his parents' home at 13 King William Street, London; there were two other children. He died in 1923.

ix Born 16 April 1860, George Wilde took pride in being a scientific astrologer and was based in Halifax. He was a railway signalman before turning to astrology and becoming the author of several astrology books and producing *Antares* almanac. Wilde married Phyllis Dickenson and had a daughter, Emily, born in 1885 who worked as a cotton reeler.

x In addition to his rapidly growing family, and musical commitments, Lacey led a double life. By 1901 the Laceys had twenty-five-year-old Nellie Higgs (Ellen Lizzie) as a general domestic servant and she became Lacey's mistress and the mother of nine 'Williams' children. By this time, four further Lacey children had been born. It would be easy to become distracted by Lacey's shenanigans, and his story is still being untangled by his descendants. Suffice it to say, although Lacey had said he'd marry Nellie once Florence died, this marriage never took place. Florence died in 1915, and before his death in on 11 December 1932, Lacey had fathered three more Williams children, the last when he was sixty.

magazine. Apart from having limited free time, Lacey also found Alan hard to work with. 'His ideals were always lofty: "his heart would run away with his head," and in consequence unprincipled people pressed upon him; they would "tell him the tale," and he assisted these parasites. It was a weak point of his; I often used to warn him about it, but there it was; our temperaments are not all alike, and I detested seeing a good man imposed upon. I used occasionally to see him after our partnership was dissolved, and when I was in "low water" … he extended a helping hand to me, as I had done to him in the early days of our acquaintance.'[21]

For some time, some readers had complained about the amount of theosophy creeping into the *Astrologers' Magazine*. Rather than listen to them, Alan decided to make the magazine more staunchly theosophical, renaming it *Modern Astrology* in July 1895 and pledging to modernise the 'ancient system of Astrology.' He also rented an office in Bouverie Street, off Fleet Street and raised the price per issue to 6d.

From now on, he was determined to establish a more spiritual and psychological form of astrology, concentrating on character rather than prediction. As a later assistant, Annie Barley, said, 'His life work was to cleanse the Augean stables of astrology, and only those who worked in close touch with him know what an accumulation of filth there was in those stables, and what slime he waded through.'[22]

Or as Charles Carter later commented, Alan wanted to 'set out to purify Astrology from dross and superstition, to rescue maiden Urania from the dragon.'[23]

Alan was ready to fight any dragons that came his way.

CHAPTER SIX

IMPULSIVE SOULS

A POOR OLD MAN BESSIE called 'Bentley' who had been one of her clients, and who had two sons at Adyar (the headquarters of the Theosophical Society), said to her, 'I have something you will like, a book after your own heart.'[1]

He gave Bessie a copy of A P Sinnett's *Esoteric Buddhism*. That night, she climbed into bed, lit the gas lamp and read throughout the night, 'Except for intervals when tears literally rained from my eyes and I could no longer see the print.'[2]

Bessie had been regularly attending the local synagogue but only to please her father. And she'd attended talk after talk on a variety of religious subjects—none of which enlightened her. And now: 'I pressed the book to my bosom as a well-loved friend,' said Bessie, 'crying: I have found the truth … Oh, God, I thank Thee for the light.'[3]

The next morning she woke up as a theosophist. 'Out of the darkness of ignorance the light flashed forth, and I who had been so blind, saw.'[4] Everything made sense! Karma, reincarnation …

Unfortunately, Bentley was found dead the following Monday.

A month later, Bessie attended a lecture by Annie Besant in Southampton. 'I felt my heart go out to her in admiration and worship, for she was a most wonderful speaker, and wished I knew her personally—when a little voice I have often heard interiorly said quietly, "You will know her later on".'[5] A month after that, Bessie joined the Theosophical Society in Bournemouth.

Bessie claimed this happened in 1890. However, it was actually December 1891 when Annie Besant spoke in Southampton. She lectured on behalf of the *National Secular Society*, talking about hypnotism in the morning, Christianity in the afternoon and theosophy in the evening—it was the second lecture that had gained an overflowing hall.

Does it matter? Perhaps not. Except that on 8 May 1891 Helena Blavatsky died, which was reported widely in the press—it's unthinkable that Bessie wouldn't have come across reports.

> Madame Blavatsky, the well-known co-founder and head of the Theosophical Society, died the other day in London, in her 60th year. Madame Blavatsky had been ill for about three weeks, an attack of influenza having led to a serious infection of the kidneys.[6]
>
> There is no immortality, I fancy, for the name of Blavatsky, the arch-priestess of the belief known under the name of theosophy ... [7]

Not all the press coverage was flattering. In fact:

> A protest against the reflections cast by a portion of the Press upon the late Madame Blavatsky has been issued, signed by Mrs Besant and several leading members of the Theosophical Society.[8]

There was a degree of kudos associated with joining the Theosophical Society in the Blavatsky days. You had to have been there ...

What is indisputable is that Bessie embraced theosophy with the same enthusiasm she'd previously had for phrenology. 'I tried vainly to give a little of the Theosophic teaching to my father ... but he begged me not to tell anyone of these ideas but himself, or they might put me under restraint as a lunatic.'[9]

Although Spark had suggested he should join the Theosophical Society as added ammunition to get Bessie to marry him, he doesn't appear to have done so. However, the membership records show Bessie applied to join 14 September 1892 and her diploma was issued on 1 October 1892.[i]

Bessie attended the Bournemouth Theosophical Lodge, the closest to her home in Southampton, before she applied for membership. The secretary of that lodge was Henry Selby Green. Green had persuaded Charles Whitting, a friend of his in the Bournemouth Theosophical Lodge, to subscribe to the *Astrologers' Magazine*. Whitting, a freemason

---

i She was successively an unattached member and later a member of the Bournemouth, Blavatsky, Hampstead, HPB and Bedford Lodges. Her sponsors were J H Moore and C J Whitting.

and Liberal political activist,[ii] was extremely impressed by what he read and asked Bessie if she believed in astrology.

'I don't know that I do,' Bessie replied. 'I have had my horoscope cast several times, but a great deal of what the professors said was not true!'[10]

'I know a man,' Whitting informed her, 'who is simply a wonderful astrologer; what he tells you is most accurate, and he is also a theosophist.'

Bessie politely asked for more details and Whitting pointed out that if she subscribed to the *Astrologers' Magazine*, she would get a free horoscope.

'What is his name?' asked Bessie.

Whitting said, 'Alan Leo.'

Bessie said she experienced 'a curious thrill' and went on to describe Alan.

'Then you know him?' said Mr Whitting. 'You have surely seen him?'

'No,' Bessie replied, 'But I am a little psychic and his face came in a mental picture for a moment. Now, as I want to test astrology for myself will you do me a favour? Here is 6s. 6d, the money for a year's subscription to his magazine, and here is my name, A. B., female, time, place, and date of birth. You write it and say nothing! Promise me!'[11]

Whitting did precisely as she asked, and about three weeks later Bessie received her horoscope, an extract of which is reproduced below:

> Born under the just sign Libra, Venus is your ruling planet. Ability for occultism is shown; in fact it is the feature (♆ ⚹ ♅ △ ♄).
>
> I judge you possess clairvoyant powers. You will, if you seek it, gain financially through occultism.
>
> There is a tendency to disaster when under ill directions (♄ MC).
>
> The disposition seems to be a good, sympathetic and kind one (☿ ☌ ♀), but there is at times a tendency to melancholia (♀ □ ♄), and this at periods may act on health.
>
> The logical and intuitive faculties seem fairly balanced.
>
> I judge the throat will cause you trouble and at the appointed time a throat disease will usher in the *terminus vitae*[iii] suddenly.[12]

Bessie was impressed. 'It was so very true, so very accurate in every detail.'[13] Being an 'impulsive soul'[14] she immediately sat down and wrote to Alan asking whether he ever came to Southampton, and if he did so, would he consider calling to see her? And did he give lessons?

---

ii Born in 1861, Whitting was the author of a history of the Hengist Masonic Lodge, published in 1897. Samuel Lidell Mathers had been initiated into this lodge in 1877.
iii End of life.

The delineation had actually been written by Lacey, although later when Bessie realised Alan didn't write the horoscopes, she made a point of saying that what she received was in Alan's handwriting. Apparently, Lacey had said, 'You do this one, Alan; it's a somewhat difficult one to decipher.'[15]

Obligingly, Alan did, and commented, 'This girl would suit me exactly as a wife. Look, her Sun and my Moon are exactly in the same degrees, and all our major planets trine each other.'[16]

Alan wrote back to Bessie saying carefully that although he didn't see clients, he did have a friend he planned to visit in Bournemouth, so he could call when travelling through Hampshire.

In February 1893, Alan arrived in Southampton. But before calling on Bessie, he visited a friend to ask if he'd heard of 'Miss A B'. It might have put some people off to hear she was a witch. But the fact she was also a 'professor' of palmistry and graphology, and a phrenologist—and more relevantly, very successful—made her sound like Alan's sort of person.

After dinner in his hotel, Alan walked to Bessie's house. It was getting late, too late to call on a stranger, and when he arrived the house was dark, so assuming everyone had already gone to bed, he pushed his card in the letter box and rang the bell. Alan was descending the steps in front of the house when a door in the area below opened and a maid asked what he wanted and who he was. As Alan was explaining himself, Bessie called from behind the front door telling him to wait as she was about to open it.

Ushering Alan indoors, Bessie explained that her father went to bed at nine o'clock and insisted on lights out before he retired. Unless Bessie wanted to sit by the fire in the kitchen, she had to spend the evening alone in her bedroom. The maid rushed to turn on the gas in the drawing room—obviously, a guest couldn't be expected to sit in the kitchen, even though it was probably much warmer. Then until midnight, Alan chatted at length about astrology and theosophy and Bessie told him about palmistry and phrenology.

As Bessie was letting him out, Alan said, 'I am going to Bournemouth tomorrow to a Lodge. I am a theosophist.'

'So am I,' Bessie promptly replied.

'Then we shall meet again very soon,' he said. 'You are a true Libran, and a daughter of Venus.'[17]

Bessie couldn't sleep. 'It was all too wonderful. How I admired Mr Leo's mind!'[18]

The next day they met in Bournemouth, and after Alan gave his talk, he chatted with Bessie, agreeing to teach her astrology. She was thrilled. Alan would later deny he had first met Bessie that evening and he only went to speak to her because someone pointed her out as the daughter of a rich man.

A flurry of letters began to pass between them, and every week they met at the Bournemouth Lodge. 'I had my first lesson on the Signs and Symbols of the Planets written on the sand of the sea-shore. I need not say I listened breathless, absorbed and enthralled by the wonders that were opening out before me.'[19]

Bessie told Alan she was engaged, and when she asked if he was married, Alan responded diplomatically by saying, 'If I could meet with a woman with whom I could live platonically, I would marry her.'[20] What a coincidence! It was exactly what Bessie wanted.

Alan said he'd decided he'd never marry—although he knew there'd be a close call that year. '[He] judged that when the Sun came to sextile of Venus in his 33rd year, followed by very powerful marriage aspects in the 35th year of life, he would meet a female friend, and probably be drawn into an engagement, which he intended to resist. The rulers of destiny thought otherwise.'[21]

Whatever the rulers of destiny thought, the British census offers another reason for Alan's resistance. In 1891, he was living in Lugard Road with his 'wife' Sarah[iv] and her mother Elizabeth.[v] Although she called herself 'Sarah Allan,' Alan and Sarah were never legally married. However, those who married away from the Anglican Church—non-comformists, Catholics and others—didn't necessarily play by the rules and also have a civil wedding, so they may well have been married as far as they were concerned.

And Alan got along well with his mother-in-law, whom he described as his housekeeper. 'At seventy-five she would pass for sixty quite comfortably; she is so nimble and active. It is her kind disposition that keeps her so young ... Now, she has two sons, one by adoption, which is myself (and a better mother I would not wish to possess).'[22]

---

iv Sarah, who was actually Mary Ann Wilson, was born in 1851 in Crowland, near Peterborough. She came from an agricultural family and spent time in service before ending up in London. (If you aren't English, or you're geographically challenged, it might not be immediately obvious that Peterborough is on the Lincolnshire borders, near to where Alan's mother Caroline's family came from, which may or may not be relevant.) No mention of Sarah appears in any of Alan's writing.

v Known as 'Betsey'.

Usefully, a dispute over ownership of Lugard Road after the death of Alan's landlord had meant there was no-one to pay rent to. After a year of living rent-free (until 1892), the deeds still couldn't be found and it took still longer—although it isn't clear how long—for Alan to be persuaded to give a 'deaf and dumb'[23] woman, who was a ward of the late landlord, the title of the property by paying rent to her.

Alan didn't bother pointing out he lived in Upside-Down World, and there's no way of knowing whether Bessie was aware of Sarah's existence.

When it came down to it, perhaps Alan had hit the nail on the head when he'd said, 'Magnetism is responsible for the majority of unions.'[24] Alan and Bessie clearly had plenty of magnetism bouncing between them. And as Bessie said, 'The strength of affection between some mortals is so overpowering that they cannot live apart from each other; the company of each is joy and strength to the other. To such, separation seems to be the loss of all good, it is death, and sometimes ends in death.'[25]

Despite Bessie's sense of drama, they did manage to live apart. Letters flew backwards and forwards between Alan and Bessie about their shared metaphysical interests and he visited her for a second time a few days before her wedding. And on 24 May 1893, Spark and Bessie married in Southampton synagogue.

It was a big affair. Bessie wore a cream brocade satin dress, trimmed with orange blossom and lace with a Honiton lace veil and was followed by four flower girls. She was given away by her cousin Amelia (who wore dark heliotrope brocade) and Amelia's husband, Harris Levy, acted as Spark's best man.

> When the ceremony commenced the bride and bridegroom took their places beneath the canopy, their relatives and friends standing close by. The marriage service ... was, of course, performed in Hebrew, although a translation of the marriage contract was given in English, and the Benediction was also pronounced in that language. Special interest attached to the symbolic portions of the ceremonial, where the contracting parties drank from the cup of joy and the cup of sorrow, the bridegroom, with his foot, broke a wine glass in token that would remain faithful until the shivered pieces of glass should again come together in their former shape. Then, again, the bridegroom placed the ring first upon the index finger of the bride ...[26]

Amongst the crowd of Bessie's friends who were present, and who apparently showered her with expensive gifts, were Hannah and John

Thompson. It's not clear why Michael Phillips didn't give her away, but he was certainly present and stepped forward to kiss Bessie as soon as she was married.

Directly after their wedding, the Sparks boarded the *Columbia* and travelled to New York where they arrived 1 June. Bessie never said what they did in the USA, but they travelled back on the *Augusta Victoria*, arriving back in Southampton 23 June. Although they travelled in the second cabin, rather than first class, both ships were luxurious, especially the *Augusta Victoria*, the first luxury liner at Hamburg America which introduced the concept of the 'floating hotel': 'She had 'a rococo stairhall, illuminated by a milky way of pear-shaped prisms and naked light bulbs clutched by gilded cherubs, a reception court choked by palm trees and a dark and gothic smoking room.'[27]

On their return, Bessie settled in Bournemouth with Spark. She spent every weekend with her father but kept an office and reception room in Bournemouth for clients and spent long days performing readings and giving lectures. It didn't take long for Alan to call at their office—he still hadn't met Spark at this point. A customer came in and Alan and Bessie moved into an adjoining study to let Spark deal with them. They were chatting about 'very deep subjects'[28] when the room became filled with a 'peculiar subtle influence enveloping them in a psychic aura'[29]—apparently, this recurred whenever they met, which must have been a nuisance. On the positive side, after talking to Alan, Spark decided to take up astrology as he could recognise its money-making potential. Indeed, he worked as an astrologer from time to time after this.

Bessie's and Spark's relationship began to show cracks almost immediately. She resented having to work so hard to keep their business going, especially as she had to hand over the money she made to Spark. Bessie thought he was mean, like her father.

But worse, Spark wanted sex. And to Bessie, it was obvious he had married her because he was after her money. 'My first partner declared that he had the same ideals, but I discovered that this was only a bait to get me and a possible fortune, for at that time my father was a very wealthy man. I discovered later when the knot was tied that my first husband wanted to live the usual married life, but I refused to consent to this.'[30]

Bessie held firm—no sex. It soon became obvious that their marriage was doomed to failure. Eventually, Bessie consulted her family doctor who advised her to sue for nullity of marriage on the grounds that Spark was impotent. 'This was done as much for my husband's sake as my

Bessie Burch

own,'[31] Bessie said, which was probably true as there were limited ways of ending a marriage.

They were still working together and Bessie performed at St James's Hall in Piccadilly in March 1894, sharing the stage with singers and musicians and offering consultations at the Piccadilly Hotel. She more likely than not met Alan while she was staying in London.

On 7 May 1894, Bessie filed a petition for nullity. (Spark agreed to pay the petitioner costs of just over £113—equivalent to about £12,000 today, so his economising had clearly been successful.) The same month, Alan placed a note in the *Astrologers' Magazine* asking if someone would look at Bessie's horoscope. He wasn't slacking; Alan beavered away choosing the best dates for proceedings and choosing counsel, and reassured Bessie that her horoscope showed the best course of action was for her and Spark to separate. This was one point on which he had Spark's full agreement.

The following month, Spark and Bessie succumbed to medical examinations to confirm he was incurably impotent and she was still a virgin. Inspectors examined Spark's 'parts and organs of generation to see if [he was] capable of performing the act of generation and whether his impotency can or cannot be relieved or removed by art or skill' according to their divorce papers. Precisely what this entailed is unclear (the inspection was held in camera) but everyone was satisfied with the results (it may be worth noting that a refusal to consummate a marriage could be defined as impotency). Bessie worked under her maiden name when staying weekends with Phillips in Southampton, but continued to live in Bournemouth with Spark during the week.

By the end of 1894, Bessie and Alan had become close enough for her to invite him to spend Boxing Day and the following day with her and Spark. But on Christmas Day, Spark received a telegram saying his father was dying and he needed to go home. (At least, that was his excuse. His father lived a hale and hearty life, cared for by Spark's sister Annie, until his death at the age of eighty-nine in 1914.) Spark left for Scarborough the next morning before Alan arrived.

In the afternoon Alan and Bessie chatted about occult matters to again find themselves in a room filled with a golden mist for an hour. Alan later said it seemed as though a Mighty Presence stood between them.[32] Unfortunately, Alan was taken ill the next day, due to a chill. He couldn't even leave the house for two days, and didn't return to London until 6 January. There's no indication of when Spark returned, but the implication is that it wasn't before 7 January.

Bessie and Alan met frequently as they were both members of the Esoteric Section of the Theosophical Society and attended its fortnightly meetings in London on Sunday mornings, afterwards having lunch together where they spent hours chatting about theosophy and astrology.

There was plenty to talk about on the theosophical front. Walter Old had developed a fit of meddling that caused a split in the Society. In 1892 he'd travelled to India and joined Colonel Olcott at Adyar, taking with him documents relating to activities of W Q Judge, then Vice President and resident in the US. He claimed to have received precipitated letters from the Mahatmas confirming his claim to the presidency. Blavatsky had relied heavily on precipitated letters from the Masters to help her make decisions. These letters manifested in a variety of ways: they appeared from thin air to drop into her hand, they were found hidden in a pile of papers or up a tree, etc. Now Judge was claiming to receive messages in the same way. A long and complex series of events led to a judicial inquiry into Judge's conduct and to Old's suspension from the Esoteric Section of the Theosophical Society. To Old's horror, the inquiry found that, as belief in the Mahatmas was not a theosophical tenet, it had no power to determine the veracity or otherwise of the letters.

In 1894 Walter returned to England and contacted an old friend of his, Edmund Garrett, who was a journalist on the *Westminster Gazette*, explaining what had happened. In October 1894, numerous eminent theosophists choked on their tea when the *Gazette* began publishing a series of articles entitled 'Isis Very Much Unveiled—The Great Mahatma Hoax'. It was clear where the information must have come from. The net effect was to force the secession of the American branches. The Theosophical Society was torn into fragments and it would be years before it could regain the power it had held in the Blavatsky days.[vi]

The Coryns resigned from the TS worldwide in 1895 over its handling of the Judge affair and the Brixton lodge gave their support to Judge, which was presumably why Alan stopped attending.

Bessie had continued to study astrology via Alan's correspondence course and began writing a column entitled 'Palmistry Astrologised' for the *Astrologers' Magazine* in 1895 under the name of 'Viola', introduced as a 'lady gifted with spendid intuition and a large experience in the

---

vi Telling the truth did not make Old popular. He was obliged to move out of London and decided he needed a new identity. In April 1895 he changed his name to Walter Gornold. The Judge affair kept Theosophists busy for months and was only really over in March 1896 when Judge, President of the Theosophical Society in America, died. By June, Old had eloped with, and married, Marie Moore and begun a life as a family man.

delineation of character.'³³ The *AM* also carried advertisements for Bessie's services.

Given that her cousin Amelia had returned to London from Manchester where she'd been working as a visitor, frantically trying to improve the lives of Jewish women, and her husband Harris Levy was stabbed outside a music hall in June 1895, Bessie had plenty of reasons to spend much of her time in London.

Alan had love, or at least marriage, on his mind. He'd received several enquiries from readers asking if he could use astrology to help them in their search for a partner. For five shillings, readers could be included on an introductions list, and Alan would compare horoscopes to 'prevent any likelihood of serious mistakes being made'³⁴ when it came to matters of the heart. (Whether those introductions were successful—or if any were actually made—is unknown, but the idea was attractive enough for Alan to attempt it again in 1904.) And in June 1895 Bessie and Spark received their decree absolute.

And here we leave the phrenologists behind. Although Bessie continued to practise and write on palmistry, she ceased to be a phrenologist after her divorce.

Spark remained in Bournemouth for a while, and the following year published the book he was to become best known for, *Scientific and Intuitional Palmistry*, a copy of which Arthur Conan Doyle had in his library. For a number of years Spark continued to travel as a phrenologist and palmist, primarily the former as he said, 'I am always readier to read heads than hands, because it is much easier.'³⁵ ᵛⁱⁱ

Alan suggested that they should marry now Bessie was free, and they could do more occult work together—'He will at times be prone

---

vii Not only was it easier, it was also safer. In September 1900, Spark would be one of three palmists charged under the Vagrancy Act (the other two were a Madame Verona and Alexander Davies). For reasons unknown, Spark decided to defend himself, without a solicitor, even though the Occult Defence League had offered its assistance. A Sergeant Jones had sought a reading to be told he 'wouldn't set the Thames on fire' and there was nothing special about him. Spark addressed the bench at length, extolling the scientific virtues of palmistry and insisted he only outlined indications. He was fined £5 and asked in frustration how he could continue working in the future. It was suggested he might want to consult a solicitor. Spark married May Susan Woodrow (1876–1950) from the Isle of Wight in 1899 and had two children, Winifred and Gladys. He moved to London, living in Catford from around 1909, and subsequently moved to Norwich in 1912, where he died in 1918. Eventually, he found he could no longer make money from reading bumps and lines and, in a strange echo of reversed circumstances from Alan, Spark became a travelling salesman, dealing in cards and calendars.

to act on impulse; in fact, more from the heart than the head,' pointed out Lacey[36]—she demurred, saying she had already had one unhappy experience and didn't like the idea of another.

But Alan pointed out, 'According to astrology, my Moon and your Sun are in the same degree of Aries, and all my planets in Leo trine yours in Aries, therefore, this time you will not make any mistake,' and added, 'Do you remember the question you asked when we first met?'[37]

Of course she did, and Alan went on to expound the attractions of a sexless marriage, saying, 'I shall not deceive you, Bessie; this is my desire. I realise that I have a work to do for the world for which celibacy is essential, but I love you with all my heart and soul, and I know you could help me in the work. Think it over. You do not love me yet, as I do you, that I am well aware, but I am quite sure you will, and ours will be an ideal union.'[38]

That was all very well, but Bessie knew Phillips would never consent to her marrying a non-Jew. And his lack of consent would mean losing her inheritance—plus, she added as an afterthought, he'd be extremely upset.

Adopting Judaism simply wasn't an option so far as Alan was concerned. 'I am really an Astrologer and the Great Solar Logos and the star angels are my religion.'[39] But if Bessie's main concern was money, he didn't believe they had a problem. 'You will not need your father's money. I shall always be able to keep you very comfortably indeed, and that is a point I am very strong upon. If you decide to marry me, I will not let you work any more for money. You must give up your professional work, for I hold that a woman should be sheltered, protected, and guarded within the home, and that she should leave the fight for maintenance and work to the man; then she has more power to develop her spiritual nature and can help him to unfold his. If we both work in the world we shall meet in the evening, both positive, both perhaps rather tired and irritable, and our finer vibrations will be disturbed, and so cause disharmony. You can help me very much in the quiet of the home if you will, for I have many books to write and much work to do. You will find plenty of scope in the Theosophical Lodge that you want to form, and also in speaking and writing; your work for Theosophy is a labour of love, I know. We will unite Theosophy and Astrology, and do our best together to become helpers of the world.'[40]

Perhaps it was the mention of the finer vibrations, but Bessie was convinced. She'd marry Alan, but on one condition—they had to keep it secret. After all, Phillips was now elderly and the shock could kill him. At his age, he might not live much longer, anyway. Alan agreed immediately.

On 23 September 1895, Alan and Bessie quietly married by licence at London City Register Office in Islington. Obviously, as a Jew, and a divorcee, Bessie couldn't marry in church. Marrying by licence was popular amongst those who wanted privacy, and had a degree of kudos as many of the upper classes chose a registry office wedding for precisely that reason. Assuming you were willing to pay the extra (£2/17 as opposed to 9/6), you could marry with one day's notice. However, there may have been more behind their choice. Alan married under the name of 'Alan Leo', rather than his original name[viii] (perhaps because William Allan was already married to Sarah), and gave his father's details as 'William Leo, gentleman', which would have astonished his family had they known. He also gave his office address at Bouverie Street as his residence and the witnesses' (P Nicholls and G H W Davenport) names don't appear elsewhere in Alan's writings—they may well have simply been pulled off the street. It would have been hard to have had a more private wedding.

Alan rented a small flat at 50 Ingham Road, West Hampstead, and when Bessie went into London, ostensibly to lecture, they spent a week or ten days together before she returned to Southampton. For two years she split her time between Phillips and Alan. However, Bessie had underestimated Phillips. When in London she attended one meeting after another with Alan, making no attempt to be discreet. Someone told Phillips, saying that if she wasn't married to Alan, she ought to be. When Bessie arrived home, Phillips confronted her, saying, 'Tell me the truth, are you married?'[41]

Bessie admitted she was and Phillips demanded to see her marriage certificate. Once she'd produced it he said, 'You have married a Christian, which you have no right to do, as a Jewess; and now I shall show you my displeasure.[39] You have pleased yourself, now I will please myself. I won't leave you any of my money, and you can go back to your husband.'[42]

The will Phillips had made in 1887 left Bessie everything—he was then worth about £80,000 (although he had lost about £10,000 in 1890 due to poor investments). It's hard to say precisely what that equates to in modern terms, but Phillips would certainly be a multi-millionaire. He tore up his will in front of Bessie and she packed and left, despite Phillips

---

viii In a letter to *Light*, 21 June 1906, Alfred Barley said 'Alan Leo' was his name and not a pseudonym, so it appears that Alan had completely adopted his new identity.

saying he wouldn't turn her out or refuse to see her as she'd been punished enough—although he had no intention of seeing Alan.

And that was that. No more need for secrets—except for one. In July 1894, after Lacey had resigned from his role as editor of the *Astrologers' Magazine,* Alan had felt it prudent to print a notice stating he didn't live at Lugard Road. Ostensibly, this was because he'd now rented offices in Bouverie Street. However, the Lugard Road address was still used for correspondence until at least 1896, several months after he'd married Bessie.

And in 1901 Alan appears on the census as living with Bessie in Hampstead—as well as at Lugard Road with Sarah.[ix]

We'll never know for how long Alan's relationship with Sarah continued. We'll never know the exact basis of their relationship or if Bessie knew about it. And we'll never see Sarah—or her mother—mentioned again.

---

ix He is listed as a commercial traveller, which suggests he may not have been physically present. At this point, Sarah uses the name 'Moore' and is described as a widow and domestic worker. She is also listed as older than on the 1891 census. It stretches credulity to suppose two William Allans born the same year in Westminster lived with two different Sarahs born near Peterborough at the same address, which is also the address given in the *Astrologers' Magazine.* Sarah doesn't appear again in public records until 1911 when she's living as a lodger at Shards Road, a short distance from Lugard Road. She died in 1917.

CHAPTER SEVEN

COUNT ON MY SUPPORT

According to Lacey, Alan was 'quiet in speech.'[1] Perhaps he was, but he had plenty to say—the problem was, he didn't have enough people to say it to.

Astrologers have long been fans of creating societies, despite the fact that most of these were abysmal failures. And, at this time, people were frantically organising themselves into groups, clubs and societies—why should astrologers be any different?

Right from the start, Alan made it clear he wanted to sort out wayward astrologers and get them organised. 'The question of Astrological Societies always appealed to him,' said Lacey. "We had many discussions on that subject, he was always in favour of them, and I was not entirely against them. I gave it as my opinion that there would always be jealousy and conflicting interests, and further I doubted whether any of them would have a lengthy existence.'[2]

Lacey had a point. Astrologers were renowned for bickering amongst themselves. But London had always had some sort of astrological society. The astrologer Raphael (Robert Cross Smith) had belonged to a group called the *Mercurii* (sometimes known as the *London Astrological Society*) in 1824, along with Zadkiel (Richard James Morrison), Thomas Oxley, John Varley, R J Morrison, George Graham and John Palmer. And the *Astrological, Cerebral and Mesmeric Society* had one hundred subscribers in 1845.

There'd even been a school of astrology in Lambeth, which still existed in 1853. Apparently, the noisy astrologers who threw their money around with abandon tended to spend most of their time in Lambeth or Walworth. In 1860 Richard James Morrison established the *Astro-Meteorological Society* and another London society was set up in 1879.

And there were less formal gatherings of those interested in the subject, especially in London. Some took place in drawing rooms and salons, such as at the Countess Blessington's[i] home in the first quarter of the nineteenth century. John Varley and Edward Bulwer-Lytton were amongst the regular attendees, along with Charles Dickens and Israel Disraeli. And there were numerous occult and masonic groups that discussed astrology in addition to their other interests.

Of course, Alan couldn't join forces with any old astrologer. It's likely that the thought of a society was in his mind when he set off on a tour of England with Bessie so together they could call on every astrologer he knew of with a view to: 'Discovering how far it was practicable to amalgamate and co-operate in the common cause of spreading a knowledge of Astrology throughout the British race.'[3]

Not far, it turned out.

'The results, to say the least, were most disappointing,' Alan said miserably. 'Some few astrologers there certainly were, who studied their science with reverence, but the majority paid more attention to the paper upon which their maps were drawn than to the Spiritual Intelligences connected with the planets.'[4]

To be fair, an almost stranger and his wife descending on your home or workplace and demanding your credentials doesn't seem the best way to make friends.

During his travels, Alan was impressed with David Lund[ii] from Keighley, Yorkshire who Alan believed had advanced views about

---

i Marguerite Gardiner, Countess of Blessington (1 September 1789–4 June 1849) was born Margaret Power in County Tipperary, Ireland. Married at fifteen, she left her husband to live in Hampshire. Four months after her husband's death in 1817, she married Charles John Gardiner, First Earl of Blessington. After the Earl died in 1829, Lady Blessington supplemented her income by writing. Her home in Kensington, now the site of the Royal Albert Hall, became a centre of attraction for all that was distinguished in literature, learning, art, science and fashion.

ii Lund wrote under the name of Zanoni. He was Secretary of the Ros Crux Fratres, or Brothers of the Dew and Light, the 'bogus occult society' condemned in *Lucifer* for raising elementals, practising magic and sacrificing goats. A self-taught mechanic who co-owned a small engineering business with his brother Thomas at Albert Foundry, Lund held a degree in Political Economy and was a member of the Keighley Foreign Affairs

astrology. He also spoke highly of Martin Ringrose[iii] from Halifax (who worked under the name of 'Helios'). Apparently, he had impressed Alan with his belief that the planets were gods or angels. Alan had planned on visiting George Wilde, but after a chat with Ringrose, he decided to call incognito. He booked an hour's consultation and was surprisingly pleased, but at a later date Alan accused Wilde of being over-hasty and not clear. Worse, he used a rubber stamp for his charts rather than buying printed chart forms. Also, what was apparent was that Alan thought Wilde was too lower-class to spend much time with: 'Where his clients were of the working or lower middle class order he was generally successful in his judgements, but when they moved in refined surroundings and were of the higher intellectual order his judgements were faulty and did not allow for the facilities that come through culture and opportunity,' he said pompously.[5]

To Alan's frustration, Wilde was highly successful as a professional astrologer and was friendly with such leading lights as Richard Garnett (A G Trent), Keeper of Books at the British Museum, and for many years friends with Robert Cross. As far as Wilde was concerned, astrology was a science and ideas such as karma and reincarnation were meaningless clutter. By this time Alan was moving away from the various systems and techniques advocated by the majority of astrologers in favour of developing his own system.

Alan also met up with Walter Old, Heinrich Daath,[iv] Casael,[v] a Mr Taylor and R H Penny. It's unlikely he called on A J Pearce, the editor of *Zadkiel's Almanack*, despite including him in his list of modern-day astrologers, although he may have visited 'Raphael', then doing astrology in his retirement years, including writing books and editing his almanac.

Committee. He'd long been an astrologer and earned a supplemental income casting horoscopes, including some for the Liberal MP for Oakworth and Keighley at the time, Sir Isaac Holden. In the late 1880s, Lund suffered several prosecutions related to his astrological services. In May 1890 he was sentenced to spend a month in Armley Jail near Leeds and was the first theosophist to be incarcerated at Armley. Following his release, he lived a solitary, hermitic existence whilst continuing to practise astrology until his death in January 1903.

iii Born 23 November 1855 at 1:44 in Yorkshire.

iv Henry (Harry) Durrant. He had medical training and was born 19 September 1872 in Peterborough—the data given actually points to Huntingdon.

v From Barnstaple and also worked as a herbalist. Casael's identity isn't clear. He was primarily a horary astrologer and was the author of *Your Future Foretold; or the Whole art of astrology*, published in 1875. He lived in London from where he commuted to an office job from Watford.

'Of the other practitioners, said Alan, 'they are all younger students, many of them untried and inexperienced.'[6]

In other words, they weren't worth bothering with. And in October 1896 he travelled to Scotland to call on astrologers with the same results.

Right from the start of the *Astrologers' Magazine*, the idea of a national astrologers society had been bandied around. As Lacey said, 'We had many letters from students and others favourable to the idea ... although nothing practical came of the notion at the time.'[7]

Some of the local societies set up in the days of the *Astrologer* remained active—the Hull society continued until at least 1893—and other small groups were set up, floundered and died. But no-one had succeeded in setting up a national astrologers' society.

However, things had changed drastically over the last few years. Travel was infinitely easier—zapping around on the train was second nature to Alan. But more importantly, the age of communication had begun. The telegraph started in the 1840s and soon become part of everyday life. And from 1876 the telephone appeared, although it wasn't widespread until the 1900s. But what we tend to forget is the postal service. In 1889, mail in London was delivered twelve times a day. People complained if they didn't receive their letters within a couple of hours. You could write a letter home asking what was for dinner, receive a response saying fish, and write back insisting on mutton. And possibly get a response refusing. The first delivery began about 7:30 am and the last one came at about 7:30 pm. Other cities had fewer deliveries—Birmingham, for example, had six—but the postal service was fast, regular and cheap throughout most of the country.

Astrologers loved their letters, and wrote dozens pointing out how nice it would be to meet up.

When Raphael commented in his 1891 almanac that a society would be a spiffing idea, and he'd be happy to throw in a decent amount of money to get it going, Lacey said, 'We should very much like to see such a Society formed, but we have grave doubts whether it will exist, except on paper, at all events for some years to come.'[8]

What was the problem? Well, some astrologers followed Zadkiel, others Raphael. And that meant they didn't use the same method of directions (prediction technique). And if you were to hold an exam, how would you get past thorny issues like Zadkiel using the Sun for the hyleg in a woman's chart—a conclusion Raphael would heartily disagree with. (If that makes little sense to you, don't worry. It made little sense to people at the time.)

But wasn't it the point? So they could get together and talk over such minutiae? Lacey didn't think so. He wanted to get a few astrologers to meet up, thrash out the problem areas and tell everyone what the rules were. Anyone would have thought he'd never met an astrologer; they were not then, and are not now, renowned for sitting down and agreeing to work in precisely the same way. To play it safe, Lacey thought it was probably easier to settle for a local group, a huddle of friends meeting around each other's houses as he and Alan had done.

And letters flew back and forth—many of them finding their way into the *Astrologers' Magazine*.

One thing you could rely on was that if there was a venture doomed to failure, Walter Old would be in on it somehow. In fact, early in 1895 he said he'd like to be president of a society if anyone got around to forming one. But there'd have to be fifty members signed up first—it really wasn't worth considering it otherwise.

It was a call to action, however, so in January 1895, Alan got a group of astrologers together to discuss the concept. But they did get a little carried away, and the astrology warned against it. Alan said, 'The plan of operation suggested was very elaborate and far-reaching, the principle object being the employment of a staff to obtain reliable data and full details of important events, also an examination and instruction class. But on my suggestion to take a figure for the result of the scheme, it was found that it could only be carried on at a great financial loss, and, none of us being wealthy men, the idea was abandoned.'[9]

Old didn't give up easily. In April 1895 he wrote a long article for the *Astrologers' Magazine* summarising the details of what an astrological society—in his view—should entail. He opposed having an inner and outer school as some had suggested, seeing it as inegalitarian. But, echoing Lacey's views a few years earlier, he did favour having a badge for members—or a seal in the form of a rubber stamp.

Henry Selby Green saw the role of a society as collecting data and reading horoscopes for members, in addition to tuition. Casael was unimpressed. 'If I thought such a thing probable, or even possible, I would throw my whole energy into the subject; yet, knowing the jealousy existing between the majority of astrologers, I fear it will ever remain a "suggestion," and, like an unfertilised egg, it will never be hatched.'[10]

Robert Cross was simply befuddled by the whole discussion, saying, 'The Astrologers' Bureau was a splendid idea ... I do not see where the great financial loss comes in. The Astrologers' College is also good, but I do not know where the esoteric instruction is to come from, or what is intended to be meant by this term. However, you may count on my support.'[11]

Whether to address this befuddlement or not, Old set out a detailed plan that suggested hiring three researchers (to be paid), two recorders (responsible, for example, for placing current events on record with the predictions which may refer to them), and three artists who made calculations for members. In his view, Alan should be in charge of this, along with any publications.

Some people worried about whether the Society was to be theosophical in nature. As G H Lock said firmly, 'If we are to have Theosophical tenets placed before us at every step, you will simply succeed in founding a very limited school, which will certainly lead to the formation of rival schools. ... To myself and others the Doctrine of Re-incarnation is so much "rot."'[12]

It may have come as a relief to everyone involved in the discussion when finally, after a lot of fuss and detailed plans from Old, an initial meeting was planned. On 14 January 1896, the *Astrological Society* was born at Alan's offices in Bouverie Street.[vi] Cross agreed to become its vice-president, Harry Green its treasurer, and A V Birch secretary. Bessie was present along with J B Rowley, Robert King,[vii] Miss Essex Browne and W A Bishop-Culpeper.[viii] Lacey wasn't there, but considering his third child, Wilfred, was born that year, he was probably busy elsewhere.

Also absent was Walter Old. Although he was instrumental in setting the Society up, by 1896 he and Alan were no longer getting along. By October of that year their relationship had deteriorated so much that Alan had felt compelled to announce in *Modern Astrology*:

> Owing to the fact that letters addressed to Sepharial continue to come to this office, it becomes necessary for me to announce that he is no longer connected with this magazine.[13]

---

vi Alan said at noon while Green said it was formed at 12:30.
vii Robert King (1869–1954) was an occultist and mystic who was well-known as a lecturer. From 1909 to 1913 he was the principal medium and psychic for W T Stead's Julia's Bureau, a spiritualist group, and was said to have acted as a means of communication with the Masters and other discarnate beings. He became an auxiliary bishop in the Liberal Catholic Church in 1916 from which he resigned in 1921. King led a small group of disciples whom he taught and trained in magic and spiritualism. He was the first teacher of the occult writer, W E Butler.
viii William Alleyne Bishop Culpeper (9 April 1844–8 April 1931) changed his name to William Alleyne Bishop-Culpeper-Clayton in 1914 in accordance with his grandfather's will. He was called to the bar 11 June 1867. He specialised in astro-meteorology.

The Society ran fine without Old. Meetings took place on the first Friday of every month with the committee meeting on the third Friday of the month. Free classes were held on the fourth Friday. The Society had one hundred members by the end of the year and *Modern Astrology* served as its mouthpiece.

Robert King

One of the most celebrated of the new society's members was Lady Malcolm.[ix] A pupil of Helena Blavatsky's, despite ill health she frequently offered up her home in Cumberland Place for theosophical gatherings. In 1895 she hosted the European Section of the Theosophical Society, where a new society was formed that elected Judge President for life.

Lady Malcolm gave the Society kudos—and the suggestion of practical support. Alan probably hoped she would be as generous with her home to astrologers as she was with theosophists. Unfortunately, she died in October 1896 and appears to have taken no active role in the running of the Society.

A year passed, and the Society had big plans for their first AGM. Alan was so sure it would be a success that he hired a room much bigger than the one that had been agreed on by the committee. But when the day

---

ix Born the Honourable Alice Frederica Irby (25 July 1861–12 October 1896), Lady Malcolm was the wife of John Wingfield Malcolm, the first and last Baron of Poltalloch Member of Parliament for Boston in 1860. Lady Malcolm left a large legacy to the School for the Revival of the Lost Mysteries of Antiquity, the educational enterprise established at Point Loma by Katherine Tingley.

came, he began to have doubts. It was a miserable day and rain poured down. Telegrams began to arrive offering excuses for non-attendance.

The Meeting of Rogues and Vagabonds,[14] or what Alan and his cohorts referred to as the first annual general meeting of the Astrological Society, was held on 5 February at the Memorial Hall in Farringdon Street.[x]

There was a shuffle of committee members and Miss Essex-Browne stood down from the committee to be replaced by Mr Melville. Alan, Green, Rowley, King and Bishop-Culpeper accepted re-election, along with Annie Watson, who replaced Lady Malcolm. Forty members attended this meeting.

There were big ideas for this society, and plans were made for students to sit qualifying exams in natal, esoteric, meteorological and horary astrology, although there clearly wouldn't be enough money to set up the college of astrology Alan wanted. Once formal business was over, a general discussion took place with Mr Larkman from Liverpool saying there should be more on offer for those from the provinces, and Harry Green suggesting a manuscript be made up of photos and horoscopes. A long discussion on whether five or three people should form a branch was surpassed by an even longer discussion on whether astrologers should wear a special pin, and if so, what it should look like.[xi] Eventually, a pin was agreed on, consisting of the symbol of the planet Mercury within a circle. However, none were ever made.

Once the door was open to the public, a hundred and fifty people swarmed in and Culpeper introduced Alan who began by saying that astrologers had been called quacks, humbugs, and charlatans, but that was because people didn't know what this wonderful science of astrology was. Astrologers had a mission to teach people why they suffered and show the world that every child could have a chart by which he could 'steer clear of many dangers.'[14]

Then he got into his stride, saying, 'During time inconceivable the unmanifest is manifesting and only when manifestation is complete will we recognise our origin, but through that unwritten law which is in the sky we may trace by faint symbology the progress of the infinite to the finite, thence back to infinitude again, taking with us the self-conscious realisation of ourselves and the universe ...'[15]

---

x The Congregational Memorial Hall was built on the site of the Fleet Prison and opened in 1875. It was a popular meeting place and the Labour Party was founded at a meeting there on 27 February 1900. The hall was demolished in 1968.
xi Discussing pins was a default position once a group of astrologers gathered.

Fortunately for the audience, Alan also said while scribbling on his blackboard, that astrology 'was built upon a beautiful symbology, the symbols of which were the same to-day as at the beginning ; the circle, which represents the Sun; the half-circle, which means the Moon; and the cross, representing the Earth. A cross over the circle is Mars or War, a cross under the circle, Venus or Love. The Sun, Mars, and Venus represent the Spirit. In the half-circle are all the planets relating to the mind. A cross over the half-circle is Saturn or the Devil the half-circle over the cross is Jupiter or Jehovah, the Higher Mind. Every person is born under some influence, and the study of astrology enables people correctly to see the qualities they have in them.'[16]

Then he got a little excited and challenged anyone in the audience to show astrology wasn't true. 'Sooner or later it will become the religion of the world!' he insisted.[17]

Green followed up by offering an address on 'The degrees of the zodiac and their theoretical value' and then Bishop-Culpeper and King spoke.

Alan had made sure there was plenty of press coverage, although it wasn't as positive as he'd probably hoped. The *Pall Mall Gazette* for one was less than impressed:

Was there ever such a farrago of nonsense? Talk about charlatans! Your modern man is a quack … without a duck behind it.[18]

Some commentators were bemused, others indignant.

The queer old times are back.[19]

Astrologers were born not made, Alan had commented. Which the *Daily Telegraph* later said 'was a regular knock down blow for any persons supposing they are capable of being imported cheaply from Germany.'[20]

Unfortunately, the meeting hadn't attracted any 'professors' (professional astrologers), except for 'Helios'—Martin Ringrose, who'd travelled down from Halifax. But Society members were happy enough. They continued with their Friday night gatherings, and also scheduled quarterly socials, although it isn't clear precisely how they socialised. (They probably discussed pins.)

Around July of that year, Alan and Bessie moved to 9 Lyncroft Gardens, in West Hampstead. The area was filled with new housing and near several transport links—ideal for Alan and Bessie. They had to scrabble together the money to buy the property, but it helped that the Astrological Society had established a 'hall fund' intended to go towards paying for somewhere for a hundred or so astrologers to meet. Alan thought it reasonable to spend it on building works at his new house, although this room was only big enough to hold seventy people. Apparently, the builders did a good job.

> Within a few minutes' walk of Hampstead Heath, a grand view of the heavens can be obtained; the meeting room faces the east, where all the stars may be seen rising; at the back of the room through a large French window, there is a very long garden ... in which open air meetings may be held in the summer, and where astrological garden parties will be held directly the weather is warm enough. The room in which the meetings are held have been astrologically designed; in the centre of the room, an archway of artistic design contains all the symbols of the planets, which have been carved out of the arch by a well-known firm of decorators. At the end of the room ... a splendid pair of curtains, with all the signs of the zodiac wonderfully designed and worked by Miss Emma Windsor,[xii] as a special gift to the Astrological Society.[21]

Now Alan and Bessie had a meeting room, it made sense to have plenty of meetings. In September 1897 the press carried announcements of a discussion about the 'Law of Equilibrium,' which turned out not to be a discussion at all, but a lecture given by Alan on astrology.

> Mr Leo treated the question from an astrological point of view, his contention being that every life was under the influence of a certain planet. Mrs Leo then gave an interesting discourse on 'The Eastern wisdom,' which she stated was not a religion, but the study of which cleared many things that before were not understood. The law of equilibrium she described being the law of cause and effect, contending that people sowed so shall they reap their next life. The Eastern wisdom taught that there was no death, but only a change of consciousness from one body to another, reincarnation.[22]

[xii] A textile designer based in South Kensington.

From this small start, the Hampstead Lodge of the Theosophical Society was born.[xiii] By now Lacey was fast losing interest in theosophy and so didn't join them. Its members included John William Sidley[xiv] and his wife Lilian, George Coleman,[xv] Sarah Dexter,[xvi] William Pinchin[xvii] and Emma Windsor. They elected Bessie as their President and Alan as Secretary.

> Modern astrologers ... have fallen upon evil times. Their peculiar situation exposes them to two conflicting forms of discouragement. The police take them too seriously, while the rest of the world will not take them seriously enough.[23]

---

xiii Charter granted 9 December 1897.
xiv Born in Limerick in 1857, John William Sidley was a cotton manufacturer's agent. His children were taught by C W Leadbeater. In 1903 Sidley had shares in an establishment that cured ailments by electrical with electric-light baths—it closed in 1915. His daughter Marguerite was active in the Theosophical Society from childhood.
xv Born in 1863, George Coleman was apprenticed to a London printer at the age of fourteen and then continued his training in New York. He moved back to Britain in 1889 and married in 1893, his wife dying three years later. He was a friend of G R S Mead and a practising phrenologist, having trained at the Fowler Institute. In 1906 he moved to India and became a printer for the *Times of India*. He returned to Britain in 1919 and enrolled in art school; some of his paintings were exhibited at the Royal Academy.
xvi Phrenologist and part of the Fowler Institute, for which she acted as examiner.
xvii A carpenter and joiner, born in Wraxhall, Wiltshire in1860.

Bessie Leo

CHAPTER EIGHT

MRS GASKELL'S COSTUME

*E*VEN VEGETARIANS NEED TO be entertained.

The competition wasn't especially strong, however. An account of a *Women's Vegetarian Union* reception in September 1897 says, 'The most noteworthy items of the entertainment were Mrs Gaskell's costume ...'¹

Unfortunately, no further details are given and, although Mrs Gaskell was no doubt dressed delightfully, it comes as something of a relief for the history of vegetarian entertainment that attendees also experienced, 'Mrs Leo's "Distinguishing Features"—a very humorous sketch, with appropriately dramatic actions and topical allusions, of the outlines of physiognomy.'²

Apparently, there was also music, and biscuits accidentally made without eggs turned out to be popular.

The event was an alternative to tea and *conversazione* at St. Martin's Town Hall organised by the *Order of the Golden Age* and was part of the Vegetarian Congress. It took place at the offices of the women's newspaper *Shafts*,ⁱ under the command of its editor, Margaret Shurmer Sibthorp who

---

i *Shafts*, one of the few feminist periodicals available at that time, was founded and edited by Margaret Sibthorp and first published in November 1892. She was also the founder of the Pioneer Club (later the Lyceum Club) with Emily Massingberd. The magazine's name was actually *Shafts of Thought*. An article explained the cover illustration of woman firing shafts of wisdom, justice and truth from a bow to carry germs of purity into dark places of sin, injustice and ignorance. *Shafts* had moved from its original base in the Strand, first downstairs to a single, poky room, and later to the Sibthorps' home. Sibthorp had lived on Finchley Road, a short distance away from Alan and Bessie. 'Mercifully,there was no "speechifying"'[3] and both men and women were present, chatting in French, German, Italian and English.

The Vegetarian Congress's exhibition opened at the Memorial Hall, on 13 September, displaying food, vegetarian boots, a new vegetable fat called, 'Albene', which apparently had no taste or smell (and sounded more worthy than tasty), soap and candles.

The President's (Arnold Hills[ii]) address outlined the success of the vegetarian movement and pointed out that the *Vegetarian Athletic and Cycling Club* would attract younger members and prove that vegetarians weren't eccentric and had long hair—which suggests many of them were and did.

Following this was a *conversazione* which was interrupted every time it got going for someone to burst into song and the room to listen politely. The next days comprised a number of papers, discussions and presentations. It's possible Alan and Bessie were present at the lunch that 250 people attended at Crystal Palace on the Thursday, where everyone congratulated each other for doing such a good job. And they probably were part of the seven hundred strong audience present at the evening's theatre turns where speeches were inserted between such delights as, 'An aerial graphoscope,[iii] shown by Miss May Yates.'[4] [iv] All the performers were—obviously—vegetarians. Afterwards, they went outdoors for the fireworks.

---

joined the TS in 1891, and was a member of the Blavatsky Lodge and worked with Edith Ward, President of the Athene Lodge in Bradford from 1893 to 1896 when she moved to London to become Treasurer of the TS. Numerous theosophical articles sprinkled the magazine's pages. Gradually, *Shafts* faded, becoming a bi-monthly magazine in 1898, and disappearing altogether after committing to appear on a quarterly basis in 1899.

ii Arnold Hills (1857–1927), the managing director of the Thames Iron Works, a large shipbuilding business, made a huge contribution to the development of vegetarianism in the late nineteenth and early twentieth centuries, working with people such as Gandhi and George Bernard Shaw. He became the first President of both the London Vegetarian Society and the Vegetarian Cycling and Athletic Club in 1888. The following year he launched the *Vegetarian* magazine. Hills encouraged his workers at the Iron Works to participate in sports, especially athletics and football. He funded the works football team from 1895. In 1898 they turned professional and in 1900 changed their name to West Ham United.

iii A type of magic lantern or photographic projector that cast images into space without the need for a screen.

iv Organising secretary of the London Vegetarian Society. Also founder of the Bread and Food Reform League.

Not everyone was in complete agreement. On the final day of the congress:

> The paper by the Honourable Mrs F J Bruce, on 'Our Mistakes as Vegetarians', was read, with most humorously interjected disagreements, by Mr H L Bathgate, of Glasgow ... Vegetarians occasionally had, as she knew from personal knowledge of herself, very troublesome tempers ... Mrs Bruce next proceeded ... to deprecate the 'too sweeping condemnation' of those agreeable little indulgences, wine, beer, tobacco, tea, and coffee, which have nothing to do with Vegetarianism, and would therefore be better left unattacked [cries of 'No, no' from the audience, and of 'I say "no" too,' from the unfortunate victim who was reading the paper]. Now these things, continued the paper, are neither harmful nor degrading to any one if taken in moderation, and when articles appear in the Vegetarian press hotly denouncing their use, the Vegetarian believer frequently thinks them too extreme, while the anti-Vegetarian unbeliever simply laughs at such madness and goeth onwards rejoicing ... the use of tobacco in moderation was, Mrs Bruce declared, very good indeed for the temper, was not, as some have asserted, stupefying, and tobacco, in her opinion, certainly does not, as some have imagined, lead to drinking—with all of which sentiments the reader of the paper found himself in helpless disagreement. To her sister-women, Mrs Bruce whispered that if they loved their own way, to make war upon tobacco was madness—the masculine breast was never so maleable as under the influence of tobacco.'[5]

Alan wouldn't have been convinced by such an argument. He embraced vegetarianism and became anti-smoking and a teetotaller that year. Henry Selby Green was already a vegetarian by the time he and Alan became friends, and others from the Theosophical Society would have been persuasive—especially John Sidley.

A member of the *Spiritualist Alliance,* Sidley had joined the *Northern Heights Vegetarian Society* (founded in 1889) in late 1890 and become its secretary the following year.[v]

---

[v] Sidley's vegetarianism led to his adopting the Bahai faith. He met Abdu'l-Bahá (23 May 1844–28 November 1921), eldest son of Bahá'u'lláh, the founder of the Bahá'í faith, in 1913.

John Sidley

There had long been an association between vegetarianism and spiritualists. The founder and first president of Northern Heights, William Theobald, came from a prominent spiritualist family. Although the Vegetarian Society had been founded in 1847, there had been a decline in membership and support after the initial growth and enthusiasm of its early years. However, vegetarianism had shifted to become more of a middle-class movement, and by the 1870s a number of food reform groups had been established in London, and the *London Food Reform Society* became the *National Food Reform Society*, which angered the Vegetarian Society's officers. By the 1880s the membership of the Vegetarian Society had increased to 2,000 members (it had dwindled to 125 in 1870); 3,000 members attended its conference in 1881. At this time, Anna Kingsford (1846-1888) was Vice President of the Society—she was also President of the London Lodge of the Theosophical Society in 1883. Trained in medicine in Paris, Kingsford was one of the first women doctors. Her thesis on the physiology of the vegetarian diet was published in 1881 as *The Perfect Way in Diet*.

On the Vegetarian Society's revival, women took a more prominent place in organising local associations and formed a sizeable proportion of its membership. Many became trustees, including Charlotte Despard, or addressed Vegetarian Society meetings, such as Annie Besant. Gradually, vegetarianism became increasingly associated with the emancipation of women. Charlotte Despard, in her presidential address to the London Vegetarian Society in 1918, said, 'Vegetarianism is pre-eminently a woman's question because it will do away with the most degrading part of her work.'[6]

A vegetarian diet was regarded as natural and ordained by God. By following such a diet, and leading an appropriate lifestyle, you could avoid illness and premature mortality. Meat is polluting to the body and 'dead', and therefore vegetarianism was often linked with other campaigns for physical purity such as the anti-tobacco movement and teetotalism. (However, although the temperance movement had become popular at the same time, while it was regarded as part of the mainstream of society, vegetarianism was still largely viewed as extreme.) Meat was seen as responsible for inflaming the desire for alcohol, carnal desire and war, which were best suppressed by vegetarianism. It was also believed to encourage masturbation—a Victorian fascination. For example, Ellen G White said, 'Flesh Food also is harmful. Its naturally stimulating effect should be a sufficient argument against its use ... It tends to irritate the nerves and to excite the passions, thus giving the balance of power to the lower propensities.'[7]

The Theosophical Society would hardly want to power the lower propensities and so from the 1880s, they were heavily behind promoting vegetarianism.

On the plus side, a vegetarian diet was associated with gentleness and pacifism, an avoidance of an animal nature. As (or perhaps, more) important to spiritualists and theosophists was the idea that consuming flesh creates a barrier against the spiritual and communication with God. Spiritualists believed vegetarianism was beneficial, if not essential, to mediums. Hence, Anna Kingsford and Edward Maitland stressed the importance of vegetarianism in allowing the receipt of messages and visions. Maitland believed that meat eating was the cause of our failing to reach our true natures, 'Since only when man is purely nourished can he attain clearness and fullness of spiritual perception.'[8]

Many of the vegetarians of this period are what we would call 'vegan' today—that word didn't come into usage until the mid-1940s. For example, Anna Kingsford wrote in *Dreams and Dream Stories* in 1886, 'For the past fifteen years I have been an abstainer from flesh-meats. Not a vegetarian, because during the whole of that period I have used such animal produce as butter, cheese, eggs, and milk.'[9]

And vegetarianism had become highly fashionable. Meat was thought to cause disease and an interest in animal welfare was on the rise with people turning against meat eating, hunting, vivisection and the wearing of fur and feathers (murderous millinery). Plus, switching to a simple grain, fruit, and nut diet saved an enormous amount of time—essential for women who were charging around and saving the world in one way or another. There were children's groups (the children's section of the Vegetarian Society was called the *Ivy Leaf Society*), a rambling society, and the aforementioned Vegetarian Cycling Club.

Only a few weeks after Mrs Gaskell had displayed her stunning costume, on 7 October 1897, an 'at home' was hosted by Alan and Bessie on behalf of the Womens' Vegetarian Union.[vi] Founded in March 1895 by Alexandrine Veigelé, a French woman living in London, the Union aimed its efforts towards women. Veigelé was a member of the London Vegetarian Society and founder of the Women's International Progressive Union. She became a vegetarian in 1888 and was supported financially by her daughter Adrienne, after Alexandrine gave up teaching to concentrate on her philanthropic work. Since women so greatly influenced the household diet, it was necessary to overcome opposition to the diet's success, and Alexandrine placed great emphasis on this work, saying in 1895, 'Women are the mothers of the human race, and as they are at the head of every household, it is but right that we should appeal to them to help us in our difficult task.'[10]

Although the Union had grown to 350 members by the time of its sixth annual report, and included overseas members, membership never flourished and the Union was poorly funded. However, the major difference between the Union and other similar organisations was that it allowed honorary male members.

The Union aimed to promote a 'purer and simpler' diet and 'at homes' were regularly held at the homes of members. Everyone gathered in the garden for refreshments and then—perhaps because of the vagaries of the English autumn weather they returned to the house where the Secretary of the Union, Adrienne Veigelé, gave a speech saying vegetarianism was a step to spiritual power; by giving up 'flesh food' you could become aware of your latent spiritual powers.

Alan then spoke, saying vegetarianism was needed for the evolution of the human soul. 'There were many refined people,' he said, 'who would not eat meat, if they had to prepare the flesh with their own hands, yet they would allow whole classes of their fellow-men to do for them the

---

vi The WVU started at 96 Crawford Street before moving to 87 Praed St in 1898 and then Bayswater. Despite the Union's plans, its international outreach was limited to a Belgian branch.

debasing and degrading work of slaughter and were thus instrumental in retarding their outward and upward growth.'[11]

In July 1898, a vegetarian fete was organised by Mrs McDonall and John Sidley, assisted by a large number of stewards, at Wembley Park. Happily, the weather was good, and the event attracted a large number of vegetarians—about 500 attended. It helped that there was plenty of entertainment. There were concerts by the popular soprano Madame (Nina) Menzies, the singer Arthur Edwards, and Professor Bacon's Family Band; the play, *A Bed of Roses*, and Alan sat in the Hall of Stars ready to delineate horoscopes. Bessie was, of course, on hand for phrenology readings. There were fountains, and fireworks, and, of course, plenty to eat, including a fruit tea at four thirty, and a marquee filled with food.

Of course, not everyone approved. The *Thanet Advertiser* spoke disapprovingly of 'peculiar people' and the sight of the 'bloodless faces of the women and children.'[12]

During the next few years, vegetarian restaurant after vegetarian restaurant would open in central London; in the Edwardian era there were thirty-four. Because no alcohol was served, many suffragettes gathered safely to discuss tactics. The most famous of these was the Eustace Miles restaurant[vii] at 40 Chandos Place, in Covent Garden, where many astrologers and theosophists retired to after events. And where you could eat egg and mushroom fillets; Duxelles sauce with asparagus and new potatoes; pine kernel quenelles and onion sauce with spring cabbage and potatoes; or hazelnut sausages and gravy with cauliflower and roast potatoes. Some of the dishes sounded better than they tasted.

But this was to come later. Vegetarianism in the late 1890s meant bloodless faces, bland beige dishes and hoping the entertainment was going to improve.

---

vii Eustace Miles was a Cambridge-educated health guru, tennis player, author and vegetarian. He opened the restaurant, with his wife, Hallie, as a food reform restaurant in May 1906, a few months after their marriage. In March 1907, the WSPU chose it as the venue for a breakfast celebrating the release from Holloway of the prisoners who had been arrested when taking part in the deputation from the first Women's Parliament. Eustace Miles also rented space for meetings and offered ozonized air for attendees to breathe as they listened.

CHAPTER NINE

GOLDEN CHARIOT

IN MAY 1898 THE GOLDEN CHARIOT of the deposed King Theebaw of Burma (which he apparently used once before it was seized by the British)[i] was bought at auction for £12[ii] by Ebenezer Roberts and Sons, Alan's employer. Although Alan was earning £500 a year,[iii] the company had been struggling since Roberts had died in July 1895. In fact, in January 1897 the *South Shields Gazette* described it as a 'poor investment'.[1]

After Roberts' widow had decided the company was too much for her to handle alone, she'd transferred it to her sons in late 1896 and shares were sold in March 1897 to enable the company to expand. It didn't. Sales weren't helped when two boys were rumoured to have died in Willesden in July after eating ice-cream—although neither of the boys did in fact die, and the ice-cream was from an itinerant seller and not Roberts and Sons.

The chariot appeared on the streets of Norwood as part of a grand procession to raise money for charity in July 1898 (the man and woman who collected the most were awarded the prize of an umbrella each). By then, Alan had decided to become a full-time professional astrologer. It wasn't necessarily his decision to make. He may have been let go or might have decided to get out as the company sank.

---

i The coach had arrived in England in 1886 having been sold to some London merchants who displayed it privately in Upper Thames Street.
ii About £1,500 in today's terms.
iii Equivalent to between £45,000 and £50,000 in modern terms.

The golden chariot appeared in public on two more occasions—in January 1899 it was driven through Bristol to advertise Bovo gravy powder, and in April 1899 Ebenezer Roberts and Sons was fined for attracting a large crowd in Leadenhall when the chariot was pulled through the city by two bullocks. Or more accurately, they were fined for not having the right permit.

The following month it was announced that the company was to be wound up and in July 1899 a liquidator was appointed, a reformed company created, and Leonard Ebenezer Roberts declared bankruptcy. The saga continued into January 1901 when the company ended up in court twice. Firstly, due to financial irregularities, including making overpayments for a worthless invention, and secondly for breaching the Factories Act by having young girls work for longer than legal hours. It struggled on for a short time but eventually collapsed.

Alan's version of events was, of course, slightly different:

> With the increased responsibility incurred by the editorship of *Modern Astrology*, the writer decided to abandon all other work and devote the remainder of his life to the practice of Astrology, believing this to be the best means of spreading a knowledge of the science amongst those who could only be convinced as to its truth by first-hand experience.[2]

It had been some years since Alan had been out of work, but by now he'd ensured he'd appeared often enough in the press to (almost) become a household name—depending on what sort of household you lived in. Subscribing to a clippings service to ensure he spotted every mention of astrology in the press, Alan also sent out press releases, especially when the *Astrologers' Magazine* covered horoscopes of the day's celebrities, many of which were picked up and reported in gossip columns.

> AN ALARMING HOROSCOPE. The Duke of Fife should lay in store of paregoric if he has any faith in astrology, for the 'Astrological Magazine' contains horoscope of his infant daughter of an alarming character, in which the writer says, 'I should not be surprised to find that during the dentitional period stomachic trembles will manifest themselves.' Ah, yes, they generally do, but fathers' families do not usually want Saturn and Jupiter and Gemini and all the rest of the heavenly host to tell them that much.[3]

Plus, a bit of romance never did any harm to sales:

> As regards people's personal affairs, however, the *Astrologer's Magazine* is so good as to settle them with preciseness, and even to enter into minutiae. A lady wishes to know what hinders her marriage. To which she gets the following reply: 'For the description of the person who stands in the way must look to Mercury as lord of your trine, he having recently left the square of Mars, and almost square to the Moon, your signification.' This change of residence is not very intelligibly stated. But in terrestrial matters, when persons leave a square it is not generally to better themselves, and their association with the Moon is described (if they leave in a hurry, by night, and without paying their rent) as 'shooting it'. However, whether in difficulties or not, 'it is quite patent' (says the astrologer) that this individual wrote your intended adverse letter, and is himself robust and inclined to corpulency, with swarthy complexion and dark-brown hair ...
>
> Some admirable hints are given to young students in astronomy: 'In predicting death, do not hastily arrive at decision,' and have due regard to 'whether the afflicting planet is dignified.' I don't know about a planet, but if any person sought to afflict me it would be no kind of consolation to know that he was dignified; I would much prefer him to be humble—and weak. In casting the horoscope of a lady, the student is recommended 'especially to regard the Moon,' which seems a little ungallant.[4]

More exciting had been the prediction written by Old in the *Astrologers' Magazine* of April 1893 accompanying Queen Victoria's horoscope and saying she'd probably die in 1895.

> In the fateful year of 1895, about October-November, an appalling calamity will fall upon the British nation, and there will be weeping.[5]

> The Union Jack will be half-mast high, the drums will be muffled, and the bells will toll, for the storm will come, and the British oak will be uprooted; the mourners will go about the streets, the song and dance will give way to the funeral dirge, the glory of England will have departed, for the silver cord will be snapped asunder, if we read the astrological omens correctly. The end will be ushered in by an accident, and that suddenly about the period have written.[6]

The Government will be unpopular, and foreign allies will shew signs of unfaithfulness. The same astrologer so predicts evil for her Majesty in the autumn of this year, and especially urges her to avoid the public streets in October, and to safeguard herself from accident.[7]

A year later, Old had excitedly added that the Prince of Wales was likely to succeed to the throne in early 1896, which presumably required a dead queen. By 1895 when the horoscope was reprinted, the analysis had changed to dire warnings about 'great troubles and sorrows' with the chance she'd be able to overcome her planets. She did—for her, it was a particularly uneventful year.

The Astrological Society had completed its second year to hold an AGM on 19 February 1898 at the Memorial Hall. There was a shuffle of the committee, with Robert Cross resigning, Robert King re-joining and many people yawning. Both Alan and Bessie gave a talk, but the excitement had faded. About twenty people attended the meetings held on the second and fourth Fridays of the month at Alan and Bessie's house. And a society journal was circulated along with *Modern Astrology*, in which the objectives of the Society appeared for the first time:

> To band together all those interested in the science of astrology
> To purify and re-establish the Science of Astrology
> To study astrology in all its various branches
> Unity is strength[8]

And by 1898 Alan was confident enough to ensure that *Modern Astrology*'s political predictions were stamped all over the press—even if the majority of them were actually made by Old.

> In the map for Washington there is grave danger of foreign complications.[9]

> According to 'Modern Astrology', the climax of 1899 will be a great war.[10]

> ROUND THE GLOBE. WILL THERE BE WAR THIS YEAR? SOME REMARKABLE FORECASTS. MANY SERIOUS CONFLICTS PREDICTED.

> England will be engaged in serious warfare during the Summer of 1899, in which France and Turkey will be involved, but in which England will hold her own, and come out victorious.

The prediction does not stand alone. In every quarter in which the verdict of the stars is professed to be given it is prophesied that the booming of cannon and the clash of steel will soon be heard, and will not cease till this luckless year has sped its course.[11]

The Second Boer[iv] War was declared on 11 October 1899.[v]

Africa ruled by this sign (Mars) will be the cause of great bloodshed ... A hit! A hit! A very palpable hit![12]

Now on a roll, he also said that France would 'attract the eye of the world' vindicated by the Dreyfus affair, the political scandal that divided the Third French Republic from 1894 until 1906 following the treason conviction of Captain Alfred Dreyfus. Evidence came to light in 1896 that a French Army major named Ferdinand Walsin Esterhazy had been the real culprit, although Dreyfus was then accused of additional charges based on falsified documents. After pressure on the government, Dreyfus was re-tried in 1899 and convicted again but later pardoned and set free. Eventually, the accusations against Dreyfus were demonstrated to be baseless and he was exonerated and reinstated as a major in the French Army in 1906.

Another hit? Perhaps, but considering that *J'accuse!*, a letter written by Emile Zola had been published in a Paris newspaper in January 1898, and anyone who was anyone had something to say about the case, it wasn't a difficult one.

---

iv *Boer* was the common term for Afrikaans-speaking white South Africans descended from the Dutch East India Company's original settlers at the Cape of Good Hope.
v Commonly simply referred to as the Boer War, since the First Boer War (December 1880 to March 1881) is less well known, in South Africa it is officially called the South African War. Lasting until 31 May 1902, the war was fought between the British Empire and the South African Republic (Republic of Transvaal) and the Orange Free State, over the Empire's influence in South Africa. It didn't go well for the British in the early stages, although they finally seized control of the Orange Free State and Transvaal as the civilian leadership went into hiding or exile. This was the war in which concentration camps came into being.

When Boston-based Catherine Thompson[vi] launched her magazine the *Sphinx* in July 1899, Alan, along with Old, Green and Lacey contributed articles. The *Sphinx* looked very much like *Modern Astrology*—both in terms of its design and its contributors. It was never very popular, however, perhaps in part because of Thompson's hectoring editorials regarding why one should believe in astrology (her small audience already did) under titles such as: 'Try This'; 'Try Another'; 'Go On Trying'; 'Try, Try Again'; 'Now We Are Getting On'; 'Now We Shan't Be Long'; 'Go Ahead'; Now We Are Getting There' and 'Still Getting There.'

Apart from ensuring his new career was financially viable, there was another reason for Alan to make successful predictions based on scientific astrological methods—what he was doing was illegal.

It had been a few years since R H Penny had been convicted under the Vagrancy Act, but astrologers still hadn't forgotten it. And David Lund had suffered three prosecutions related to his astrological services, despite his insistence that he charged for time making calculations and not telling fortunes. In May 1890, police were so desperate to arrest him for something that they consulted a local antiquarian society to ascertain legislation under which Lund could be prosecuted, finally using the Vagrancy Act. He was sentenced to spend a month in Armley Jail near Leeds.

The legislation in question was the Vagrancy Act of 1824, which came into being as a response to people sleeping on the streets of London. It had a long history, but in its late nineteenth century form, it was derived from King George II's Vagrant Act 1744, which divided beggars and idle

---

vi Thompson (1858–1934) had been born into a well-off family, although she was orphaned by the age of twenty when her twin brother and parents died. She was the daughter of Christopher Walton (1809–1877), a writer on theosophy. Later in life, she married a wealthy American, with whom she had two children and homes in Newport and New York City. The marriage didn't last, and, after her husband left her, she took a job as a hostess to a widowed Washington senator. She studied astrology with Luke Broughton in Boston and focused on market forecasting, attracting an important business clientele. Thompson also gave astrology lessons to Evangeline Adams, although they didn't get along well. From July, 1899 to May 1901 she edited and published the *Sphinx*. Thompson was known for her difficult personality, often referring to herself with the royal 'we' and believed herself the reincarnation of Queen Elizabeth I. She infamously supported the Germans in WW1, isolating herself from the British astrological community. Thompson was 'exposed' in the *Ladies Home Journal* of August 1933 as 'Madam Zamos' and it was reported she gathered information about her clients through spies to use in her readings. By 1934 Thompson was down in her luck; she owed rent and was given a notice of eviction. Shortly after, Thompson had a stroke. She was taken to the pauper's ward where she died penniless.

persons into two categories of 'rogues and vagabonds' (the unemployed without means of support, those refusing to work 'for the usual and common wages' and those not supporting their families) and 'incorrigible rogues' (those already convicted of one or more offences).

'Rogues and vagabonds' meant anyone whose lifestyle the authorities disapproved of, including 'any persons wandering abroad in alehouses, barns, outhouses or in the open air, not giving a good account of themselves.' Actors, buskers, pedlers, and fortune-tellers in particular were targets. Although rewards for rounding up vagrants ceased in 1822 (prior to then, stalking actors could be financially lucrative), conditions following the Napoleonic Wars made homelessness as big an issue during the early nineteenth century as it is today.

Section 4 of the Act was the one astrologers feared. It covered: 'Every person pretending or professing to tell fortunes, or using any subtle craft, means, or device, by palmistry or otherwise, to deceive and impose on any of his Majesty's subjects.'

When Walter Old wrote, 'The sooner we bring the science [of astrology] down from the clouds where the would-be esotericists have incontinently harried it, the sooner will it gain a proper recognition in the practical world,'[13] his intentions weren't as noble as they might sound. Classifying astrology as a science meant astrologers would be no longer covered by the Vagrancy Act—possibly.

In Penny's case, the question of whether an intention to deceive was necessary for a conviction and how good faith might be established in court was raised. The justice cited *res ipsa loquitur* (the matter itself speaks), the common law doctrine of criminal negligence, writing it was 'absurd' for anyone to believe in the causal relationship between the heavenly bodies and human life. Therefore, the judge's opinion of the scientific status of astrology nullified the legal question of the good faith of the practitioner.

Astrologers were now in greater danger of prosecution and imprisonment than they had been for years, as prosecutions were actively sought by the constabulary and judiciary. They often used paid informers to entrap the astrologer, and the penalty was usually severe: a prison sentence of up to three months, accompanied or followed by hard labour. Plus, appeals weren't usually allowed.

Recently, 'Bruce the Great American Astrologer' (Henry Harding) had been convicted for the third time at the end of 1892; James Alger, who felt degraded by having to work as an astrologer was convicted in 1893; William Wallace was also convicted in 1893 after taking up astrology professionally because he was unemployed; and Charles Bright of Lambeth had admitted he was guilty and said he wanted the matter done with in 1895.

There had been attempts to fight the Vagrancy Act. After James Bradshaw from Manchester was imprisoned in November 1842, the then-Zadkiel, Richard James Morrison, set up the snappily-named *British Association for the Advancement of Astral Science &c., and the Protection of Astrologers*, which advertised 107 members by 1845. After his appeal, Bradshaw was released and the magistrate forced to pay him £35 in compensation. Others were less fortunate. Unfortunately, this society soon folded. Morrison didn't give up. He hoped to make it legal for enfranchised householders to practise professionally in their own homes. On the advice of Christopher Cooke,[vii] a solicitor and astrologer, in 1852 he wrote a petition which MP William Ewart presented to Parliament as a private members' bill. It sank without trace.

And in 1845 the Astrological Society brought a case against the magistrates who charged William Coulson with vagrancy.

> The action had been brought by the Astrological Society of London against the defendants, to ascertain the right they had to imprison persons charged with such an offence as Coulson was alleged to have committed ... His friend (Mr Humfrey) would attempt to turn the case into ridicule. He was already laughing—the attempt had begun—he could not restrain the champagne till the time had come for drawing the cork; but ridicule the matter be would, and laugh at it as he might, was not a laughing matter to the plaintiff, who had been imprisoned for two months, and been obliged to associate with felons ... These various qualities would enable his friend turn the matter into a joke; but it was no joke for his poor client, who had been sentenced to two months imprisonment at the tread-wheel.[14]

Little else appears to have happened until 1888 when after Lund's conviction 'Albertus Magnus' (possibly Lund himself) gave a lecture on astrology in Keighley entitled 'Astrology: is it a true and faithful science?' after which Jos Blackburn moved, 'That this meeting is of the opinion that the decision of the magistrates in the recent fortune-telling case by astrology was unjust, tyrannical, and contrary to the spirit of British law.'[15]

---

vii The author of *A Plea for Urania* (1854) and *Curiosities of Occult Literature* (1863), which describes his relationship with Morrison and views on astrology.

A collection was immediately held towards establishing an astrologers' defence fund—which also sank without trace. But Yorkshiremen are persistent, and a solicitor from Halifax, Joseph Dodson, recognised the need for astrologers—and, indeed, others covered by the Act such as palmists—to form a united front. Dodson knew the occult scene well; he was friends with George Wilde and operated the Occult Publishing Company, which published works by Wilde amongst others. He also needed someone who knew how to attract publicity, wasn't scared of losing his job, and who was passionate about what he did. In short, he needed Alan.

The first meeting of the *Occultist's Defence League* was held 9 May 1899 at Alan's house. They appointed the barrister William Bishop-Culpeper as president and he outlined the objectives of the League as being to offer legal aid, promote study and expose frauds. Things had come to a head because of the recent case against the palmist Georgina Jones for whom Dodson had lodged a failed appeal. Jones had been represented in court by Thomas Probert Perks,[viii] described as 'a sort of standing counsel to those fortune tellers throughout the country.'[16] Perks had said, 'People might honestly believe that they could foretell the future; pretending does not necessarily involve deception, many people believe in palmistry.'[17] And the previous month, Dodson had also defended the palmists Emily (Madame Emily, the Lady palmist) and Thomas Livesey, winning the right to appeal.

People still couldn't make up their minds whether astrology and palmistry were inherently illegal, or if some sort of fraudulent activity needed to take place for it to be covered by the Vagrancy Act. Culpeper feared that no astrologer would be safe while noting things were safer in Scotland. Dodson, as the League's general secretary, responded with, 'Our judges were apparently paid to play skittles with each other's decisions.'[18][ix]

The problem was that a lack of occult knowledge made a fair judgment impossible—hence the need for education. Robert King offered a speech, the publisher William Foulsham had words to offer, and Alan also gave a talk.

After they'd heartily agreed with each other, Alan read out a letter of support from Robert Cross and brandished the cheque for ten guineas he'd enclosed. That meant Walter Old's letter of support—which was free from any financial donation—wasn't received as excitedly as it might

---

viii Perks (c.1861 in Bilton, Breconshire–1 December 1949) married Alice Lydia Hawkins in 1892 and lived in Skipton. He was a freemason from 1863.
ix W T Stead was made Vice-President, but it's unclear whether he attended the first meeting. The treasurer was G W Bibbings.

have been. It was probably a grudging letter of support, anyway. Old was publically scathing at what he saw as Alan's efforts of self-aggrandisement. This culminated in a lengthy attack he made in the March 1900 issue of his magazine *Coming Events*.

> The 'Oracle' has spoken, not in the sententious manner for which the Sybillines were once famous, but in the incoherent croakings of the roadside hag whose refuge is that of the ignorant—the fulsome platitude ... Let him go back into his hole in the corner and not presume to criticise one who, in any and every department of his astral knowledge can and will assert his undoubted birthright, unprejudiced, uncompromised, and indisputed, as against the colossal and well advertised incompetence of the notorious PAS.[19][x]

To be fair, Old did apologise later when he heard that Alan had been ill—he didn't want to appear unmanly enough to hit a man when he was down.

Before the ODL parted company at their first meeting, they agreed to hold an annual conference in London. Soon afterwards, the League appointed Roger Dawson Yelverton,[xi] the ex-Chief Justice of the Bahamas as counsel.

It was rather jolly, but if Alan had any further direct involvement in running the ODL after its inaugural meeting, it goes unrecorded. However, Dodson was unstoppable: 'We have both law and justice on our side, and we shall not much longer be denied either.'[20]

He charged around the country, offering legal advice and engaging barristers. With the rise of the holiday industry and seaside fortune-tellers, he was never short of something to do, and in 1901 he attempted to set up an occult college. Dodson never moved from his hometown of Stainland in Halifax where he lived with his sister. In 1903 he was in debt to the tune of £1,000 and at the bankruptcy court it was revealed he had sold mortgages on properties that already held mortgages—a scam he managed to operate by delaying registration of the deeds after a property

---

x President of the Astrological Society.
xi Roger Dawson Yelverton (15 June 1845-5 July 1912) was forced to resign in 1895 after he imprisoned a newspaper editor, Alfred Mosely, for contempt of court when he published a letter mocking Yelverton and refused to reveal the identity of its anonymous author. Yelverton also wrote a pamphlet and a letter to the *Pall Mall Gazette* accusing the Governor of the Bahamas, and other high officials, of corruption and perversion of justice. Yelverton's requests for an official investigation resulted in Joseph Chamberlain deriding him as egotistical and eccentric.

sale. It didn't help that one of his victims was Thomas Perks. Dodson had also used the books he was publishing as security against loans.

But as stated above, Dodson was unstoppable. He continued to defend occultists wherever he could find them, and in 1904 was involved in his biggest case to date—defending the 'Keiros', Charles Stephenson and his wife Martha. It's worthy of note that Stephenson held 660 signed and 700 unsigned documents stating:

> Keiro hereby gives notice to all who wish to consult him that he has no intention to deceive or impose upon any one; that any consultant is at liberty to believe or not his statements as to character, past life, or prediction, of foretelling of the future; and anyone who consults him must do so on the understanding that he has no intention to deceive or impose upon any one or to obtain money by false pretences ... Having consulted you I hereby declare my belief that in all you have said and written you have had no intent to deceive or impose upon me or to obtain money by false pretences, and I pay your fee accordingly.[21]

This was a clear, although doomed to failure, attempt by the ODL to save occult practitioners from prosecution. And the annual meetings continued:

BOND STREET FORTUNE TELLERS AMUSING MEETING. MASTERS OF THE BLACK ART

One of the funniest meetings ever held in' connection with the advocacy of imposture was that, which took place on 6th July at no. 8 Inverness place, Bayswater.

It was a secret meeting, called together by the Occultists' Defence League, a society founded in 1898 'for the purpose of defending professors of physic, occult, and predictive arts or sciences against wrongful prosecution'. Among its members are 'Keiro,' 'Sphero,' 'Xante,' 'Zoralda,' and 'Vita.'

The object was to arrange for the meeting of protest against the "Daily Mail" revelations concerning clairvoyance, palmistry, astrology, and other kindred' "sciences." This is to take place at St. James' Hall, Piccadilly, on Saturday afternoon.

The astrologer pot called the palmist kettle black, and with ample reason. At the outset a very natural question was asked by a gentleman who practises the gentle art of astrology.

'Why did not you clairvoyants detect who this "Daily Mail" fellow was, and his object?' he queried.

This was a poser, indeed. The lady clairvoyants fenced it, and, in turn, demanded, with indignation in their voices, 'Why did not you astrologers find him out?'

It is not surprising that neither question was answered, and that by general consent the meeting passed on to other matters.

One fair lady volunteered the information that our investigator ought to be horse-whipped. This remark met with general approval.

A member of the sub-committee explained that so soon as the league was properly established the secretary would forward a list of the members to the police, so that police and fortune-tellers may work hand in hand towards the elimination of the pretenders.

A lady asked whom among them was to be the judge of the true and the false. This delicate matter was left to the subcommittee.

An astrologer who was present proceeded to mystify the clairvoyant section. On the black-board he exhibited a horoscope of Saturday's meeting. The stars showed that while at one time the police threatened trouble, another star, powerful and benign, has become ascendant, and now nothing was to be feared from the authorities.

A certain conjunction of the stars, however, indicated that there would be a difficulty over money matters. No one seemed to doubt the truth of this prediction. It was already true.

The league is going round asking for funds, but none are forthcoming.[22]

Maybe Alan was the astrologer who mystified the clairvoyant section. Or perhaps he had other things to worry about, because in 1899 that the palmist Cheiro[xii] wrote to him with the prediction that Alan would die in 1917.[23]

---

xii William John Warner, (1 November 1866, Dublin, Eire–8 October 1936) was known as Count Louis Hamon. Several colourful versions of his early life circulated: in one he was kidnapped by gypsies when young. His entry into high society was due to his lover Lady Valancy Crawford, previously Daisy Skimp, dancer and acrobat. In 1889 Warner met Blavatsky, although he didn't join the Theosophical Society. In 1900, he was awarded the Order of the Lion and Sun by the Shah of Persia for saving his life by foiling an assassination attempt. He was the founder of the newspaper *L'Etente Cordiale* in Paris in 1901 and proprietor and editor of the *Anglo Colonial American Register* from 1900 to 1914. Warner worked as a press correspondent in Japan, spent a number of years in the USA, and claimed to have travelled in Russia, Japan, China, India, Egypt and South America. In 1920, he married Mina Dixon Hartland. For a number of years he operated from a London West End address before moving to Hollywood in 1930.

CHAPTER TEN

ALL KINDS OF PRETENDERS

*T*HE TROUBLE WITH BEING a professional astrologer was the people Alan had to deal with. Not all (if any) responded to a higher calling of any sort, which exasperated him. Indeed, clients in general exasperated Alan, especially when the nature of their problem was distasteful.

> A man called to see me at Lyncroft Gardens ... in great fear. He said detectives were after him, and that he wanted help ... He had been guilty of unnatural practices with newspaper boys and was being sought by the police. I told him to go abroad and change his name.[1]

Then there was the 'gentleman engaged in betting' who offered to pay Alan £1,000 a year for help. Alan refused, saying, 'What shall it profit a man if he gain the whole world but lose his soul?'

The bemused man responded with, 'I didn't know you were a Christian as well,' and promptly left.[2]

It was easy for Alan to be pompous when his supporters held views like those of his student Charles Moore: 'His knowledge of human nature was so vast and profound that many say that their burden of anxiety was lifted and their problem solved by simply going into his office for a little private talk. He was so sociable that in five minutes you felt as though you had known him all your life.'[3]

Perhaps so, but Moore's account of one consultation made Alan sound like someone who deserved a poke in the eye with a sharp stick.

> A hard, worldly type of woman desiring to gain an unjust advantage over another, called upon him for counsel and assistance to realise her selfish desire. She was prepared to remunerate him handsomely, but she did not know Alan Leo. Of clear discernment, he quickly penetrated to the heart of the affair, and said, 'Madam, you are contemplating an immoral act, and I cannot help you; but I warn you that one day you will bitterly regret if you follow your evil course. My advice to you is to go home, and in the privacy of your room, fall upon your knees and pray earnestly that God may forgive you and grant you the strength to walk in paths of righteousness.'
>
> The woman dumbfounded at his discovery of her hidden secret, and impressed by his demeanour did as she was told. Sometime after she called again and thanked him with deep gratitude for having turned her thoughts and life toward better ends.[4]

Alan warned another client that in a few weeks' time he was going to lose a large sum of money. 'He transferred all into his wife's bank account and a few weeks later she ran off with the chauffeur.'[5]

Now convinced of his superior talents, Alan had little patience for people who tried to pick his brains so they could set up in competition:

> A man came to me desiring to have lessons; after the second lesson he stated that he proposed bringing out a weekly journal on Astrology. He had only one idea respecting the lessons he wished to take, and that was to earn money by becoming a professional astrologer; he was a tailor by trade, but could not make money fast enough to satisfy his greed. Failing to raise his consciousness to the point where he might gain some respect for the study, I wrote declining to give him any more lessons, and although I spent much time in corresponding with him I could not get him to realise the high moral standard required to fit him to become an astrologer.[6]

These people clearly needed lessons in how to approach their astrologer, lessons which Alan was only too happy to offer:

> Nearly every transaction with an astrologer may be successfully conducted by correspondence, for all that the astrologer actually requires is the exact time, day of month, year, and place of birth,

or the latitude and longitude may be substituted for the place. It is not necessary to give the name of the person, initials, or a nom de plume may be used instead, but the sex should always be stated ... In the majority of cases, the Astrologer is much more successful when he neither sees nor knows the person for whom the work has to be done; the map of the Heavens alone being his only guide. [7]

On balance, he preferred not to have actual people clutter up his office, unless they really, really insisted. After all, astrology was, in general, a postal service. As soon as the penny post had begun in 1840, adverts had appeared in the press offering readings for a few postage stamps.

Previously, postage had depended on distance and the number of sheets of paper (with an envelope counting as a separate sheet); now a single penny guaranteed delivery anywhere in the country provided the letter satisfied the weight condition. This was a vastly lower rate than before, when the cost of postage was usually more than 4d (four pence).[i] Postal communication was now more affordable to the increasing numbers of people capable of reading and writing. During the first year of the new postal service, the number of letters sent more than doubled. Plus, it was an easy way to send money as stamps were transferrable into cash.

Astrologers took advantage of this. For example, in 1880, John Major[ii] had offered a seven-year prediction for seven postage stamps—a love charm warranted thirty stamps, as did a complete horoscope. When arrested, he was found to have 9,000 circulars and 1,000 photographs to hand, so this clearly was a sizeable business.

And in 1883, John Hartwell from Birmingham who went under the names of 'Methratton' or 'Anna Ross, the Seeress of New York' was arrested for fortune telling after upsetting the local vicar after advertising 'News from the invisible world for twenty stamps.'[8] He also offered a glimpse of your future for 7d 'marriage and other particulars, 2s 6d.; wonderful supernatural records, 1s 8d and 5s.' In fact, Hartwell offered a dizzying range of services, including selling photos of both Methratton and Anna Ross. When Hartwell was arrested, he was in possession of around 300 letters requesting assistance and containing postal orders or stamps. In fact, as he was leaving his house in the company of the

---

i The reform did not completely settle the issue of who paid for the postage, as it still remained optional for a number of years and letters could be paid for on receipt at a higher cost. Financially, the penny post scheme was a disaster, and more than thirty years elapsed before revenues were back to the pre-1840 level.
ii Described as a thirty year old fruit seller from Bermondsey.

arresting detective, the postman handed over more letters that were immediately confiscated.⁹

However, unlike Major, Hartwell appears to have believed in his own prophetic abilities and told magistrates, 'I have always noticed that my being imprisoned has been attended with great national disasters, and I have been informed that unless I am discharged this country and its rulers will be ruined.' He also claimed to have started the battle of Armageddon and pointed out, 'Those who have wronged me have been punished by death or something otherwise very dreadful.'¹⁰ He was also reputedly the descendant of Lord Lovell.ⁱⁱⁱ

Frederick Wilson ran a similar business, advertising himself as a professor of graphology and physiognomy, and had thousands of letters testifying to his ability when he was charged under the Vagrancy Act in 1891.

Although some people had made a success of it, Alan knew that unless he established himself quickly, he was almost guaranteed to be short of cash. 'Astrology, as a profession, is not remunerative, nor can it be until it is realized that the lowest fee which should be paid for a carefully judged horoscope is £5 5s. 0d ...ⁱᵛ The fact is that the public do not appreciate the skill and labour necessary to produce a full and extended judgement,' Alan said plaintively. 'To supply something approaching a true reading smaller fees have to be accepted, but this opens the field to all kinds of pretenders.'¹¹

Quite.

Despite Alan's desire for qualified astrologers who could command high rates of pay, reality dictated that most people preferred to answer a newspaper ad and pay a few shillings for a quick reading. And they had plenty of ads to choose from. Plus it was a little rich to insist on well-schooled astrologers when Alan had admitted, 'For my part I never boast of any education.'¹²

The test horoscopes had brought in some money, although they weren't an original idea. It's impossible to say who first came up with the notion of selling cheap and fast horoscopes to act as a taster for bigger things. George Wilde liked to think they were his idea back in 1893, and he made that point in his advertisements again and again, especially in

---

iii Hartwell was imprisoned twice. He disappeared from view for several years and returned to Northamptonshire via a metropolitan Poor Law Union who had been paying for his keep in an asylum at Bethnal Green. He was moved to Berry Wood Asylum, where he was maintained at the expense of Daventry Union. His death in the asylum was reported at the meeting of the Guardians in 1904.
iv At least £500 in modern terms.

Old Moore's Monthly Messenger, the forerunner of the *British Journal of Astrology*.

Providing anything more detailed than the test horoscopes was impossible to do in large numbers at any decent speed—until the invention of the copying machine.

Stencil duplication was a cheap method of producing documents that worked by forcing ink through waxed-paper stencils on to target paper. In the past, copyists spent hours copying documents, which then had to be carefully checked to ensure their accuracy. It was a slow, expensive and unreliable process. The Hungarian David Gestetner filed his first copying patent in London in 1879 and set up the Gestetner Cyclograph Company in 1881. By 1891, he had patented his Automatic Cyclostyle, a rotary machine that retained the flatbed which passed back and forth under inked rollers and allowed more automated, faster reproductions. Gestetner's inventions became an overnight and international success. By the turn of the century, a variety of mimeographs had come into use.

It revolutionised the office. And it also revolutionised astrology.

In the midst of this revolution was Ernest Bailey,[v] 'that great controversionalist'.[13] Writing under the name of Wilfred E Stanley, Bailey documented his experience of working for Alan in a fictionalised account published in his magazine *Destiny* in 1904.

> My story is a strange one, but it is nevertheless true. It is the narrative of how a young and earnest astrological student became the tool and dupe of an unprincipled and unscrupulous professor of the science; how he was betrayed and ruined through the treachery of his master's wife; of his resolution to devote a certain part of his time to the unmasking of his betrayers; how he won his way, step by step to a more prominent position than his former master, and how the avenging hand of NEMESIS, though long delayed fell with a terrible justice on those who had wronged him.[14]

---

v Ernest Henry Bailey (29 November 1876, East Kent (51N15; 1:18E) according to *Old Moore's Monthly Messenger* February 1914; incorrect data is given at *Astrodatabank* quoting a rectified time of 18:20 from *Astrology Quarterly* Winter 1945–26 January 1963, not in 1959 as is often reported due to confusion between him and the astrologer G H Bailey). During this period he lived in Ashford, Kent with his wife Edith, mother-in-law Harriet Pond and his children Alice (1892), Harold (1898), Edith (1900) and Ernest (1901). Bailey was most well-known for his work on, and controversy surrounding, the pre-natal epoch.

Bailey had always wanted to be an astrologer, although his mum disapproved:

> 'It is a pity you don't get on with your French and Shorthand instead of wasting your time over that rubbish,' said a pale faced lady, looking up from her needlework one evening to her son, who was engaged in some intricate mathematical problems. 'You will never earn your living by Astrology."
>
> 'Don't you be too sure about that, Mother,' said the young man, without raising his eyes from the paper. 'I am not doing this work for nothing, and no one can tell but that it may be a source of employment some day.'[15]

This was in 1895 when Bailey was nineteen. The son of the village schoolmaster in Kent, Bailey was of a 'sensitive and retiring disposition.'[16] From fifteen he'd worked in the offices of the Clerk of the Guardians of the Poor of the Union in which his home was situated, devoting his evenings to studying astrology and the occult. He worked for the Superintendent Registrar and had access to the registers of births and deaths—and he took advantage of that access. Trawling through the registers, he searched for details of birth times and corresponding death records. Soon, he had a collection of 500 cases together with the causes of death, later adding 400 more. He set to calculating as many horoscopes as he could find time for.

Unfortunately, he didn't know the time of his own birth. His parents told him they'd forgotten it, but Bailey was convinced they didn't want him to know it. Bailey had a high view of his abilities, believing he was 'endowed with talents far above the average.'[17] But his parents had failed him by not being able to afford to 'give him a good start in life', meaning he had to work, and 'His consciousness began to expand, and his whole life became illuminated by the wonderful knowledge of his own humanity and destiny which astrology had brought home to him.'[18] Which was nice, but back in the real world ...

In 1897 Bailey had begun a new job and soon got involved in an argument with the office boy. Apparently, the boy was friendly with some of the village girls who Bailey had snubbed for being unladylike. Due to the gossip, Bailey stopped socialising to focus on his astrology. Unfortunately, the demands of his job placed him under stress and he offered his resignation. At least part of the stress was down to him being accused of neglecting his work. As soon as he left, the office boy he had previously clashed with was re-instated, so Bailey wrote to Alan, suggesting he might work for him.

Alan had sought help for his business from 1896 when he'd placed an advertisement in *Modern Astrology* saying he needed an apprentice, someone who would pay for the honour. That year he'd hired Henry (Harry) Perhouse, a draper from Basford, Nottinghamshire with whom he'd corresponded since the early days of the *Astrologers' Magazine*, after Perhouse had won a competition. Before long, Alan had a network of helpers as Lacey said, 'In order to secure more leisure for editorial demands and astrological calculations he introduced a method of delegating the other work to subordinates employed by him in different parts of the country and responsible only to him. He called them his "curates" jocularly; they did the work and reported to him, and he visited them when necessary.'[19]

Some members of Alan's staff were gleaned from his classes. In 1897 Florence Higgs contacted Alan after reading the *Astrologers' Magazine*. It was at her request that Alan began students' classes at his office in Bouverie Street once a week. Ten people attended, including Higgs along with her sister and brother, Bessie, and Robert King. Higgs soon began working for Alan and said, 'When, as is my custom, I used to enter the office at 8.45 a.m. he was always to be seen at his desk, busily writing, for the after-hours of the day brought clients, dictation and business generally, and this was the one time when he could work undisturbed. He had no idle moments.'[20]

Florence Higgs

Indeed, he didn't. And what was clearly missing was textbooks—easy to follow and cheap. Unfortunately, there wasn't enough money floating around to fund such a venture. Therefore, in 1898 Alan announced in

Modern Astrology that he planned to publish a series of manuals. To do so, he needed three astrologers who were willing to subscribe £5 to his syndicate. They could write a book and would receive either 5% interest on their down payment or a percentage of profits per thousand copies sold. In 1901 the first of his small manuals of the *Astrology for All* series appeared. Alan beavered away, writing as much as he could himself. 'On an average he wrote a book once every three months rising as early as 6 o'clock in the morning and working till 9 o'clock at night.'[21]

Alan liked to encourage up and coming astrologers, and in writing to Bailey, who had managed to find himself a new job, Alan praised his work and sent him gifts of books saying, 'Your zeal and devotion to the science shall not go unrewarded.'[22]

A little flattery goes a long way. It persuaded Bailey to throw all his spare energy into helping Alan, despite his rapidly growing family. From 1899 he edited a monthly almanac which was printed as a supplement to *Modern Astrology* and had his articles published within its pages.

But what he really wanted to do was work as an astrologer. In June 1900 he again wrote to Alan asking for work and Alan responded saying he wasn't taking on any more staff just then, but he'd keep him in mind. That polite, non-committal response caused Bailey's imagination to run riot. He envisioned Alan and Bessie discussing him at length, working out how they could take advantage of him. The conversation opens with Bessie:

> 'I have been anxious to hear about him, for somehow I am interested in that young man, I do not know why.'
>
> 'He has written me a most peculiar letter … asking if I can give him work to do in connection with Astrology. He seems to be in a very unsettled state … I feel a bit sorry for the lad, but I do not see what I can do for him at present."
>
> 'Couldn't you have him here … and train him up to do the extension horoscopes, and help you in one of the other departments? … Surely with his splendid ninth house he would easily master the working of the system and do the horoscopes as well as you can.'
>
> 'That is just the point, my dear … he would do the horoscopes as well as I could and perhaps better … I have sunk a heap of money in this business … and it would be suicidal to put a young man who has equally high abilities for Astrology as myself, into an important position here. He might bring us ideas which I could not accept, and if any friction arose between us, and I had to dispense with his services, he could carry my secret away with

E H Bailey

him and use it for himself to our hurt, and he might even improve upon it ...'

'Yes, but you could easily silence him ... you know how Clariss Ridgie ... tried to bounce you, and threatened all sorts of things. You remember how you frightened him by writing a sharp letter ...'

'Yes, I could silence him, if any friction arose ... but I do not know whether in this case it would be to my advantage ... I must try and have him here later on as he is one who will be practical enough in his methods to make a financial success of this concern ... I am not quite such a fool as to run a business year after year without trying to make a considerable profit out of it.'²³

In reality, Alan was recovering from a bout of rheumatic fever that had left him seriously ill at the start of 1900. He probably had other things on his mind.

Bailey persisted. He visited Alan twice in 1901 and finally Alan offered him work. Alan was then:

A short thick-set man of some forty summers, possessing an open countenance, hair slightly grey, and a pair of small steel grey eyes which always twinkled when he spoke. There was an air of dignity about his personality, which tended to make him somewhat proud and self-important, but on the other hand he possessed much geniality and there was a certain magnetism about his presence which had a soothing influence on all around him.²⁴

Bailey was appointed assistant editor of *Modern Astrology*, and believed that in the near future he would be promoted to manager and later made a partner in the business. He began work at Alan's house on 13 January 1902.[vi] To his disdain, Alan presented him with a backlog of horoscopes to calculate, but he rolled his sleeves up and got on with it. 'The work room is at the top of the house, a small square room, the door cutting off one of the angles. There is one small window, and here at a table sits my companion, one Harold Stratton,[vii] a tallish, thin young man, a year older than myself, wearing glasses and having a peculiar dreamy demeanour.'²⁵ For much of the time, Bailey prepared horoscopes as described in the following:

---

vi At 9:30 am.
vii A pseudonym. It's unclear who this actually is.

MODERN ASTROLOGERS

The morning mail had just been delivered, and Albanus Leon was busily engaged in sorting a large pile of letters ... Most of them contained money orders, for Leon had an immense clientele, and the income from his business had now reached four figures a year and bid fair to greatly increase as time went on.[26]

Arranged round the walls of a room at the top of his house were upwards of one hundred of Stones' Patent Drawer Boxes,[viii] the hour drawers of each box being filled with mimeographed sheets of the various planetary positions and configurations.

I was told by the inventor of this 'scientific system delineating horoscopes' that it was founded on the same lines as the Hindu Nadigranthams—a baseless and unfounded assertion ... Certainly, the work, for it comprised nearly 700 different sheets, was a most remarkable one, and credit must be given to the inventor for his ingenuity, but it was neither a honest nor legitimate method of delineating horoscopes.

The method of delineating horoscopes was to take out of the boxes the address containing the required delineations and merely to fasten them together.

The professor's name would be affixed to the last sheet by means of a rubber stamp, and the sheets would be fastened and forwarded to the client.[27]

Nadi astrology is practiced in Tamil Nadu, India. *Nadi granthas* are writings on a variety of subjects, including astrology, written down on palm leaves. The records were of the life cycle of an individual, containing predictions and other astrological data. The data is available in a number of volumes and in every volume, there are approximately a hundred predictions that could be referred to by future astrologers. Basically, Alan was claiming to be using an ancient system. At other times, he claimed that one of his assistants, had come up with the idea. Neither was true.

It isn't clear who was the first to come up with the idea, but in 1898 H Carrington Bolton came across a crowd of people on Pennsylvania Avenue looking at a large chart which was an advertisement for the 'Faust Institute of Solar Biology, Occult Science, Astro-Phrenology, and Biblical History' in Philadelphia.

---

viii Stones' boxes had patented drop-down drawer fronts to allow easier access to documents.

> The chart itself consisted of vividly coloured concentric circles divided into twelve segments, corresponding to the twelve constellations, surrounding a man's head marked to show phrenological development. At intervals on the chart appeared the signs of the planets and of the zodiac, the symbolic figure of man's anatomy, and other astrological characters. Beneath the chart were twelve wooden pigeon-holes filled with printed folders. On approaching the exhibitor he inquired, 'In what month were you born?' In response to the information, he handed me a folder for Aquarius, with my horoscope, which contained the usual platitudes about 'how to succeed,' 'latent talent,' and a promise to write a fuller horoscope for one dollar.[28]

Maybe it wasn't Alan's idea, but he could still try to fight off the competition.

> This same professor was an extensive advertiser of test horoscopes, all of which were done by means of his mimeographed sheets. He was a great stickler for 'originality,' and was continually running down other astrologers because he said they were 'copyists.' A more colossal piece of impudence and hypocrisy it would be hard to beat, for all the while he was accusing others of what he did himself. The whole mimeographed sheets comprising his test horoscopes were copied, in many cases verbatim from Sepharial's *Prognostications from the Rising Sign* and H S. Green's *Planets in Signs and Houses*, while the greater part of the other sheets of his system were copied and paraphrased from Butler's[ix] *Solar Biology*.[29]

---

ix Hiram Erasmus Butler (1841–1916), a 'sexual mage and astrologer' was a Civil War veteran, and a survivor of a post-war sawmill accident that cost him several fingers. Unable to work, he retreated to the New England woods to live as a hermit, meditating and praying in the wilderness, and studying with the Hermetic Brotherhood of Luxor. After fourteen years, he reappeared in Boston. Butler made sacred sexuality the core of his doctrines, insisting that to truly achieve higher consciousness, not only orgasm but any sexual contact had to be avoided. In 1887, he dubbed himself 'Adhy-apaka, the Hellenic Ethnomedon', and founded the 'Genii of Nations, Knowledge and Religions'. This angered Blavatsky and she attacked Butler in *Lucifer*, saying he was no better than a cheap pseudo-spiritual hustler, and his group's initials stood for "Gulls Nabbed by Knaves and Rascals." She also accused him of siring 'astral plane children' with female elementals. The scandals that erupted when he and Eli Ohmart were convicted of fraud and initiating women by seducing them forced Butler to leave Boston and head to California where he established the Esoteric Fraternity in 1893.

Hiram Erastus Butler's *Solar Biology*[x] (and accompanying magazine *The Esoteric*) was published in 1887 and offered astrological character delineations. The basic premise of his work is that the Sun is central to this system of character analysis. Although Butler claimed his system was based on heliocentric astronomy, and not astrology, it's difficult to see his work as anything but astrological. It offered interpretations of the Sun in each sign, in a way indistinguishable from Sun sign astrology texts of today. Each Sun sign was delineated with its accompanying Moon sign, and the other planets were interpreted according to their sign. There was no need for complicated calculations as a quick glance at a set of tables would give the planetary positions—if you could be bothered. For some people, the interpretation of the Sun sign was enough.

Although reference to what was known as *zodiology* (what we understand as Sun sign or popular astrology) predate this period, it wasn't until the cosmology of theosophy took hold that the Sun became central to astrological interpretation. (Prior to that, when someone said they were 'a Libran' they meant they had the sign of Libra rising in the east at the place and when they were born, not that they were born during the dates when the Sun is in that sign.) Blavatsky was profoundly influenced by the Hermetic heliocentric cosmology of the first and second-centuries BCE, the structure of three heavens, and the centrality of the Sun, and she was influenced by the works of writers such as Max Müller who argued a solar basis for all religions.

Butler's work was highly popular and spawned imitators. Sun sign delineations were easy to understand and work out, and offered yet another method of character reading. Later authors focused on those alone, such as Eleanor Kirk[xi] who wrote the highly successful *The Influence Of The Zodiac Upon Human Life* in 1894.

Using Butler's work as one of his main sources, Alan began to gradually shift the emphasis of his interpretations, ignoring physical characteristics to focus on inner character and emphasising Sun signs—although he wasn't convinced this was a good idea. The first edition of *Everybody's Astrology*, Volume 1 of his Astrological Manuals published in

---

x The term 'solar biology' first appeared in Robert Buchanan's 1883 novel *The New Abelard*. After Butler adopting it, the term was commonly used to describe what we now call Sun sign astrology. In *Lucifer* in 1889, Blavatsky referred to it as an invention of Butler's.

xi Eleanor Maria Easterbrook Ames (7 October 1831–1908), better known by her pen name, Eleanor Kirk, was a writer from Rhode Island. She wrote a number of books and published a magazine entitled *Eleanor Kirk's Idea*, a self-help journal. She also wrote *Libra: An Astrological Romance* in 1896.

1904, comprised chapters on the Sun in each of the twelve zodiac signs with no discussion of other astrological factors. In the second edition material was added to include Sun signs combined with Moon signs as well as short chapters on the other planets, leading to complaints about the Sun sign interpretations being reduced in length. By the tenth edition an appendix had been added to extend the Sun sign interpretations.

No-one would accuse Alan of being original but he knew what sold—astrology that rejected fatalism and celebrated the qualities of the individual.

Before long, Bailey realised Alan's business wasn't as financially successful as he'd assumed. In fact, money was tight and Alan was constantly worried about how he'd pay his bills. Bailey 'helpfully' recommended changes to save money, 'Very possibly, so I am told, I may be put in entire charge.'[30]

He wasn't. It isn't totally clear precisely what did happen as Bailey never completed his exposé, but:

> It was clearly a case of building up a business on the brains and life blood of young and capable people, and if friction or dissatisfaction arose, just simply dismissing them and then threatening them with vile letters if they attempt any remonstrate. 'White Lion' was undoubtedly a strong-willed man, but he used his strength for his own selfish ends, and not for the good and usefulness he would have others believe ... hundreds of people in a higher social and intellectual scape had been taken in by this man's vanity and self-approval. 'There is only one Astrologer in England and I am he,' that was his heart's cry, 'the others are only mountebanks and frauds. Is not this Astrology which I have made?'[31]

Bailey had always been a little paranoid, illustrated by a later occasion when he sought Walter Old's advice about his fears, saying, 'I dreamed that my house was being burgled. I was aroused, surprised the thieves and they bolted ... I put the facts before a friend who was both psychic and clairvoyant, and he gave me his interpretation ... someone would attempt to rob me of the fruits of my astrological labours.'[32]

It didn't help that the Astrological Society had floundered. 'It came to an end in spite of its very promising beginning,' said Harry Green, 'strangled to death by too many rules too few who were willing to do any practical work for the good of the Society.'[33]

This was to set a pattern as Florence Higgs commented: 'An Astrological Society was started, was dissolved, re-started, again dissolved, and again restarted.'³⁴

And as Bessie later pointed out: 'From the point of view of research, astrological societies are a complete failure and always will be. They invariably centre around a prominent member who is usually a very able astrologer and the position resembles a schoolmaster and his class ... The number of serious students and workers is extremely small; and the majority of members have no inertia whatever of doing anything more strenuous than talking.'³⁵

Despite the negativity, Alan persisted. In 1899 Walter Old had suggested in his magazine *Coming Events* that there was room for another astrological society, and a meeting on 5 December 1902 led to the foundation of the Society for Astrological Research. The committee consisted of Old, Alan, Bessie, Harry Green, E H Bailey, Robert King and Godfrey Turnbull Elliot.ˣⁱⁱ Bailey became its secretary and Alan its president after resigning as President of the Astrological Society. Also present were David Christie-Murray,ˣⁱⁱⁱ Mr F Brown, Nelson Turner,ˣⁱᵛ Robert Hoare, Esther Woodˣᵛ and a gentleman from the *Psychological Society* whose name no-one could later remember.

The intention was to examine astrology from a scientific and practical viewpoint. Certain of success, the committee decided that Bailey would be paid for his role as secretary once 150 members had enrolled. There is no record of this ever happening. Although invited, Zadkiel (A J Pearce) refused to attend because he could only work with those who used a Placidean system of primary directions.ˣᵛⁱ Alan's abrupt resignation from

---

xii Son of a vicar, a mechanical engineer who lived in Lewisham; (1 February 1861–23 March 1923).
xiii Murray (13 April 1847–1 August 1907) was a journalist from Birmingham, who had been a war reporter before turning to fiction. He was a frequent contributor to the *Occult Review* and was known as 'Merlin' of the *Referee*. Murray wrote a stage adaptation of Bulwer-Lytton's *The Coming Race* which premiered at Saint George's Hall in London on 2 January 1905. Nevil Maskelyne and his father John Nevil Maskelyne collaborated on the play's special effects. It closed after eight weeks.
xiv Possibly J Nelson-Turner, the actor who was married to the actress Nora Temple (Florence Nelson).
xv Writer on art, socialist, theosophist and co-mason who wrote for *Borderland*, the *Social Democrat* and the *Labour Prophet*.
xvi Old's definition of primary directions from *Primary Directions Made Easy* was: 'What are known as "Directions" in Astrology are arcs of a right sphere measured in the plane of the Equator. They are counted from the point of Right Ascension occupying the Midheaven at the moment of birth to the point which occupies the Midheaven when

the Astrological Society caused it to be wound up at the same meeting. Despite a change of name to the 'Uranian Society',[xvii] the Society was doomed to failure by 1903, reputedly because of Alan's insistence on focusing on theosophy. Another problem was that the original society was too local and astrologers wanted something less London based. Bailey announced that he planned to reorganise the Society and turn it into the Society for Astrological Students, but few people took any notice of him. Adverting for new staff—as Alan did in June 1903—might not have been the most tactful thing to do considering Bailey believed his talents were sadly under utilised.

And in July 1903, believing Alan had conned him, Bailey led the nine staff of *Modern Astrology* out on strike complaining about their workload and the increasing commercialism of their work. That marked the end of Bailey's working relationship with Alan and he continued to rail against him for the rest of his life, most notably in the *British Journal of Astrology* which he later edited. He immediately contacted Robert Cross and ended up helping to compile Raphael's ephemeris for the next twenty years.

Alan was frustrated with recent events and moaned about 'people who are not unselfish or spiritual minded enough to share their knowledge with others,' adding, 'It is necessary and essential that we all work together, for we are all working for that wonderful and glorious future that is slowly opening up before us ... Those who have so generously given help in the past will in that wonderful future that awaits us shine out as brilliant stars to light the pathway of the student.'[36]

---

the Direction is completed. The process of directing is the means by which we compute these arcs. To direct one celestial body to the conjunction or aspect of another in the zodiac we have to find the equatorial degrees which will pass over the meridian of a place while the first of these bodies moves to the place of the second, either by Right Ascension or by Oblique Ascension.' To many people then, as now, such instructions were incomprehensible. Although a mainstay of astrological prediction for over a thousand years, the complicated mathematics involved meant that 'primaries' fell out of favour and more straightforward methods were used—usually either 'secondary' directions (or progressions), which symbolically equate one degree in the chart with one year of life and move the planets forward accordingly, or 'transits' which compare current or future planetary positions to those in the birth chart. Alan's antipathy towards primaries had long-lasting effect as astrologers rarely use them today (usually those calling themselves 'traditional' astrologers or who have an unhealthy fascination with mathematics), especially as astrological software doesn't usually incorporate them as an option.

xvii Not the best considered choice as 'Uranian' was a euphemism for homosexual in the late nineteenth and early twentieth centuries. It's likely that in this instance it was intended to refer to the planet Uranus and its associated meanings of science and innovation.

CHAPTER ELEVEN

NO TROUBLE AND ANNOYANCE

ALTHOUGH *MODERN ASTROLOGY* announced in 1901, 'Bessie Leo will pour out her sympathetic vibrations,'[1] Bessie was fast running out of sympathetic vibrations.

Michael Phillips was now in his nineties and old age was taking a toll on him. And he'd become a curmudgeon. Although he accepted visits from his relatives, Phillips didn't attempt to hide his relief when they finally left. For some time after the Leos' marriage, he refused to have anything to do with Alan. There were rumours that Bessie used to sometimes sneak him in through the back door of his home in Southampton, although Alan vehemently denied this.

But Phillips couldn't keep it up forever. Finally, at Christmas 1898 he allowed Alan into his house. This change of heart was followed by him changing his will on 20 March 1899 to leave Bessie an annuity of £75 a year—not a huge amount, but enough to make a difference, although a notable drop from the £200 per year he'd left her in 1889. It might have been more if bad investments hadn't whittled away at his money. In 1890 he told Bessie he'd lost £10,000. By late 1899, he was worth about £50,000—still nearly half a million pounds in today's terms and an amount not to be sneezed at.

And he was rich as far as Alan was concerned. Not only Alan—Henry Thomas, Phillips' bank manager called at his house to deal with Phillips' finances and mused on why he lay on an iron bedstead; surely with his money he could afford a nice brass bedstead? Anyway, Alan thought it was worth asking as he wrote:

> Dear Bessie, Do you think it well to ask O for 25 or show him the letter I enclose? I have a dread of money affairs this year, and wish I had paid up all my debts.[2] i

Phillips knew there'd be plenty of interest in where his money went after he died, and decided it was best to get his affairs sorted out. He wrote to Bessie's cousin Amelia in 1901 saying he needed the full name of her and his other nieces—just his nieces, as 'the men could work for themselves, but the women folk he must look after.'[3] He wrote again to Amelia on 10 February 1902:

> My dear niece, I am sorry to tell you that my house was broken into at midnight and robbed of all my silver and plate, valued at between £30 and £40.[4]

Although the burglary shook his confidence, Phillips didn't welcome visitors. He'd had enough of his family; his brother Henry had died recently and there'd been a row about the funeral arrangements which still irritated him.

Tweaking his will had long been one of Phillips' hobbies—he had little else to do. Although he asked for his letters, the days had long passed when he could expect to receive piles of correspondence. And Alan dictated what he should write on his cheques. From time to time Phillips went out in a bath chair pushed by Alan and submitted to Bessie's public displays of affection. It had become easier for Bessie to bestow kisses on her father after having studied Phillips' chart along with Alan. They were sure he'd die by the autumn.

Except he didn't.

Bessie had to spend more and more time in Southampton looking after Phillips who was slowly deteriorating. When his brother Henry's daughter Rachel Markson visited in January 1903, Phillips didn't recognise her at all. He stared at her vacantly and said, 'You are the woman who ran away and got married.'

She replied, 'You don't know me, Uncle.'[5]

Phillips was clearly upset so Bessie said to him, 'I will mesmerise you to sleep.'[6] and waved her hands to and fro over him.

---

i It was unclear whether he meant shillings or pounds, but in context it was likely to be pounds.

Things grew worse as the next month Phillips fell ill with thrombosis. He told Bessie he was going to make her executor of his estate—he wanted someone he could trust. And wanting to acknowledge her efforts in nursing him, in March 1903 he transferred a mortgage of £800 to her—less due to generosity than making life simpler. Bessie went to stay with him for six weeks with Alan visiting from time to time.

In April 1903, Henry Harman, husband of Phillips' brother Solomon's daughter Maria, arrived in Southampton to share the sad news that his father-in-law was terminally ill. The servants told him no-one was allowed to see Phillips. He insisted, however, and on being led upstairs he found Phillips strapped to his bed. Alan was holding his head while Bessie was pouring champagne down his throat. They told the astonished Harman that this was on doctor's orders. On seeing Harman, Phillips said, 'If you don't look out, you will get seven years for forging cheques.'[7] Bessie dismissed his comment saying he'd been reading the newspapers, and Harman observed that Phillips wasn't right in the head

Champagne was clearly something Bessie thought essential to Phillips' health. She later wrote to Maria saying, 'Dear Maria, [he] now drinks three large glasses of champagne, together with two eggs daily.'[8]

Harman was understandably worried about what was going on and insisted on looking at Phillips' finances, noting he had investments worth about £30-35,000 at the time.[ii] Phillips thought it would be a good idea to transfer all his property into Bessie's name before his demise, as she'd then avoid paying the ten per cent inheritance tax that would be due because she wasn't his legal daughter. Alan went to a solicitor to get a deed drawn up, which was sent to Phillips to sign, but Phillips' solicitor advised against him simply handing everything over to Bessie and instead advised making a new will—which Phillips did; so although a brief codicil was added to his will in April 1903, it was completely rewritten in May. When Phillips' doctor, John Fraser, attended to witness the signing of the will, Phillips told him it was, 'all for Bessie.'[9]

He also wrote to his bank saying Alan would call in to arrange his affairs so there'd be no 'trouble and annoyance' when he was gone. Everything was to be left to Bessie, so there was no reason to assume Alan would do other than make sure the capital was safely invested. Ernest Locker, a clerk from Phillips' bank, called to discuss Phillips' finances with him and made sure his investments of about £4,500 were immediately handed over to Bessie.

---

ii Other reports say Phillips had debts amounting to about £40,000.

Whether they were protecting their investment or Phillips preferred the company of the Leos to his other relatives is unclear. Things didn't always run smoothly and Phillips resentfully said to his nurse, Mary Roberts, of Bessie, 'She wants me to do things I do not want.'[10]

When Amelia Levy and Maria Harman wrote and offered to help nurse Phillips through his illness, they were told that he was well looked after by a nurse and they should visit later—plus there really wasn't space for them. When Amelia's next letter went unanswered, she was worried and travelled down to Southampton. To her horror, she found Phillips' house locked up and completely deserted. Immediately, she called the police.

Scotland Yard found Phillips at Cowes on the Isle of Wight. He was annoyed at having the police descend on him and said archly that he would write and say when he wanted a visit from his relatives. Apparently, he'd recovered a lot better than anyone could have expected by the summer, and happily sat and discussed his stocks and shares with anyone who cared to listen—and many who didn't. Maria travelled with her husband to visit Phillips in Cowes but he refused to speak to her. He had begun to act very oddly. When a nurse showed him a baby, Phillips said, 'That child will be King of England.' Bessie brushed the comment aside saying that, 'The old fellow was always thinking people were lords and ladies or something of that sort.'[11]

The nurse who accompanied Phillips to Cowes, Mary Shoesmith, wrote to his previous nurse, Mary Roberts, saying, 'You may think yourself lucky to have got out of it. Oh! The night I had with the old man on Friday. He was like a madman; abused me shamefully all night. He has evidently been made to think that nurses are a bad lot, and says he wants none of them.' Referring to Alan and Bessie, she added: 'I do not trust them in the least.'[12]

Shoesmith was convinced that Alan and Bessie were trying to turn Phillips against her. She'd had a row with Bessie about the *benger*[iii] when Shoesmith threw away the meal Bessie had prepared in preference for her own.

---

iii Benger's Food was one of several 'artificially digested' foods developed at the end of the nineteenth century. A diverse set of products that included malted foods, dextrinised foods, and peptonised foods, artificially digested foods contained digestive ferments (pancreatic enzymes). Benger's Foodwas a white powder (similar to Complan or Horlicks) that could be mixed with milk or drunk with tea, cocoa or coffee, and was a wheat-based powder.

Phillips never returned to Southampton but instead moved into a house Bessie procured—'Felsted' in Surbiton. He darkly remarked that there would be trouble when he was dead, as there was jealousy on the part of her father's relatives.

In March 1904 Phillips wrote to his bank saying:

> Sir, I have requested Mr Leo to call and see you on Friday to arrange my affairs so there should be no trouble or annoyance after I have gone. I have left everything to my adopted daughter, Mrs Leo, and having decided to live with Mr and Mrs Leo for the remainder of my life, Mr Leo has kindly consented to see my remaining capital properly and safely invested. Therefore, deal with Mr Leo when he calls as you would deal with me, and consider him fully authorised to act as he thinks best for me, and also for the future benefit of my adopted daughter, Mrs Leo.[13]

On 30 June 1904, Phillips added a codicil to his will confirming all he owned had been transferred into Bessie's name 'in order that all disputes and controversy after my decease may be avoided.'[14]

The Leos felt secure. Money might be tight now, but the situation was temporary. However, Phillips still showed no sign of dying. On the contrary, it seemed as if he would live forever. While staying with Phillips for a while, Alan and Bessie did the only thing they could. They established another theosophical lodge in Surbiton on 24 December 1906.

Annie Besant

CHAPTER TWELVE

MAGNETIC AND ELECTRIC

*S*AYING THAT ALAN AND BESSIE were theosophists is akin to mentioning that fish swim in water. Being theosophists wasn't a hobby, something they dipped into from time to time. It influenced every area of their life. Theosophy informed and supported Alan's astrology, as he said when someone complained about how much it did so, 'If you squeeze Theosophy out, you squeeze me out.'[1] After all, he also said, 'Personally, I cannot estimate the value of Astrology apart from Theosophy.'[2]

And like all good theosophists, they loved talking about it.

Although firmly embedded in theosophy, Alan's lectures had at least some astrological elements. Bessie's subject matters were wider ranging and included such tantalising subjects as 'Mental Aberrations.'

In addition to talks at the Hampstead Lodge on Monday nights, plus study classes on the first and third Saturdays of the month, in 1901 Alan and Bessie went into a lecturing frenzy and charged around London speaking at every London (or near London) theosophical lodge that would have them—the North London, Adelphi, Chiswick, Battersea, Croydon, Lotus, West London and the Blavatsky Lodge amongst others—sometimes at different lodges on the same night. Once in a while, Bessie was a little more adventurous—she spoke twice in Birmingham in 1901. And in 1899 she gave a talk in Hamburg.

Plus, there were discussion groups where they could offer their opinions, 'at-homes' and dinner parties to attend, as well as theosophical meetings, congresses, and conventions at which they weren't speaking.

This meant that Alan and Bessie hung out with all the best theosophists. They'd become friendly with A P Sinnett early in their theosophical careers and soon met Annie Besant and Charles Webster Leadbeater. As Bessie later said:

> I had the good fortune to be able to found a Theosophical Lodge in my own home in Hampstead and there Mr Leadbeater spoke twice a month ... it was a large drawing room and was always full. Both Mr Leo and myself had for some years close personal touch with Mr Leadbeater who helped my husband with his articles in *Modern Astrology* and corrected the proofs for him, as did Mrs Besant later on.[3]

If Leadbeater spoke there twice a month, it must have been at the study classes, because he certainly doesn't appear that often on the list of lecturers published in the *Vahan*, the theosophical publication that listed upcoming talks. But this is probably no more than an example of Bessie's hyperbole. What is certain is that both Alan and Bessie were starry-eyed when it came to Leadbeater:

> I place on record that we ever found in Mr Leadbeater a friend and a most wonderful teacher, the soul of honour and truth ... one of the noblest men and a fine character. He set an unselfish example which we tried to follow. He spoke ill of none, he had a serene, joyous and restful disposition, and we always felt it was a great joy and a privilege to have his presence among us.[4]

If anything, they held even higher views of Besant who had been one of the first speakers at the Hampstead Lodge—two months before it was granted its charter.

Alan idolised Besant and Bessie was perfectly aware of this: 'My husband had her portrait, life size, beside him in his office as he worked, saying she was at once his greatest inspiration and living ideal.'[5]

To be fair, Bessie was also a fan saying, 'She is both magnetic and electric in magnetism ... Mrs Besant is above our criticism.'[6]

Although his name might not be familiar to those outside theosophical and occult circles, Leadbeater's[i] influence has informed occult ideas since the end of the nineteenth century. Modern ideas about chakras and auras

---

i 1854–1934.

Charles Webster Leadbeater

(to take two examples) can be traced directly to his writings, which were hugely popular in his lifetime. He'd joined the Theosophical Society in 1884. By 1894 he was a popular lecturer and that year saw the publication of the first of his books, *The Astral Plane*.

The story of Leadbeater's life prior to joining the Theosophical Society is where truth and fiction diverge. Despite his claims, he wasn't born in 1847 but in 1854. He didn't have a brother called Gerald or go to Oxford. Disappointingly, he also didn't have wild adventures in Brazil, driving railway engines or engaging in sword fights with rebel generals. However, during a period when bureaucracy hadn't taken hold, he'd never have been required to prove any of his assertions.

When Leadbeater joined the Theosophical Society, he found himself amongst people drawn from the upper-middle-classes and the professions. A clergyman, ill-educated and the son of a Manchester book-keeper, who'd died of tuberculosis, Leadbeater felt compelled to re-invent himself. For example, he explained his failure to attend a good school due to being in South America with his family; he'd enrolled at Oxford but had to leave due to a financial crisis. As time went on, he embellished his stories with more detail, introducing lost secrets and treasures of the Aztecs and an older brother. And he also claimed to have been a pupil of Helena Blavatsky's, although no records exist to suggest anything more than a formal connection.

Leadbeater and Besant had met in April 1894 at the London Lodge of the Theosophical Society in Sinnett's house, and they soon became close co-workers in the theosophical movement, Leadbeater later claiming he'd helped Besant develop her clairvoyant skills. Together they clairvoyantly investigated the universe, matter, thought-forms, and the history of mankind, and co-authored *Occult Chemistry*.

Alan and Bessie also attended the gatherings at Sinnett's home, and it's likely that this is where they met Leadbeater and Besant. Leadbeater was friendly with John Varley, the painter and grandson of the painter and astrologer John Varley who had been friends with the artist William Blake. And in 1894, Varley described a vivid dream he'd had to Leadbeater.

> He narrated that he was on the top of some building of an unusual shape which had a flat roof, and that he was dressed in some robe or garment which was novel to him. But the part of the dream which was most real to him was that he held in his hand a rod, whose end seemed to produce light when it touched the ground, and that he marked on the ground the astrological symbol for Jupiter.[7]

He asked Leadbeater 'What kind of an astral experience could it have been?'

The answer was, 'Well, I don't know. I will look up your dream.'[8]

According to Leadbeater, Varley had been in an incarnation as a priest in ancient Chaldea and was invoking star spirits. Working together for several afternoons and evenings, Leadbeater investigated clairvoyantly the lives lived by Varley. (This was the first of the 'Lives' which Leadbeater would later become renowned for investigating.)

Alan and Bessie were extremely impressed and asked Leadbeater for more information, so Leadbeater began to clairvoyantly investigate astrology in ancient Chaldea.[ii]

> In Chaldaea the faith was sterner and more mystical, and the ritual far more complicated. It was not the Sun alone that was reverenced there, but all the Host of Heaven, and the religion was in fact an exceedingly elaborate scheme of worship of the great Star-Angels, including within it, as a practical guide to daily life, a comprehensive and carefully worked-out system of Astrology.[9]

This comment is surprising given that Sun sign astrology was nowhere near as ubiquitous as it now is, although anyone with an interest in astrology would have come across it. Still, the message was that Sun sign astrology wasn't true astrology, an assertion common amongst astrologers to this day.

Leadbeater's views on astrology are recorded in Chapter XX of *Man: Whence, How and Whither* and some of the points he made are worth repeating here as they provide the foundation of Alan's astrology from the 1890s onwards:

> The Astrology of these Chaldaean priests therefore devoted itself chiefly to the calculation of the position and action of these spheres of influence, so that its principal function was rather to form a rule of life than to predict the future; or at least such predictions as it gave were rather of tendencies than of special events.
>
> What Astrology could do, then or now, is to warn the man of the circumstances under which at such and such a time he would find himself; but any definite prophecy of his action under those circumstances can, theoretically, only be based upon probabilities

---

ii These investigations were first published in the *Theosophical Review* February, March and April 1900 and were later incorporated into *Man: Whence, How and Whither*.

even though we fully recognise how nearly those probabilities become certainties in the case of the ordinary will-less man in the street.

Some day in the future, when once again the Third or Astrological Ray will influence mankind, true astrology will be the predominating religion of man-kind.[10]

Besant had other fish to fry. For one, she had speaking engagements that took her all over the world. Theosophical congresses and conventions abounded in the early years of the twentieth century. Groups formed, amalgamated, separated and joined in federations. And European gatherings got bigger and bigger. The decision to hold European congresses was made in July 1902 and the first was planned for London in the following year.

We can safely assume Alan and Bessie were amongst the attendees at each event. They certainly attended the second International Congress of European Sections in Amsterdam 19-21 June 1903. The Sidleys accompanied them, and, oddly, Walter Old attended, although by then he was persona non grata with the TS.

During the 1903 Congress, Alan met the astrologer Adolph (A E) Thierens[iii] and this led to a Dutch version of *Modern Astrology* being published in 1906 under the joint editorship of Alan and H J van Ginkel. This was changed to *Urania* the following year under Dutch editors. The publication of *Urania* marked the start of modern Dutch astrology and in 1907 the Association for Modern Astronomy and Astrology was founded.[iv]

The next European Congress was held in London 8-10 July 1905 at the Empress Rooms, High Street, Kensington, the day after the British Section Convention. The cost of attending was 2/6, excluding the dramatic presentation, including refreshments. Around six hundred or a thousand people attended, depending on which account you read. An arts and crafts exhibition opened the events on Thursday afternoon:

> Specimens of exquisite workmanship in gold, silver, and other metals, in wood-carving, weaving book-binding, painting and sculpture—nearly all the works of members of the Theosophical Society—formed a most satisfactory collection and showed how

---

iii Adolph Ernestus Thierens (20 December 1875–30 December 1941) was an officer in the Royal Marines, astrologer and author.
iv Later the Nederlandsch Astrologisch Genootschap (Dutch Astrological Association).

the principles of Theosophy are permeating and directing the various activities and necessities of daily life.[11]

The exhibition stayed open for a week, and that evening Annie Besant lectured on 'Qualifications for Discipleship'.

On July 7 the British Section Convention took place in Queen's Hall and, as E A Houston said, 'Mrs Besant's beautifully modulated voice thrilled through the great auditorium, the eager listeners sat as entranced, except when, stirred by some outburst of eloquence, silence gave way to thundering applause.[12]

> She stood alone on the great platform, clad in a flowing robe of cream-coloured silk, with a kind of scholastic hood of lace, a long necklace of beads or berries, a brooch in the shape of the mystic crossed triangles, and a large seal ring on the third finger of her left hand. Her face has become tanned like a Hindoo's, and her grey hair, short for a woman but long for a man, gives her very much the look of a holy man of the East.[13]

The European Congress opened the next morning with a choir singing 'Hail to the Day Star,' a song specially written for the Congress by Lily Nightingale Duddington:

> *Hail! Thou Day-Star from on high,*
> *Hail! Creation's Destiny!*
> *Lowly sod and loft soul*
> *Upward climbing to their goal,*
>
> *Lowly soul and lowly sod*
> *Soaring surely to their God;*
> *Hail! Thou Day-Star from on high,*
> *Hail! Creation's Destiny!* [14]

Then everyone settled down to listen to Bertram Keightley's welcome address followed by Besant's speech. The next section required serious stamina. Representatives from thirteen different countries each gave short speeches in their own languages. It's likely each was followed by polite applause. Rudolph Steiner wasn't impressed with how this was done: 'Mrs Besant … would always add a few pompous remarks to everything that was said.'[15]

Rudolf Steiner

Of course, Steiner's view may have been a little jaded as he wasn't that well-received:

> The sympathies of the audience were not at all on my side. What I said was drowned in a flood of words and clichés, while what the audience wanted was more in the line of the Buddhist dandy Jinarajadasa[v] ... Having spoken about something which was ... of historical significance for the world ... I sat down again. The Buddhist dandy Jinarajadasa then came tripping and staggering down from his place somewhat higher up—I have to say 'tripping' to describe the matter quite exactly—stamping with his walking-stick on the floor. He gained the sympathies of the audience, but the impression I retained was like a torrent of words.[16]

It's worth remembering that for many of the audience, Steiner's German would be no more understandable than Jinarajadasa's Singalese, no matter how historically significant it might have been.

Saturday evening saw theatrical performances in the Royal Court Theatre, Chelsea. *The Shrine of the Golden Hawk* had been written by Florence Farr and Olivia Shakespeare: 'The little work proved to be not without a certain weird impressiveness.'[17] The play was set in a cave in Mount Bakhua near Sinai in 4000 BCE. 'The great magician, Gebuel has made a talisman in the form of a golden hawk...to the god Heru in the hope of overcoming the power of Zozer, king of Egypt.'[18]

This was followed by W B Yeats' *The Shadowy Waters* and music from Handel, Dolmetsch, Rameau, Boccharini, Tchaikovsky and Grieg. 'The strangeness ... was all on the stage and there it was strange enough ...[19] We were still in a strange country ... in dreamland ... What did it all mean?'[20]

---

v Curuppumullage Jinarajadasa (16 December 1875–18 June 1953_ became a member of the Theosophical Society in 1893. In 1895, Annie Besant invited Leadbeater and Jinarajadasa to join the staff in her house at 19 Avenue Road, St. John's Wood, and they lived there until she sold the lease at the end of the century. Jinarajadasa became a student at Cambridge in 1896, graduating in 1900. He was awarded a Masters of Arts in 1913. He returned to Ceylon where he became Vice-Principal (1900–1901) of Ananda College in Colombo, but in 1902 he returned to Europe to study in Italy. In 1904 he went to America, beginning a long career as an international lecturer of the Theosophical Society. He was companion and tutor to Krishnamurti and Nityananda from 1911 until the end of 1913. He became President of the Society in 1945.

There wasn't really time to work it out. Sunday offered a choice of thirteen lectures in the morning, and the afternoon was taken up by a *conversazione* starting with madrigal renderings of Shelley's poem 'Music, when soft voices die' followed by more music and songs in a variety of languages.

More lectures followed the next day and Steiner's followers became offended by the idea that he was expected to keep to the allocated time. He therefore decided to hold an impromptu lecture back at the hotel. The event concluded with a concert comprising Blake's 'Songs of Innocence' set to music, more music and a selection of business meetings.

Life tootled along much as it had done within the Theosophical Society for the remainder of 1905. And in January 1906, Besant received a letter from Helen Dennis, Corresponding Secretary of the Inner Section of the American Theosophical Society, detailing charges of 'immoral sexual practices' made against Leadbeater in respect of two boys—Robin Dennis and Douglas Petit—who had travelled with Leadbeater on his American lecture tours, and demanding a full investigation.

Dennis accused Leadbeater of teaching boys given into his care to masturbate under the guise of occult training and demanding secrecy from the boys. Robin Dennis said Leadbeater had told him 'it would make me grow strong and manly' and Douglas Petit said, 'I think that was the worst part of the whole thing, somehow he made me believe it was Theosophical.'[21]

Besant's response stressed her certainty of Leadbeater's good faith and pure intent:

> Your letter causes me some grief and anxiety, and I think I shall serve you, Mr Leadbeater and the Society best by perfect plainness of speech. Mr Leadbeater is intimately known to you, and you have definite experiences in connection with him on superphysical planes; you know something of his relations there, and the impossibility of the existence of such relations with deliberate wrong-doing. All this must not be forgotten in the midst of the terrible [sic] to which you are subjected. I know him better than you can do, and am absolutely certain of his good faith and pure intent, though I disagree with the advice he has in rare cases given to boys approaching manhood.[22]

She went on to discuss how some boys are ruined by self-abuse and others by seeking immoral women, and how others are simply tormented by sexual thoughts. Masturbation was a means given by nature to provide for the relief of such torment. Leadbeater's recommendations were only made when a careful diet, exercise, and other methods had failed.

There must have been a mistake—or perhaps it was a conspiracy.

Sex was often on the minds of theosophists—or at least the requirement to avoid it. Plus homosexual desire was subject to increasing scrutiny. Therefore, during the 1906 scandal, the central issue was that of Leadbeater's morality. The homosexual nature of Leadbeater's offence couldn't be stated other than in allusions and inferences. Discussing the accusations openly would cause untold damage to the Society, and the obscenity laws meant documents had potentially offensive terms replaced by asterisks, and many theosophists had no idea what the accusations against Leadbeater actually were.

To everyone's surprise, Leadbeater refused to answer his critics. For some this was evidence of his high occult status, others saw it as an admission of guilt. Douglas Petit later offered a sworn statement giving his version of events:

> Mr Charles W Leadbeater and myself occupied the same bed, habitually sleeping together. On the morning succeeding the first night that we slept together and before we rose to dress, Mr Charles W Leadbeater explained to me the practice [of masturbation] and urged me to engage in the practice, giving as a reason therefore that it would aid me in overcoming any desire to have sexual intercourse with women—which desire, he told me, would develop in the course of nature at my age very soon. Mr Charles W Leadbeater also told me that the practice was recommended by his Master and teacher for that reason and advised me not to speak of the matter to anyone. This reciprocal practice continued for the greater part of seven months.[23]

Many theosophists regarded the charges as unsubstantiated and false, and they were shocked when a letter allegedly from Leadbeater to one of the boys was found in a house in Toronto.

> PRIVATE: My own darling boy, there is no need for you to write anything in cipher, for no one but I ever sees your letters. But it is better for me to write in cipher about some of the most important matters [. . .]
>
> Turning to other matters, I am glad to hear of the rapid growth and the strength of the results. Twice a week is permissible, but you will soon discover what brings the best effect.[24]

Part of the passage that caused consternation was written in code, which when translated read:

> The meaning of the sign is urethra. Spontaneous manifestations are undesirable and should be discouraged. If it comes without help, he needs rubbing more often, but not too often or he will not come well.
>
> Does that happen when you are asleep? Tell me fully. Glad sensation is so pleasant.
>
> Thousand kisses, darling.[25]

When confronted with the letter, Leadbeater admitted he recognised it but:

> I certainly did not write the thing in the form in which it at present appears, and I equally certainly never used the phrases attributed to me in the sense which is there put upon them. I have never seen the original, but I did see a written copy ... the document ... was divided into two parts, the first part referring to some psychic experiences, and the second to sexual difficulties ... The second half contains such advice as I think I might have given, though I do not definitely remember giving it; but the closing phrases are not in the least my style.[26]

Some theosophists, including Besant, suggested it was a forgery, and Edith Ward, in a circular letter to the British Section of the TS, called for a full investigation.

The British Section met 16 May 1906 at the Grosvenor Hotel in London. Leadbeater attended, having been assured that the proceedings would be confidential. The Committee was to consider not only the two cases described above but also the general subject of Leadbeater's relations with his pupils.

> Leadbeater: I want to call up quite clearly the exact incidents. I scarcely recollect. There was advice but there might have been a certain amount of indicative action. That might be possible.
>
> Mead: The boy suggests in the most distinct way that the difference between 'Z' [Dennis] and you was that in the case of 'Z' he spoke of these things, and in your case something was done to him.
>
> Leadbeater: Nothing was done to him. You can't be suggesting what seems to be the obvious suggestion.
>
> Mead: You say the boy lies?

Leadbeater: He has misrepresented. I don't like to accuse people of lies, but a construction has been put upon it which is not right.

Thomas:[vi] Your reply as to scarcely recollecting suggests that there were so many cases. I would like to know whether in any case—I am not suggesting sodomy—there was definite action.

Leadbeater: You mean touch? That might have taken place.

Thomas: You admit giving advice to more than the two boys?

Leadbeater: You are to take it that the same advice was given to several.

Olcott: How many? Twenty altogether?

Leadbeater: No, not so many.

Mead: The second charge read: 'That he does so with deliberate intent or with the promise of the increase of physical manhood.' The evidence of these boys says nothing about applying to him for help. I want to ask whether this advice was given on appeal or not.

Leadbeater: Sometimes without, sometimes with. I advised it at times as a Prophylactic.

Miss Ward:[vii] I suppose from what you saw on the other planes?

Leadbeater: From what I saw would arise.

Olcott: That is not within our discussion."

Bernard:[viii] Since Mr Leadbeater was teaching these boys to help them in case of need, considering that men may be in the same difficulty, has he ever taught this to any grown-up men? Has he taught the same thing in the same personal way to grown-up men as to children?

Leadbeater: I believe that at least on two occasions in my life I have given that advice to young men as better than the one generally adopted.

Olcott: Since you came into the Society?

---

vi President of the Middlesborough Lodge, William H Thomas was later secretary of the Quest Society.
vii Originally from Bradford, Edith Ward was known for her stand on social purity, which she articulated in *The Vital Question*, published in 1891, a year before she joined the Theosophical Society. In 1891 she was living with Mary Pope and working as an outfitter through E. Ward and Company, which had been founded by her father. Ward was a lead writer for *Shafts* and in 1897 established the West London Lodge. She resigned from the TS in 1909 due to the Leadbeater crisis.
viii Pierre E Bernard from the French Section of the Theosophical Society.

Leadbeater: I think not, but one case might have been. You are probably not aware that one at least of the great Church organisations for young men deals with the matter in the same manner.

Mead: Do you deliberately say this?

Leadbeater: Yes.

Mead and Burnett:[ix] What is its name?

Leadbeater: I am not free to give this. I heard of the matter first through it.

Mead: Mr Leadbeater states then that there is an organisation in the Church of England which teaches self-abuse.

Olcott: Is it a seminary for young priests or a school?

Leadbeater: It is not a school but I must not give definite indications ...

Mead: This last statement of Mr Leadbeater is one of the most extraordinary things I have ever heard. It is incredible to me that there is an organisation of the Church of England which teaches masturbation as a preventative against unchastity. I ask, what is the name of this organisation?

Leadbeater: I certainly should not tell.[27]

Leadbeater left the room and the Committee decided to accept his resignation, although they were divided over whether he should be expelled, what sort of publicity should be given to the case, and what sort of official announcement should be made. Bertram Keightley commented, 'Unless in some public manner the Society is informed that Mr Leadbeater is no longer a member, he will be visiting branches and giving lectures and picking up boys, as he has done in the past.'[28]

Besant agreed that Leadbeater should have resigned, and said she might do so in protest. She intended to expel from the ES everyone who had taken part in action against Leadbeater and to cancel her American tour, certain that Leadbeater had acted with good intentions. However, on 9 June she wrote to the Esoteric Section of the TS saying:

> Mr X denied none of the charges, but in answer to questions very much strengthened them, for he alleged that he had actually handled the boys himself and that he has thus dealt with boys before puberty as a prophylactic. So that the advice supposed

---

ix R A Burnett from Chicago representing the American Section of the Theosophical Society. He was married to Mary Weeks Burnett.

to have been given as a last resort to rescue a boy in the grip of sexual passions, became advice putting foul ideas into the minds of boys innocent of all sex impulses; and the long intervals, the rare relief, became twenty-four hours in length—a daily habit. It was conceivable that the advice as supposed to have been given had been given with pure intent, and the presumption was so in a teacher of Theosophical morality; anything else seemed incredible. But such advice as was given, in fact such dealing with boys before sex passions were awakened, could be given with pure intent only if the giver were, on this point, insane.[29]

What did Alan think? According to a later account, he was heard to have said (although it was claimed this was slightly elaborated on):

Let Mr C W Leadbeater be sent to some picturesque sanatorium in Samoa, where he can, in most congenial surroundings ... devote himself to the pursuit of clairvoyant investigation and astral journeyings, and to the writing of books on the akashic records, the past, present and future civilisations of Uranus and Neptune, and the glories of human races yet unborn ... Let there be well-ventilated bathrooms with automatic bolts, so that his leisure-hours may be devoted to the hygienic education of delightful Samoan boys—so long as Mrs Besant isn't there to foist them on the whole civilised world as bodhisattavic vehicles.[30]

At least the matter seemed to be sorted prior to the next European Congress which took place in Paris in 3-5 July 1906. Although Olcott was supposed to preside over this event, he fell ill and Besant stepped into his shoes. There was, again, a mix of nations but the Congress was dominated by English and Dutch theosophists. The Germans were also well-represented and Steiner scheduled additional talks both before and after the Congress.

In January 1907 Olcott said he'd been visited by two Masters who'd told him Annie Besant should succeed him. As the constitution of the TS allowed for a new president to be appointed during the last six months of the outgoing holder's term of office, he sent notices to recording and general secretaries asking them to take votes on the nomination. Unfortunately, he only received responses from the Netherlands and Italy before he passed away on 17 February.

Of course, not all theosophists were happy with the idea of Besant becoming president, some of them describing Olcott as 'deluded'. Sinnett took charge as Vice-President until the voting was over. He managed to annoy Besant immediately by changing the arrangements Olcott had put in place and removing any authority from Besant, saying that as she was the agent of Dark Powers, he could leave her in authority.

So when the European Congress took place in Munich 18-21 May 1907, everyone was waiting to see if Besant was going to take over the TS. Rudolph Steiner had been in Munich for six weeks, arranging décor and the performance of a planned mystery drama, casting, directing, giving instructions for scenery and costumes. In short, he tried to do practically everything himself. That way he could ensure it was done right.

Steiner favoured a less scholarly approach to the Congress with more artistic surroundings and spiritual activity. The room was draped in red surrounded with shields and other artistic devices representing cosmic truths relating to Rosicrucian symbology—at the front of the hall stood two pillars of kabbalistic and masonic lore. The so-called seven apocalyptic seals were placed on the walls (on both sides and on the posterior wall) in a size corresponding to the space. They represent in the image certain experiences of the astral world. He'd also hoped to drape blue material across the ceiling but was prevented from doing so by his rental agreement.

Steiner had met Besant in London in 1902 and had become head of its newly constituted German section in 1902. The German Section of the Theosophical Society grew rapidly under Steiner's leadership as he lectured throughout Europe. Through his lecturing to Theosophists, Steiner met Marie von Sievers, owner of the Theosophical headquarters in Berlin, who became his spiritual partner and second wife. By 1904, Steiner had been appointed by Annie Besant as leader of an Esoteric School for Germany and Austria. Steiner made it clear this school would teach a Western spiritual path harmonious with, but differing fundamentally in approach from, other theosophical paths. These and other differences with Besant became particularly pronounced at the Theosophical Congress in Munich in 1907—its focus on artistic expression was a sharp departure from the Blavatsky tradition. This was the first opportunity theosophists had had to meet en masse since Olcott's death, so Steiner opened with a speech of appreciation. Around six hundred theosophists attended, including twenty-seven British delegates.

> The gentlemen looked very grand and ancient, some even had long white beards.[31]

The Congress had opened with music and Steiner's address: 'dark, slim, upright, gaunt, in a long almost priest-like coat—a countenance full of inner fire, full of intense concentration and mastered will.'[32] He welcomed Besant and emphasised the importance of the fact that the Munich Congress enjoyed her visit. As in previous congresses, every speaker spoke in their own language.

Alan's lecture took place on the Saturday afternoon and he spoke on 'Astrology and Personal Fate' focusing on the esoteric nature of astrology. Steiner later said Alan's talk contained 'highly valuable information.'[33]

After further talks, everyone attended a recitation from Marie von Sivers from the beginning of the second part of Goethe's Faust's 'The Life Pulse Freshly Live' and more music.

Sunday opened with music again, and Besant's main lecture, 'The Place of Phenomena in the Theosophical Society' followed by Steiner on Rosicrucianism. That afternoon saw what Steiner had been working so hard towards—the mystery play the *Sacred Drama of Eleusis* by Edouard Schuré, performed by members of the German section.

Monday was initiated by the recitation of Goethe's poem 'Song of the Spirits over the Waters' and 'Prometheus' by Richard Jürgas, followed by Besant's second lecture, and later that day, Steiner's second talk on planetary evolution, to be followed by yet more compulsory music.

Tuesday brought yet more music and small discussion gatherings on the necessity of supporting occultism within the TS, ending in closing music and song. The next event was planned in Budapest in 1909.

At the close of the Congress, it was clear that Steiner still had plenty to say, so he offered a selection of post-conference talks.

Finally, on 6 July 1907 Besant was elected President by an overwhelming majority. Alan was a little put out as he'd interpreted her chart for that year as suggesting she would die, and he told her that by not doing so, she had 'knocked the bottom out of English astrology'.[34] Presumably glad to be alive, Besant appointed Sinnett as Vice president.

After all this excitement, it was time for a holiday. In mid-July Alan and Bessie packed their bags and went to spend a nice few weeks by the sea in Brighton, staying at Harrison's hotel on the seafront until late September.[x]

---

x At 25 King's Road, previously known as the Old Ship and Gun, Harrison's was demolished in 1984 and the Ramada Hotel built on the site in 1987. It's now the Hospitality Hotel.

B by August 1907, Leadbeater and Besant were again working together on their occult investigations at Weiser Hirsch in Germany. They continued to exchange letters after this, and Leadbeater explained how he'd tried to contact Helen Dennis on the astral plane, but she was avoiding him. Leadbeater was beginning to take the role of a martyr, quietly awaiting reinstatement as he thought was his due. By the end of 1907 he was answering questions in the American *Theosophic Messenger*. After objections were received, a referendum was held resulting in an overwhelming vote in favour of Leadbeater's articles. The tide had already begun to turn. Perhaps Leadbeater should be allowed back?

Dr van Hook, inspired, so he said, by the Masters, issued a series of letter calling for Leadbeater's reinstatement. The first appeared in April, 1908, and was snappily entitled 'The Enemies of Mrs Besant are the Enemies of Charles W. Leadbeater, of the Masters and of the Future Religion of the World.'

British Theosophists were less impressed. The 1906 transcript was published and sent to members. At the annual convention of the British Section, a motion allowing for the reinstatement of Leadbeater produced violent arguments. A special committee was appointed to prepare a report on the matter. Herbert Burrows demanded that, 'The last vestige of this foul teaching which audaciously calls in the Masters to its aid, must absolutely disappear from the Theosophical Society'[35] while Mead said that the TS was on "the brink of an abyss" into which it would be 'inevitably plunged, if an imperative halt is not instantly called.'[36] And he declared:

> At all times of great spiritual revival, the foul reflection, the distortion, the perversion of the most Sacred Mysteries accompanies it; at all such times the true Mysteries have been surrounded and besmirched with the foulest of sex crimes. For the High Mysteries have to do chiefly with the Mystery of Regeneration.[37]

Besant had already referred to Leadbeater as a martyr, wronged by her and by the Society, and she declared 'never again would a shadow come between her and her brother Initiate'. A ready explanation was found for the difficult events of 1906-7: 'this dreadful ordeal which he had to undergo was the symbolic crucifixion through which every candidate for the Arhat Initiation must pass.'[38]

The proceedings of the 1906 committee were reviewed by the nine members of the Executive Committee of the British Section:

> We, the undersigned responsible members of the Theosophical Society, have considered all the documents submitted in 1906

to the Advisory Board, and also the papers in possession of Mr Mead and Miss Ward. Further, we have considered certain other evidence obtained since last July, and in face of all this, we give it as our deliberate opinion that there is nothing to show that in what he did Mr Leadbeater was not actuated by the highest and purest motives, and nothing to warrant the insinuations of personal misconduct which have been so freely made. We see no good reason, therefore, why the President should not incite Mr Leadbeater to resume again his membership.

Signed: S. Maude Sharp; Hodgson Smith;[xi] Annie Larmuth;[xii] Esther Bright;[xiii] E. Maud Green;[xiv] Ethel M. Mallett;[xv] James I. Wedgwood;[xvi] Herbert Whyte[xvii]—and Alan Leo.[39]

To be fair, Alan and Bessie were a little distracted during these discussions. On 30 March 1908, Michael Phillips had died.

---

xi (Walter) Basil Hodgson-Smith (1887–1929) was President of the Harrogate Lodge. He met Leadbeater (who became his tutor) when he was eight and lived with him at TS Headquarters ,before moving to Ealing and sharing a house with Dr Arthur Wells and Jinarajadasa.
xii Larmuth (1854–?) was Wedgwood's landlady for several years.
xiii Esther Bright was the daughter of Ursula M. Bright, who corresponded with Helena Petrovna Blavatsky. Born 19 February 1868, her father was Rt. Hon. Jacob Bright, MP. She joined the Theosophical Society in 1891.
xiv D.25 May 1928.
xv Ethel Mary Mallett (1869–1966) married George Whyte in 1909. Annie Besant was one of their witnesses.
xvi James Ingall Wedgwood (24 March 1883–13 March 1951) was the first Presiding Bishop of the Liberal Catholic Church. He became a theosophist in 1904 and was General Secretary of the Society in England and Wales from 1911 to 1913. Wedgwood initiated Leadbeater into freemasonry. Wedgwood had what he described as an 'almost unbelievably strong' sexual urge (he once visited eighteen public toilets in two hours, explaining to police he had been 'searching for a friend'). In 1919, along with several other priests and bishops of the Liberal Catholic Church, he came under investigation for sexual activities involving boys. The scandals led to jis resignation from the Theosophical Society and the Liberal Catholic Church. He enrolled as a doctoral candidate at the Sorbonne, and while in Paris became addicted to cocaine and that the symptoms of secondary syphilis manifested themselves. In the late 1920s, Wedgwood resumed his activities with the TS, with increasingly frequent claimed visions and meetings with masters and angels. He died from a fall which broke several ribs and ruptured a lung.
xvii George Herbert Whyte (1878–23 December 1917) is best known as co-founder, with his wife Ethel, of the International Order of the Round Table in 1908. He was born into a family of theosophists in 1878, and joined the Society in 1894. In 1895 Whyte worked as Leadbeater's secretary. For several years he was Assistant Manager of the Theosophical Publishing House in London. He died in World War I and was posthumously awarded the Military Cross.

Bessie Leo

CHAPTER THIRTEEN

TO THIS HIGH END

BESSIE'S COUSIN AMELIA was a busy woman. After training as a teacher,[i] she worked for the *Jewish Working Men's Club*, the *Ladies Conjoint Visiting Committee*, and as a health visitor for the *Jewish Association* in Manchester. In addition, she was part of the *Jewish Association for the Protection of Girls and Women*,[ii] became Vice President of the Jewish Hospital, and set up the Jewish Library in Whitechapel. Her 'oratory and debatory powers ... were much too brainy for a woman of that period'[1] and were used to powerful effect. Eastern European Jewish women were at the bottom of everyone's list, working for half the wages of men (in industry—these women generally refused to become domestics). Amelia was behind movements that fought sex trafficking and supported women who had been raped, provided medical treatment (in years to come, the local maternity ward would be known as 'Old Mother Levy's' in her honour), and set up bathhouses and libraries.

Living in the East End of London for most of her life, Amelia whizzed around rescuing young women, especially those who'd arrived from

---

i Amelia completed her education at Queen's College and worked as a teacher at the Portuguese Jewish School.
ii The Jewish Association for the Protection of Girls and Women was founded in 1885 as the Jewish Ladies' Society for Preventive and Rescue Work by Constance de Rothschild (Lady Battersea; 1843–1931) and a group of influential friends and relatives. The JAPGW came into being when women taking shelter in a Christian mission in London refused to eat non-kosher food or listen to Christian sermons.

overseas alone and without English. She campaigned tirelessly for better sanitation and education, especially for young Jewish women. She also adopted her brother's three children.

Although no-one in her family could compete with Amelia's list of activities, the idea of joining things and doing good works must have been catching. Her husband, Harris Levy (when not working as a tailor's machinist), as well as her brother Sydney, was a druid. (Oddly, however, while Amelia was outspokenly Jewish, Sidney was so quiet about his background that his friends denied 'rumours' of his being Jewish.)

The *Ancient Order of Druids* was a fraternal organisation founded in London in 1781. After a split in 1833, half the Order became a registered friendly society, offering sickness, unemployment and other benefits to its members under the name of the United Ancient Order of Druids while the remaining part became the Ancient Order of Druids, continuing as an unregulated fraternal society. This appears to be the branch Levy belonged to. From an early date it also had an 'inner' order, the Royal Arch—basically, it was freemasonry on a budget, primarily appealing to immigrants in inner cities.

As well as having druids in the family, Alan would have known freemasons due to his occult and theosophical connections. Plus, Bessie's first husband, John Joseph Spark, had joined the Hengist Lodge in Bournemouth on 4 December 1890, the same lodge Charles Whitting (who had been responsible for introducing Alan to Bessie) had been a member of since 1888 and had written a history of in 1897. And Frederick Lacey had been initiated into the Citadel Lodge in Harrow on 20 January 1883 and into St Mark's Lodge, Camberwell on 15 September 1891. He acted as organist for St Mark's Lodge and played the organ at the Royal Albert Hall for masonic events.[iii]

Given Alan's propensity for joining societies, it would come as no surprise to find out he'd been a freemason—except he hadn't. That changed when Annie Besant made it possible for women to become freemasons, and for Bessie to become a mason alongside him.

Theosophists were used to the idea of women taking an equal share in lecturing, travelling and writing on behalf of the Society, as well as supporting it financially. Plus, the Theosophical Society explicitly rejected sexual discrimination. Not so the world of freemasonry, which was very much a male reserve.

---

iii Lacey resigned from St Mark's Lodge in 1892.

When the first Grand Lodge of modern freemasonry adopted its constitution in 1723, it decided women shouldn't be admitted. France operated differently—mixed lodges were established from the 1730s onwards, although they tended to be more lightweight and their rituals omitted key masonic elements. Their proceedings usually culminated with a banquet and ball. Some of these societies became associated with specific masonic lodges and, because each lodge was under the 'protection' of a male Craft lodge and male officials from a regular lodge had to be present at their ceremonies, they became known as *Lodges of Adoption*.

Co-masonry, which admitted men and women, started on 14 January 1882 in France when Maria Deraismes was initiated into a Lodge called 'The Free Thinkers' (*Les Libres Penseurs*). By all accounts, it was a marvellous event, and a huge banquet followed the ceremony, attended by over four hundred guests.

After considerable opposition, on 14 March 1893 Deraismes initiated sixteen women masons and on 4 April *Le Droit Humain* came into being, spreading rapidly throughout Europe. Deraismes died a year later.

The first Englishwoman to join the French Lodge was Marie Martin, who had married a French doctor, Georges Martin,[iv] who had assisted in the initiation of Maria Deraismes in 1882. Marie Martin was also the sister of Francesca Arundale[v] (a close friend and co-worker of Annie Besant) who joined a mixed French lodge on 21 July 1895. Arundale said:

> My sister was an ardent feminist, and I sympathized most strongly with her views, and the fact that in this movement men and women could work together and that once again women could triumph in a disability removed, was sufficient to draw me within the Order.[2]

It didn't take long for Besant to approach Arundale:

> I was travelling with her on the District Railway between Ealing and London when she said, 'I have been told to join the Masonic Order. I know there is a section that admits women, but I do not know where it is to be found.'[3]

---

iv 9 May 1844–1 October 1916.
v A former spiritualist, Arundale (1847–23 March 1924) had joined the Theosophical Society in 1881. Her house at 77 Elgin Crescent, London, became the nucleus of the London Lodge of the English Section. In 1902 she moved to Adyar, and was active in the Benares) branch of the Society. Arundale was very well-regarded by early theosophists, and frequently entertained them at her home. George S. Arundale, her great-nephew and adopted son, succeeded Annie Besant as the third president of the Theosophical Society.

However, Besant knew more about freemasonry than she let on. For one thing, Charles Bradlaugh had been an enthusiastic freemason when they'd worked together. Initiated in England by the French *Grande Loge des Philadelphes*, Bradlaugh had sought involvement in a type of freemasonry that campaigned for social justice and was open to working men. He became the Orator of the Philadelphes and a member of a craft lodge in Paris, and used the pages of the *National Reformer* to denounce English Freemasonry and argue in favour of the French example. When the Prince of Wales became Grand Master of the English Grand Lodge in 1874, Bradlaugh resigned his membership.

And like theosophy, freemasonry professed a belief in universal brotherhood—there was an obvious commonality. But as Besant pointed out, it couldn't accomplish its object if it refused entry to one half of humanity.

> The entry of women into Masonry, hand in hand with men, is full of the fairest augury for the future, for it will reknit the ancient tie between Masonry and the inner worlds, will reopen the ancient channels in which the water of life can flow, and shed once more the pure white light on all who pray for its bestowal. Masonry, thus restored and revived, will play a great part in preparing the world for the future, in proclaiming and popularizing the ideals necessary for its melding, in shaping the new order in which wisdom as authority shall wed with liberty, and ensure cooperation and progress. To this high end is Co Masonry ordained.[4]

In later years, Besant downplayed Arundale's role in establishing the English co-masonry movement, saying she'd been invited to join by Deraismes herself in 1893 but had refused. Fortunately, in 1902 she had been instructed by one of the theosophical Masters—the Head of All True Freemasons—to become a freemason and discuss it with Francesca Arundale who by 1902 had reached the thirty-third degree.

In summer 1902, Besant was living in the home of Ursula Bright and her daughter Esther at 31 St James's Place, London. The Brights were a prominent Quaker family and active in feminist causes.[vi] Esther Bright said later:

> Doctor Annie Besant became deeply interested in the possibility of starting a Co-Masonic movement in England in the summer of 1902 … she asked us if we would be willing to co-operate with

---

vi Ursula was the widow of Jacob Bright, who had introduced the first Woman Suffrage Bill in 1870.

her in the formation of such a movement. We were of course only too willing to stand by her and do all we could to help. I well remember those early days when she chose those whom she thought suitable to be the founders of the new movement, workers whom she trusted.[5]

Arundale accompanied Besant, Arundale's nephew George, Ursula and Esther Bright, and Colonel and Mrs Lauder to Paris to be initiated in Le Droit Humain. There was sulking and haranguing from people who felt excluded from the party as Besant pointed out in a letter to Ursula Bright.

Poor old Faulding! The very simple reason for not asking him and his wife to Paris was that we only wanted 7, and I chose those who were available at the moment, the Arundales, you and Esther and myself, and for the remaining two the Lauders, who could easily afford it. Everybody can't do everything and go everywhere! The Meads were cross, and Mrs Oakley, because I had not asked them!'[6]

Besant and the Brights stayed with Georges Martin, the Founder Orator of Lodge Maria Deraismes No.1, and Maria Martin, the Grand Secretary of the Supreme Council, and were horrified by the lack of a bath in the house. (The number of grand banquets planned for the guests went some way towards compensating for this.) The party was initiated in Paris on 27 July 1902.

On their return to England, they decided to set up a provisional Lodge at the Bright's home to prepare for the founding of the first British Lodge. A meeting took place 29 July 1902 when the seven founding members (those who had travelled to Paris) drew up and signed the Petition for the Lodge to the Supreme Council. The title of the Lodge was to be *The Scotch Symbolical Worshipful Lodge of England: Droit Humain, No. 6 Human Duty.*

On 22 September, the Martins visited the Lodge to help prepare for the inauguration and installation on 26 September 1902 at the Theosophical Society headquarters, 28 Albemarle Street, Piccadilly. Esther Bright was the secretary and said:

Many meetings and rehearsals were held in our home... and when the great day came for our first real Lodge meeting in a big hall we were all slightly nervous, anxious to play our parts as well as possible. I drove in a hansom cab with Dr. Annie Besant and for the first time she was going to do without her ritual book! It was a great occasion, but all went well![7]

Indeed, it did. (S) Maude Sharpe, Ursula Bright, William Lauder, Ivy Hooper, Edith Ward, Florence Faulding, Esther Bright, Alfred Faulding, Max Gysi, George Whyte, Evelyn Lauder and Francesca Arundale became the founders of the first co-masonic lodge in England.

From the start, Besant was careful to establish an important principle. French freemasonry was associated with radicalism and atheism. At first, a translation made by Francesca and George Arundale of the French ritual was used. Besant decided it would be necessary for British co-masonic lodges and candidates to acknowledge they believed in the existence of *The Great Architect of the Universe* (TGAOTU), in other words, that they accepted the existence of a deity. It was arranged with the Supreme Council in Paris that co-masonry in Britain and its dependencies should have a large degree of autonomy in constitutional affairs which allowed them to include this requirement—to become known as the *Besant Concord*.

From the start, Besant favoured Leadbeater's interpretation of freemasonry, later saying gleefully, 'Instead of fragments of half understood traditions, confused and uninterpreted, we find in our hands a splendid science and a reservoir of power which we can use for the uplifting of the world.'[8] She worked with Leadbeater in India in 1904 to revise the French ritual which became known as the 'Dharma' (also the 'Besant-Leadbeater' and now the 'Lauderdale') ritual. And that same year, Alan and Bessie joined the Human Duty Lodge.

The Human Duty Lodge had begun to consecrate other lodges almost immediately. The first in London were the Golden Rule and Hermes lodges—and the Hermes lodge, a venture of Alan's and devoted to astrology, was inaugurated 6 September 1905.

Present were Alan, Bessie, Alfred and Florence Faulding, Alfred Barley,[vii] Ethel Mallet, a Mr Elliot, S Quinton and Frederick Lacey, and the lodge began to operate under the leadership of Alfred Faulding. Once the speeches, where they agreed everyone was really nice, were over, the names of six more candidates were brought forward: Sarah Dexter, Annie Watson,

---

vii Alfred Henry Barley was born 7 February 1872 in Stoke Newington, London at noon. Barley studied music at Stuttgart and later took a pharmacy degree. In 1910 he married Annie Lewton. Barley was sub-editor of *Modern Astrology* and briefly became its editor after Alan's death. In 1918 the Barleys left the Theosophical Society. In spring 1926 they met Brother Twelve (Edward Arthur Wilson). They gave him all their belongings and followed him to Vancouver Island to meet the coming of the Age of Aquarius. In 1933, Brother Twelve left on an eleven month trip, appointing Barley head of the colony. After his return, the Barleys amongst others dissented against the abuse they'd experienced, only to be banished. Destitute, they sued Brother Twelve, and were returned the $14,000 they had donated as well as the land itself.

Alfred Barley

Maude Ruth Higgs, SC Tibbles,[viii] Alfred Ellerbeck and Mrs W Shutes,[ix] all of whom were initiated at the meeting on 4 October 1905. At later meetings, Robert King and Sydney Old (Walter Old's brother) were added.

The members' astrological studies began with Alan presenting papers on temperament, with Sarah Dexter inserting some phrenology. However, things didn't run as smoothly as they could have.

> Many difficulties arose in those early days. They were greatly owing to enthusiasm (not always wisely directed), impulsiveness and inexperience. The amount of work being done at each meeting was enormous, often two degrees being worked at one sitting, with perhaps six Candidates for each degree.[9]

---

viii Sidney Tibbles (born c.1878) was an illustrator primarily remembered for his illustrations in books of stage magic, including *The Magical Entertainer* by 'Selbit', his brother whose real name was Percy Thomas Tibbles. Selbit (17 November 1881–19 November 1938) is credited with being the first person to perform the illusion of sawing a woman in half.

ix American-born Elizabeth Weed Shutes (or Shute; 30 April 1871–27 October 1949) was governess to Margaret Graham on the Titanic in 1912. She survived and later wrote an account of her experience.

The worst of the Lodge's problems were solved by the simple solution of requiring meetings to end at 9:30 pm and setting out a few rules. Whenever the subject of 'Why study astrology' came up—as it did regularly—Alan must have been tempted to point out anyone who felt they had to ask that question might be attending the wrong lodge. That, of course, didn't prevent him from making long speeches telling those present that this was the time of the group, rather than the individual.

> While Humanity will become perfected under the Aquarian influence, individuals will return to incarnation under Capricorn as 'Saviours'—hence the universality of the tradition that Christ was born in December.[10]

Things tootled along happily on their monthly Wednesday evening meetings at 13 Blomfield Road, Maida Vale with Alan taking over from Alfred Faulding on 3 October 1906, to be replaced by Bessie on 2 October 1907 for two years. Alan was an 18° in 1907 and a 30° in 1908. And Alfred Barley kept things jolly by playing the organ at meetings; it isn't clear why that role didn't fall to Lacey.

Francesca and George Arundale visited the Hermes Lodge in May 1907 to talk about co-masonry in India. That same month, rumblings of complaint against Besant's control of the co-masonic movement began to cause problems, exacerbated by the amount of time Besant was spending overseas. However, Besant said, 'Co-Masonry is not democratic, and if it is to be an instrument hereafter for the M[aster] Rágoczy, in the Seventh Ray time, it can't be. It must be a hierarchy, through which the guidance comes from above to below, and not from below to above.'[11]

The main protagonist objecting to Besant's rule was the Reverend Doctor William Frederick Cobb,[x] who wanted a representative and democratic body, free from France's control. During his lifetime, Cobb was most well-known for his work in the cause of equality for women, and he was one of the few priests to marry divorced couples.

Besant simply saw him as a troublemaker: 'Off with their heads as soon as is quasi-constitutionally possible.'[12]

In May 1907, Cobb proposed and J W Sidley seconded that a Grand Lodge be formed to govern the three craft degrees; the proposal was carried. Besant later suggested the formation of a craft council, composed

---

x Cobb (1857-1941) was an Anglo-Catholic and Assistant Secretary of the *English Church Union* for most of the 1890s. He worked in Winchester and London parishes before being appointed Curate-in-Charge of St Ethelburga Within Bishopsgate in the City of London in 1900. The following year he became Rector, a position he held until his death in 1941.

of past masters, senior brethren and lodge wardens, to draw up bylaws for the guidance of craft lodges, subject to her approval. She soon retracted this, but Cobb and others continued to meet.

Life went on as usual for the Hermes Lodge, and Annie Besant visited it to speak on 3 July 1907. Although she hadn't yet been confirmed as president of the Theosophical Society, it was clear this was about to happen. Besant spoke for an hour about temperaments, which the Lodge had been studying for eighteen months by then. Although a complete transcript of her hour-long talk was never made, notes were taken. Most of the content would be familiar to those who were adherents to Alan's system of esoteric astrology and theosophical tenets, but Besant also made some surprisingly specific astrological statements—surprising because although she'd taken lessons in astrology from Alan in 1900, she had more than once made the point that she wasn't very knowledgeable about the subject. Her mention of a technique known as the 'pre-natal epoch' suggests otherwise.[xi]

> Where a horoscope shows mental abilities hampered by the physical it indicates that one should set to work to improve the mediocre body. The physical body will come to birth at the particular time when the planetary conditions are suitable for it and when its future is mapped out in the stars.
>
> Now in regard to the building of the body of birth, and the conditions affecting the same. In the *Upanishads* reference is made to five symbolical fires. King Soma, the Causal body, is first thrown into fire and the Mental body is formed, then into water, and the Astral body is formed, then to the earth, not yet however to the father and mother, but into the food, which is to say the Physical Permanent Atom enters into the food and the father eating the food (he is the 4th fire) passes the permanent atom into the mother. This reveals the importance astrologically of the first moment when the astral vortex is formed between the parents (the moment of pre-natal epoch as it is called).

---

xi The pre-natal epoch is a symbolic conception chart. Its basis (a chart cast for when the ascending degree is held by the Moon at birth, and the Moon is the place of the ascending degree at birth) is ancient. After Walter Old had written a number of articles on the subject for the *Astrologers' Magazine*, E H Bailey researched the method, writing numerous articles on the subject, and finally a book. At the time Besant spoke, it was a popular astrological technique although it soon fell out of favour.

The use of a well-drawn horoscope lies in its ability to show us where we may guide the attempts of nature in her spiritual alchemy to transmute by raising the consciousness from the lower pole (vice) to the higher pole (virtue), always working with the vice to change it into the one related to it, i.e. the virtue; never by changing over to some other virtue unrelated to it.[13]

Once the talk was over, they retired happily for a banquet held at Eustace Miles' restaurant.

By November, Cobb's Craft Council were to hold no more meetings at the Headquarters in 13 Blomfield Road, Maida Vale. Alfred Faulding had been indiscreetly canvassing, although unsuccessfully, in his Lodge Emulation to find members willing to join an outside co-masonic Lodge. Cobb continued to ask awkward questions about finances and suggest changes to the ritual.

Besant wrote to Ursula Bright from Benares:

Cobb's whole policy is to make trouble in order to show that a Craft Council is necessary ... But we shall have no peace until Cobb, Faulding & co. leave us. With love—I am sorry these people are so disagreeable, dear.[14]

It had become clear compromise was impossible, so Cobb and his wife, Alfred and Florence Faulding, J W Sidley and several others resigned from lodge Human Duty No.6 and the Co-Masonic Order in November 1907.

By this time, Besant was firmly implanted as President of the Theosophical Society, and Alan had made it clear he supported her—and Leadbeater. And the defection of members from Besant's co-masonic group coincided precisely with the calls for Leadbeater's reinstatement.[xii]

---

xii On 20 June 1908 the first meeting of the Grand Lodge of England of the Honourable Order of Antient Masonry was held at 1 The Mall, Notting Hill Gate. Its founding members were Cobb, Sidley, Alfred and Florence Faulding, Horace P Geddes, John A Johns, T. Anderson Marks, F W Schon, Lacey, Edward Greenfield and Peter Birchall. Three founding Lodges were consecrated: Golden Rule No 1, Emulation No 2 and Lodge of Unity No 3. Their aims were: (1) To spiritualise Masonry; (2) To give women their proper place in the Brotherhood of Masonry. In 1909 Sidley and Faulding were empowered by the Grand Lodge to make masons and grant provisional charts in the US. These activities were brought to the attention of the United Grand Lodge of England and in March 1910 UGLE issued a directive outlining the sanctions that would be invoked for those participating in the new Orders. When Lodge Stability No 5 was consecrated in April at the Gordon Rooms at the Holborn Restaurant in London, where several of the UGLE Lodges had their meetings, Sidley and Lacey were observed attending and were suspended from UGLE. Matters went from bad to worse and on 17 March 1912, Cobb resigned his membership of Lodge Golden Rule No.1, and, as it was his mother lodge, his membership of the Order.

CHAPTER FOURTEEN

TORCHBEARER OF TRUTH

*I*T WAS TIME FOR a new Astrological Society. Walter Old had been badgering everyone again, and a society was finally formed 25 April 1909. Seventy-five people out of the hundred invited attended its first public meeting on 16 June[i] at the Memorial Hall in Farringdon Street. Arranged in groups according to their Sun, Moon and ascendant signs, people out of the hundred invited listened as Alan explained why this society would work, although others had failed. It's a shame to ruin the plot, but it can't be a great surprise he was wrong. And that he was beginning to feel exasperated.

> I have always found that those members of a society who do nothing are constantly finding fault with the method of those who are carrying the society on; the busy ones have neither the time nor the disposition to grumble.
> A headless body is a dead body. The last astrological society I was connected with was such a body. A man was elected to the presidency rather against his wishes … [it] fell to pieces within the year …[1]

Although the Society soon had two hundred members, it was to go the same way as past societies. Astrologers simply weren't as enlightened as Alan and Bessie would have liked, so they turned their attention to

---
i At 15:39:15.

something more exciting—the coming of the World Teacher, who was going to change the world as they knew it.

There had been mutterings for some time about the coming of the Messiah within occult communities. In fact, Blavatsky herself had told a group of Theosophical students in 1889 that the real purpose of establishing the Theosophical Society was to prepare humanity for the reception of the World Teacher.

> The next impulse will find a numerous and united body of people, ready to welcome the new torch-bearer of Truth. He will find the minds of men prepared for his message, a language ready for him in which to clothe the new truths he brings, an organisation awaiting his arrival, which will remove the merely mechanical, material obstacles and difficulties from his path.[3]

Alan and Bessie were eagerly awaiting the Age of Aquarius, which would begin with the arrival of the World Teacher, who would herald the start of an evolutionary shift back to spirituality. And they expected it soon, because as Alan said:

> Every Two Thousand Years a human being is born in whom every human principle is personified ... [4]

Or as Bessie said at greater length, in case anyone hadn't got the point:

> Once every two thousand years or thereabouts ... a new dispensation commences; the "wise men" of that by-gone period saw in the heavens a luminous star rise, and studying the heavens they predicted the coming of the Great Teacher ... today... astrologers find similar influences prevailing, and ... it appears likely that the events which took place 2,000 years ago may be repeated in the present century.
>
> If we look around us we cannot but notice that we are in a period of transition, of change, of flux and movement. With the gradual conquest of the air, everything has been rapidly widening and changing before our very eyes; with the increased facilities of travel, and ability to communicate with those at a long distance, the slow and set conditions of the past have all broken up.
>
> Those of us who are quite young ... may have the glorious privilege of seeing the Christ in His second coming.
>
> The world is slowly moving nearer in harmony by its very discords; for the Master of Music is coming, once again the melody of a New Heaven and a New Earth will sound.

Astrologers should let their wisdom shine forth as a beacon light into the darkness of the world around; should become a lifting force in evolution, and as pioneers eagerly point again to the star about to rise in the East, proclaiming anew the advent of a World Saviour.[5]

Both Alan and Bessie were in agreement—this was the sort of astrology that really mattered. Alan emphasised that:

I have been swinging very much in the direction of the esoteric side of astrology, for, to speak candidly, it is the only part of the science that really interests me.[6]

Except if someone was paying. Like Alan, Bessie wasn't averse to making the occasional prediction that was anything but esoteric.

A GOOD YEAR FOR LOVERS Lady Astrologer's Forecast

The year 1907 should be a 'bright one for lovers ... Love, indeed is the dominant keynote of the astrological figure, for Venus, the Goddess of Love is its ruler, and the fair sex may look: forward to romance entering their lives to a large degree. Reading the horoscope, Venus is seen to be occupying the fifth house: of the figure—an eloquent sign that 1907 will be a record year of romance ...

A long list of divorce cases is premised; some will be; 'causes célèbres,' and much excitement will prevail in aristocratic circles ...

Essentially a Woman's Year.

The most favorable days to 'pop the question' are:-
January 16; July 28; February 15; August 22 ...

Ladies, make the most of your opportunities in 1907.[7] [ii]

But on balance, everything faded into insignificance when compared to the search for the World Teacher. And no-one could have been more active in seeking him out than Leadbeater. His involvement with Curuppumullage Jinarajadasa was a prelude to later activities in this sphere. Born to Sinhalese Buddhist parents near Colombo, Jinarajadasa discovered theosophy at the age of thirteen in 1888 when he met Leadbeater who was principal of the school he attended. Leadbeater said Jinarajadasa was the reincarnation of his dead brother Gerald—who he'd been told would return as a Sinhalese. He'd interviewed a few students before settling on 'Raja' as he was known. Unfortunately, as already mentioned,

---

ii The dates given are when the transiting Moon conjoins Venus in the ingress chart for 1907.

Leadbeater never had a brother called Gerald. Notwithstanding this, he decided to take Raja to England. Unfortunately, Raja's parents objected so Leadbeater decided to kidnap him. Raja swam out to a schooner in the harbour of Colombo where he was to wait until it set sail. Leadbeater was to meet him in the English Channel. Raja left his bag with a sailor who had been persuaded to take it on board, and swam out to the boat that was to take him to the schooner.

Curuppumullage Jinarajadasa

Bit by bit I collected a few clothes, which were put in a carpet bag, and on a certain afternoon I took them to a particular place in Colombo where a sailor from the ship met me, and I gave the bag to him. That evening I slipped away from home, and went to the beach, where I found C. W. L. It was utterly dark, and a monsoon wind was blowing, with huge waves. I was told that the ship's boat was out there beyond the waves, and that I was to swim out. I had on only a dhoti and a coat. I stripped and gave these to C. W. L. and plunged into the waves. Just beyond the breakers I saw something white, and this was the boat. Two sailors hauled me in. I still vividly recall the sensation of cold and shivering as I lay crouched at the bottom, with a strong wind blowing. The boat took me to the ship, and the Chief Mate conducted me to a cabin, where I found my carpet bag. I stayed locked in the cabin that night and the whole of the next day and night, also a part of the following day.[8]

When he didn't return home, Raja's parents searched for him and his father threatened Leadbeater with a revolver, demanding to know his son's whereabouts. However, after talking it over, Raja's parents agreed to allow him to accompany Leadbeater on 28 November 1889.[iii] Shortly after his arrival in England, Jinarajadasa met Madame Blavatsky.

Leadbeater took Raja with him while acting as tutor for A P Sinnett's son Denny and George Arundale. They spent the next eleven years together:

There was a period when his income was so low, that he and I lived in a tiny room, for which seven shillings were paid for rent. It had just enough room for two beds, a table, a couple of chairs, a box or two, and a wash-stand. His considerable collection of books was tied up in bundles and placed under the two beds. I had my classes to attend and he his lessons to give or his office to go. Fortunately he had still some good clothes left, for it was de rigeur that at the meetings of Mr Sinnett's Lodge ... all should be in full evening dress. There were occasions when his dress suit and gold watch were pledged with the pawn-broker ... I recall a day when the only money in hand was one half-penny, though [a] few shillings were expected in the evening.[9]

And then Leadbeater met Hubert van Hook, the son of Drs Weller and Anna van Hook, and decided Raja wasn't the World Teacher, after all. In fact, he was a little problematic now. Jinarajadasa's membership of the Theosophical Society had been suspended by Olcott, then President, in 1906 for his public defence of Leadbeater, although he was fairly quickly restored to membership by Besant.

Weller Van Hook was a Chicago surgeon. He'd given up his practice in 1894 and spent some months engaged in postgraduate study. In 1907, Weller became General Secretary of the Theosophical Society in the United States and the van Hooks met Leadbeater who was on his American lecture tour.

In the summer of 1907, Hubert and Anna went to stay with Leadbeater near Dresden in Germany, after visiting Italy and Sicily, where some of Hubert's past lives were written out and he was given the name 'Orion'. Besant

---

iii This story was later denied by Jinarajadasa, although in later years still, he accepted it.

met him for the first time, and along with Leadbeater believed Hubert was the appropriate vessel for the indwelling of the expected Lord Maitreya.

They returned to the US and Besant saw Hubert again in Chicago on 11 August 1909 while she was there to give a public lecture, and, 'She was so struck by him that she prevailed on his mother to leave her husband and bring the boy to Europe and India for special training for his marvellous destiny.'[10]

Anna van Hook never saw her husband again. Unfortunately, what they didn't know was that Leadbeater had already lined up yet another potential World Teacher.

Leadbeater had arrived at the TS headquarters in Adyar at the beginning of April. Shortly after he got there, Besant left for other parts of India, returning briefly in early April. Basically, Leadbeater was left to his own devices.

He was living in the Octagon bungalow, and in a room adjoining the bungalow lived his secretary Johann van Manen. Nearby lived another assistant, Ernest Wood. And next to Wood lived a young Indian, Subrahmanyam Aijar, who introduced him to his friend Jiddu Narayaniah and his two sons, Krishnamurti and Nityanda. Wood and Subrahmanyam helped the two boys with their homework.

In the evenings, van Manen and Wood would go down to the beach to bathe with friends, and the boys, along with other local children, would often accompany them. One evening, Leadbeater decided to go along with them. He patted the head of a thin, unhappy looking child, and commented to B P Wadia[iv] that he felt a sense of well-being with him. When he returned he told Wood one of the boys had the most wonderful aura he'd ever seen and would one day become a great spiritual leader.

'How great? As great as Mrs Besant?' asked Wood.

'Much greater,' said Leadbeater.[11]

Wood told Leadbeater that Krishnamurti was dim-witted and was without any great potential. Indeed, as Mary Lutyens noted, he wasn't particularly attractive.

> Apart from his wonderful eyes, he was not at all prepossessing at that time. He was under-nourished, scrawny and dirty; his ribs showed through his skin and he had a persistent cough; his teeth were crooked and he wore his hair in the customary Brahmin fashion of South India, shaved in front to the crown and falling below his knees in a pigtail at the back; moreover his

---

iv Bahman or Bomanji Pestonji Wadia (8 October 1881–20 August 1958).

Jiddu Krishnamurti

vacant expression gave him an almost moronic look ... Moreover, according to Wood, he was so extremely physically weak that his father declared more than once that he was bound to die.[12]

Krishnamurti's father, Narayaniah had retired from his employment in the Civil Service in 1908 to work for the TS, and lived just outside the Adyar estate. Narayaniah was a widower, the father of thirteen children, only four of whom had survived.[v]

Leadbeater didn't tell Besant of his discovery right away, although they corresponded regularly. On 1 August 1909, he later related, he was instructed by the Master to take Krishna and his brother to the Master's house, in their astral bodies, whilst their physical bodies were asleep, and there they were placed upon probation as the Master KH's pupils.

At the time he met Krishnamurti, Leadbeater was already working on clairvoyant research into past lives, along with Besant. Someone suggested he should examine the past lives of Nitya and Krishnamurti. It was obvious to Leadbeater that Krishnamurti and his family had been brought to Adyar for a special reason, and he enthusiastically took up the suggestion.

In the long run, Leadbeater's explorations of past lives would culminate in two large volumes, detailing thirty lives of Krishnamurti under the name of *Alcyone*. Headquarters bubbled with excitement about the news of this occult research, and an audience of enthusiastic theosophists ascended to the roof of the headquarters building every evening after dinner to hear the latest revelations, all hoping their past lives would be featured—hopefully, in a flattering way.

While this was going on, Besant, along with numerous other theosophists, possibly including Alan and Bessie, attended the International Theosophical Congress from 31 May to 1 June in Budapest. The gap between hers and Steiner's approach was turning into a yawning chasm, as while Steiner insisted Christ couldn't be compared to other great leaders as they were only forerunners, Besant was starry-eyed about the arrival of the World Teacher. Whether or not Alan and Bessie attended this gathering, it's unimaginable that they hadn't heard of the Lives. But they had more mundane issues to attend to.

---

v All four were boys, and one of them, Sadanand, was 'mentally deficient'. Krishnamurti, the eighth child, was born 11 May 1895, in a small town about one hundred and fifty miles to the north of Madras, and was thirteen when the family moved.

Bessie had been with her father when he died. Phillips had reached the grand old age of a hundred and one and was still well-known in Southampton and Salisbury, as the papers pointed out. His will was clear enough—while everything had been left to Bessie, a codicil confirmed there was little to be left to anyone as Phillips had, 'transferred the whole of my possessions to my dear (adopted) daughter Bessie Leo ... [I] wish to affirm that I have acted in the above described manner in order that all disputes and controversy after my decease may be avoided.'[13]

Unfortunately, disputes and controversy were precisely what happened. Amelia challenged the will, asserting Phillips had been of unsound mind and that Bessie and Alan had placed undue influence on him. The case finally reached the probate court on 23 June 1909.

Apart from a donation of £50 to the Southampton Synagogue, he'd left everything to Bessie. The case was heard before Sir John Bigham[vi] and a special jury. Montague Shearman KC[vii] and Mr Bayford represented Amelia while Mr Barnard KC and Mr Middleton represented Bessie. Earlier versions of the will were produced and Bessie admitted Phillips had gifted her £4,500 shortly before he died—in the region of half a million pounds in today's terms. Oddly, Alan later said he'd considered not contesting the challenge made by Phillips' nieces, but it hadn't been his decision to make.

Once the background to the case had been detailed, Bigham asked what the estate was worth.

'Practically nothing,' said Barnard.

'When we last heard of it, it was about £40,000,'[viii] added Shearman.

'If the property is nothing, what are you fighting about?'

---

vi Bigham (the Right Honourable The Viscount Mersey; 3 August 1840–3 September 1929) came under fire himself in 1902 when he was criticised for a sentence in a criminal trial which was seen by some to be unduly lenient. 1909 he was appointed to the Probate, Divorce and Admiralty division, but he did not find the work as fulfilling and the following year he decided to retire. Upon his retirement he was a raised to the Peerage as Baron Mersey of Toxteth. As a peer, he continued to hear appeals in the House of Lords and was a regular attendant at the Judicial Committee of the Privy Council. He was created a viscount in 1916. Lord Mersey achieved his greatest fame in 1912 when he was appointed commissioner to inquire into the loss of the Titanic.

vii Sir Montague Shearman (7 April 1857–6 January 1930) was an English judge and athlete. He is best remembered as co-founder of the Amateur Athletics Association in 1880. He practised on the Midland Circuit for twenty-two years before becoming a King's Counsel in 1903 and was a specialist in common law and commercial cases.

viii About £4,500,000 in today's terms.

Shearman pointed out, 'We cannot find out what these people have done with the money, unless we set aside the will.'[14]

From then on, Alan and Bessie were on trial for being astrologers and theosophists. Shearman said it was clear Phillips was under the influence of the Leos and 'by a deep design [they had] tried to get the old gentleman into their hands and get everything they could from him.'[15] He added that the only evidence he'd willingly given his fortune to Bessie came from the Leos themselves, and they'd tried to prevent anyone from inquiring into it.

Bessie's background was addressed in detail, and it was pointed out that although Phillips referred to her as his 'adopted' daughter, she was actually his illegitimate daughter. However, there was no doubt as to the truth of their relationship. A series of witnesses speculated on the state of Phillips' finances and outlined the various wills and codicils.

Phillips' doctor, John Henry Pearson Fraser took the stand and said firmly that far from being easily influenced, Phillips was stubborn. Fraser seemed happier, pointing out, 'Mr Phillips was wont to wear a curious old dressing gown and was a stubborn man'[16] than dealing with questions relating to Alan and Bessie's occult activities, initially describing Alan as an 'astronomer' only to be swiftly corrected.

'I suggest to you,' Shearman said to Fraser, 'that Mr Leo's income came from practising on the credulous in prophesying the future.'

'I do not know that.'

'Have you heard of Madame Blavatsky?'

'Yes, I believe she dealt in the occult.'

'You know this gentleman was a pupil or practised her system?'[17]

Fraser knew nothing about this but agreed he knew Alan was an astrologer and he ran a magazine. 'Perhaps you will be interested in seeing a picture of the testator in it? Is that like him?'[18]

Bigham brightened up at this point and suggested the jury might like to take a look. He added that according to *Modern Astrology*, 'he saw saw the old gentleman was born under Scorpio,[ix] and they threatened to publish his horoscope in a subsequent number of the paper'[19]

In fact, everyone had brightened up. Mentions of astrology, phrenology and palmistry drew laughter, especially the exchange between Mary Shoesmith, who'd nursed Phillips in 1903.

'Did Mrs Leo say anything about foretelling the future?'

'Yes. She said Mr Phillips was going to die on a certain date. I believe she said it would be the following autumn.'[20]

---

ix Apparently, a Scorpio was particularly difficult to describe or understand.

MODERN ASTROLOGERS

Bigham took whatever opportunity he could to drop witty quips into the proceedings—some more witty than others. When Phillips' doctor, Henry Chambers, said Phillips had simply died of old age, Bigham offered, 'I should scarcely say he died. He stopped living.'[19] And when Henry Thomas, manager of Phillips' bank in Southampton, at the end of a very long first day of the hearing, gave evidence about the transactions he'd had with Phillips and described him as 'stingy', Bigham ignored that to respond instead to Thomas' comment that Phillips had told him he remembered seeing Napoleon's army retiring from Moscow. Bigham said, 'Well, we have traced him from Poland to Russia, and I begin to wonder if he is any relation to the Wandering Jew.'[21]

That ended the first day on a high note.

The next day, Ernest Locker, from the London City and Midland Bank at Southampton, described how he'd facilitated the handover of the Union Discount Company's shares to Bessie, later visiting Phillips to find him sane and clear minded. It was rather dull. As was the evidence offered by Kate Oliver, Phillips' housekeeper, confirming details of Phillips' wills. Things finally livened up when Louis Becker[x] took the stand.

Becker, introduced to the court as a merchant from Surbiton, although German, described Phillips as an intelligent old man who could speak several languages.

'Did you understand that the Leos were cheating the old man of his money?' asked Shearman.

'I understood they had his money and were keeping it in trust to take care of it and provide for him.'[22]

---

x Although the name 'Louis' appeared in newspaper reports, this was Wilhelm Becker (2 July 1869–?) who operated an astrological publishing house under his own name in Berlin-Steglitz, until the late 1930s. He translated and published Alan's books in German. Becker stayed in London for several years as one of Alan's students, and it appears he lodged at Phillips' house. Under the name of Frederick William Becker he applied to join the Blavatsky Lodge 18 March 1898, then living in Woodford Green. Alan was his only sponsor. He later switched to the Surbiton Lodge and transferred to the German section on 14 April 1914. Becker returned to Berlin in 1910 where he opened his astrology shop. He is primarily known for his involvement the group active in Berlin during the 1930s called the *Wahrheitsgesellschaft* (Truth Society), which sought to gain control of the mysterious power of 'vril'. Post-war books on the Nazi-occult connection claimed that the organisation, renamed the *Vril Society*, was closely affiliated with the *Thule Society* and the Nazi hierarchy itself and played an important role in the Third Reich's plans for world domination. In reality, the Vril Society had the formal name of *Reichsarbeitsgemeinschaft: Das Kommende Deutschland* (Reich Working Group 'The Coming Germany') and was one of hundreds of occult societies active at that time. It was, however, sponsored by Wilhelm Becker.

Shearman ignored the question of the will and the state of Phillips' mind completely as if he'd forgotten what the case was about and instead harangued Becker about theosophy. Becker agreed he was a theosophist, although he said he'd known Alan prior to his joining the TS.

'Are they meetings where bodies, ghosts—I not know what you call them—of reincarnated persons are supposed to appear?'

'I do not think so.'

'Then what is it takes place at these meetings?'

'Discussions on religious subjects.'

'Have you never attended a meeting where the soul of one body supposed to pass into another?

'Yes.'

'But you have never attended a meeting where there was a practical illustration? Do such practical demonstrations take place on occasions?'[23]

To Shearman's apparent disappointment, Becker denied having seen a ghost at a theosophical meeting, and when asked if he and Alan had ever been to a séance said he'd never attended one. This was getting dull, so Bigham interjected, asking if Becker knew anything about astrology and was connected with Alan's magazine. Patiently, Becker said he was no more than a subscriber.

'Is Leo one of the signs of the zodiac?' asked Bigham to laughter. 'Is Leo the right name of Mr Leo—we know it means lion—or has he adopted it?'

'I cannot say,' responded Becker.

'Oh, I think you can if you search about,' said Bigham, leading to more laughter. 'Where does Mr Leo hail from? Is he a foreigner?'[24]

Although, boringly, Becker said Alan was born in London, Bigham had no intention of dropping the astrology angle. Indicating a copy of *Modern Astrology*, he continued to question Becker, finally getting him to admit he had studied astrology.

'Do you agree that "the wise man rules his stars and that the fool obeys them"?' asked Bigham.

Becker was becoming frustrated. 'In what sense? It is all according to the sense you put on them.'

'Oh, I do not know what sense is put on them,' Bigham said, playing to his audience, as this brought more laughter.[25]

Shearman tried to regain control. 'Do you know what Mr Leo was before he became an astrologer? ... A traveller in sweetstuff?'[26]

By now it seemed the whole court had got the giggles as even this innocuous query gained laughter.

'It was remarkable that these people who had abused justice by distorting the mind of the old man were not anxious to go into the witness box,'[27] commented Shearman. It wasn't, of course. At this point in the hearing, there'd been no need for Alan or Bessie to give evidence. But there was nothing wrong with planting some doubt. Shearman added that Phillips' fortune had amounted to £100,000 at one time—a huge amount of money—and it may well have been speculated away.

After a few days' adjournment, it was time to address the case for Amelia, now the background had been dealt with.

The first witness, Henry Harman, commented that Phillips seemed to be out of his mind when he last saw him. Janet Roberts, one of Phillips' nurses, was in full agreement.

'When you first went there, do you think he was capable of transacting business?' asked Shearman.

'Certainly not. Sometimes the old man was sensible, and sometimes not. At night he was very delirious.'[28]

Roberts further added that Phillips was always in the company of one of the Leos. One by one, Phillips' family gave evidence attesting to Phillips' lack of capability. Finally, it was time to call Bessie. Alan was asked to leave the court while Bessie testified.

Bessie was keen to emphasise her close relationship with her father. 'I loved him,' she said, and added she 'did everything one soul could do for another.'[29] Through tears, she explained Phillips had decided to gift his money so she'd be able to avoid the ten per cent inheritance tax she'd otherwise be obliged to pay, not being Phillips' legitimate daughter. Bayford commented, 'The old man told her there would be trouble when he was dead, as there was always jealousy on the part of her father's relatives and herself.'[30]

'Have you ever kept any of Mr Phillip's relatives from the house?' asked Bernard.

'Never, I swear before God.'

'Did you ever force Phillips to make a will?'

'I never forced him to do anything. It was he who always forced me to do everything he wanted.'

Bigham had questions of his own. 'Your husband managed your father's affairs?'

'Yes, my lord.'

'And now he manages your affairs?'

'Yes, my lord, and I am quite safe.'

'Did you ever tell any of his relatives about this will?'

'I do not think I did.'

'And I don't think you did.'

'Have you a banking account? ... Where is it? ... What is the name of it?'

'Well, really, you may not think I am speaking the truth, but I can't remember. My husband can tell you; I am not a business woman.'[31]

Bessie went on to describe how Alan had changed his name on becoming an astrologer and answer questions about her own background, emphasising that Shearman had got it wrong when he'd stated Alan had become a Jew.

But what everyone was interested in was Bessie's occult credentials.

She explained she'd worked as a phrenologist and graphologist and later a palmist, and that she had qualified as a phrenologist. Her offer to read Bigham's handwriting resulted in a sharp, 'I should be afraid of that.'[32] Bessie then said she'd taken up astrology after meeting Alan.

'Have you a certificate for that?' asked Bigham curiously.

'No; unfortunately there is no-one clever enough to examine us.'

'Your husband?' asked Bayford.

'He is going to do it.'[33] Bessie then agreed that she and Alan had cast Phillips' horoscope.

'What did he say?'

'That it might or might not be true. You cannot put a ladder up to the stars and see.' Bessie added that she had been a theosophist since she was twenty-three.

'Does theosophy teach you to despise riches?' asked Bayford.

'Not to despise or love them, but use them wisely for others.'[34]

And then came one of the oddest moments of the hearing. Bigham called an adjournment so they could retire for lunch. When he returned, he was accompanied by Oliver Wendell Holmes Jr,[xi] the US Supreme Court judge, who in times to come would be remembered for his long service and his concise and pithy opinions—he is one of the most widely cited Supreme Court justices in history and had inherited his father's disdain for astrology and similar subjects. Holmes was accompanied by his lover, Irish born Lady Clare Castletown, the daughter of the fourth Viscount Doneraile who died from rabies when bitten by his pet fox.[xii] They sat next to Bigham on the bench to observe the proceedings.

Described as an 'iron grey haired man of middle age with an expansive forehead'[34] Alan was next to give evidence and he described his friendly

---

xi 8 March 1841–6 March 1935.

xii Holmes and Lady Castletown corresponded for over twenty years.

relations with Phillips, and denied that any undue influence had ever been used to get property from him.

'When you first saw Mrs Leo, was she pointed out as being the daughter of a very rich man?' asked Shearman.

'She was not.'

'Do you say that at the time you married your wife you did not know she had great expectations?'

'No, I did not.'

'You are the happy possessor of a motor car and good house? Has that come from journalism?'[35]

Alan insisted his money was his money and Bessie's was Bessie's, and he'd never been hard up, although he was forced to admit he might have been pressed by his printers.

In summing up, Shearman described the Leos as the 'rankest possible humbugs' saying that Bessie 'Was at one time making her living by one of the rankest forms of imposture—feeling people's bumps and telling them their fortunes by their hands, and Mr Leo had been engaged in another form of imposture, talking about the scorpion and the lion, and various signs of the zodiac, which were said to influence people's fortunes so that one could tell what was going to happen. and whether one was going to win when making a bet on the Derby.'[36]

Barnard tetchily said that the jury had been asked to ignore evidence and find against the Leos because they happened to be connected with astrology. And phrenology and palmistry had nothing to do with the issue.

Bigham reminded the jury that the real question was whether Phillips had been in sound mind and knew of and approved the contents of the will. The jury retired but only took fifty minutes to reach a decision. They found in favour of the will dated 8 May, 1903 and negatived the charge of undue influence. The costs were paid from the estate for investigating the will, but Amelia had to pay the costs for the case of undue influence.

It was finally over, and the Leos could rush off to the British Convention of the Theosophical Society on 3 July, able to relax in a suitably theosophical fashion.

Probate was finally granted 27 July 1909 for the final value of the estate of £126-11-6.

As had been pointed out during the court hearing, Alan was the proud owner of a car. He liked to keep on the move and used to cycle at least once a day, but the age of the car was beginning—especially in London, as Annie Besant had noted:

> London is a good deal changed as regards its traffic. Private carriages have almost disappeared, and motors have taken their place. The hansom and the four-wheeler are in a small minority and taxi-cabs fly about in every direction, and crowd the cab-stands everywhere. They go very fast, but are driven with great skill and care, and very rarely meet with or cause accidents; but a whole crowd of these packed closely together in a street-block, offer a curious sight to unaccustomed eyes. They add unpleasantly to the smells of the streets, but are otherwise innocuous. But London is certainly more noisy than ever, with the continual rush of the motors of all kinds and the incessant tooting of their horns. One feels as though one were in one of H G Wells' stories.[37]

Besant was used to travelling everywhere in a carriage or on horseback:

> Mrs Besant had a horse named Sultan. Like the early motor-cars it had the defect of possessing no self-starting arrangements. She would sit in the carriage all ready to start, and several coachmen and syces would coax and pull and push, sometimes for ten or fifteen minutes before it would go. When it did go it went like the wind, with a splendid high-stepping display. She would never allow the whip to be used, but would sit smiling in her carriage, confident of reaching her meeting or train in time, as she invariably did—partly, I think, because she always used to go much earlier than was necessary to the railway station or to any appointment.[38]

> At 60 she could ride as well as any person a third of her age ... She never rode astride, though a large number of women had begun so to ride even then. She rode like the ladies of old, mounted on one side of the saddle ... She trotted and cantered and galloped and could be long hours on horseback.[39]

A carriage wasn't good enough in Alan's estimation, so he undertook to chauffeur Besant around himself. Besant was more than happy with the arrangement, and Alan and Bessie managed to have some welcome timeout while the hearing was progressing:

A little party of us travelled down to Brighton on Monday, June 14th, where the Lodge had arranged a public lecture in the afternoon, and a gathering afterwards in the Lodge room ... The next day I motored down to Letchworth, the Garden City, with Mr and Mrs Leo.[40]

On Wednesday some of us went by train, and others, including myself, by motor, to Cheltenham. Mr and Mrs Leo were kind enough to take us, and we had a delightful drive of over forty miles through lovely country.[41]

On July 16th, the Masons met in the afternoon, from Leeds and Manchester as well as from Bradford, and I gave an address after which we gathered at a modest banquet of tea, and cakes and fruit, and then away past fields and over hills and dales, through the pleasant air and beneath the setting sun to Harrogate, with Mr Leo's skilful hands on the wheel of the motor car.[42]

During this driving around, a likely source of conversation between Besant and the Leos was Besant's plan to set up a society to investigate psychic phenomena. Besant set up new societies at the drop of a hat, but hadn't as yet established one concerned solely with spiritualism.

'I understand,' said Ralph Shirley in the *Occult Review,* 'that the attitude of the club towards spiritualistic revelations will be somewhat more advanced than that of the Society for Psychical Research, many prominent members of which, however, are taking up the project with ardour and enthusiasm.'[43]

Rather than simply a society, Besant had in mind a club with a room for séances, doing work similar to that of *Julia's Bureau,* which had been established on 24 April by Besant's old friend W T Stead.

Stead had become increasingly interested in spiritualism from the 1890s and in 1893 he'd founded a spiritualist quarterly called *Borderland,* which he edited for four years. In 1890 he'd met Julia Ames, an American temperance reformer and journalist, who died shortly after they met. Immediately after this, Stead began a spiritual correspondence with her.

As Julia's communications became so constant, Stead decided to establish a Bureau. Julia's messages would be taken down by shorthand writers, and those who wanted to communicate with loved ones in the beyond could avail themselves of the services of Bureau staff. Stead converted his old offices in Mowbray House, Norfolk Street, just off the Strand, into a public office for communication between the living and the dead. A small circle of sensitives reputedly chosen by Julia herself met there every morning at ten.

One of these mediums was Alan's friend Robert King. King had acted as a medium for A P Sinnett, with whom he served on the *Daily Mail* committee for the investigation of psychic photography in 1908. Through King, Sinnett had learned from a discarnate entity claiming to be Pierre Simon Laplace,[xiii] an eminent French astronomer, that Mars was still inhabited by members of Earth's humanity, who lived in ignoble, degraded conditions and the animals on Mars consisted solely of reptilians, inhabiting the canals.[xiv]

The results of the communications received via Julia's Bureau fascinated theosophists, and Besant's decision to launch a similar, although more up-market, venture was unsurprising. By the autumn of 1909, membership of over a thousand for the *International Club for Psychical Research* had been assured, and those behind the project were actively searching for premises. However, finding suitable accommodation proved to be more complicated than had been anticipated, and the project had to be put on hold.

Clairvoyant journeying would also have been near the top of the list when it came to chatting on long drives.

Leadbeater hadn't told Besant what was going on with Krishnamurti until a letter dated 2 September 1909 when he commented that one of Narayaniah's children had a past of great importance: 'A better set of lives even than Hubert's, though I think not so sensational.' Later that month, he wrote again saying, 'The set of lives upon which I have been engaged proves of quite enthralling interest, and of the greatest importance.'[44]

His reticence was understandable: 'I must carry out the instructions given to me, but after all that has happened within the last three years, I must not take too prominent an interest in boys of thirteen!'[45]

Besant had received copies of the completed versions of the ten Alcyone lives Leadbeater had prepared in October, along with a private list giving the key to the meanings of the 'Star names' under which people were known. In addition to compiling details of the relationships and adventures of theosophical heroes, Leadbeater had also produced genealogical accounts showing the interrelationships between individuals

---

xiii 1749–1827.

xiv In 2017 photographs taken by NASA were believed by alien-chasers to show a lizard-like creature on the Curiosity rover droid on Mars, although it was later explained as being a dust removal tool, a rock or an optical illusion—anything but a lizard. This wasn't the first claim—several 'sightings' of lizards have been claimed in NASA photos. The idea of lizards on Mars has been firmly planted in our consciousness since Sinnett's revelations.

across different lives. Were Alan and Bessie in the Lives? It's never been clear who precisely was included, although a variety of lists circulated as Ernest Wood described:

> Mr Leadbeater kept a list of pseudonyms, which came to be called the 'star names' of the people concerned, because they were mostly names of stars. The identities were supposed to be kept secret, but they somehow leaked out, and members used to go about with little books exchanging discoveries with one another to complete their lists![46]

Numerous people went into a snit when they felt excluded. Those who Leadbeater liked, admired or otherwise approved of were granted more than their fair share of lives. It has to be said that not all theosophists were overwhelmed by the marvellous revelations of the Lives—in fact, some were distinctly underwhelmed.

Besant and Leadbeater working on the Lives in 1901

In the Lives, in the Lives,
I've had all sorts of husbands and wives,
I've been killed and reborn,
Many bodies I've worn,
But my higher anatomy thrives.

In the Lives, in the Lives,
We've been busy as bees in their hives—
Whether Arab or Turk,
We were pining to work,
In the Lives, in the Lives.[47]

The lives were made open to a wider audience from April 1910 when they began to appear in *The Theosophist* under the title of 'Rents in the Veil of Time' and later as part of *Man. Whence, How and Whither.*

Whether or not they were taken seriously, the Lives offered wildly entertaining purple prose:

> For another influence was playing upon him, and his blood ran hotly in his veins. Ill-pleased at his indifference to their worship—nay, at his shrinking from it, even in its outward rites of animal sacrifice and poured out oblations of strong drink—his father and Oduarpa had conceived the plan of drawing him into the secret mysteries by the allurements of a maiden, Cygnus, dark and beauteous as the midnight sky star-studded, who loved him deeply, but had so far failed to win his young heart with her charms. Between her dusky brilliant eyes and his half-fascinated gaze would float the splendid face of his vision, and he would hear again the thrilling whisper: 'Thou art mine.'[48]

Now his finances were secure, Alan could afford to splash out a little. On 28 November 1909 Besant arrived in India with the Leos to visit the World Teacher. Waiting for them was the car Alan had bought for Besant.

And Hubert van Hook, who had found out that he wasn't the World Teacher, after all.

CHAPTER FIFTEEN

REVERENCE AND OBEDIENCE

*N*EVER HAVING TRAVELLED any great distance, Alan may well have taken Thomas Cook's advice regarding his wardrobe.

They recommended travellers should pack ordinary summer wear—tweed and flannel suits, possibly without a waistcoat, morning and dress suits made from thin black cloth, white and flannel shirts, pyjamas, woollen drawers and vests, linen collars, merino socks, walking boots, brown shoes, a light and heavy overcoat, and rubber-soled shoes. There was no need to carry a sun hat or umbrella as these were easy to purchase in Bombay. Not that this advice worked in reality as Ernest Wood noted:

> I soon committed two solecisms in the matter of dress; the first, when I went out in the garden in a tennis shirt and grey flannel trousers; and Mrs Besant told me it shocked the Indians to see the lower part of the trunk not loosely draped; the second when I took to Indian dress and failed at first to drape the lower cloth sufficiently over the ankles! There was no eight-inch skirt-line for men. Two inches was quite a maximum, unless you were willing to be mistaken for a workman![1]

Bessie's recommended wardrobe was equally extensive, although described in less detail—and this was travelling light. Their luggage would be collected a few days before they set off.

In November 1909 their journey, of about 50-60 hours, began at Liverpool Street station from where they made their way to Tilbury Dock (or they may possibly have caught the more expensive express from Charing Cross). Alan and Bessie arrived in Brindisi in Italy and met Annie Besant who had just travelled there from Turin, accompanied by Isabelle Cooper-Oakley,[i] Arthur and Hilda Powell,[ii] and the British Consul, Reginald MacBean.[iii]

On the morning of 17 November, they boarded the *Morea*[iv] to Aden, leaving MacBean behind and adding to their party the American Gertrude Kerr,[v] the French Cecile Bayer, and Fred Harvey.

Once in Aden, they transferred to the smaller *Salsette*, which speeded its way to Bombay. Never one to miss an opportunity, Besant managed to squeeze in a lecture on board. The Powells left them as soon as they arrived as they'd found they had to return to Aden. Harvey also left them as he'd decided to take a more leisurely journey.

The trains at Bombay's Ballard Pier Mole station connected directly with the P&O ships, so they got straight on the postal express. No-one else did, so they had the train to themselves. Considering the station was a major hub for British officials arriving for postings in India, that was a surprise. Everyone settled down for the twenty-four-hour arduous journey. Toilets were introduced on trains that year, so they may have been lucky in that respect. And there was room enough to lie full-length so you could sleep. As far as refreshments went, they were available at the stations en route and the guard could wire ahead to book meals on request.

Then as they reached Dudhni, one side of the train went up, and then the other. Besant said:

---

i Isabelle Cooper-Oakley was an English Theosophist who went to India with her husband A J Cooper-Oakley and Blavatsky in 1884. She returned to England the next year while her husband stayed on in India. She was a member of HPB's Inner Group in London.

ii Lt. Col. Arthur E. Powell (1882–1969) was a Welsh-English writer who had married Hilda Mary Hodgson-Smith the previous month in Harrogate. Hilda's father was head of the Harrogate Lodge, and her brother was Walter Basil Hodgson-Smith, who travelled with Leadbeater as his secretary.

iii Reginald Gambier MacBean (1859–1942) was British Consul in Palermo, for Sicily. A prominent freemason, he knew Aleister Crowley. He later became a co-mason, later awarded the thirty-third (and highest) degree of co-masonry by the Supreme Council in Paris in 1921, and admitted Leadbeater, Wedgwood, George Arundale, Oscar Kollerstrom and Jinarajadasa to the Rite of Memphis.

iv A passenger liner built for long distance mail services to India and Australia.

v Born Gertrude Lizzie Giles (d.1941) and second wife of the artist Charles Henry Malcolm Kerr (1858–1907), best known for his illustrations for the adventure novels of H Rider Haggard.

We were running very fast. The engine or mail-vans struck the points, and in a moment we were derailed; it was a curious sensation to see the side of the carriage rise up, and for a moment overturning seemed inevitable. Then the carriage steadied itself and the train stopped. The poor guard was stunned, having probably been flung out, as he was found on the permanent way; the rails were broken and fragments of wood and iron strewed our passage. But we found ourselves safe and whole with deep gratitude for a wonderful escape.²

Bessie immediately rushed out and 'ministered' to the guard. Eventually, three hours later, they were transferred with the mail to another train. The poor guard was still out of it, so Bessie's ministering clearly wasn't that great.

Then a pipe burst in the engine of the new train. Another three-hour wait until they managed to get on a passenger train to Madras. And there they were greeted by a big crowd. A crowd that had been waiting for six hours. Amongst them was Krishnamurti who'd been standing with a garland of roses in his hands, waiting impatiently and uncomfortably for Besant to arrive.

> Some of us were barefooted, and that part of the platform unprotected by the roof became very hot. My feet grew so uncomfortable that, after dancing about for some time, I took refuge on Don Fabrizio Ruspoli's feet.[vi] At last she arrived and everybody pushed towards the railway carriage from which she stepped down. There was such a rush that I could hardly see anything of her at all and was only just able to get near enough to her to throw the garland over her and salute her in our India way. Then three other people came up and [I] doubt she noticed me at all.³

Besant got into a car with Leadbeater, probably joined by Alan and Bessie, and Krishnamurti and others followed in a carriage as they made their way to the theosophical headquarters at Adyar.

Adyar, in south Madras (now Chennai), is located on the southern banks of the Adyar River and is (and was then) one of the costliest areas

---

vi Don Fabrizio Ruspoli (1878–1935) was an officer of the Italian Navy (some sources say a Lieutenant, others Vice-Admiral) and joined the Theosophical Society in 1902. He assisted Leadbeater as a secretary by writing down his dictation as he undertook clairvoyant investigations for past life research.

in Madras. It had belonged to the Theosophical Society since 1882 when Colonel Olcott and Helena Blavatsky had bought what was previously Huddleston Gardens, an estate with a large colonial style building and two outhouses for £600—about £55,000 in modern terms. The Society soon began improving the estate, and within four years Headquarters Hall had been built, followed by Adyar Library in 1886 with its striking outer panelled wall with eight sculptured elephant heads. When Besant became President in 1907, she immediately began expanding the estate from its original twenty-seven acres—eighty acres were added in 1908 and it would reach 253 acres by 1911. The high school Olcott opened in 1894 and shrines, temples and churches were scattered around the grounds.

More importantly, the Adyar estate was a naturalist's paradise. Gardens and wooded areas sheltered indigenous and exotic plants and trees. Coconut trees, including 300 planted by Olcott along with a selection of fruit trees, casuarina and mahogany trees abounded in the compound. Copper pods, cannon-ball trees and baobabs from Africa, along with bodhi trees and several banyans, flowers and palms, covered large areas. But the pride of the estate was the Great Banyan Tree, believed to be around 350 years old which came with property acquired in 1908. Its branches covered 40,000 square feet of space and were once held up by a 40-foot tall trunk. Thousands could sit under its canopy to listen to lectures. It was also a sanctuary for a wide variety of birds and animals—fruit bats, snakes, jackals, wild cats, mongooses and hares, butterflies and squirrels.

> The most interesting part of the grounds to me in walking from the headquarters to our bungalow is the cocoanut palm grove. These graceful trees are extremely tall and up among the leaves at the top are many cocoanuts. Some buildings are in course of erection near the grove, and I understand they are private houses for some Hindu members, who are coming to live here with their families.
>
> Here you can watch the eastern at work. Most of the labourers are coolie men and women, for both sexes work together here in the building trade. The women are beautifully developed physically, and they seem quite happy at their work. They carry to the men all the mortar, bricks, and so on, in round baskets on their heads. The Indian coolie seems to be able to carry almost any weight on his head. The female coolies sing and play tricks on each other while they work. They are to all appearances quite happy. There is equal work between the sexes, but the men get about five annas a day, while the women receive only about three annas ...

These women ... wear bright-coloured saris, which twisted around forms skirt and drapery for the upper part of the body. One arm is always left bare. (Some of the women wear silver bangles, rings on fingers and toes, sometimes some ornaments. They look strong, healthy, and happy. Food and clothes are all the coolies seem to require. They live in *cadjau* (plaited coconut-leave huts), require no furniture, and need no fireplaces, as they cook outside their huts. They have no responsibilities, and never seem to worry about the future; hence they are happy if they only get food and clothes ...

The flower gardens around our four big bungalows, as well as at headquarters, are beautifully kept. An army of coolies are employed in watering and so on, all day long. They carry the water in big earthenware jugs. These are supported on the hip or shoulder, and all the water supplied to our bathrooms is carried in this way. From morning until night numerous sweeping women are employed sweeping up leaves ... The life of the coolie sweeper woman is, however, healthy, as she is out in the fresh air every day, and lies down to sleep for a while.[4]

And for a reason best known to themselves, once they finally reached Adyar, the household burst into song.

After a long chat with Besant, Leadbeater went onto the veranda and called Krishnamurti and Nitya. Shortly afterwards they met Besant for the first time. 'We both prostrated ourself at her feet,' said Krishnamurti. 'She lifted us up and embraced us.'[5]

They couldn't spend long together as a meeting for the Esoteric Section was due to be held in the drawing room. Within moments Alan and Bessie also saw Krishnamurti for the first time, sitting at Besant's feet.

Also present at Adyar were Anna and Hubert van Hook. Anna spent much of her time teaching Hubert, Krishnamurti and Nitya. After discovering Krishnamurti, Leadbeater had become interested in Hubert, eventually banning him from touching Krishna's bicycle in case bad vibrations entered it. However, apart from Nitya, Hubert was the only boy Krishnamurti was allowed to see, and they had little choice but to spend time together.[vii]

---

vii In later years Hubert would claim Leadbeater had 'misused him' (had sex with him) but some viewed this allegation as a case of sour grapes. Hubert was accepted as an initiate in December 1912 and he and his mother remained at Adyar for five years. Hubert's mother eventually took him back to America, where he grew up to become a lawyer. He died at 61 in Chicago, leaving behind his widow Lucille and one daughter.

Bessie was smitten with Adyar: 'All in the East moves slowly,' she observed later. 'The eastern characteristics of calmness, serenity, patience, and the entire absence of any kind of hurry, turmoil or haste, are curiously effective in quieting the lower or concrete mind ...'⁶ There was something in the very atmosphere that was restful and peaceful, and life was simpler and more natural. No Hindu ever seemed to hurry, and he always had time to be courteous and polite.'⁷

She hadn't forgotten she was a phrenologist. 'The Indian head is shaped quite differently from that of his Western brother, reverence and obedience being the larger organs. There is an entire absence of conventionality, everyone doing as he wishes.'⁸ That sounds a little unlikely, but true or not, what was even better was that everyone seemed to have heard of—and accepted—the idea of reincarnation. Lest anyone should think theosophy was responsible for introducing Alan to the idea of reincarnation, he took pains to point out that 'At seventeen I was present at a discussion between my mother and a gentleman ... who had just returned from India, in which the theory of reincarnation was mentioned. I told my mother that it was the most reasonable hypothesis.⁹

And Alan hadn't forgotten he was primarily an astrologer. He'd brought along a number of books to donate to the library, including several volumes of his own work and copies of *Astrologie Restored* by William Ramsey (1653), noted to be 'a very rare and costly work'.¹⁰ He also made sure to get Krishnamurti's birth data from Narayaniah, which he later published in *Modern Astrology*.ᵛⁱⁱⁱ

Hindu astrology wasn't new to Alan. Right from the start, the *Astrologers' Magazine* had included articles on Indian astrology. Lacey had been in correspondence with N Chidambaram Iyerⁱˣ before he and Alan had met, and when Iyer translated the *Brihat Samhita of Varaha Mihira*ˣ from Sanskrit into English, Lacey suggested that he and Alan became agents and sold the books through the *Astrologers' Magazine*. In return, Iyer had persuaded people he knew to subscribe to the *AM*. Alan and Lacey also corresponded with J T Chitnis, another Hindu astrologer, who contributed articles to the *AM* in 1892. And, of course, Walter Old had contributed material about Indian astrology while he was staying at

---

viii 12 May 1895, 0:30, Bellary–17 February 1986.
ix A renowned theosophist, astrologer and palmist, who knew Blavatsky well, Iyer fought vigorously for calendar reform in India. He died in 1892.
x Meaning 'natural astrology', the *Brihat* comprised two lengthy texts that dealt with a variety of astronomical and astrological material, especially covering forecasting techniques such as planetary periods, and rectification.

Adyar in 1893. He especially revered the Indian approach to *prasna*, or horary astrology—the art of answering a question by casting a chart for the moment the question is asked, saying, 'In this branch of astrology the Hindus excel everything I have ever heard of.'[11]

We shouldn't mistake any of this as suggesting Alan had a less colonial attitude towards India than his contemporaries. Far from it. Back in 1894 he had commented that he had, 'recently enlightened the Indian astrologers of a system of predicting long lost to them.'[12] Which was nice of him.

Besant was fascinated by Leadbeater's accounts of Krishnamurti's past lives and immediately launched into helping Leadbeater out with his work.

Besant in the car Alan had bought for her

However, we can't forget Alan's passion for driving. Now he had given Besant a car, the next obvious thing was to teach her how to drive. Besant said in a letter to Esther Bright, 'I think it will amuse you to know that I am learning to drive the motor-car; I have had four lessons, and am getting on quite gaily. Mr Leo is very proud of me, and says that I am a very good pupil, and that it is Hershell.'[13] [xi] 'One is never allowed to have any credit

---

xi 'Hershell' here means the planet Uranus, then more commonly called Herschel after its discoverer, William Herschel who discovered it in 1781. In Besant's horoscope, which Alan had spent many hours studying, Uranus is close to the rising sign or ascendant, suggesting she would have an affinity for machinery and find it easy to acquire technological skills.

for oneself,' continued Besant. 'It is always "One above"; as bad as popular Christianity. I negotiated a really difficult corner this morning, and heard Mr Leo murmur behind me: "Quite remarkable, but there—it's Hershell." I felt inclined to say, ungrammatically and proudly, "No, it is me".[14]

Besant soon got the hang of it, and became a good driver, taking people out for short drives in the early mornings.

The annual convention proper opened on 27 December, but delegates began to arrive several days before. On the evening of 26 December, a large crowd filled the hall at the Central Hindu College to hear Besant lecture on mysticism and occultism.

At eight o'clock the next morning, the Anniversary Meeting took place with a presidential address followed by reports from lodges all over the world. 'It was a long but very interesting meeting,' insisted Besant.[15] As hundreds of theosophists were spread around the compound, it was probably longer than it was interesting.

The talks began that afternoon, with the first of a series of four on 'The Laws of Manu in the Light of Theosophy' delivered by Babu Bhagavan Das Sahab. Meeting followed meeting followed lecture followed speech. This was serious work. Although lectures being delivered in Bengali was admirable, it was probably less than thrilling for the European attendees. Apart from quick breaks for photo opportunities and Q & A sessions, there was little time to breathe. Indeed the talks continued on into the evenings. Alan and Bessie delivered talks together on the 31 December and 1 January.

Besant also gave a talk on 31 December, saying a great 'Teacher and Guide … will deign once more to tread our mortal ways.'[16] She probably felt more confident in her assertion due to the fact that she'd received a telegram from Leadbeater saying that the Master Koot Hoomi was going to accept Krishnamurti as his pupil that night and he wanted her to be present—astrally, of course.

The next day Besant telegraphed Leadbeater to share her recollections of the ceremony and asked him if it was true that the Lord Maitreya had given Krishnamurti into hers and Leadbeater's charge. She soon received a response confirming that was the case. And she obviously told him how well the convention had gone. Perhaps Besant wasn't as taken with the Leos as they believed. Leadbeater's response of 3 January hinted as much. 'I am very glad to hear that the Convention was so harmonious. I think you are right to move Mrs L. for she is not at all a suitable person to live so near the Shrine.'[17]

On 8 January telegrams flew back and forth between Leadbeater and Besant discussing the fact that Krishnamurti was to be initiated by the

Master on 11 January. They would need complete seclusion from the night before—to which Besant gave her blessing.

If anyone asked Alan's opinion, his response goes unrecorded. However, chances are he would have nodded agreeably and said he wasn't surprised in the least. For several years, something special had been expected to happen on 11 January. The astrologer and theosophist George Sutcliffe had said as far back as 1899 that the date heralded the arrival of a great spiritual teacher, and the idea was common knowledge amongst astrologers. As he pointed out, 'There seems to prevail ... a very strong feeling amongst the spiritually minded that the present century will see the advent of a great spiritual teacher.'[18]

Yorkshire-born Sutcliffe[xii] came from a family whose fortunes relied on the cotton mills. A clerk in the family firm of Ely Sutcliffe and Son, he first went to India in 1901 where he managed mills in Bombay and Solapur. Sutcliffe wrote and lectured extensively on theosophy, including occult chemistry, but was best known for his astrology. While in India he invested a great deal of his time in studying Indian astrology, but some of his theories belonged to no standard astrological system. He proposed two hypothetical planets that he'd discovered clairvoyantly—Isis and Osiris—and in 1900 was lecturing on two intra-Mercurial planets, which he called Vulcan and Adonis.[xiii] Sutcliffe was a regular contributor to *Modern Astrology* from 1906, although it's likely Alan met him for the first time in 1909. Despite having three children, fathered on his rare and short visits back to England, Sutcliffe spent most of his time in India. More relevantly, in 1908 he had written *An Appeal for Restitution and Peace to Indian Theosophists* which attempted to justify Leadbeater's sexual teachings.

Why was Sutcliffe so excited? He'd explained to anyone who wanted to listen that this precise planetary configuration occurred only once every ten thousand years. The Sun, Moon and Uranus were together in Capricorn, opposite Neptune and square a Mars/Saturn conjunction which was opposite Jupiter—in other words, they formed a cross. A similar pattern had occurred around April 25 CE, although Uranus and

---

xii Born in Elland, near Halifax (1859-1933). Sutcliffe finally returned to the UK in 1924 and died after being knocked down by a motor bike in Croydon.
xiii Vulcan was the standard name for an intra-Mercurial planet; Jacques Babinet had used it in 1846, and Urban Le Verrier hypothesised a planet by that name as an explanation for the perihelion advance of Mercury later found to be due to general relativity. An apparent observation of Vulcan was made by Edmond Lescarbault in 1859, although it is now realised to have been erroneous.

Neptune were in opposite positions to those in the 1910 chart and there was a full rather than new Moon.

This was the dawning of the Age of Aquarius. 'Astrologers believe, too, that the second coming of Christ is near at hand, because we are nearing the end of the two thousand years' cycle. It takes 25,000 years for the cycle of the Zodiac to go round, and at each twelfth division a new teacher is supposed to appear on the earth and a new cycle starts. This time it is believed to be the second coming of the same spiritual intelligence.'[19]

That would have been enough to excite most astrologers, but in addition Halley's comet had come into view in September 1909 and been photographed, although it wouldn't be visible to the naked eye until 25 April. Its passage in 1910 was particularly close to Earth, which would pass through its tail on 19 May. Many British thought it heralded an invasion by the Germans, and later that it was responsible for killing King Edward VI who died 6 May. Theosophists thought it was connected to greater things. The French astronomer Camille Flammarion warned that poisonous cyanogen gas in its tail might impregnate the atmosphere and snuff out all life on the planet, and some people bought anti-comet pills, but on balance few believed the world was going to end.

In fact, theosophists believed a new world was beginning.

From the evening of 10 January until the morning of 12 January, Leadbeater and Krishna were shut up in Besant's bedroom while a group kept watch outside. When they emerged, Leadbeater announced that Krishnamurti had been received by the Masters into the Brotherhood. Those outside the room prostrated themselves at the announcement.

Later Besant said about the date, 'A great peace brooded over the earth, and a deep solemn joy pervaded Adyar and Benares. For all was well,'[20] which covered most eventualities.

To be fair, she was later to add, 'January witnessed at the rare conjunction of the planets noted by all astrologers the Occult birth of the young child who in due time shall be the vehicle for the blessing of the world. 2,000 years have run their course since a similar gift was vouchsafed to the sorrowful star,'[21] and 'The remarkable arrangement of planets on January 11, 1910 offered magnetic conditions of the most favourable and unusual kind and that was the date chosen for the Initiation of our loved Alcyone, of him who had been marked out, by the acceptance of his vow by Lord Buddha twenty-five centuries ago, as one of those to be used specially in the great work of teaching the world, of carrying the message of the wisdom to many lives to come.'[21] [xiv]

Exciting though the news was, the work at Benares had to continue. On 14 January a ceremony took place to lay the foundation stone of a new lodge in Gaya. The local lodge had bought a piece of land in the centre of the town, and the foundations were already dug. At nine in the morning, they gathered to the sound of chanting of Sanskrit shlokas—Hindu verses—followed by Khaja Muhammed Noor's readings from the Quran. It fell to Bessie to read from Corinthians 1 of the New Testament (she appeared to have forgotten she was Jewish by now):

Charity suffereth long, and is kind; charity envieth not; charity vaunteth not itself, is not puffed up,
Doth not behave itself unseemly, seeketh not her own, is not easily provoked, thinketh no evil;
Rejoiceth not in iniquity, but rejoiceth in the truth;
Beareth all things, believeth all things, hopeth all things, endureth all things.
Charity never faileth: but whether there be prophecies, they shall fail; whether there be tongues, they shall cease; whether there be knowledge, it shall vanish away.

More solemn chanting and some singing were followed by dropping coins, the plans of the buildings, and copies of the alphabets in use in the province into a cavity awaiting them, and, as Besant said, 'The mortar was spread and the stone lowered; a few words from myself and the mystic taps consecrated the building ...'[22]

As ever, Besant delivered a lecture in the nearby tent. Schoolchildren showed off their work and the day concluded with an evening lecture.

Back at Adyar in March, Besant persuaded Narayaniah to sign a letter to grant her guardianship of Krishnamurti and Nitya. Narayaniah wasn't happy at first, although after some discussion he agreed—hoping this would mean the boys had a good education. After some travelling, Alan would have come to the realisation that laying foundations with great ceremony was a relatively frequent occurrence. On 17 March 1910

---

xiv The star Alcyone (the Central One) in the Pleiades is associated with vision and the revelation of secret and hidden things, or alternatively blindness. The Great Year of the Pleiades describes the cycle of precession (the twenty-five centuries referred to). In the third millennium BCE Alcyone marked the vernal equinox and is hence also associated with a New Age. The Pleiades (Weeping Sisters) signify sorrow, especially from bereavement. In the *Secret Doctrine* the Pleiades, especially Alcyone, are described as the central point around which our universe of fixed stars revolves.

the foundation stone of new students' quarters were laid with Masonic rites by Besant at eleven in the morning—the precise time chose by Alan according to the astrology of the day. After gathering at ten, a long line of co-masons joined in procession behind a parsi carrying the sacred fire. After a brief halt to declare the new office for *The Theosophist* formally open, they went to the site of the new building where Besant stood with her two chief officers in the sunshine to hear solemn Masonic knocks and the words, 'Except the Lord build the house, their labour is but lost that build it.' Apparently, there was a 'stirring invocation' and a box containing that day's *Madras Times*, a coin and some precious stones was placed into the cavity. Corn and salt were scattered, oil poured and the fire laid on the stone to the sound of further invocations—which may or may not have been stirring.[23]

Besant returned to Benares early April. Although Narayaniah had initially been excited about his son's initiation, his distrust of Leadbeater's motives soon resurfaced. In early April he was angry to discover Leadbeater planned to go away from Adyar on a two days' excursion taking Krishna and Nitya with him, although he hadn't asked for permission. But worse, one of Besant's servants, Lakshman, who told him about finding Krishna naked in Leadbeater's presence. Lakshman also said that Leadbeater had been in a state of semi-nakedness, washing Krishna's hair while the boy was naked. He lost his temper and Leadbeater wrote to Besant suggesting that Narayaniah had lost his sanity and asking her to return to Adyar, saying, 'He seems to have had a bad fit of his insanity two days ago, but it does not last long ... is it not odd that he cannot let things alone? It seems such an easy thing to do, just to keep quiet and mind one's own business.'[24]

Narayaniah wanted to remove the boys but Subramania Iyer (Vice-President of the Theosophical Society) advised him to wait for Besant's return.

It's helpful to have the situation summed up in a song. Ferdinand T Brooks,[xv] who lived at Adyar 1909-1911 wrote a long satirical poem about Leadbeater and Krishnamurti, addressing the allegations made by Lakshman. It was apparently to be sung to a 'simple pastoral tune':

---

xv From 1901–1904, Brooks (5 April 1873–1916) was tutor to Jawaharlal Nehru, later the first Prime Minister of India. Paris-born Brooks joined the Society in 1896. He met Leadbeater in London in 1898 and served as his interpreter. In December 1900 he went to India at Besant's invitation. Brooks resigned from the Esoteric Section of the TS and began a career as antagonist of Besant. His body was found in a river in August 1916, the cause of his death unknown but commonly believed to have been suicide.

The Sage flung wide the bathroom door:
'Pray step in here, my dear.
Those lice tonight shall bite no more
Their corpses shall lie here ...'
The Sage then stripp'd his humbler half
(Lest little things crawl up)
And showed a plump and fair-hair'd calf
(Let Mrs Grundy[xvi] *gup.*[xvii]*)*
 Quoth he, "My son, lest lice should fall
And in your clothes get stuck,
Pray doff at first your garments all
While I the varmints pluck.[25]

The rest of Krishna's story was to play out after the Leos had left. Besant returned to Adyar on 24 April and arranged for separate bathrooms for Nitya and Krishna and that their lessons should be given in her presence, on the verandah.

But it was time for the Leos to return to London, while Besant remained in India for the rest of 1910.

The trip had been a success on many levels, but events hadn't worked out in the way everyone had hoped. Although he had learned that his 'ray' was Venus, Alan was nursing his disappointment regarding the sad state of astrology in India:

> Whilst travelling through India in search of facts concerning Astrology, I was surprised to find that semi-clairvoyance, a few psychic impressions, and hand readings, to say nothing of other questionable means of divination, passed under the name of Astrology. The few real astrologers I saw, those who were able to distinguish between science and psychism, assured me that without the aid of some genuine Astrology, there was small hope of once again restoring the ancient science to its rightful position in the eyes of men.[26]

And as Leadbeater was to observe in later years, 'The Coming had gone wrong'.[27]

---

xvi Mrs Grundy is a figurative name for an extremely conventional or priggish person and originated as an unseen character in Thomas Morton's 1798 play Speed the Plough.
xvii Hindi for 'gossip'.

A SPECIALITY.

In every profession there is a tendency to specialise. This is due to concentration of the endeavors in the direction of producing the highest grade of work that attention and experience can produce. During the past seven of his twenty years' public practice, MR. ALAN LEO has been concentrating his attention upon the judgment of FIVE GUINEA HOROSCOPES—after realising that a correct and careful judgment could not be given for a less sum—with the result that a Five Guinea Horoscope has become a speciality in his hands.

With this class of work the experimental stage has now been long passed, and therefore a GUARANTEE will be given WITH EVERY HOROSCOPE *where the birth time is known*, that if not true in every detail the FIVE GUINEAS WILL BE REFUNDED. Can any offer be more fair or honest?

GUARANTEE FORM: No............ *(for office use only.)*

This form may be filled in and forwarded to ALAN LEO for his signature.

THE undersigned will, on acceptance, undertake to give the applicant remitting Five Guineas ($26·00) for a Special Horoscope a correct and truthful delineation, or otherwise refund the amount remitted.

Date.................................. Signature..

Name of Applicant..

Address...

This is not only an opportunity to prove the truth of Astrology, but also an option for those who wish to have the best work of the author while in practice. The time is drawing near when the work undertaken must necessarily be limited.

Full particulars of what may be expected for the outlay will be forwarded, if required, on application to the office of *Modern Astrology*.

N.B.—*This form must be used. Tear out the whole page. No letter is necessary.*

Application for "Modern Astrology" Special Offer.

To the EDITOR, *Modern Astrology*,

    42 & 43, IMPERIAL BUILDINGS, LUDGATE CIRCUS, LONDON, E.C.

DEAR SIR.—Enclosed you will find the sum of FIVE GUINEAS (or if from America $26·00, to cover postage of book and registration) for which send my Horoscope as above.

    Name in full...

    Address in full...

    Time of Birth *(state clearly whether morning, noon or night)*..........

    Date of Birth *(please make the figures very distinct)*..................

    Birthplace in full..

"What is Astrology?" and "How to Study Astrology" free on application to "Modern Astrology" Office, 42 & 43, Imperial Buildings, Ludgate Circus, London, E.C.

CHAPTER SIXTEEN

ALL IS JUST A VIBRATION

*I*T WAS BACK TO WORK as usual. By 1909, Alan's workload had increased so much that he had decided to take on offices at 42–3 and 50 Imperial Buildings, Ludgate Circus. Renting offices wasn't as straightforward as it should have been—back in 1906 he'd been refused a lease in the Strand owing to the nature of his business.

Getting the work done was less onerous than it might have been due to the eagerness of his fans to become involved, as Annie Barley described:

> I knew Alan Leo first in this life in 1907, and very shortly after I first saw him, I was fired with the idea of the greatness of his work, and I felt I wanted to help in that work, though then I was totally ignorant of Astrology and literally did not know the difference between Aries and Taurus, nor even how to make the symbols. What I did know was that I wanted to work for this man or for his cause, I didn't mind which, and on the second occasion of seeing him, I took my courage in both hands and went up to him and asked him if he could give me 'something to do'.
>
> He smiled and said, 'We'll find you something some day,' and there, so far as I could see, the incident ended. However, some twelve months afterwards he asked me one day if I would come to his office and give him a little help.
>
> 'Yes, certainly,' I said; 'What work is it?'
>
> 'Oh never mind that,' said he, 'people who want to do work mustn't pick and choose what work they'll do.'

And when I got to the office I found it was only a job of sorting some papers, and though I did it I don't know that the work was ever used—I fancy not.[1]

On balance, life was good. Alan had bought a pianola, a self-playing piano that contained a mechanism that operated the piano action via pre-programmed music recorded on perforated paper. Foot-operated bellows provided the vacuum needed to operate a pneumatic motor driving the take-up spool while inrushes of air through a hole in the paper roll were amplified to strike a loud note. He spent many happy hours listening to Beethoven, Chopin, Wagner, Mozart, and others and even occasionally played himself. Otherwise, he would read a little, play draughts, or potter around his garden. 'He loved the evening shadows and walked amongst the trees and flowers musing and meditating.'[2]

However, his work took precedence as Annie Barley pointed out. 'Frequently when in the presence of people not directly connected with the work, he would keep up a light kind of airy banter, immediately dropping it as soon as they had gone with the air of—"Now then, let's get to business." For with him the work was everything, and all the rest was mere bubbles on the water; though I sometimes suspected that he had a deeper motive underlying the apparently easy chit-chat.'[3]

His tactic of sending review copies of *Modern Astrology* to anyone who showed the slightest of interest—or no interest whatsoever—had long ago paid off and resulted in coverage of his predictions (or at least, predictions published in *Modern Astrology* as he was generally given credit no matter who came up with them). His prediction that, 'The Government likely to be very unpopular, and it will come near to being defeated, if it is not actually so. Changes are likely to take place in the Government.'[4] was widely published, given that the January 1910 general election, called in the midst of a constitutional crisis after the Liberal's 'People's Budget' which sought to tax the wealthy to fund social welfare had been blocked by the House of Lords. At the time of Alan's prediction, Britain was under a Conservative/Liberal hung parliament and it was widely known that a second election would take place soon, as it did in December 1910.

By now, the concept of duplicated horoscopes had been copied again and again and they were no longer lucrative—even as tasters—so Alan ceased offering his shilling horoscopes in 1910. Plus he'd been shown a copy of an article that had appeared in the journal *Truth*, reporting on the popularity of cheap horoscopes and suggesting the law should be involved. London was undergoing an epidemic of fortune-tellers and many people were agitating for a clampdown.

Alan now sought a much more upmarket (and therefore safer) audience and recommended that for a full horoscope you should expect to pay £5/5- (about £500 in today's terms) and a life horoscope that covered the 'whole of the future' should cost about £10/10- (about £1,000 today). Whether he actually received that sort of payment seems unlikely.

In 1913 Alan gave a full horoscope to his secretary, May Robbins,[i] as a gift. The extracts below should give a taste of what he expected people to pay so highly for.

One ship drives east and another drives west
With the self-same winds that blow.
'Tis the set of the sails
And not the gales
Which tells us the way they go.

Like the winds of the sea are the ways of fate
As we voyage along through life:
'Tis the act of the soul
That decides its goal
And not the calm or the strife.

The following pages are written to help you rightly to guide your course through life in knowledge of your latent powers, and to enable you to judge the significance of the precept 'KNOW THYSELF.'

The judgment is based upon the assumption that the birth data, from which the nativity has been cast, is correct, for unless this is so, no true horoscope can be given. It should be read as much between the lines as literally, for the most any astrologer can do is to interpret the planetary influences according to the light of the spirit that is within him; he cannot, without assumption, say that his judgment is infallible, neither can he say that all his reading will be correct. For the stars incline they do not compel.

Now with regard to your marriage, I judge a late marriage, although some romantic love affairs are indicated, but marriage is not a strong feature of this nativity, for if you marry, you would marry a man much weaker than yourself, for his significator is weaker than your own. But marriage in your case would require a special judgment for the man for you is denoted by Uranus rising in Libra, since the Sun first applies to this planet by direct sextile.

---

i Matilda Robbins (later Minnear) joined the City of London Lodge 20 May 1913.

1914. (Nov).

The Sun in sextile to Mars will give you an abundance of energy and vitality, thus strengthening your constitution and bringing a healthy period in which you should feel fully energized, very enterprising and well able to cope with your surroundings. There is nothing very special in the aspect, beyond its increase of energy and activity, so that all opportunities that come in your way while this aspect is operating should be made the most of, since you now have the strength to deal with all the conditions around you. It sometimes brings important changes into the life, and they are usually connected with enterprise or adventure, so that on the whole this will be a favourable period.[5]

The work done in compiling material for the test horoscopes wasn't put to waste. Alan compiled it into a book, *The Key to Your Own Nativity*, published in 1910. For an extra 2/6 (the book cost 10/6 with postage) he would include a copy of your chart. If you had a copy of your chart and were baffled by it, you could send it with your book order and receive instructions on how to read it—which seemed pointless as this information was included in the book. Selling horoscopes alongside subscriptions to *Modern Astrology* or book sales seemed designed to move the spotlight. There was also advice regarding how to set out your horoscopes:

> In cases where a written delineation is given, it is worth while to arrange that every paragraph has a page to itself. As each contains just enough to go comfortably on a page of an ordinary exercise book, there need be no difficulty about this, and the advantage of having the reader's attention focused on one paragraph at a time is obvious.[6]

It was, as Alan pointed out, a false economy to write on both sides of the paper. Many people simply copied out the interpretations and combined them in the way they'd been used for the test horoscopes. Indeed, the text was presented in such a way to enable you to do just that:

> Aries was rising at your birth. This is a cardinal, moveable and fiery sign. This gives much energy and activity, both of body and mind, much impulse and enthusiasm, with many changes in the course of life. You are courageous, enterprising, frank and outspoken. You face difficulties promptly and bravely; you know your own mind, and are seldom at a loss what to do or

say when called upon to decide. You are ambitious, self-reliant, and adventurous; and you will win your way in the world largely through these qualities and through your confidence in your own ability to succeed. You are a great lover of freedom and independence, and you get along badly when you are in any way hampered, restricted, or interfered with. You are generous and quickly responsive to appeals to the emotions. You are a zealous and energetic supporter of any person or cause that enlists your sympathies. Most of your misfortunes will arise through too much hastiness and impulse, whether in action, in judgement, or in the feelings. You are somewhat lacking in coolness, in calm deliberation, and self-restraint, and you do not find it easy to give way to others, even when justice or prudence demands it. Mars is the ruling planet of the sign Aries.[7]

Alan was in a writing frenzy. 'On an average he wrote a book once every three months rising as early as 6 o'clock in the morning and working till 9 o'clock at night,' said Bessie.[8]

By now, Alan had fourteen of his shilling manuals for sale. The pocket-sized guides offered instruction on a variety of astrological matter, all written by astrologers associated with *Modern Astrology*. For many people, and for years to come, these books served as their first introduction to astrology. Those with more money to splash out could buy a range of textbooks, some of which had already gone through multiple editions: *Astrology for All, Casting the Horoscope* and *The Art of Synthesis* amongst them. He'd also now published his pride and joy *Esoteric Astrology*, later described by Charles Carter as 'a big volume containing virtually nothing'.[9]

Alan made no claims as to originality. In fact, he was often 'criticised for picking other people's brains,' as Ralph Shirley pointed out.[10]

However, viewing the Sun as the single most important factor in the birth chart, Alan had gradually discarded the centuries old list of zodiacal attributes and he ignored physical characteristics to focus on inner character. His descriptions of the signs set the tone for future Sun sign descriptions. For example, Aries:

> Represents undifferentiated consciousness. It is a chaotic and unorganised sign, in which impulse, spontaneity, and instinctiveness are marked features. Its vibrations are the keenest and most rapid, but without what may be called definite purpose, except towards impulsiveness and disruption. It signifies explosiveness,

extravagance and all kinds of excess. Its influence is more directly connected with the animal kingdom, in which life is full and without the directive power of fully awakened self-consciousness.[11]

Alan's prime motivation was to encourage people to interpret their own horoscopes rather than pay someone to do it for them. To this end, the Astrological Institute, with Bessie as its President, offered a series of classes, lectures and lessons at 5 Upper Woburn Place in Bloomsbury. That ran alongside the newly resurrected Astrological Society (of which Bessie was also president) which held its first annual meeting 28 May 1910—maybe, just maybe, there'd be an astrological college in the future, but that time was yet to come.

And a comprehensive correspondence course was available for those who couldn't attend meetings, offering qualifications on completion, at a cost of five guineas for seventy lessons.

The correspondence lessons were typed and sent out lesson by lesson to subscribers:

RULES FOR STUDENTS.

1. This lesson is the property of Alan Leo, and may be kept by the student for ten days, during which time the student is advised to make a copy for his private use.

2. After ten days the lesson must be returned with, or without, the answered questions.

3. No further lessons will be sent out until this lesson is returned.

4. The correct answering of all the questions is necessary if a certificate of qualification is desired.

5. Students must write on one side of the paper only.

The questions weren't easy, but neither were they surprising:

1. What planetary positions and aspects account for the complaints and accidents during infancy?

2. What significance has the ninth house in this horoscope?

3. Account for the sympathy or for the lack of it, existing between the native and her father and mother.

4. What were the natal influences in this horoscope that pushed the native into publicity?

5. How would you expect Jupiter conjunct Uranus to translate itself in the native's life?

Alan Leo

However, once the student reached a more advanced level, they were expected to address such questions as:

> Why are we born into this world?
> Why do we live to suffer and enjoy?
> Why do we die when we are just beginning to learn how to live?
> And why are there so many inequalities in the human race?[12]

Fortunately, Alan pointed out:

> From an astrological standpoint there is only one hypothesis by means of which we may expect to answer these questions.
>
> Every human being in a 'Divine Fragment', a centre within the Universal Divine Consciousness, inseparably united with every other centre, and ultimately all blended in one by the Universal Life and Consciousness in which they are centred. If we compare the Universal Life with a flame, the human soul is a spark of that flame, not really separated from it. If we use the comparison of a diamond, the soul is a facet of that diamond. If we employ the symbolism of sound, the soul is one note in the mighty chord that sounds throughout the whole of creation. It is beginningless and endless but apart from the Universal Life it is nothing.
>
> The small blank circle is the 'Self' and all that exists apart from the 'self' or 'That' in the circle of the horoscope is the 'Not Self'. I know this sounds very metaphysical, but the idea should be grasped, if we wish to penetrate into the mysteries of esoteric astrology, that the 'Self' is eternally pure, immortal and divine. In essence it is one with God, and until this essence has identified itself with a form in which first self-consciousness, and afterwards super-consciousness is reached it does not know itself as part and yet 'one' with its source.[13]

That would obviously be clearer to theosophically inclined astrologers than it would to any other type of astrologer—or indeed, any other sort of person. Fortunately, (or unfortunately, depending on your point of view) Alan rarely simply held a conversation. He always had one gem or another to offer as Annie Barley commented, 'Curious little "pearls" would often drop from his lips, which proved extraordinarily useful and illuminating in times of difficulty. For instance, if a hail of bombs were dropping around, I am certain that his quiet and half-amused remark would be "Well, it's all experience!" ... "Take it all as just a vibration," he would say ...'[14]

The vibrations were keeping Alan and Bessie firmly in the theosophical camp. They attended meetings, gave lectures and rushed around organising activities with fervour. In with the in-crowd, they zapped around to ensure they were seen at all the best events.

> On Saturday afternoon, the lawn of Mrs Cedric Chivers was very gay, when members and friends of the Theosophical Lodge gathered together, at the invitation of Mrs Chivers, and the committee. Mr Alan Leo, London gave a short lecture on Astrology, and the influence of the starry world on our lives, while Mrs Leo gave character readings to those who cared to have their virtues and weaknesses brought to their notice.[15]

To ensure a party atmosphere, there'd often be a singalong, a pianist and recitations that may not have been as humorous as the reciter would like to have believed.

And those happy vibrations led Alan and Bessie back to India. In November 1910, they set off for Adyar.

CHAPTER SEVENTEEN

KIND AND DEAR SOULS

WHETHER MONEY WAS tight at this time for Alan and Bessie, or they'd simply learned to be more frugal, they rented out their flat to a South African family while they were away. Immediately before they left, in November 1911, Alan had rented new offices in Imperial Buildings in Kingsway, London and left his eager staff to deal with the constant requests for chart interpretations.

Although theosophy was high on the Leos' agenda, with their second visit Alan was more determined to investigate astrology in India.

> It was not until I had made a second visit to India that I was able to obtain the clue to the central idea that could unify all my numerous thoughts upon the subject of Esoteric Astrology. In one of the Holy Places, I met a sage whose mind and my own were in complete harmony. I had only to express a few ideas to this marvellous Pundit and he would run through the whole sequence of my thought and in a few words link those ideas into a consecutive whole to achieve which I have laboured many years. At one of our meetings he spoke but a few words, but he conveyed to my mind ideas which illuminated my thoughts to such an extent that I instantly saw light to which I had been formerly blind. On one occasion we rode many miles in an old gharry to visit an ancient Temple, and while he chanted his sacred hymns continuously, my mind was filled with beautiful thoughts suggesting the very questions a sage alone could answer.[1]

Alan found it frustratingly difficult to obtain the information on astrology he wanted. He later commented on 'the peculiar method of drawing up horoscopes and an instrument that is used which saves a great deal of calculation'.[2] He also said:

> That in India a knowledge of Astronomy was considered necessary as well as Astrology, that he found the Singalese more friendly and broadminded than the Hindus who were absolute fatalists and that it was the opinion of some of the Astrologers he met that it would be a good thing if the Astrology of the East and West could be worked together otherwise the Astrology of India would be lost or extinct in about fifty years.[3]

With this in mind, when he visited B Suryanarain Rao in Madras, Alan told him that he wanted to participate in the Astronomical Conference due to be held in Kalady. Suryanarain Rao[i] had set up *The Astrological Magazine* in 1895 and was the first writer in English on astrology in India, producing nearly seventy books. He was also a theosophist.

Rao was also clearly difficult to impress and told Alan he wouldn't be speaking at the conference. 'He being an Englishman, it was felt, he would not be able to adjust himself to local conditions'.[4] Plus, 'Alan Leo was somewhat narrow-minded in the sense that while freely borrowing Hindu astrological ideas, he never had the fairness to acknowledge his indebtedness to the Hindus.'[5]

The easiest option was for Alan to hold his own conference, which he did. Over two days, he challenged Indian astrologers with a statement that Indian astrology was inferior to Western and led a debate, backed by George Sutcliffe. The Indian astrologers sought to convince Alan by interpreting his chart using his methods—although he stated he was unconvinced, Alan wrote to Charles Carter asking him what he thought about a prediction he would marry twice.

This took place at Seth Dharamsey Morarjee Gokuldas'[ii] house, where on 11 March Alan met Ella Wheeler Wilcox.[iii] An adherent to New Thought and fascinated with the occult, saying, 'The study of people gifted with occult powers has interested me for several years. I have met and consulted scores,'[6] Wilcox had recently arrived in Bombay and was eagerly accepting every invitation that came her way. She is primarily remembered today for her poem 'Solitude':

---

i 1856–1937.
ii A manager of textile mills and staunch theosophist and freemason.
iii 5 November 1850–30 October 1919.

Laugh, and the world laughs with you;
Weep, and you weep alone;
For the sad old earth must borrow its mirth,
But has trouble enough of its own.

Shortly afterwards, Besant left Adyar in the car Alan had bought for her.

> Miss Wilson, my two Indian wards and myself left beautiful Adyar on March 22nd, in the motor-car so generously given to me by Mr and Mrs Leo; the occupants weren't the same as those in our illustration, save the driver at the wheel, and the chauffeur who is standing beside the car; besides me, on our outgoing, where Mr Wadia sits in the picture, was Miss Wilson, and the tonneau was occupied by Mr Leadbeater, Krishnamurti, and Nitya. For the last time for many months to come I drove the car which has proved so faithful a servant, never misbehaving, and with absolutely no injury to its account to man, animal or object since it arrived in India in 1909. We steamed away with the setting sun from Madras.[7]

Presumably, Alan and Bessie took the train. In any event, they also travelled to Bombay and joined Besant in a spot of serious lecturing. Both Alan and Bessie spoke at the Blavatsky Lodge: on 13 April Bessie spoke on 'Stars and human destiny', on the 18th Alan on Theosophy and astrology' and on the 19th Bessie spoke again, this time on 'The three paths of human evolution' and 'The new race and the world teacher.' Happily, the front seats were reserved for ladies. Besant herself spoke on 21 April on 'The Masters and the Way to them' at the Gaiety Theatre.

The World Teacher was what everyone—at least, all theosophists—was talking about.

In 1910 the Theosophical Society had published the first work *At the Feet of the Master* by 'Alcyone' a pseudonym for Krishnamurti, although much, if not all, of the text had actually been written by Leadbeater. The book had become very popular among theosophists, and a flurry of organisations sprun up in its wake. The *Yellow Shawl Group* consisted of Krishnamurti's special pupils. The group was so called because members wore yellow silk shawls at their meetings. When the number of members increased, an inner group emerged, known as the *Purple Shawl Group*, because members wore purple shawls, purple sashes embroidered in gold and bearing the initials 'J K' and a silver badge on a purple ribbon. On 11 January 1911 the *Order of the Rising Sun* was founded at Benares by George Arundale, a prominent theosophist and Principal of the

Central Hindu College, to prepare for the coming World Teacher, on the understanding that Krishnamurti would be the 'vehicle' of the 'Coming Christ-Maitreya-Bodhisattva.' Arundale had enthusiastically adopted the Order of the Rising Sun as an extracurricular activity for the students, and it soon reached about 170 members.

It was alleged that many pupils were neglecting their studies, and staff and parents protested to Besant, as President of the College. Arundale was given leave to accompany Besant to England, and about half of the College staff resigned. The Order of the Rising Sun was formally disbanded by Besant in May 1911.

While these arguments were going on, in April the *Order of the Star in the East* had been founded—again, to promote Krishnamurti as World Teacher. Intended as a less intellectual organisation than the TS, the OSE soon became wildly popular, attracting membership from non-theosophists.[iv] An *Order of the Servants of the Star* was also established for those members under twenty-one.

On 22 April Alan and Bessie accompanied Besant, Krishnamurti and Nitya on board the P&O steamer *Mantua*. Also in the party was George Arundale, the Raja of Rajapala[v] and his medical attendant, George Sutcliffe, Shri Prakasha,[vi] the Raja of Kanika[vii] and Lieutenant Colonel John Stratchey.[viii]

The *Mantua* was crowded as numerous people were travelling to attend the coronation of King George V which was to take place in June—they'd had to book well in advance. Besant had ordered her tickets the previous September. And ever observant of the right way to go about things, Besant had made sure that Shri Prakasha as well as Krishnamurti and Nitya were suitably dressed before going on board, buying a selection of suits and other items from Asquith and Lord in Bombay.

Although there was a holiday atmosphere, Besant wasn't going to allow an opportunity to lecture slip by and took over the dining room to speak on karma and reincarnation. It may not have gone down as well as she hoped considering that Shri Prakasha pointed out it was, 'Far beyond the ideas of the ... holiday crowd that filled the saloon that night.'[8]

---

iv In late 1913, the Order had about 15,000 members worldwide. Its journal, *The Herald of the Star*, began publication in January 1912.
v Maharana Shri Sir Chhatrasinhji Gambhirsinhji Sahib (1862–1915).
vi Politician and activist (3 August 1890–23 June 1971) in the Indian independence movement, Prakasha was later to become India's first High Commissioner to Pakistan.
vii Rajendra Narayan Bhanja Deo (1881–1948).
viii Controller of the household to Lord Curzon when Viceroy of India. So many members of the family were in the Indian government that sarcastic mentions were made of the 'Government of the Stracheys'.

Fortunately, there were also dances on board and a variety of sports in which passengers could participate.

At Port Said, the party transferred to the smaller *Isis*, and after a day and night's rough journey on the swell of the Mediterranean, they reached Brindisi in Italy, from where the remainder of the journey was made by train in comfortable Pullman coaches which made their way to Calais and on to Dover and London.

Finally, on 5 May they reached Charing Cross where a crowd of theosophists, journalists and photographers lay in wait. *The Lives of Alcyone* had preceded them and excited and wealthy theosophists were eager to open their doors to Krishnamurti. One of those waiting was Lady Emily Lutyens[ix] who 'had eyes for none but Krishna, an odd figure, with long dark hair falling almost to his shoulders and enormous dark eyes which had a strange vacant look in them.'[9] In the press photograph of the party, Besant looks grim and is flanked by Nitya and Krishnamurti. Alan and Bessie don't appear in it.

Once the fuss was over, Shri Prakasha left with Alan and Bessie to spend a few days with them. 'Mrs Besant asked them to take me in for a few days in their own house in order to accustom me to English ways ... Mr Alan Leo and Mrs Bessie Leo were kind and dear souls, noted astrologers and staunch Theosophists. I often enjoyed their hospitality

---

ix Emily Lutyens (1874–1964) was married to the architect Edwin Landseer Lutyens (1869–1944) who designed some of New Delhi and was the daughter of Edward Robert Bulwer-Lytton. Two of the Lutyens' children were close in age to Krishnamurti and Nitya, who spent much time with the Lutyens family. Her daughter Mary is known for writing books about Krishnamurti.

during the years I was in England ... They were a most devoted pair.'[10]

Besant went to stay with Esther Bright and on 8 May Krishnamurti made his first appearance at the Theosophical Society headquarters in Bond Street, announcing the formation of the Order of the Star in the East. One of the first to enrol was Emily Lutyens. She sat on the floor at Krishnamurti's feet marking an obsession with him that caused her in the years to come to dedicate herself single-mindedly to Krishnamurti, following him around the world. She was involved in the production of the Theosophical journal *Herald of the Star,* and was English representative of the Order of the Star in the East.

There was a small delay in getting things going with the OSE. Members were required to wear a five-pointed star suspended on a ribbon. High officials of the Order were permitted to wear gold stars, everyone else wore silver. The ribbon, according to Leadbeater, had to be the same shade of light blue as the aura of the Lord Maitreya. Unfortunately, only Leadbeater could identify this spiritual colour and numerous samples had to be submitted to him for examination (those higher in the order could wear a purple ribbon, which was apparently less of a problem). Finally, after eighteen months, Emily Lutyens found the right colour ribbon in Paris. It was promptly ordered and cut into lengths which were magnetised by Krishnamurti before being sent out to members.

On returning to London, Besant had immediately launched into a whirlwind of sightseeing, socialising and theatre visits—punctuated by talks here and there. On 18 May she wrote to her son:

> We are now established in London and the dear boys are quite happy. Enclosed is a newspaper snapshot taken on our arrival in London, where we were met by a big crowd. It appeared in a number of papers, the boys have begun their regular lessons again. Mr Arundale taking charge of them. One of our members has lent me a motor car, so we can get about very comfortably, and another has given us seats in one of the Government stands to see the Coronation Procession. We go to Oxford this day week and the boys are much looking forward to it.[11]

As soon as Alan returned to work, he was told there'd been a minor problem. The police had called at the *Modern Astrology* offices and said they'd had a complaint, adding to the clerk working that day that he should tell Alan that casting horoscopes and fortune telling through astrology was an offence. Alan didn't think it was worth worrying about and promptly forgot the incident.

CHAPTER EIGHTEEN

DREAMING WONDERFUL DREAMS

*L*ADY DAISY WARWICK[i] was one of the most celebrated hostesses of her day. A long-term confidante of and mistress to the Prince of Wales (who later became King Edward VII), she was also the inspiration behind the popular 1892 music hall song 'Daisy Bell'.

Daisy, Daisy
Give me your answer, do.
I'm half crazy
all for the love of you

—ending with the words 'a bicycle built for two'.

Lady Warwick was also very fond of campaigns. An active and beneficent socialist, she financed schools for the disadvantaged and arranged parties dedicated to a reinvention of supposed folk traditions, pageants, dances and dialect plays. Her activities allowed her to forge friendships with such leading lights as H G Wells, Ramsay MacDonald, J M Barrie, Gustav Holst and George Bernard Shaw. That she knew Annie Besant was therefore no surprise to anyone, and that it was her money that allowed the International Club for Psychical Research to finally get off the ground simply confirmed how the world worked.

---

i Frances Evelyn 'Daisy' Greville, Countess of Warwick, née Maynard; 10 December 1861–26 July 1938.

On the day the club opened, 29 May 1911, Lady Warwick gave her welcoming address and listened to Besant state the necessity of avoiding superstition and narrowness 'in all intercourse with the unseen world'.[1] Members were told that the club held appliances and apparatus for studying mediumship and special rooms for rapping manifestations with bespoke tables.

Esoteric Buddhists, followers of W T Stead and 'people who believe there are more things in heaven and earth than are dreamed of in their philosophy and are willing to devote time and money to seeking them out … young men and women brought up in the faddist atmosphere which permeates London'[2] plus 'countesses and viscountesses, retired army and navy officers, schoolteachers, literary men and women, suffragists and antis, spiritualists and scientists'[3] comprised the rumoured 600-strong membership of the club founded by Robert Colgate[ii] of New York, Lyman J Gage,[iii] Colonel Count Gleichen,[iv] Sir Francis Younghusband[v] and Major General Sir Alfred Turner.[vi] And, of course, amongst the members and present that night were Alan and Bessie Leo—plus Robert King, an almost required presence for such a venture.

Based at 22a Regent Street (on the corner of Jermyn Street and next to the site that would become the Regent Palace Hotel in 1915; the largest hotel in Europe), opposite the statue of Eros in Piccadilly Circus, the International Club was at the heart of London, surrounded by shops, theatres, restaurants and an ever-moving throng of men and women. It was

---

ii From the American Society for Psychical Research and part of the toothpaste family.

iii Lyman Judson Gage (28 June 1836–26 January 1927) was an American financier and was President of the First National Bank of Chicago and later Secretary of Treasury in Presidents McKinley's and Roosevelt's cabinets. In 1906, Gage in purchased property on and subsequently lived at Lomaland, a theosophical retreat in California.

iv Major General Lord Albert Edward Wilfred Gleichen (15 January 1863–14 December 1937) was a British courtier and soldier. Born Count Albert Edward Wilfred Gleichen, he was the only son of Prince Victor of Hohenlohe-Langenburg (a half-nephew of Queen Victoria) and cousin of the late King Edward.

v Francis Younghusband (31 May 1863–31 July 1942) was an explorer and spiritual writer, most remembered for his travels in the Far East and Central Asia; especially the 1904 British expedition to Tibet, led by him. During his retreat from Tibet, Younghusband had a mystical experience which convinced him that 'men at heart are divine'. He was British commissioner to Tibet and President of the Royal Geographical Society.

vi Major-General Sir Alfred Edward Turner (3 March 1842–20 November 1918) was a British Army officer of the late nineteenth century, who served in administrative posts in Ireland. He attended séances with the medium Cecil Husk and during one of the séances he stated that he had witnessed the materialisation of W T Stead. Turner also claimed to have experienced apports and spirits in his own home.

also the address of numerous clubs and societies over the years, including at various times the Anti-Vivisection Society, the London Spiritualist Alliance, and the Society for American Graduates.

George Knowles, who managed the Club, already had experience of managing clubs in the same building—including that of the American Graduates. It was run under the auspices of the AIU Company Limited, with the intention of later turning it into a member-run company, although it's unclear whether this actually ever happened.

It had numerous large rooms, although the idea of bedrooms on the premises had temporarily been abandoned—they were to come later. Spiritualistic research was firmly located in the cellar where there were no hangings or recesses and only one door. Above this was a lecture hall and library, a dining room and kitchens with a cook (strictly vegetarian), writing rooms and smoking rooms.

Afternoons and evenings were filled with lectures, music, drama, readings and discussions. Studies of concepts related to auras and incarnations were frequently interrupted by a drawing-room tea:

> Nor are there wanting those who possibly exhibit more zeal in the way of inquiries as to how to withdraw from one's body than they do for the just performance of all due achievements when in the body; but all these are somewhat negligible, and for the greater part the deliberations of the International Psychic Club contribute suggestions and speculative theories that are not unimportant.[4]

The newly-opened Club attracted plenty of attention from the press:

> Up several flights of stairs in Regent Street there is one of the weirdest clubs in London the International Club for Psychical Research. It has no concern with merely earthly things. Its members are pledged to the higher thought, the thought that lifts you off the earth, and makes you see visions, dream wonderful dreams, talk with the spirits the beyond, and walk absentmindedly into motor buses ... Every possible "ist" is represented. There are theosophists, spiritists, phrenologists, psychologists, spiritualists, mesmerists, and so on ... The world that is so pressing a reality Regent Street is looked upon as a fantastic shadow, an intangible thing of no account, and the theosophists, spiritists, and all the others find the real world in two dark and creepy cellars, where strange shapes flit to and fro, where chairs and tables walk if alive, and sounds grow out of the darkness. There do the members of the Club hold séances, and listen in the darkness to mysterious voices.

It is the only club in existence that sets apart its cellars for so other-worldly purpose. It is, indeed, the only club given up entirely to psychical matters. There are numbers of psychical societies, but there is no other place where theosophist can drop in for chat with a hypnotist, where spiritist can compare notes with a psychologist, or where a phrenologist can run the risk of lunching with a mesmerist.[5]

It was all rather marvellous.

But within weeks of the Club being established, everyone's attention was distracted by the coronation of George V. Not because it was an excuse for a good party and they were staunch monarchists, but because the co-masons were major participants in the demonstration which took place in London five days before the coronation.

London was already crowded with visitors when on the afternoon of 17 June 40,000 women formed up along Westminster Embankment in the fifth, the last and biggest procession ever seen in the campaign for the vote.

It was soon impossible to move along the pavement as women crowded the streets, climbed up lamp-posts, stood on ladders and scaffolding, perched atop cars, taxis and other people along the streets.

At 5.30 p.m. the procession moved off—seven abreast and five miles long—to the strains of Ethel Smyth's 'March of the Women',[vii] led by Florence Drummond (famous for chaining herself to the railings in Downing Street and nicknamed 'the General') on horseback, followed by a colour-bearer and Joan Annan Bryce (an MP's daughter) representing Joan of Arc, in full armour on a white palfrey.

The forty-five separate contingents represented all aspects of women in society and throughout the ages and were (unique in these demonstrations) drawn from the full spectrum of the suffrage societies. Contingent Number 35, between the Ethical Societies and the women pharmacists and health visitors, were the co-masons in full regalia and led by Annie Besant, bare-headed and dressed in a yellow silk sari. Although her presence is unrecorded, it's unimaginable that Bessie wasn't a member of the party.

When normality resumed, life went on at the International Club. By 1912 it had launched the *International Psychic Gazette*.[viii] The journal

---

vii It was composed by Ethel Smyth in 1910, to words by Cicely Hamilton and became the official anthem of the Women's Social and Political Union (WSPU) and more widely the anthem of the women's suffrage movement, not only sung at rallies but also in prison during hunger strikes. Smyth produced a number of different arrangements of the work.
viii The monthly periodical ceased after a few months but was revived as an independent publication, the *Psychic Gazette*, by John Lewis which survived for over twenty years.

contained short accounts of the conferences and séances held at the Club's rooms, together with notes on palmistry, feminism and the occult. Astrology was often on the agenda, and indeed, Walter Old spoke there on 18 June 1912. More interesting to many members, however, was the report from W de Kerlor[ix] who excitedly announced he'd spoken to the then deceased W T Stead who had materialised and chatted with him in front of a room of twelve people.

His death casting a severe blow to the world of spiritualism, Stead had been on board the Titanic when it sunk on 15 April, travelling to take part in a peace congress at Carnegie Hall at the request of President Taft. Apparently, Stead had chatted throughout the eleven-course meal that fateful night, telling thrilling tales, including one about the cursed mummy of the British Museum before going to bed at 10:30 pm. After the ship struck the iceberg, Stead helped several women and children into the lifeboats and gave his life jacket to another passenger. He was later seen clinging to a raft but the cold forced him to release his hold. Stead's body was never recovered.

The following year de Kerlor announced his invention of a machine to measure human magnetism. And the ghost dinners where everyone attending related their own ghost story were highly popular.

And later still when war broke out, in an attempt to be useful, the International Club placed in its windows horoscopes of the German and the Austrian Emperors, with bulletins of telepathic war news regarding the movements of troops. (Nearby, was the Krishnamurti shop.)

By 1919 the International Club had begun to collapse and it was taken over by Lieut Col W J Roskell and reinvented as the *Delphic Club*. Largely similar in make-up to the International Club, the Delphic Club contained a higher proportion of theosophists than its predecessor. However, it's clear that its connection to Alan's followers had been sustained as Florence

---

ix Wilhem de Kerlor (Willem de Wendt or Willie Wendt) legally changed his name in England to Wilhelm Frederick Wendt de Kerlor, a combination of his father's last name and mother's maiden name. Claiming to be part Breton, Swiss and Polish, he was a French national. At various times, he claimed to be a detective, criminal psychologist, doctor and lecturer. He met the fashion designer Elsa Schiaparelli when giving a theosophical lecture and they became engaged the next day, marrying on 21 July 1914. In July 1915 they were forced to leave England after de Kerlor was deported following his conviction under the Vagrancy Act for fortune-telling. They lived in France before leaving for the USA in 1916. In New York, de Kerlor came to the attention of the FBI on suspicion of harbouring anti-British and pro-German allegiance during wartime. In 1917 he was on the government radar as a possible Communist. After his daughter was born in 1920, de Kerlor abandoned Schiaparelli and they divorced in 1924. In 1928, de Kerlor was murdered in Mexico.

Higgs, who took over as President of the Astrological Society after Alan's death, spoke there on 1 October 1919.

But this was yet to come. Astrologers were worrying about falling foul of the law again. In 1912, the number of fortune tellers in London had risen rapidly and it was estimated that between six and seven hundred were operating. The Metropolitan Police Commissioner responded by issuing an order that fortune tellers of all types within his jurisdiction must remove all words such as 'palmist', 'clairvoyant' and 'astrologer' from their doorplates, window signs and other public advertisements. Public concern was heightened enough for questions to be asked in the House of Commons in 1911 and 1912.

> Mr Charles Duncan asked whether the commissioner of police for the metropolis of London has issued an Order to the effect that palmists and other practitioners of psychic arts in his jurisdiction must remove all words such as palmist, clairvoyant, or astrologer from their door-plates, window-signs and other public advertisements; and whether he will state under what Act such action has been taken?

> Mr McKenna: The police notified to palmists, clairvoyants, astrologers, and similar persons that any advertisement by them that they were carrying on their calling would be held to bring them under the preview of the Vagrancy Act, 1824 for the purpose of proceedings.[7]

In other words, if you were fool enough to practise as an astrologer, it was best to do it really, really quietly. Alan and Bessie were anything but quiet.

Firstly, in 1912 Alan had founded the Astrological Institute. At its meeting in March, the subject under discussion was 'Should Astrology be studied as an independent science and kept apart from all theosophical interpretations?' Obviously, Alan thought it shouldn't.

There was regular press coverage of his predictions, plus since returning from India Alan and Bessie had gone into a whirl of lecturing. In addition to their regular spots at the Hampstead Lodge and similar, they were travelling further afield. For example, on 10 April 1912 Bessie spoke in Southsea on the types of characters indicated by the different planets; in June they both spoke in Cardiff, where confusing Bessie referred to herself as a 'follower of Christ' and referred to the second coming, which she hoped some present in the audience would live to experience; in September Bessie spoke about 'Evolution and Theosophy' in Hastings; and in October Alan spoke in Bedford—which made some people indignant.

> The lecture ... would have been truly interesting if the gentleman had given any evidence that he had solved the problem, even by 'the supreme intelligence of the sun'. Mr Leo has but an imperfect apprehension of his stupendous theme and of the logical intelligence of Bedford, if he thought that rehearsal of the astounding credulity of astrologers would suffice for light upon the transcendent subject, or justify his audacity to palm upon us, and also to propagate, such amazing assumptions without adequate demonstrative evidence. To pose as 'the father of modern astrology', whose 'information' was 'obtained first-hand', and that had any amount of proof of his allegations, is no substitute for argument; neither will such tactics count in scientific spheres of thought in our justly critical and sceptical age, which is wisely contemptuous of mere professions, by which the world has been already deluged for ages ... it is obvious that the learned (?) astrologist represents a retrogression, with which modern thought has sympathy, except as in a petrified mummy of remote antiquity.[8]

By now, Alan was focusing on selling esoteric horoscopes. His correspondence course cost five guineas for seventy lessons (although other plans were available) and he also taught esoteric astrology at the Theosophical Society. Esoteric was where it was at for Alan, and a symposium at the Astrology Society debated at length whether or not this was the right approach, deciding that on balance it was—although Alan was aware enough to plead for scientific validation saying:

> It is my intention ... to bring out a book on the purely scientific aspect of Astrology ... I have a few friends who will help me, and we will see what we can make of it. We will see whether we can get scientific proof for our astrology... To justify Astrology from the scientific standpoint you do not want anything more than the effects of Wireless Telegraphy. If you can understand that vibrations can go through the ether from the planets to this earth just as in wireless telegraphy the electric vibrations pass from one station to any other that can respond, you have the best explanation you can want of planetary influence.[9]

However, he ended by saying he couldn't understand why anyone should object to a theosophical 'colouring'. And despite Alan's mention of science, everyone knew that reincarnation was the point. Indeed, he'd said so on a number of occasions:

> I am quite convinced that until the fatalistic notions that are usually associated with the science are completely broken up, and the theory of Reincarnation universally accepted by astrologers, there will continue to be confused ideas with regard to 'Directions'. Only a few seem to have the courage to honestly state that Character is Destiny, and adhere to the principle that the stars incline, they do not compel, or as the time-honoured maxim has it: 'The wise man rules his stars, the fool obeys them'.[10]

Bessie wondered, 'What would an Astrologer who did not believe in reincarnation... say if he had placed before him the chart of an idiot? How could he account for such a thing if there were only one life? He might ask himself: Why should I be perfect in body and brain and my brother an idiot? The question demands an answer and no rational answer is forthcoming that does not involve the great truths of Karma and Reincarnation.'[11]

So there.

It took Bessie's sort of determination to remain a theosophist at this time. In late 1912 Rudolf Steiner left the Theosophical Society and most German-speaking theosophists followed him into the newly-formed *Anthroposophical Society*, founded between August and December 1912. In a telegram sent to the Theosophical Society they justified this step by stating it was: 'Based upon the recognition that the President has continually and even systematically violated this highest principle of the Theosophical Society, "No religion higher than the truth," and has abused the presidential power in arbitrary ways, thus hindering positive work.'[12] As Steiner's exclusion of Star in the East followers was a contravention of Theosophical Society statutes, the charter of the German Section was revoked.

And in July 1912, Narayaniah found out his sons had a continued association with Leadbeater and wrote to Besant demanding the boys' return. (This letter was published by *The Hindu*, leading to attacks on Leadbeater, Besant and the OSE.) In October, Narayaniah submitted a written statement to the Court of the District Judge of Chingleput, including charges that despite assurances from Besant, Leadbeater had continued to have access to his sons. He also claimed to have witnessed 'an unnatural act' between Leadbeater and Krishna.

The case was heard on 20 March 1913. Leadbeater admitted teaching masturbation, but denied any sexual contact with either Krishna or

Nitya. The judge found that the allegations of unnatural acts between Leadbeater and Krishna were unfounded, but said Leadbeater was an unsuitable person for the boys to associate with and he declared them wards of court.

Aleister Crowley said about the case, 'I am no prude. But I am a stickler for the value of words, and I deem that the French slang, 'Petit Jesus'[x] is being taken too seriously when a senile sex maniac like Leadbeater proclaims his catamites as Coming Christs.'[13] He wasn't alone in his views.

After an appeal, in January 1914 the Privy Council granted a stay of execution, and during the interim, Krishna and his brother would stay in England. Meanwhile, Leadbeater had made another discovery at the annual TS convention in December 1913—a thirteen-year-old Brahmin boy named Desikacharya Rajagopal Acharya[xi] who was, according to Leadbeater, destined to become a Buddha on the planet Mercury and was the reincarnation of Saint Bernard of Clairvaux. In February, Leadbeater embarked on a tour of Burma, Australia and New Zealand, and by the end of August had settled in Sydney. Alan and Bessie never met him again. Rajagopal became a close friend of Krishnamurti's, and his wife Rosalind (the three lived together) was Krishnamurti's lover for many years.

And of all those mentioned in this chapter, the greatest legacy may be that of Daisy Warwick's. The song named for her was the first to be sung by a computer (the IBM 7094 in 1961) and honour was paid to that moment when it was sung again by the computer HAL in *2001: A Space Odyssey*.[xii]

---

x 'Petit Jesus' was slang for a gay man, sometimes a male prostitute—used where we might say 'rent boy' today. (Given the context, an irresistible pun.) In ancient Greece and Rome, a catamite was a pubescent boy who was the intimate companion of a young man, usually in a pederastic relationship.

xi Rajagopal (1900–1993) became Krishnamurti's business manager, secretary, literary agent and editor.

xii 'Daisy Bell' by Harry Dacre was first recorded in 1893. An 1894 phonograph recording performed by Edward M Favor can be found on YourTube at https://www.youtube.com/watch?v=PqvuNb8DevE. There are innumerable recordings of the song and you might prefer a more recent version by Blur from 1993 https://www.youtube.com/watch?v=x7kUuXR7pKw&start_radio=1&list=RDx7kUuXR7pKw&t=28. In 2014, an album composed entirely of covers of 'Daisy Bell' entitled *The Gay Nineties Old Tyme Music: Daisy Bell* featured covers by Katy Perry, Tyler, the Creator, Weird Al Yankovic, Nick Cave, Kirk Hammett of Metallica, Mark Mothersbaugh of Devo, Wall of Voodoo's Stan Ridgway, Danny Elfman and others.

Alan Leo

CHAPTER NINETEEN

EARLY MIMOSA IN THE GARDEN

*I*N 1913 ALAN WAS WORRIED about his secretary, May Robbins. Specifically, he was worried about her reaching old age because he saw her standing alone 'amidst desolation'.

May Robbins

The prediction came true, but it was nothing to worry about. When my grandma was very old, we were living in a house that was due for demolition. The house had been under compulsory purchase in the 1970s because the council wanted to knock down the old houses and build a new industrial estate, but we had held out longer than any other house in the street and most of the houses had already been knocked down. One morning my mum looked out of in my grandma's bedroom and saw that someone had written on the wooden hoardings opposite: 'Desolation Row'. We got a good price for the house in the end and moved to the lovely house I still live in now. Grandma died surrounded by her family.[1]

Many of Alan's predictions were of doom and gloom—or at least, those reported in the press were. For example, Alan had been predicting revolution in Russia for a number of years. In 1905 he prematurely said it was likely soon. And in 1913 it was widely reported that in a 1912 issue of *Modern Astrology*, he'd predicted disaster for the Czar:

> Russia, he said, was influenced by Aquarius, and Japan by Libra, and Libra was the dominating planet for the present. The positions of the planets also pointed to a great revolution inside the Russian Empire. The horoscope of the Czar showed that 'Nicholas II is in himself a humane and peace-loving, monarch, but he is in the clutch of destiny, and has very little opportunity to exercise his own free will. The obstacles in his path are insurmountable. This war is the 'beginning of the end' for the Czar; indeed, it is an open question if he will live to see its end ... Will he survive the present year? It is doubtful. And, even should 'he do so, his country is threatened by an internal revolution which will go to hasten his end.'[2]

With such disaster forecast, Alan and Bessie needed a holiday. They decided to spend a few weeks in Cannes in December 1913 with their friends Rosa Praed and Nancy Heyward.

Rosa Praed[i] was an Australian novelist and theosophist who wintered

---

i The author of over fifty books, mainly romances, Rosa Campbell Praed (27 March 1851– 11 April 1935) had moved to England with her husband in 1876, and within a few years of their arrival she decided, due to her husband's extramarital affairs, to live a separate life. In the 1880s she began to attend and host Theosophical Society meetings. She'd met A P Sinnett in 1887, and he mentioned Nancy Harward, an Anglo-Indian medium in Portsmouth who Arthur Conan Doyle had told him about. Hayward wanted to move to London to further her writing career and Praed invited her to London. A few weeks later, Hayward moved in with Praed in 1899. A succession of mediumistic conversations with Hayward were recorded and became the basis of the novel *Nyria* (1904). According to Praed, these resulted from the discovery that Nancy could be assume the personality of a former incarnation, that of a Roman slave girl. All her children except her deaf daughter Maud predeceased her and all died tragically: one killed in a car accident in California; one gored to death by a rhino in Africa; and a third committed suicide after developing terminal cancer. Maud survived her but had been committed to an asylum.

on the Riviera, or in Algeria or Morocco, due to her weak lungs. She lived with the medium Nancy Hayward, and they had met Alan and Bessie at a dinner party after which Hayward had taken astrology lessons from Alan, although Praed was less keen saying, 'Astrology never particularly appealed to me. I am afraid I classed it with fortune-telling, for which in truth I have no liking.'[3]

Alan and Bessie wrote to Praed and Hayward asking them to find them accommodation in the Hotel Californie where they were staying at Cannes. The grand hotel, built in 1876 on a plot of over two hectares, overlooked the Bay of Cannes and had all mod-cons, including a hydraulic lift and telephone. They chose:

> The big south room, on the same floor as our own rooms ... A delightful room full of sunshine—palms, late roses and early mimosa in the garden below.[4]

After an overnight journey, Alan and Bessie stepped down from the bus as Praed and Hayward watched their arrival. After a short time, Alan knocked on their door and he and Bessie joined them for a chat.

> This was the first of many an informal gathering, either in our rooms or in theirs—sometimes a quartette, sometimes a larger party when other friends interested in Astrology or attracted to the Leos themselves, would come in for a sort of picnic tea provided from Mrs Leo's tea-basket and our spirit-lamps and teacups. Sometimes there were not chairs enough to go round, and, occasionally, Mr Leo would seat himself Buddha-fashion, cross-legged on the floor. Then we would overflow into the balcony, where, at tea-time, there was the beautiful sunset over the Esterels to admire, and anyhow, we much preferred our funny little tea-parties in our own quarters to the hotel teas in the smart palm-decorated lounge where our talk might puzzle uninitiated listeners.
>
>   Unfortunately, evil transits in Mrs Alan's case caused her to be ill for some little time, and though Mr Alan was the most devoted of nurses, he had to have meals and to take occasional exercise and recreation. During his wife's absence from the dining-room, we persuaded him to eat his vegetarian fare at our table—he never touched meat in any form nor alcohol, nor did he smoke, but he would sit with us after dinner in the lounge. Among strangers he was always rather silent, but he observed everything.[5]

Alan's claims of past lives, and talk about functioning on other planes, prompted Praed to persuade him to agree to meet her one night in the dream world. The following morning she recounted her dream in which Alan appeared. Less forgiving people might have thought Alan had no idea what she was on about.

> He nodded as if it were quite true, but when I asked him to fill in the blanks, he only nodded again and smiled oracularly.[6]

Holiday or no holiday, Alan continued to give Hayward astrology lessons. In the mornings, the four of them went for a walk. Alan and Praed strolled along chatting while Bessie spent her time with Hayward. When they passed a flower farm, as they often did on one of their routes, Alan stopped to buy a bunch of violets or carnations for Bessie.

Alan and Bessie Leo in Cannes

Unfortunately, Alan's predictions still caused him problems, even on the French Riveria. In an issue of *Modern Astrology*, he had invited readers to delineate 'a horoscope which has been productive of many confusing statements'.[7] Apparently, astrologers had interpreted a series of adverse aspects in different ways:

> One saying the native would be shot, another that he would lose his wife, a third that he would be ruined in business, a fourth that he would suffer a severe illness, a fifth that he would soon meet with an accident, and a sixth that he would elope!!![7]

The subject of the horoscope was so upset by these suggestions that he travelled from Birmingham to Cannes to challenge Alan who:

> Was fortunately able to convince the native that erroneous judgements had been given, although I must confess it was a painful task to show the superficiality of the work turned out by those who would by the length of their practice have been capable of giving better judgments.[8]

This event may have been behind Alan's frequent assertions that he was on holiday and didn't want to discuss business with Praed. In fact, he would leave the room to avoid doing so. On the new moon, Alan and Bessie took the evening express back to London, possibly now more aware that in general terms, predictions were dangerous.

The threat of the Vagrancy Act still hung over astrologers and the Occult Defence League was no longer active to help them out. Worse, the potential damage to anyone's reputation had increased. Although clauses of the Act had long always included indecent behaviour, the 1898 amendment had added clauses to include in Section 1:

Every male person who
(a) knowingly lives wholly or in part on the earnings of prostitution; or[ii]
(b) in any public place persistently solicits or importunes for immoral purposes.

Although the intention was to address prostitution and sex trafficking, these clauses were primarily used to convict gay men.[iii] Instead of having to convict for sodomy, it was now possible to seek convictions for flirting, worrying body language and being dressed in an inappropriate way. The clause heightened the significance of behaviour that wasn't not explicitly sexual and was focused on places with a reputation, such as Piccadilly. Men could be arrested not for what they did, but on the basis of assumptions. And in 1912 the sentence of one month in prison was increased to six months with a discretionary whipping for a second offence. Being convicted under the Vagrancy Act now carried a new taint.

---

ii Although 1898 had seen a new Amendment to the Vagrancy Act passed, which made 'living off the earnings of a prostitute' (or pimping) an offence, in 1900 only 165 'pimps' were sentenced while 7,415 women were convicted under the solicitation laws.
iii In 1912 these provisions were extended to Scotland and Ireland.

On 29 April 1914 Alan worked in his office until 10 am when he set off for the law courts where he was completing jury service. On his return later that day, he'd just sat down to attend to his mail when he was told, 'Two gentlemen had called from the Jury.'[10] Assuming the visit was related in some way to his jury service, Alan asked that the men be shown in, whereupon they handed him a summons.

> Information has been laid this day by Hugh McLean of the City of London Police for THAT YOU on the 27th day of February 1914 did UNLAWFULLY PRETEND TO TELL FORTUNES to DECEIVE and IMPOSE upon the said Hugh McLean and others of his Majesty's subjects contrary to the Statute ... YOU ARE THEREFORE hereby summoned ... at the MANSION HOUSE on Wednesday the 6th of May at 11:15 am.[11]

Taken aback, Alan asked who Hugh McLean was. The detective who'd handed him the summons said it was him and Alan responded, 'This after twenty-live years! I have never seen you before: I do not tell fortunes.'[12] And he opened his office door to see the men out.

As soon as they had left, Alan called for one of his assistants to calculate a chart for 4:15 pm, the time the men had arrived. Once Alan got home that evening, he talked it over with Bessie and examined the chart. Alan would have noticed immediately that the planet that represented him, Venus, was in a much stronger position than his opponents'—Mars. And the Moon was void of course, suggesting the matter would come to nothing.

Chances were, this wasn't a serious problem, but to be on the safe side, and after thinking about the matter, Alan decided to consult fellow theosophist Kingsley Bayley, his solicitor. Bayley took the matter extremely seriously and advised Alan that risking prison as a martyr for the cause was probably not the best idea he'd had. There'd been too many martyrs already and the tactic could easily backfire. So on 1 May Alan engaged Mann & Crimp, solicitors and agreed to Walter Warren[iv] being appointed barrister for the case. He gave instructions that if the worst happened and he was convicted, there should be an immediate appeal so his case could be taken to a higher court and he would make the case for astrology.

---

iv Walter Richard Warren (1867–1931) stood for parliament in 1908 as a Liberal, although he lost. In March 1910, standing for the Liberal backed Progressive Party, he gained a seat from the Conservative backed Municipal Reform Party at Battersea in the London County Council election. A freemason, Warren was initiated into the Antioch Lodge in 1908. He was the father of Marjory Winsome Warren (1897–1960), who was one of the first geriatricians and is considered the mother of modern geriatric medicine.

When Alan turned up to Mansion House on 6 May ready to fight the charges, he'd gathered a number of character witnesses including Annie Besant, A P Sinnett and Walter Old. A crowd of journalists had also gathered.

Mansion House was a magistrate's court, presided over by the Lord Mayor of London, being the chief magistrate. Numerous high profile cases were heard here. It was an imposing and grand enough building enough to worry even those confident of their innocence. Alan was led up some stairs and through a hatch-door to sit on a wooden chair behind an iron railing, looking up at the magistrate. Alan was charged with having told fortunes on 27 February and 8 April 1914. He pleaded not guilty.

Thomas Vickery,[v] the Assistant City Solicitor, opened the case for the prosecution, saying that in February Detective Inspector Hugh McLean of the City of London Police had written under the name of William Hammond asking for a list of charges for horoscopes. In response to his query, he'd received a letter that outlined the various charges for horoscopes, ranging from five shillings to five guineas, the latter offering forecasts for ten years. He'd also received a booklet entitled *The Stars and How to Read Them*.

McLean wrote back and asked for a ten shilling horoscope, giving his birth data as 6 am, 22 February 1875, Isle of Wight. For his money, he received a 'Delineation of Nativity' and the advice that he could either purchase a more detailed judgment or add to it himself by studying Alan's books.

> This abridged delineation is only a brief sketch of your nativity, but it may be considerably enlarged either by purchasing a special and complete judgement or by judging it yourself from the *Key to Your Own Nativity*.[13]

The advice to keep his blood 'pure' as Vickery said, prompted laughter in court. The section of the report entitled *Future Prospects* was also read out:

> The influences operating during the next five years of your life are, on the whole, favourable. During 1914 the Sun will be in trine to Uranus. This will bring some rather important changes into your life of a favourable nature, mostly mental. You will come into contact with peculiar strangers whose influence over you will be strong and good, and your own magnetism will now increase and you will find that you can deal satisfactorily with

---

v Thomas George Vickery (1850–5 February 1935).

others at this time. You will be less conventional and orthodox and you will take a broader attitude towards life, inclining to anything which will give more freedom and independence. It is a good aspect for travel, and will in all probability bring you financial gain, especially as the moon will be going through the second house. You have just passed away from the conjunction of Saturn, and therefore I can now promise you much improvement generally in your affairs.[14]

Vickery glossed over the character analysis to emphasise the predictions made, although Warren insisted no fortune-telling had taken place. He pointed out that Alan had been in India when the letter was written—it was signed *per pro*[vi] *Alan Leo H.L.*—and Alan was a respectable man, the author of many books on astrology who had received testimonials from 20,000 people.

Warren also wasn't happy that McLean had used an assumed name, although he hastily pointed out that he wasn't suggesting that if the date had been correct, Alan would have been able to tell McLean's future. Anyway, at the time the letter was sent, Alan was abroad and therefore could not possibly have written it.

The second summons was then considered. Again, Warren pointed out there was no evidence that Alan had any knowledge of the horoscope sent to McLean, or that it was sent under his authority.

Vickery felt obliged to dismiss the charges, although he said, 'I am fully convinced in my own mind that there is no doubt that it is endeavouring to tell fortunes.'[15] Warren applied for costs, observing that Alan was a gentleman of the highest respectability and independent means with a number of people attending to speak on his behalf. Vickery refused and his decision was received with applause.

The case was widely covered in the press and an issue of *Modern Astrology* was devoted to discussing its ramifications. Although Alan wasn't convicted of fortune telling, it was a weak victory to have the case dismissed on a technicality.

And a few weeks later, on 26 May Alan's friend Charles Moore[vii] appeared in court as another of McLean's victims. Working under the name of 'Young Moore' through an office in the Strand, Moore advertised

---

vi Short for *per procurationem* and often rendered 'p.p.' Literally, it means 'through the agency of' but was often used to mean' on behalf of' and was a common abbreviation in business English.
vii Charles Walter Moore, a printer (30 January 1870–1955).

regularly in *The Tatler* throughout 1912. After complaints from the police, he took on an office at St Bride's house from where his mail was redirected to his home in Luton. The case was almost identical except Moore didn't have the support Alan had. He was fined £25 and three guineas costs.

Eventually, the fuss died down and it seemed everyone could simply get on with the business of supplying horoscopes. And Alan gave up making predictions like a sensible person—except he didn't.

In August 1914 the press reported Alan's views of the eclipse on 2 August:

> The eclipse of the sun in the same degree as the martial fixed star Regulus, which takes place shortly after noon to-morrow, is remarkable for the destructive influence it denotes, when signifies the downfall of monarchs.[15]
>
> It ... stirs the whole Europe into exceptional violence and lawlessness. It is very inimical to all crowned heads of Europe, and especially fatal to the Kaiser and the Austrian Emperor.[16]

Britain declared war on Germany on 4 August.

Alan Lei in 1917

CHAPTER TWENTY

A BOMB MORE CRUEL

Despite the war, life went on much the same for the Leos. Alan's predictions about the war were widely published in the press, and in March he compiled them into a pamphlet:

Alan Leo's 'star turn' is not very convincing, although he begins with the reassuring statement that astrology is 'based upon mathematics, the only exact science, and may be said to consist of mathematical computations…' As a matter of fact, the pamphlet is disappointing in that it does not tell us when the war will end, it merely gives various dates when it may end.

'The beginning of the end of the year,' says Mr Leo, 'should be seen during the month of June.' But that will not be the end, for 'during the month of July and all through the summer extraordinary efforts will be made to bring about peace.' Still the end is not yet. 'About October the influence of the planet Jupiter, the 'peace' planet, becomes so powerful that peace could then be secured on favourable terms to all concerned.'

Even Jupiter's influence seems to be uncertain, however, and we are told that should it fail 'the war will enter on a new phase during the autumn, and will continue until the War Lord, Mars, comes to the sign of the Balance Libra—in the spring of 1916.[1]

By the summer Alan and Bessie had moved to Dollis Lodge[i] in Finchley. Despite its name, Dollis Lodge wasn't a grand old house, but a set of apartments—one of which Alan and Bessie lived in. Finchley was an up and coming area, swiftly becoming more populated. Parades of shops were being added to, the tram system had been established since 1909, and the Edgware, Highgate and London Railway (precursor of parts of London Underground's Northern line) offered regular trains into central London. And yet they lived close to Dollis Brook and open land that still exists today.

On the evening of 13 July 1915, the Leos held an informal meeting to which seventeen other people were invited. After refreshments in the garden, they retired to the drawing room and Alan spoke saying it was time to bring together theosophy and astrology in a new theosophical lodge. Bessie wrote in the minute book:

> Mr Leo explained that it had seemed to himself and Mrs Leo that the time was ripe for the Amalgamation of Theosophy and Astrology in a Lodge of the T.S.
>
> They had already founded two previous Lodges, at Hampstead and Surbiton, with the same object in view, but in neither case had the Lodge development proceeded quite along the intended lines.
>
> There were good reasons for this third venture, as many earnest students have regarded Theosophy and Astrology as inseparable, Astrology being a demonstration of Theosophy.
>
> The present company were offered the privilege of being founders of this new Lodge of which Mrs Leo was to be the President, himself Vice President and Miss Helen Veale Secretary.
>
> Meetings would be at 12 Upper Woburn Place, and would commence on Monday, Sept 13th. It was suggested the lectures every Monday should occupy the first session, but that after Christmas a course of study would begin for members only; the third volume of the *Secret Doctrine* being proposed as a subject.[ii] [2]

---

i 14 Dollis Avenue, Church End, Finchley. Now Finchley Central.
ii Blavatsky's *Secret Doctrine* was published as two volumes in 1888. Blavatsky stated that its contents had been revealed to her by mahatmas who had retained knowledge of humanity's spiritual history. In 1897 Annie Besant published what she claimed was the third volume as written by Blavatsky. There was, and is, dispute within the theosophical movement as to whether the papers had actually been given to Besant and whether they were intended for publication. Additionally, there is dispute regarding Besant's editing.

After some debate, it was unanimously agreed to proceed with the application for a charter and W Green, Miss Emery, Mr Stanley Gritton,[iii] Mrs Earp, Miss Head, Mrs Halliday, Mrs J E Smith, Mrs Worsley,[iv] Mrs Dudley, Miss Hoffman,[v] Miss Debenham,[vi] Miss P Corus, Charles Carter, Wynter Robinson, [vii]Sydney Randall, Miss Butterton and Helen Veale[viii] signed the letter.[ix]

An advertisement swiftly appeared in the *Vahan*, a Theosophical Society newsletter that circulated with details of meetings and lectures, as well as discussions on theosophical issues.

> It requires some courage to announce yet another Lodge, holding meetings in or about Headquarters, but this one is prepared at once to justify its existence, by bringing several new members to the T.S. Its appeal is to all who are students of both Astrology and Theosophy, and it will aim at showing the former as inseparable from the latter—as indeed, an intellectual presentment, by the grandest of all symbols, of the same universal truths that have been re-translated to the world of truth by our Theosophical teachers.
>
> To some Theosophists, it seems as impossible to omit the study of Astrology as it would be for a soi-disant classical scholar to content himself with translations of Homer and Virgil! Yet this simile fails to do justice to Astrology, for it is no dead language,

---

iii Stanley Evan Gritton born 1882, Reigate, Surrey.
iv Celia Worsley.
v Maud Hoffman (1870–1952) was an actress born in Washington. For a while she lived with the theosophist Mabel Collins and collaborated with her on *The Story of Sensa*, a stage version of Collins' *Idyll of the White Lotus*. In later years she became a follower of Gurdjieff and moved to the Château de Prieuré in Fortainbleau, France in 1922. She became executrix for the estate of AP Sinnett and presented his Mahatma Letters to the British Museum.
vi Marjorie Cecily Debenham (3 December 1893–December 1990) was the daughter of Sir Ernest Ridley Debenham of the department store family, and educated at the Sorbonne. She was the founder of the *Society of Divine Wisdom*, devoted to promoting Blavatsky's brand of theosophy. Debenham was also a practising Buddhist and became a freemason in 1920. She made a lifelong study of symbolism and its role in ritual and founded a number of masonic lodges.
vii Probably the architect responsible for creating the plans for the Theosophical Society building in Auckland in 1921.
viii Helen Veale lived in the Society's headquarters in Adyar, India for many years and was principal of the Madras National High School for Girls.
ix Although his name doesn't appear in the minute book, David Freedman later claimed to have been at this meeting. He was certainly an early member of the Lodge, and his name appears in the records for 1919 and he was secretary by 1920. It's likely he was one of the non-theosophists in attendance.

writ on perishable parchment and stone, but a living fount of knowledge, blazoning itself forth in the fires that eternally lighten the darkness of the material universe—the same yesterday, to-day and forever.³

The first meeting of the Middlesex Lodge took place on 13 September in the form of a social. The Vice-President of the Theosophical Society, AP Sinnett, attended along with Francesca Arundale. Alan opened proceedings saying that theosophy showed the unity of all things and astrology the diversity. Bessie followed up by saying that Besant and Leadbeater had come to the inaugural meeting of the lodge she had formed previously, but they weren't now available—which placed a damper on the proceedings. Despite clearly being third choice, Sinnett spoke about how he had evidence that the Masters made predictions for the future based on astrology. Arundale stated that she had no time or patience for astrology (another less than helpful comment) but she was glad Alan was no fatalist. In response to this, and perhaps in irritation, Bessie pointed out that she and Alan were free will astrologers and added that the Middlesex Lodge was for bona fide astrologers and those who had not hitherto been to a theosophical lodge.

Things ran smoothly apart from the usual hiccoughs—a question evening had to be hastily re-arranged because no-one could think of any questions, attendees had to be told to stay in their chairs until the end of a lecture, and speakers cancelled at short notice. And the idea of studying the *Secret Doctrine* was soon abandoned as people found it too difficult.

At the meeting of 8 November, Alan announced that the Lodge was henceforth to be known as the *Astrological Lodge*,ˣ as the previous name lacked colour, and it was under that name that its theosophical charter was granted. A hasty committee meeting beforehand established the rules of the Lodge, which made it clear membership was open both to full members of the Theosophical Society and 'associates' (non-theosophists).

---

x Although it separated from the Theosophical Society, the Astrological Lodge continues to meet (as of 2018) and is one of only two of Alan's organisations that have survived; the other being the Hermes Lodge. Virtually all contemporary astrological organisations in Britain are its offshoots.

Alan had told the Hermes Lodge in June 1915 that:

> The part the Astrologer should play in the world was along the line of action, the acting at certain specified and arranged times, and that the present time would usher in a new era in accordance with the law and that a new era is always preceded by a great calamity.[4]

For Alan, that calamity was to come in July 1917 when he was again charged with fortune telling.

> A 'bomb' more cruel than the German air raider's bomb fell into the astrological camp at 11.5 a.m. on July 2nd, when we were served with a summons to appear at the Mansion House at 11:30 a.m. on July 9th on a charge of 'pretending and professing to tell fortunes'.[5]

Alan immediately sought people character witnesses, and a number of people agreed to speak on his behalf in court, including Sinnett and Maud Sharpe. Despite putting on a brave front, he was clearly worried.

> There comes to my mind a dream that he told me he had had during the early days of July while the Mansion-House case was pending. In his dream he found himself walking by the sea-shore, carrying something in his hand, and looking at it he became conscious that it was lifeless, and so said to himself "It's no use carrying a dead thing," and threw it far into the sea. He watched it splash into the water and disappear, but from the place of its disappearance there came up a water bird, whose head shone with vivid peacock-blue colouring; and it swam to the land and walked about, shaking itself free of water and growing larger and more brilliant as he watched it.[6]

The case was broadly similar to that brought in 1914. An Inspector Nicholls had ordered a five guinea horoscope, which included predictions. However, this time the case against Alan was treated more seriously.

> Mr Travers Humphreys, who prosecuted, said the charge was that the defendant professed to be able to forecast the future. A great many people professed in different ways to do so, and the present time, when there were very few people who had not some near relative or other in imminent peril, it was preposterous that persons should be allowed to make their living attempting to induce the belief in those who had relatives abroad that they were able for a sum of money to tell what was to likely happen to those relatives.

The defendant professed to be able to forecast the future of an individual without ever seeing him; he did not want an interview, nor did he even desire to see the handwriting. He merely wanted to know the date and hour when the person was born, and then professed to be able to tell not only the character and prospects and future of the individual, but to be able to tell him accurately what was going to happen to him within the next ten years. The defendant said he did this by astrology and the study of the stars.[7]

Humphreys went on to read extracts from the horoscope. Under the heading 'Quality and Triplicity' it stated:

These two words denote a great deal more than is ordinarily supposed when judging a nativity, because they represent seven distinct states of conditions corresponding to the planes of matter from which vibrations of the planets are constantly passing, diagrammatically represented by the horizontal lines, while the planetary influences may be represented as vertical lines passing perpendicularly through these states of matter, the whole forming a great cross upon which the drama of human destiny is being played.[8]

Which was nice, and couldn't really be classed as fortune telling. However, under the heading '1920' it said:

This year appears to be dominated by the sun's square to Jupiter, an adverse aspect that will tend to affect you socially and financially, hence you will need to act cautiously. It seems to be more in the latter half of the year that this affliction will affect you and as Jupiter governs your eleventh house at birth, trouble with friends is shown, and you may lose someone to whom you have been attached, which will cause you some sorrow or grief. Do not make any new acquaintances or push yourself forward in any way, for there will be a tendency to be misled ... it would be wise to look after your circulation keeping the blood in good condition, and do not neglect any chills or colds, but give all minor ailments attention and, above all, avoid all tendencies to worry and anxiety.[9]

Alan's defence was that his report showed only tendencies and should not be defined as fortune telling as that involved making a specific statement about the future. This approach may have succeeded if it hadn't been for a sentence saying:

At this time a death in your family circle is likely to cause you sorrow.[10]

The prosecution demanded to know whether death was a tendency or was there a tendency to death? This sentence was Alan's undoing.

Ernest Wild for the defence said astrology was a science that had been believed and practised by Orientals for six thousand years, and it was generally accepted in India, where every mother had her child's horoscope drawn for a few annas—which most people attending thought had nothing to do with the price of fish.

Alan said in his defence that astrology had proved its truth in a number of instances, and when asked if he 'extracted money from the simple-minded classes' responded: 'No, my clients are mainly among the rich and intellectual classes.'[11] 'I most emphatically say that I do not tell fortunes. I tell tendencies from the horoscope.'[12]

The hearing ended in a nominal fine of £5 and 25 guineas costs. Alan got off lightly—the maximum sentence was three months' imprisonment, including hard labour. The issue was never about punishing astrologers but about forcing legal boundaries upon the rising interest in spiritualist movements during the war. Wild asked for permission to take an appeal to a higher court which was granted.

A special edition of *Modern Astrology* covered the details of the case, and the national press, including *The Times*, carried reports. Whatever the validity of astrology, in the way Alan was trying to present it, there was no doubt in the mind of the press that he was guilty and his conviction just.

> The result of the prosecution should make clear beyond any doubt that in the eyes of the law the scientific astrologer is just as much a rogue and vagabond as any gipsy woman who asks you to cross her hand with a piece of silver. There is, of course, a vast gulf between Mr Leo and the majority of the horoscope merchants. The element of imposition was lacking in his case. He could and no doubt did draw up horoscopes scientifically accurate. Where he went wrong was in interpreting his maps for money. Rightly, I think, our laws decrees this to be an offence, for whether such interpretations are honest in intention or otherwise, they are equally likely to be harmful to persons credulous enough to believe them. Mr Leo or any other astrologer has, of course, a right to believe in and practice astrology, but he must not make his living by it.[13]

Obviously, this decision wasn't popular with everyone:

> It is clear to anyone who walks about London with his eyes open that the magistrate's decision against Mr Alan Leo, the

best-known of the astrological fraternity, will affect great many people. Most people will agree that if the obscure fortune-teller is to be prosecuted there should be discrimination in favour of those who, as Mr Leo pleads, are well-to-do and intellectual. But interference in these quarters has naturally brought about a movement protest from those who might have borne with equanimity the punishment of more humble practitioners. We have already had one meeting of protest at the Queen's Hall, and believe a campaign on behalf of 'liberty of prophesying' is to be instituted. It will not be unopposed.[14]

Alan had planned to appeal against the decision, but decided against it as he was advised his chances of success were low. Instead, he and Bessie travelled to Bude in Cornwall for their annual holiday. He'd realised he would have to revise his system of reading horoscopes to escape future tussles with the law. Only halfway through the work, he intended to rewrite much of his material while on holiday. As Harry Green said:

> It became evident that his whole system of reading horoscopes would have to be revised, because what he regarded as no more than truthful and legitimate advice to clients, the law insisted upon treating as fortune-telling. Therefore he decided to recast the whole system and make it run along the lines of character reading ... This entailed a tremendous amount of rewriting of reference-books and sheets ... when he went to Bude was found that he had finished rather less than one-half of it.[15]

Every day, Alan devoted four or five hours to writing for his anticipated book *Astrology Without Prediction*. Then on the morning of 27 August, he complained of feeling shivery and cold and said, 'I feel I have taken a chill'.[16]

Alan's condition worsened and Bessie wrote to Harry Green, pleading with him to do a horary chart to find out what was going to happen. The situation didn't seem desperate as Alan joked, 'My wife is trying to find out how long I shall live!'[17]

Although Alan claimed to be feeling better he said, 'I have a great tightness in the chest and a feeling as if there was an iron band round my throat.'[18]

After a bad night, Bessie finally decided to ignore Alan's objections and call for a doctor, who examined him and said. 'Don't be anxious Mrs Leo, your husband will be quite all right in two or three days; he has got a bad chill, and it has settled on the liver. I will send you at once some fever medicine and a pill—give him the medicine every four hours and the pill to-night, late, a dose of salts in the morning, and he will soon be all right.'[19]

Ethel Hart, the Leos' housekeeper, joined the doctor in his car to collect the medicine.

That night, Alan was uncomfortable but he slept a few hours and his temperature seemed to go down. After a drink of hot milk in the morning he said, 'Bessie, leave me quite quiet here for a little while, I want to pull myself round.'

Bessie went downstairs but within minutes heard Alan cry out. When she rushed upstairs, she found him convulsing and saying, 'What is it, what is it, where am I?'

Bessie responded with, 'Alan, rouse your will and try to pull yourself together,'[22] and told Hart to run for the doctor. She was gone nearly an hour, but Alan regained consciousness and the convulsions ended.

When the doctor arrived, Alan apologised for calling him out so early. The doctor said, 'That's all right.'

'Am I going to die, doctor?' Alan asked, 'I don't mind if I am, I'm not afraid of death.'

'No certainly not, Mr Leo, you will be quite all right by and by.'

'I believe I have been off my head for quite a quarter of an hour,' said Alan.

'Well you're quite all right now anyway,' the doctor said briskly.[27]

Bessie took the doctor outside the bedroom and said, 'If you want another opinion, get it at once, money is no consideration, his life is a very valuable one to the world.'

'Don't worry, Mrs Leo, your husband is not going to die; there is no necessity for another opinion,' came the response. 'I will come in later,' he added before leaving.

A few minutes later, Alan was sick again and said, 'Oh my poor head, it is going round; the eclipse on my Moon has done this.' He had another fit before losing consciousness.[20]

Bessie rushed out for the doctor and when she came back with him was greeted at the door by Hart who told her she was too late.

The doctor insisted no-one could have known this would happen. 'Mrs Leo, your husband died of a seizure and no one could know it was going to happen, it has been as great a shock to me as to you, I am very sorry, but believe me nothing could be done. He was only really ill for one hour.'[21]

Green did do his horary—it said that while Alan's illness was serious, the worst need not be feared, and it should pass off in a few days. Alan died 30 August 1917 due to a cerebral haemorrhage. Many of his supporters blamed the case for his death and viewed the authorities as murderers. He was cremated at Golders Green cemetery 5 September 1917.

'His soul lives and works on in the astral world in the same great field of labour that was his on earth,' Bessie insisted. 'He was called to higher work and is more alive than ever, not less; his body clothed in a finer vesture than the physical.'[22]

CHAPTER TWENTY-ONE

REACHING MODERNITY

*A*STROLOGY CONTINUED WITHOUT Alan, although it was a duller astrology. When Charles Carter[i] returned from the war in 1919, he found that most of the activities he had fostered were in a state of decline. He had no choice but to take over. Unfortunately, he held a low view of Bessie:

> Mrs Leo was a queer old body if ever there was one ... she had a great talent for what I would describe as inept interference ... Physically lazy and a chronic valetudinarian, the lady insisted on remaining its [the Astrological Lodge's] President for many years, issuing ukases from her house in Finchley, but never doing anything to help ... I have no doubt Bessie Leo was fundamentally a sincere woman, though she could stoop to making private enquiries about a person and then claiming she had found

---

i Carter (31 January 1887–4 October 1968) had graduated from London University and was called to the Bar in 1913, the same year he married. He was from a wealthy family, his grandfather, Jesse Carter, having founded a thriving brick and tile business in Poole in 1873—the Carter company produced much of the ceramic tiling used on London Underground stations built in the 1930s and eventually became Poole Pottery. On his return from the War, Carter worked with his father, helping post-war families to resettle through the Homeland's Trust initiative. He was President of the Astrological Lodge from 1922 to 1952, the first Principal of the Faculty of Astrological Studies in 1948, editor of the Lodge's publication, the Quarterly magazine and Patron of the Astrological Association of Great Britain from its foundation in 1958. He also succeeded in making badges available for astrologers to wear.

whatever it was in the horoscope ... Mrs Leo was forever making plans and then scrapping them, often by telephone the next morning. She ... used to hurry her husband home from meetings on the grounds that she had an appointment on the astral plane, usually at eight o'clock. One is glad to think our astral brethren have such a high regard for punctuality ... She was sometimes generous where it was ill deserved, and niggardly with those who merited generous treatment.[1]

She had an itch for power but she was totally incompetent and very indolent. This led to an attitude of constant ineffectual interference.[2]

In fact, Carter believed that the Astrological Lodge had been set up to give Bessie something to do in other words, to stop her interfering in Alan's work. But to be fair to Carter, although he described Alan as a man of vision, he wasn't complimentary towards him, either.

He was not impressive, being short, and in later years, tubby ... he had a somewhat plethoric appearance ... doubtless there is an inner side to Astrology as there is to many other things, but, judging by his book Esoteric Astrology, Leo had little to teach in this field. He was accused ... of picking others' brains ... I feel he was threatened with a lapse into 'wooliness'.[3]

Carter slipped comfortably into the role of Vice-President of the Astrological Lodge, taking over from Vivian Robson. The Lodge was a small and intimate group at this time, but in autumn 1920 there was an influx of new members. With these new members came new ideas and they decided to offer beginners' classes.

It wasn't as if there was a shortage of astrological classes in London. At the Astrological Institute on alternate Tuesdays at four in the afternoon, Bessie gave special classes on esoteric astrology, while a Mr Barker offered a more general class at seven. On Wednesdays, David Freedman taught a beginner's class at seven. Thursday was Carter's night and he offered tuition at six-thirty in advanced, medical and horary astrology—presumably not all at the same time. Vivian Robson taught at both four and seven o'clock on Fridays. And there were other options. The Delphic Club offered 'drawing room meetings' to discuss astrology on Wednesdays and Fridays. Monday was the only night of the week that didn't have an astrology class. It soon did.

It was possible to flit from class to class, studying with whoever took your fancy. However, there wasn't a large number of people flitting. Although in October 1920 the Institute re-organised itself in an attempt to build enthusiasm and attract more people, hiring a more expensive and larger room in Woburn Place, the number of attendees was woefully low. One week Bessie attracted only seven people to her first group and none to her second. Poor Mr Barker had to spend his evening alone. And yet people kept asking for classes, Bessie pointed out in frustration.

Bessie couldn't see any reason why the Astrological Lodge should change. It was, after all, a theosophical lodge first and foremost. Those who wanted their astrology theosophy-free could attend the Institute. It went both ways, of course, although most attendees were unworried about what organisation was affiliated with which group.

She no longer attended the Astrological Lodge, although she occasionally hosted socials for it at Dollis Lodge. On top of her work with the Institute and other organisations, Bessie was suffering from ill-health. Her high blood pressure was a problem and she was seriously ill in October 1921. Bessie was due to stand for re-election as president of the Astrological Lodge in January, but she was painfully out of touch with the current membership. And at a committee meeting of the Astrological Lodge on 15 December 1921 it was noted:

> That this meeting has heard with deep regret Mrs Leo's continued ill health and tenders its sincere good wishes for her recovery and begs her to accept the office of Honorary President of the Lodge in recognition of her long services.[4]

Bessie took the hint and offered her resignation and Carter was appointed Acting President.

Over the next year, Bessie's health continued to trouble her, and she complained about gout, flu, and an abscess in her left breast. She remained Honorary President of the Astrological Lodge until May 1923 when the title was quietly dropped. She had enough on her plate. Florence Higgs, who had been President of the Astrological Society since shortly after Alan's death, had died suddenly of heart failure on 30 December 1921, leaving the responsibility for the Society in Bessie's hands as well as the Institute, plus she had *Modern Astrology*, which she was editing with the assistance of Vivian Robson, to think about. Money was tight.

The Astrological Lodge was struggling. One of Carter's first tasks was to seek out new premises. Meetings were still taking place at Woburn Place, the Astrological Institute's home, and with Bessie no longer president, the Lodge needed to find alternative accommodation. The exercise was made more complicated by a discrepancy in the accounts—they recorded that rent of £20 was paid per anum and yet the actual rent was a little over £15. (It's unclear from the minutes how this was resolved.) However, having signed a rental agreement with Bessie, the Lodge couldn't simply leave, so for the short term they simply moved to a larger room on the first floor in the same building. They were still there in December. Bessie refused to cancel their rental agreement and they were committed to stay until September 1923. To add insult to injury, when the Lodge moved upstairs in April 1923, they discovered that a bookcase had gone missing. Bessie insisted the bookcase actually belonged to the Astrological Institute. After an exchange of unfruitful correspondence, the Lodge admitted defeat and decided to buy a new bookcase.

Bessie had become disillusioned with astrological societies and desperately missed Alan.

> Since he passed over I have come into touch with him, while both in and out of the body, and I have done my poor best to keep his work going, although mine is a broken body with failing health.[5]

The Astrological Lodge wasn't the only organisation questioning its relationship with the Theosophical Society. In 1929 Krishnamurti publicly dissolved the Order of the Star in the East and thousands of people left the Society.

By now Bessie was living as an invalid and was known locally for the trips out she took in her bath chair. According to Charles Mitchell,[ii] Bessie had asked him to predict her death and he'd told her it would be when she was seventy-two years old—as indeed it was; she died on 24 May 1931, a month after her seventy-second birthday.

Bessie made a number of bequests, including £125 to Matilda Minnear (May Robbins), £20 to Mitchell, £250 to Annie Besant, £100 to Leadbeater, her astrological curtains and oil paintings of herself and Alan to the Hermes Lodge, £1,000 to the Star Publishing Trust to publish Krishnamurti's writings, and £300 to the Theosophical Society. The remainder of her estate, valued at over £10,000 was left to Duncan McNaughton[iii] to be used by him in 'furthering the aims, scope and

---

ii Charles Everard Mitchell (1883–1967) wrote for the *Halifax Courier* and was renowned for predicting financial investments. He made a living for many years selling his patented 'Deskette Novelty', a memorandum appliance.

iii Writing under the name of Maurice Wemyss, McNaughton was a lawyer and at one point scholar in public international law at McGill University, Montreal. He became president of the Edinburgh Astronomical Society (1952), a member of the Royal Astronomical

objects of the science of astrology and in conducting my magazine *Modern Astrology* as he may think fit.⁶

She was cremated and her ashes deposited with Alan's.

And Bessie had lived long enough to witness Alan's true legacy.

In 1930 Cheiro turned down a request to write an astrological feature and passed it on to his assistant—Richard Harold Naylor.ⁱᵛ The *Sunday Express* wanted a fresh angle for their story of the birth of Princess Margaret (younger daughter of the future King George VI) and on 24 August 1930 it published Naylor's analysis of the Princess' birth chart, along with political predictions and comments based on readers' dates of birth. (Working with Cheiro, Naylor was used to the type of astrology based on character descriptions and forecasts grouped by month of birth, although at that time the zodiac signs weren't mentioned as too few people were familiar with them.)

A flood of appreciative letters persuaded the *Sunday Express* to commission a feature 'Were You Born in September?' for the following week. Naylor's success was secured when one million readers read his prediction that British aircraft were in serious danger. The BBC announced that day that the R101 airship, on its maiden voyage from Cardington to India, had crashed in northern France.

Naylor introduced his readers to Sun signs as a character type, featuring Mr and Mrs Taurus, for example, in precisely the way Alan had. Sun sign astrology had arrived. One by one, the national press took up similar features, and gradually, the twelve sign format we're familiar with today was born. And Naylor realised what he had done.

> In 1930 I commenced a series of Astrological articles which have entirely altered the orientation of the public mind towards Astrology. I am aware all this sounds egotistical and perhaps boastful, but it so happens it is true.⁷

Almost everyone in the West today can tell you the sign they're born under, and most of them can tell you something about what that sign means. The majority of newspapers all over the world carry horoscope columns, and practically all women's magazines do. There are thousands

---

Society in London and in 1943 was a Fellow of the Royal Society of Edinburgh.

iv Born Richard Harold Thropp (2 August 1889, London, 9:15–1952), Naylor was one of those rare people who had always wanted to be an astrologer. His career in astrology began in 1910 after his father gave up trying to persuade Naylor to enter the family business. His acrimonious divorce hit the newspapers in 1933. Naylor was at that time living with Phyllis 'Naylor'. The judge found the description of his profession 'absurd'.

of websites based on Sun signs and thousands of sun sign books published each year. It's hard not to be aware of horoscopes.

And every single one of these is based on Alan's interpretations, Alan's methods and Alan's astrology.

Finally, on 16 November 1989 the Law Commission repealed the Vagrancy Act without replacement. Over time it had become so ineffective and impotent that few people noticed its passing. It was only in 1991 that the astrological community realised its removal.[v]

Alan and Bessie Leo were modern astrologers.

---

[v] On 26 May 2008 the Fraudulent Mediums Act of 1951 (it replaced the Witchcraft Act, under which some astrologers were prosecuted in the past) was repealed by the Consumer Protection from Unfair Trading Regulations and the Unfair Commercial Practices Directive of 1 April 2008. Numerous laws and restrictions exist against the practice of astrology in the USA. In Australia it is a minor misdemeanour in some states, but the law is ignored.In 2011 India's Bombay High Court ruled that astrology was a science.

A CHART BY ALAN

The text below has been transcribed from a handwritten manuscript prepared in 1901. The only amendments made are the addition of full stops to the text where they were obviously intended.

The horoscope was prepared for Daniel McCarthy, born in Garraunawarrig, Upper Townland, Cork who moved to Minneapolis in 1893. At some point he was naturalised. He moved to Oakland, California before 1920 where he worked as a maths teacher. He married Gertrude (maiden name unknown) in about 1917—making Alan's prediction below completely wrong. He had three children and died on 30 May 1974.

PREFACE

There is a law that forms all things and the workings of that law may be seen by the revolutions of the heavenly bodies around the sun which is the centre of our solar system, known to all men by the name of Astrology, but this Astro Logos which means the wisdom of the stars has been buried beneath the materialism of ages.

Far back in our evolution the wise men in the east saw that star which is illuminating the whole world. That star which governs or which corresponds to the human soul shines brightest highest in the heavens of all the stars, and to those who can appreciate its sphere of influence there is wisdom and love contained in the thought that a wise hand governs the whole of our destiny.

It is the mission of the true Astrologer to explain those spheres of influences which distribute from the common centre the various principles to all humanity. In the following pages an attempt is made to the law under which every human being must sooner or later learn to obey. Our judgement is based upon the firm belief that as we sow we must also reap for the great teacher has said:

"Be not deceived God is not invoked whatever a man soweth that shall he reap."

Obedience to the law means a willing co-operation with the divine ruler in carrying out his will. He maintains that Astrology, while appearing to teach fatalism, directly proves that every one possesses a free will of their own, and that will being a fragment of Gods will either co-operates with the Lord or serves itself. Thus we postulate what may be called a theory until its truth is finally realized that the sun as verified messenger

The nativity by Alan Leo P.A.S Astrologer, London, Eng.

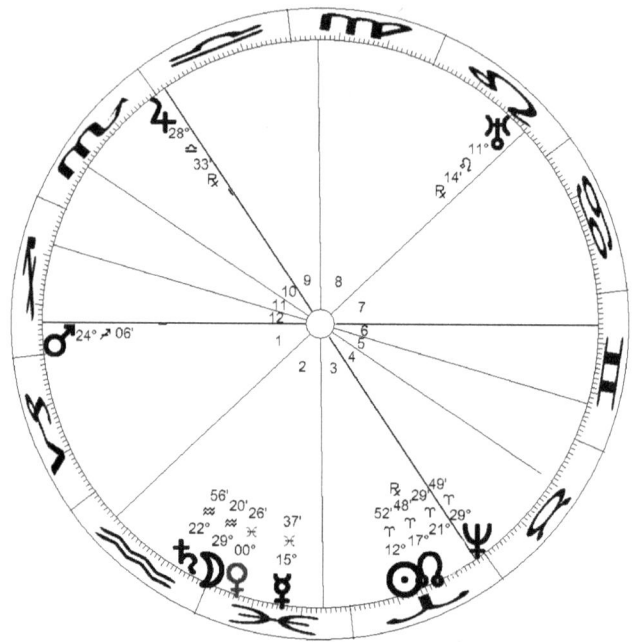

The nativity of Daniel T. McCarthy, Los Angeles, Cal, U.S.A.

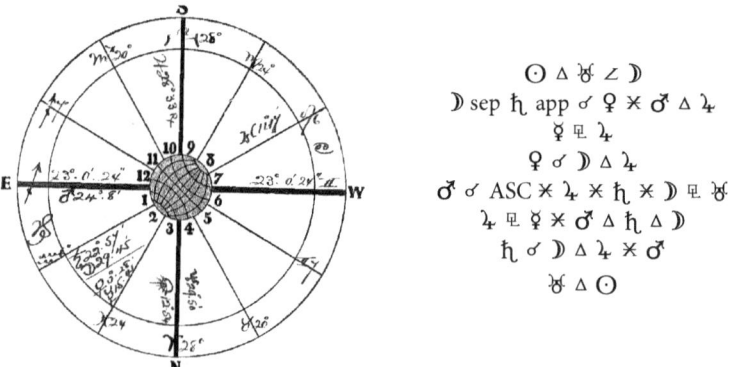

☉ △ ♅ ∠ ☽
☽ sep ♄ app ☌ ♀ ✶ ♂ △ ♃
☿ ⊡ ♃
♀ ☌ ☽ △ ♃
♂ ☌ ASC ✶ ♃ ✶ ♄ ✶ ☽ ⊡ ♅
♃ ⊡ ☿ ✶ ♂ △ ♄ △ ☽
♄ ☌ ☽ △ ♃ ✶ ♂
♅ △ ☉

D. T. McCarthy, Birth data rectified 1 am, April 3rd, 1875.
Lat 52 °. 13 N Long 8 °. 59' W Ref. No. 5046 R.A.M.C. 206 °
3 fixed; 3 common; 3 cardinal 4 fire; 3 air; – earth; 2 water

Modern Astrology, 9 Lyncroft Gardens, West Hampstead, N. W.

and the attendant beautiful star Venus are in harmony with our higher nature and that our lower or material and objective so called physical nature formed by the Moon Mars and Saturn, but paused between these two great polar opposite is the planet Jupiter as intermediary, the Jehovah of old, the God-like influence that walks amid men.

Studying as we do the Esoteric side of this divine science we will try to paint and that between the individuality and the personality there is often a wide gap. In the former we have reality coming under the solar influence. In the latter, unreality under the way of the ephermeral Moon ever changing its conditions. Every attempt will be made in the following papers to help you to understand and fully grasp the valuable import of the delphic oracle.

"Know Thyself."

INTRODUCTION

Starting from the 1.25 theory, I have very carefully rectified your horoscope and I make the time to be 1 am on the date given.

At this time the celestial sign Sagittarius at the 23rd degree with Mars in the 24th degree of the same sign was rising upon the ascendant.

Jupiter the ruling planet of the horoscope was elevated over all the planets in the meridian and well aspected.

CHARACTER

Although the ruling planet is the benefic Jupiter, placed in the sign Libra above all the other planets, the opposition of Mars and Saturn using both malefics will have to be contended against and all their claims satisfied before the Jupiterian influence can assert itself.

The period of Mars upon the ascendant extends over the first 19 years of life and then comes Saturn whose period endures for 30 years longer, making in all a period of 49 years before you can free yourself from the Karmic debts which you yourself have sought to bring down but at about your 45 year, the chain will begin to loosen and then you may come more directly under your ruling planet, which however will more or less affect your life when it has the opportunity.

I judge from these factors that in the early part of your life while but a lad you were very consequential and was more inclined to over cultivate your abilities that underrate them.

This however would wear off as you passed out of the period of Mars and came more under the Saturnine qualities, which influence is now operating upon your life bringing you into a more steady and contemplative mood. These two malefics rising make you a very difficult character for the majority of persons to understand, as you are capable of being either hot or cold as the whim suits you.

You have a very complex character and behind a some what erratic exterior there is a great deal of fire energy and spirit.

At times you are impulsive rebellious and prone to be headstrong breaking down all barriers, at others you are the reverse being inclined to take on a gloomy view of things tending to be more melancholic or misanthropic than is good for you which is really the result of re-action.

Individually you are original loving all that is free and impressive [?] but there are still some fetters around you that bind you to circumstance and environment.

You can be liberal free and serious although you have at the same time very strong selfish instinct which fires your acquisitiveness and makes you anxious to acquire.

Internally you are often very excited, when exteriorly you to be calm and collected.

You love justice and equality but might be inclined to take extreme measures to bring about your own ideas.

Your horoscope predicates that you are far too idealistic in character and you are also mentally conventional but certainly not practical enough.

You live too much in the outside of yourself and it seems with the ruling planet in Libra that the aim of this life should be to balance or equalize your conditions.

Your character is certainly a unique one and you are capable of making very great attainments but it would be well for you to put into practise some of these very lofty ideals which you undoubtedly possess, and it is possible for you while passing through the Saturnine period, to realize it by contemplation and meditation how you may bring down the ideal world into the practical, you should not deceive yourself by thinking that you really desire to be very practical as this is not really the case as you are full of ideas which you may expect others to live.

You are straightforward frank and outspoken a lover of health and a beauty worshipper and you also have sufficient determination common sense and ambition to cause you to put into practise that which it is very necessary you should do, And as a summary of your character should ask you to ponder over the following words, Occultism is the most practical thing in the world.

MENTAL QUALIFICATIONS

You have a receptive mind and good mental abilities but your brain mind which is totally different to the real mind has still many limitations around it and here again I am afraid I must lay stress upon the fact that you are not yourself sufficiently mentally practical.

In this you have somewhat of the artistic temperament, and you stand midway between art and science.

You are a good judge of human nature, and would make an expert character reader.

It is more easy for you to sense the character of strangers than those who are your real friends, but your mind is however an adaptable one, thus you are able to adapt yourself to the experiences of the moment.

There is just a tendency that you may do acts; that you afterwards mentally regret but as your Moon has many more good aspects than evil, it is quite evident you will emerge on the safe side of reason after being forced to cultivate the reflective and introspective nature.

In reality you have a very fine mind capable of the deepest understanding and decidedly occult, in all its tendencies.

Your mind will yet lead you into the realms of the very deepest thought, and as the Moon applies to the benefics and has separated from the malefic influences you are thus leaving behind you the purely personal or seeking to live the higher individualized life.

HEALTH

You have really a strong constitution and much vitality, and you will develop finally with the muscular native temperament.

The mental vital was in excess at birth, this has passed with the mental and should you attain the correct temperament for you so that you may have a healthy mind in a healthy body you must reach the temperament that is marked for you as the summit, which is muscular native. The sooner you can develop this the better for you in every way.

It is practically your own fault if you suffer in health and you may trace it to your own actions as there is some slight element of carelessness with regard to physical conditions.

There is some danger of accidents and at the close of your life it is very probably that the terminus vitae will be either directly or indirectly the result of an accident.

You are a man who would suffer much if ever you gave way to worry, as this would react upon your lungs and nervous system.

Your life will be in jeopardy and danger in the 40th year of life. This is your most critical period in life.

FINANCE

A superficial glance at your nativity would lead one to suppose that it promised wealth, but I am inclined to judge from Saturn's position in the second house that you could only acquire wealth by labor and industry; and at certain periods of your life you will have to work hard if you wish to attain a substantial income.

Your nativity also promises some gain by will or legacy, but on the whole you appear to make more money for others than self.

You would benefit your employers but I judge that it would be best for you to be in business for yourself.

You are able to spend money as fast as you earn it, and at certain periods of the life will be inclined to spend money freely on pleasure; and also personal adornment.

The opposite sex may also be a drain upon your purse but this more from an artistic and sensuous point of being most sensual.

Flirtations and romantic attachments might prove very extravagant luxuries but on the whole your financial affairs will be satisfactory.

MARRIAGE

Your horoscope is against marriage and the only serious attempt at it will come two years hence.

You will do well to give this matter serious thought, there being a certain duality in connection with your marriage which may fall out in your either courting two sisters or being engaged and then finding later some one you would prefer more.

The real time for marriage in your case is about your 28th year but you will do well to either calculate your own directions or have them cast for you so that the best time may be chosen should you marry.

There is no sign of happiness in connection with your union and I see tragedy [illegible] out of it. All flirting tendencies should be guarded.

PROFFESSION (sic)

You would have made your mark in life as an actor but the proffessions you are best adapted for is that of Estate Agent auctioneer and valuer Land Surveyor Builder or Contractor Architect also as a commercial traveller.

Electrician or Gas Engineer.

SUMMARY

You have truly a remarkable horoscope and if you can carry the cross which in all probability you have you have placed upon your self – you will succeed in accomplishing this life what many would require 7 lives to perform.

If I may speak plainly to you for your own good I would advise you to be scrupulously careful with regard to speech.

You are apt at times to say more than you actually know, this will retard your progress and cause complications to arise, which will affect you in the unseen worlds

There is a very powerful text in the ~~Voice of the Silence~~ *Light on the Path* which says "Before the voice can speak in the presence of the Masters it must have lost the power to wound." This should be your motto through life, for you need to take the sting out of some of your speech before you can impress those with whom you come into contact and give them the value of some of the depths of your nature.

You will realize this life much through the pairs of opposites.

By your physical conditions it is essential that you make practical that which is now only ideal.

Truth must be lived before it can be realized and the beauty of one's own soul must be realized before true beauty can be appreciated.

You do not know the value of your own capabilities.

On the surface and externally you can display the best side of your nature, and are well able to conceal all that is undesirable and when you dip into yourself in an introspective manner you will find much waiting for you that requires clearing out. There is much more in your mind and your mental attitude towards things than is apparent until you put them to the most severe practical tests.

It is said that those whom the gods love, they chasten. You appear to have been chastened by some difficulties and handicaps and you have many more yet to undergo.

It is not wise to seek to avert them, but amidst it all, lose everything before you lose the determined spirit.

The basic quality of your natus is Intuition and reason.

Trust your own instincts and give your own soul a chance to whisper its commands to you – don't let your brain be too active. ☉ in Aries people—all—are too alert and are mentally too active. Stop thinking for a few minutes each day or wait and listen. You have 4 planets in fire signs therefore are devotional privately.

If you have not already studied the "Wisdom religion" for you it will indeed be light in darkness as it explains the why we are here and what we are here for!

The purpose of life and manifestation is the causes of the inequality of the human race. It sets forth the truth and only by the truth can any of us be set free.

Yours truly,
Alan Leo

PSEUDONYMS

Adhy-apaka	Hiram Butler
A E	George W Russell
Agorel	Alan Leo
Alcyone	Jiddu Krishnamurti
Amherst	Henry Steel Olcott
Anael	John Rhodes
Anrias, David	Brian Ross
Aphorel	Frederick Lacey
Arokiel	John Yarker
Baretta (Professor)	Frederick Shipton (1860s-70s)
Barlet, F Charles	Albert Farcheux
Burgoyne, Thomas	Thomas Dalton
C A(quarius) Libra	Roelf Takens
Charubel	John Thomas
Cheiro/Count Louis Hamon	William John Warner
Christian, Paul	Jean-Baptiste Pitois
Cicero	George Shepherd (1860s-70s)
Daath, Heinrich	Henry (Harry) Durrant
Dubois, H	Frederick Herrick (1880s)
Flambart, Paul	Paul Choisnard
Helios	Martin Ringrose
Henderson, Joseph	Joseph Bailey (Liverpool, 1857)
H. S. G.	Henry Selby Green
Idris	Arthur Mee
Ireton, Rollo	Ralph Shirley
Kirk, Eleanor	Maria Easterbrook Ames
Kymry	Hamilton Minchin
Leo	Henry Selby Green
Lisle, Flambart	Albert Leister (1880s)
M A Oxon	Stainton Moses
Magus	Joseph Blackburn
Mars and the Goat	George Wilde
Mejnor	Peter Davidson
Mercury	James Richard Wallace

PSEUDONYMS

Merlin (of the *Referee*)	David Christie-Murray
Methratton	John Hartwell
Montague	William Osborn (1870s)
Morathiel	Francis George Irwin
Murray, Leslie	Bessie Leo
Naylor, R H	Richard Harold Thropp
Ne opp Me	Richard Henry Penny
Neptune	Richard Henry Penny
Papus	Gerard Encausse
Raphael	Ebenezer Webber (1839 Devon); Robert Charles Drummond (1840 Sheffield) [of almanacs] Robert Cross Smith; John Palmer; Dixon; Medhurst; Francis Wakely (first to use 'Edwin Raphael'); R V Sparkes; Robert Thomas Cross
Regulus	Frederick Vaughan
Ross, Anna (Seeress of New York)	John Hartwell
Sarastro	J B Shipley
Scott, Professor	John Dean Broadwood (1890s Wales)
Sepharial	Walter Richard Old (later Gorn Old/Gornold)
Stanley, Wilfred	E H Bailey
Star, Ely	Eugene Jacob
Stella, R H	Thomas Dalton
Thalaby, Professor	William Henry (1871 Manchester)
Theon, Max	Maximilian Louis Bimstein
Trent, A G	Richard Garnett
Viola	Bessie Leo
Wemyss, Maurice	Duncan McNaughton
Young Moore	Charles Moore
Zadkiel	Richard James Morrison; R V Sparkes; Alfred John Pearce
Zain, C C	Elbert Benjamine
Zanoni	David Lund; Thomas Dalton
Zariel	David Cope
Zendavesta (Professor)	John Dean Bryant (1870s)
Zephon, Alec	E H Bailey

ALAN'S FAMILY TREE

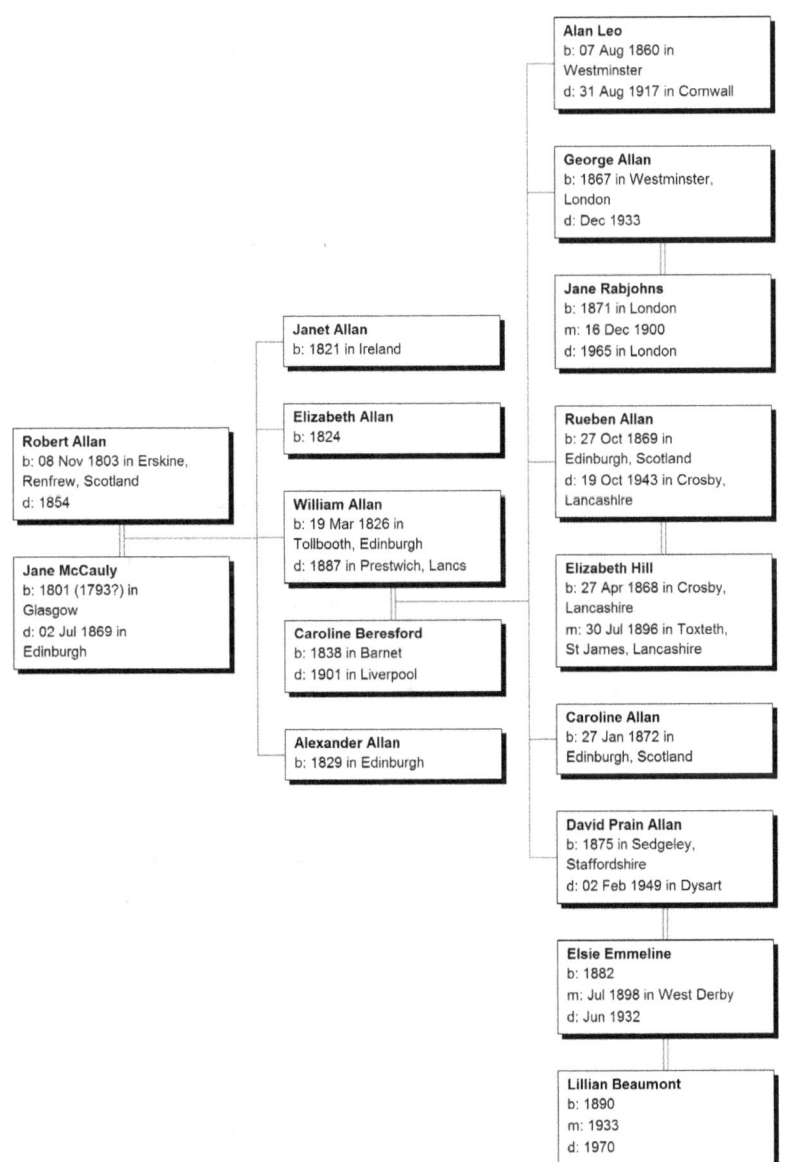

ALAN'S FAMILY TREE

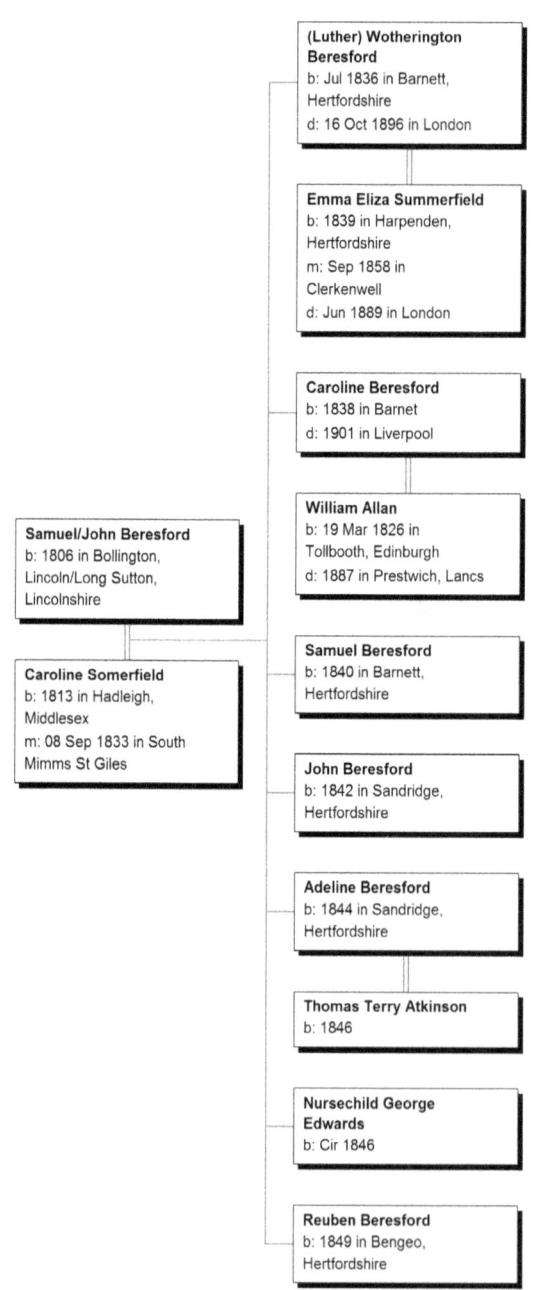

BESSIE'S FAMILY TREE

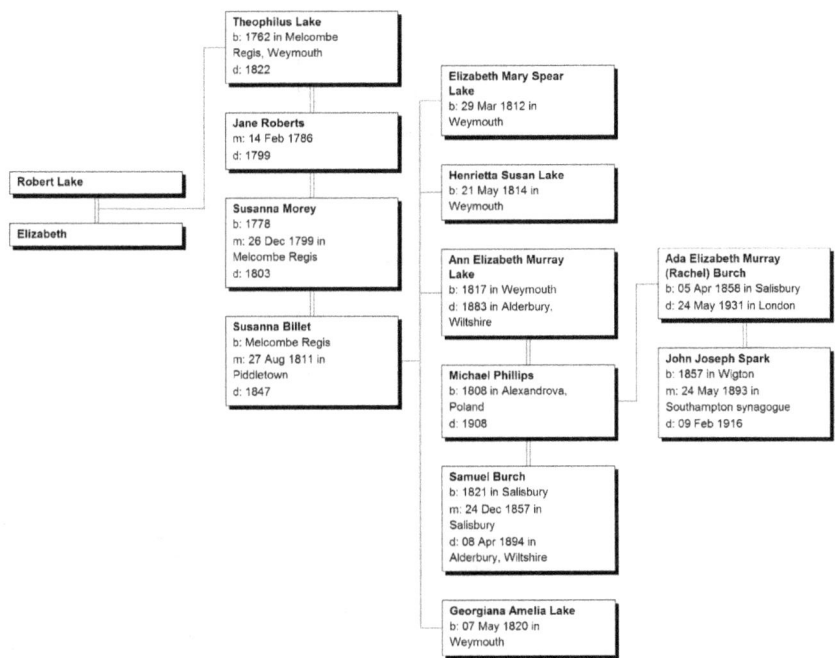

BESSIE'S FAMILY TREE

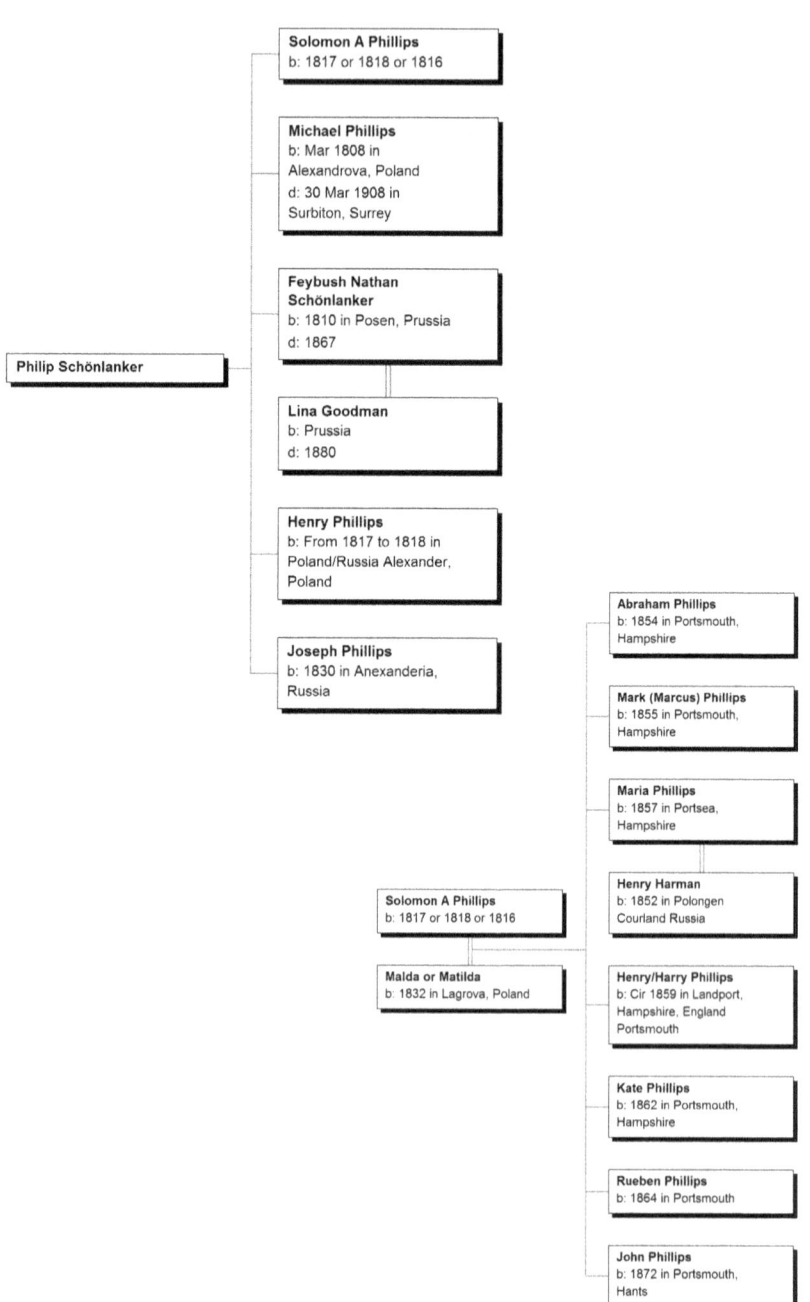

BESSIE'S FAMILY TREE

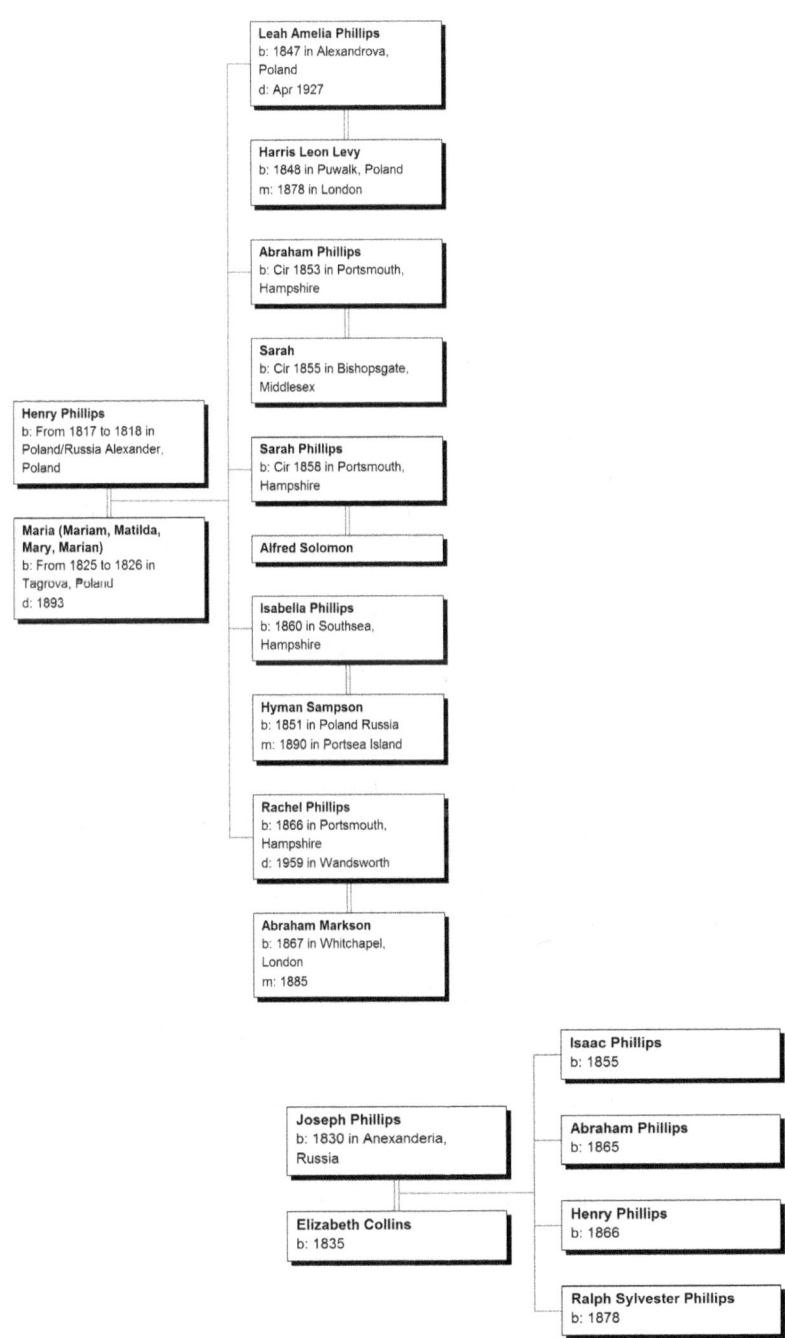

WORKS OF ALAN LEO

Alan Leo's Dictionary of Astrology. Edited by Vivian E. Robson. London: Modern Astrology, 1924.
Art of Synthesis (third edition of *How to Judge a Nativity* part 2), London: Modern Astrology, 1912.
The Astrologer and his Work. With some remarkable short stories. London: L N Fowler and Co, 1911.
Astrologers' Annual for 1906. Christmas number of Modern Astrology. London: Modern Astrology, 1905.
Astrology Explained. London: L N Fowler and Co, 1911.
Astrology for All. London, 1899. (With H S Green).
Casting the Horoscope. London: L N Fowler, 1901.
Complete Dictionary of Astrology. London: 1905.
Esoteric Astrology: a study of human nature. London: Modern Astrology, 1913.
Everybody's Astrology. London: L N Fowler and Co, 1901 (second edition).
Four Lectures on Astrology, Exoteric and Esoteric. London: 1901.
The Horoscope and How to Read it. London: L.N. Fowler and Co, 1902. (Second edition and later entitled What is a Horoscope and How is it Cast?)
Horary Astrology. London: Modern Astrology, 1907.
The Horoscope in Detail. London: Modern Astrology, 1904 (with H S Green).
How to Judge a Nativity. London: Modern Astrology, 1903.
How to Study Astrology. London: Modern Astrology, 1903.
Jupiter: the Preserver. London: Modern Astrology, 1917. (His last book.)
Key to Your Own Nativity. London: Modern Astrology, 1910.
Mars: the War Lord. London: Modern Astrology, 1915.
My Friends' Horoscopes. London: Modern Astrology, 1910.
Practical Astrology. London: Modern Astrology, 1897.
The Progressed Horoscope. London: L N Fowler and Modern Astrology, 1906.
Saturn: the Reaper. London: Modern Astrology Office, 1916.
The Stars and How to Read Them. London: Modern Astrology [n.d.]
Symbolism and Astrology. London: L N Fowler and Co, 1914.
What is a Horoscope and How is it Cast? London: Modern Astrology, 1905.
When the War Will End. London: Newspaper Publicity Co., 1915.
The Work of the Hermes Lodge. London: Modern Astrology, 1906?

Modern Astrology manuals not written by Alan

Alfred Barley, *A Thousand and One Notable Nativities*, London: Modern Astrology, 1911.
—*What do we Mean by Astrology?* London: Modern Astrology, 1910. (Originally *Rationale of Astrology*.)
—*Rationale of Astrology* with an additional chapter by Alan Leo on the Education of Children in the light of Astrology, London: Fowler and Co, 1905.
Charubel, *The Degrees of the Zodiac Symbolised* (to which is added a translation by Sepharial of a similar series found in *La Volsafer*a), London: Modern Astrology, 1898.
—*The Degrees of the Zodiac Symbolised* (to which is added *The Theoretical Value of the Degrees of the Zodiac* by H S Green), London: Modern Astrology, 1898.
Heinrich Däath, *The Art and Practice of Directing*, London: Modern Astrology, 1906.
—*Medical Astrology*, London: Modern Astrology, 1907.
H S Green, *Directions and Directing*, London: Modern Astrology, 1905.
—*The Reason Why in Astrology*, London: Modern Astrology, 1910.
—*Mundane Astrology*, London: Modern Astrology, 1911.
—*Theoretical Astrology*, London: Fowler, 1903.
—*Weather Predicting by Astro-Meteorology*, London: Modern Astrology, 1912.
Bessie Leo, *Planetary Influences*, London: Modern Astrology, 1906.
—*Rays of Truth*, London: Modern Astrology, 1904.
—*The Romance of the Stars*, London: Modern Astrology, 1914.
Zariel, *The Horoscope Revised* and Sepharial, *Prognostications Based upon the Ruling Sign* combined edition, London: Law and General Printing Co, 1895.

Articles in theosophical publications

'Astrology in the Light of Theosophy (1)', *The Theosophist*, April 1911, p. 82.
'Astrology in the Light of Theosophy (2)', *The Theosophist*, May 1911, p. 258.
'Soul of Astronomy', *The Theosophist*, May 1910, p. 1010.
'Individuality and the Horoscope', *The Theosophist*, December 1912, p. 402.
'Modern Astrology', *Transactions Annual Congresses of the Federation of European Sections Theosophical Society 1904-1923*, July 1905, p. 313.
'Past Karma in a Present Horoscope', *The Theosophist*, December 1917, p. 321.
'The Purification of Astrology', *Lucifer*, April 1894, p. 163.
'Soul of Astronomy', *The Theosophist*, May 1910, p. 1010.
'Symbology of Astrology', *The Theosophist*, June 1897, p. 557.
'Symbology of Astrology (2)', *The Theosophist*, September 1897, p. 726.
'Wisdom of the Stars', *American Theosophist*, September 1913, p. 961.

IMAGES

Adyar, 205
Astrologers' Magazine, 58
E H Bailey, 119
Alfred Barley, 159
Annie Besant, 132
Annie Besant and Alan's car, 189
Annie Besant and Krishnamurti, 211
Annie Besant and CW Leadbeater, 181
Chart by Alan, 250
Devil's Acre by Gustav Doré, 4
H S Green, 10
Florence Higgs, 117
Curuppumullage Jinarajadasa, 166
Robert King, 85
Jiddu Krishnamurti, 169
Frederick Lacey 10
C W Leadbeater, 135
Alan Leo 10, 57, 203, 222, 232
Bessie Leo, 16, 72, 90, 152
Alan and Bessie Leo in Cannes, 226
Modern Astrology, 98, 196
Walter Old, 10, 38
R H Penny 10
Michael Phillips, 22
Phrenology head, 26
May Robbins, 223
John Sidley, 95
A P Sinnett, 35
John Joseph Spark, 52
Rudolf Steiner, 40
John Thomas, 29
John Thompson, 47

ENDNOTES

CHAPTER 1

1 Leo, *Life and Work*, p. 20.
2 Ibid.
3 Ibid.
4 Ibid.
5 Leo, *Esoteric Astrology*, p. 208.
6 *Nottingham Evening Post*, 19 April 1892, p. 4.
7 Letter in the *Astrologer*, 1890.
8 Dickens, *Household Words*, 22 June 1850.
9 Jackson, 'The Rookeries of London, by Thomas Beames, 1852.'
10 Leo, *Life and Work*, p. 14.
11 Ibid.
12 Leo, *Life and Work*, p. 15.
13 Ibid.
14 *Astrologers' Magazine*, October 1894, p. 61.
15 Ibid, September 1894, p. 36.
16 Ibid, November 1894, p. 80.
17 Leo, *Life and Work*, p. 25.
18 *Pall Mall Gazette*, 30 June 1886, p. 2.
19 *Pall Mall Gazette*, 15 July 1887, p. 6.
20 *Horoscope*, 1902.
21 *Astrologers' Magazine*, November 1894, p. 110.
22 Old, 'Unremembered Self.'
23 Leo, *Life and Work*, p. 42.
24 *Manchester Courier and Lancashire General Advertiser*, 13 January 1888, p. 3.
25 *Marchylebone Mercury*, 24 June 1871, p. 2.
26 *Astrologers' Magazine*, September 1893, p.36.
27 'Alan Leo', Audactor.

CHAPTER 2

1 Leo, *Esoteric Astrology*, p. 214.
2 Ibid, p. 215.
3 Leo, *Esoteric Astrology*, p. 213.
4 Ibid.
5 Ibid, p. 214.
6 Ibid.
7 Leo, *Esoteric Astrology*, p. 215.
8 *Modern Astrology*, May 1901, p. 183.
9 Ackerman, 'Microcosm of London.'
10 *Globe*, 10 June 1837, p.1.
11 *Salisbury and Winchester Journal*, 3 September 1838, p. 1
12 *Salisbury and Winchester Journal*, 7 December 1835, p. 4.
13 *Salisbury and Winchester Journal*, 28 February 1857, p. 3.

ENDNOTES

14 *Wiltshire Independent*, 30 October 1845, p. 3.
15 *Salisbury and Winchester Journal*, 2 May 1857, p. 3.
16 Ibid.
17 *Salisbury and Winchester Journal*, 20 July 1861, p. 6.
18 *Salisbury and Winchester Journal*, 27 December 1852, p. 3.
19 Leo, *Esoteric Astrology*, p. 208.
20 Ibid.

CHAPTER 3

1 Gilbert, 'Disappointed Magus.'
2 Leo, *Life and Work*, p. 37.
3 *Occultist*, July 1886, p. 1.
4 Ibid.
5 *Leeds Mercury*, 10 January 1883, p. 7.
6 Gilbert, 'The Disappointed Magus.'
7 Ibid.
8 Ibid.
9 Ibid.
10 Ibid.
11 Ibid
12 Leo, *Life and Work*, p. 94.
13 Gilbert, 'Disappointed Magus.'
14 Ibid.
15 Howe, *Alchemist of the Golden Dawn*, p. 13.
16 Old, *Memory of Helena Petrovna Blavatsky*, p. 38.
17 Ibid.
18 Besant, *Autobiography*, p. 342.
19 Ibid.
20 Leo, *Life and Work*, p. 40.
21 Ibid.
22 Collins, *Mahatma*, p. 136.
23 Howe, *Alchemist of the Golden Dawn*, p. 59.
24 Leo, *Life and Work*, p. 97.

CHAPTER 4

1 Leo, *Esoteric Astrology*, p. 215.
2 *Star*, 6 September 1888.
3 Whye, 'History of Phrenology.'
4 Thompson, Phrenology and its uses, p. 10.
5 Eschener, 'Infamous 19th-Century Birth Control Pamphlet.'
6 Thompson, *Man and his Sexual Relations*, p. 119.
7 Thompson, *Phrenology and its Uses*, p. 57.
8 Thompson, *Man and his Sexual Relations*, p. 129.
9 Blavatsky, 'Theosophy and Sex Problems.'
10 Blavatsky, *Theosophist*, February 1881, p. 103.
11 Niemand, *Letters That Have Helped Me*, p. 174.
12 Leo, *Esoteric Astrology*, p. 216.

ENDNOTES

13 *London Standard*, 30 June 1909, p. 9
14 Leo, *Esoteric Astrology*, p. 218.
15 Olcott, *Old Diary Leaves*, p. 363.
16 Leo, *Esoteric Astrology*, p. 216.
17 *Hampshire Advertiser*, 27 May 1891, p. 4.
18 Leo, *Esoteric Astrology*, p. 218.
19 *Pontypridd Chronicle*, 4 April 1890, ad.
20 *Pontypridd Chronicle and Workman's News*, 4 April 1890, letter.
21 Spark, *Confessions of a Phrenologist*, p. 1.
22 Wells, *Vital Force*, p. 22.
23 Ibid, p.28.
24 Burch and Spark, *Marchriage a Success*, p. 2.
25 Leo, *Esoteric Astrology*, p. 222.
26 Ibid.
27 Ibid.
28 Ibid.
29 *Portsmouth Evening News*, 25 June 1909, p. 3.
30 *Daily Telegraph and Courier*, 25 June 1909, p. 14.

CHAPTER 5

1 Leo, *Life and Work*, p.28.
2 Ibid, p.29.
3 Ibid.
4 Ibid, p.30.
5 Ibid, p.32.
6 *Fate and Fortune*, July 1890.
7 Leo, *Life and Work*, p. 32.
8 Ibid.
9 *Daily News*, 28 Aug 1890, p.4.
10 *Astrologers' Magazine*, October 1890.
11 *Fate and Fortune*, October 1890.
12 *Yorkshire Evening Post*, 24 July 1893, p. 3.
13 Leo, *Life and Work*, p. 143.
14 *Astrologers' Magazine*, November 1893, p. 82.
15 Leo, *Life and Work*, p. 123.
16 Ibid, p. 44.
17 Ibid, p. 49.
18 Ibid, p. 51.
19 *Astrologers' Magazine*, December 1893, p. 98.
20 *Modern Astrology*, Aug 1895.
21 Leo, *Life and Work*, p.134.
22 Ibid, p. 136.
23 Carter, 'Reminisences.'

ENDNOTES

CHAPTER 6

1 Leo, *Esoteric Astrology*, p. 219.
2 Ibid, p. 220.
3 Ibid, p. 219.
4 Ibid.
5 Ibid.
6 *North Devon Gazette,* 19 May 1891, p. 7.
7 *West Somerset Free Press,* 16 May 1891, p. 6.
8 *Western Times,* 20 May 1891, p. 4.
9 Leo, *Esoteric Astrology,* p. 221.
10 Leo, *Life and Work,* p. 68.
11 Ibid, p. 58.
12 Leo, *Art of Synthesis,* p. 233.
13 Leo, Alan, *Life and Work,* p. 58.
14 Ibid. p. 59.
15 Ibid, p. 60.
16 Ibid.
17 Ibid, p. 61.
18 Ibid.p. 62.
19 Ibid.
20 Ibid, p.65.
21 Leo, *Astrologer and His Work,* p. 2.
22 *Astrologers' Magazine,* January 1895, p. 123.
23 Leo, *Astrologer and His Work,* p. 42.
24 *Astrologers' Magazine,* Aug 1894, p. 10
25 Burch and Spark, *Marchriage a Success.* p. 2.
26 *Southern Echo,* 24 May 1893, p. 3.
27 'View from the Hill.'
28 Leo, *Astrologer and His Work,* p. 36.
29 Ibid.
30 Leo, *Life and Work,* p. 63.
31 Ibid.
32 Leo, *Astrologer and His Work,* p. 37.
33 *Astrologers' Magazine,* January 1895, p. 1.
34 *Astrologers' Magazine,* May 1895, p. 217.
35 *Popular Phenologist,* March 1896, p. 46.
36 *Astrologers' Magazine,* September 1893, p. 36.
37 Leo, *Life and Work,* p. 65.
38 Ibid.
39 Ibid.
40 Ibid, p. 67.
41 *Evening Journal* (Adelaide), 7 Aug 1909, p. 6.
42 Leo, *Life and Work,* p. 66.

ENDNOTES

CHAPTER 7

1 *Astrologers' Magazine*, November 1894, p. 80.
2 Leo, *Life and Work*, p. 44.
3 Leo, *Astrologer and his Work*, p. 28.
4 Ibid.
5 *Modern Astrology*, November 1916.
6 Leo, *Astrologer and his Work*, p. 29.
7 Leo, *Life and Work*, p. 44.
8 *Astrologers' Magazine*, December 1900, p. 112.
9 *Modern Astrology*, letters, March 1895.
10 *Modern Astrology*, letters, April 1895.
11 Ibid.
12 *Modern Astrology*, letters, May 1895.
13 *Modern Astrology*, October 1896, p. 136.
14 *Geelong Advertiser* (Victoria), 21 April 1897, p. 4.
15 Ibid.
16 *Edinburgh Evening News*, 8 February 1897, p. 2.
17 Ibid.
18 *Pall Mall Gazette*, 24 Aug 1897, p. 4.
19 *Bedfordshire Times and Independent*, 13 February 1897, p.2.
20 *Modern Astrology* Astrology, March 1897, p. 39.
21 *Journal of the Astrological Society*, March 1898
22 *Hampstead and Highate Express*, 25 September 1897, p. 6.
23 *Daily Telegraph and Courier*, 17 Aprilil 1897, p. 5.

CHAPTER 8

1 *Vegetarian*, report 2
2 Ibid.
3 Ibid.
4 *Vegetarian*, report 4
5 *Vegetarian*, report 5
6 Preece, *Sins of the Flesh*, p. 274
7 Quoted in Calvert, 'Eden's Diet,' p. 38.
8 Maitland, *Story of Anna Kingsford and Edward Maitland*, p. 29.
9 Kingsford, *Dreams and Dream Stories*, Preface.
10 *Women's Signal*, 21 November 1895, quoted in Delap.
11 *Theosophist*, December 1897, p. 90.
12 *Thanet Advertiser*, 24 September 1898, p. 6.

CHAPTER 9

1 *Shields Daily Gazette*, 18 January 1897, p. 3.
2 Leo, *Astrologer and His Work*, p. 29.
3 *Aberdeen Evening Express*, 8 July 1891, p. 2.
4 *Illustrated London News*, 9 July 1892, p. 2.
5 *Wells Journal*, 20 April 1893, p. 3.
6 *Lancashire Evening Post*, 5 April 1893, p. 2.
7 *Banbury Advertiser*, 25 July 1895, p. 2.

ENDNOTES

8 *Journal of the Astrological Society*, March 1898.
9 *Cornubian and Redruth Times*, 24 June 1898, p. 4.
10 *Yorkshire Evening Post*, 28 December 1898, p. 2.
11 *Sunday Times* (Sydney), 12 March 1899, p. 10.
12 *Nottingham Evening Post*, 26 October 1899, p. 2.
13 Curry, *Confusion of Prophets*, p. 127.
14 *Globe*, 20 March 1845, p. 4.
15 *Leeds Times*, 29 September 1888, p. 5.
16 Davies, Witchcraft, *Magic and Culture*, p. 66.
17 Ibid.
18 *Light*, 20 May 1899, p, 230.
19 *Coming Events,* March 1900.
20 *Light*, 2 Februaryruary 1901, p. 56.
21 Davies, *Witchcraft, Magic and Culture*, p. 67.
22 *West Gippsland Gazette*, Victoria, 6 September 1904, p. 4.
23 *Astrology Quarterly*, Vol 18, No 3, 1944, p. 1.

CHAPTER 10

1 *Modern Astrology,* July 1928
2 Ibid.
3 Leo, *Life and Work*, p. 131.
4 Ibid, p. 162.
5 *Astrology Quarterly*, Vol 64, No 3, 1938, p. 124.
6 *Modern Astrology*, May 1903, p. 166.
7 Leo, *Astrologer and His Work*, p. 8.
8 *Pall Mall Gazette*, 16 Jan, 1883, p. 11.
9 Ibid.
10 *Evening News*, Portsmouth, 31 January 1883, p. 3.
11 Leo, *Astrologer and His Work*, p. 30.
12 *Astrologers' Magazine*, November 1893, p. 1.
13 *Modern Astrology*, June 1904 and *Astrology Quarterly*, Vol 65, No 4, 1935, p. 122.
14 Bailey, *Destiny*, Vol 1, No. 1, p. 14.
15 Ibid.
16 Ibid, p. 15.
17 Ibid, p. 16.
18 Ibid.
19 Leo, *Life and Work*, p. 99.
20 Ibid, p. 141.
21 Ibid, p. 72.
22 Bailey, *Destiny*, Volume 1, No. 3, p. 75.
23 Ibid, Volume 2, No 1, p. 135.
24 Ibid.
25 Ibid.
26 Bailey, *Destiny*, Volume 1, No. 1, p. 18.
27 Ibid, p. 20.
28 Bolton, 'Relic of Astrology.'
29 Bailey, *Destiny*, 1904, p. 20.

ENDNOTES

30 Ibid, 1905, p. 62.
31 Ibid, p. 157.
32 *British Journal of Astrology*, May 1925.
33 Leo, *Life and Work*, p. 116.
34 Ibid, p. 139.
35 *Modern Astrology*, May 1928.
36 Ibid, December 1904.

CHAPTER 11

1 *Modern Astrology*, December 1901.
1 Leo, *Life and Work*, p. 190.
2 *Daily Mail*, 3 June 1909, p. 6.
3 *Evening Journal* (Adelaide), 7 Aug 1909, p. 6.
4 *Southern Echo*, 24 June 1909, p. 3..
5 *London Evening News*, 29 June 1909, p. 3.
6 Ibid.
7 *Salisbury and Winchester Journal*, 26 June 1909, p. 6.
8 *Southern Echo*, 24 June 1909, p. 3.
9 Ibid.
10 *Southern Echo*, 24 June 1909, p. 3.
11 *London Evening Standard*, 30 June 1909, p. 9.
12 *Star* (Sydney), 14 Aug 1909, p. 2.
13 *London Evening Standard*, 25 June 1909, p.12.
14 Will of Michael Phillips.

CHAPTER 12

1 Leo, *Life and Work*, p. 190.
2 *Modern Astrology*, April 1903, p. 149.
3 *Theosophist*, October 1922, p. 95.
4 Ibid.
5 Leo, *Life and Work*, p. 70.
6 *Theosophist*, October 1922, p. 95.
7 Jinarajadsa, *Occult Investigations*, p. 3.
8 Leadbeater, *Soul's Growth Through Reincarnation*, p. 19.
9 Besant and Leadbeater, *Man Hence How and Whither*, p. 192.
10 Ibid.
11 *Vahan*, Aug 1905, p. 1.
12 Ibid.
13 *Tenbury Wells Advertiser*, 29 Aug 1905, p. 8.
14 Villeneuve, *Rudolf Steiner in Britain*, p. 116.
15 Ibid, p. 120.
16 Ibid.
17 *Daily Telegraph and Courier*, 10 July 1905, p. 12.
18 Villeneuve, *Rudolf Steiner in Britain*, p. 122.
19 Ibid, p.121.
20 Ibid, p. 122.
21 Tillett, *Elder Brother*, p. 78.

ENDNOTES

22 Ibid, p. 79.
23 Ibid, p. 81.
24 Ibid, p. 82.
25 Ibid.
26 Tillett, 'the 1905 Scandal (ii).
27 Tillett, *Elder Brother*, p. 84.
28 Ibid, p. 86.
29 Ibid, p. 88.
30 Brooks, *Neo-theosophy Exposed*, p. 412.
31 Zeylmans, An Inspiration for Anthroposophy, p. 58.
32 Ibid.
33 Villeneuve, *Rudolf Steiner in Britain*, p. 126.
34 Nethercot, *Last Four Lives*, p. 99.
35 Tillett, *Elder Brother*, p. 98, note 14.
36 Ibid, p. 98, note 15.
37 Ibid.
38 Ibid, note 20.
39 Ibid, p. 99.

CHAPTER 13

1 *East London Observer*, 28 May 1927, p. 4.
2 Pilcher-Dayton, *Open Door*, p. 10.
3 Pilcher-Dayton, *Women's Agency*, p. 344.
4 Besant, *Theosophic Messenger*, Junee 1909, p. 377.
5 Pilcher-Dayton, *Women's Agency*, p. 345.
6 Ibid.
7 Ibid, p. 346.
8 Leadbeater, *Hidden Life in Freemasonry*, foreword.
9 Wilcox, 'Early History of Hermes Lodge.'
10 Ibid.
11 Pilcher-Dayton, *Women's Agency*, p. 383.
12 Ibid.
13 Minutes of the Hermes Lodge.
14 Pilcher-Dayton, *Women Freemasons*, p. 42.

CHAPTER 14

1 *Modern Astrology*, July 1909, p.7.
2 Leo, *Life and Work*, p.139.
3 Blavatsky, *Key to Theosophy*, p. 307.
4 Leo, *Esoteric Astrology*, p. 116.
5 *Modern Astrology*, March 1909.
6 Ibid, May 1907.
7 *Chronicle* (Adelaide), 2 March 1907, p. 2.
8 Jinarajadasa, *Occult Investigations*, https://www.minhtrietmoi.org/Theosophy/Jinaradasa/OCCULT%20INVESTIGATIONS.htm (accessed July 2018).
9 Jinarajadasa, *K H Letters to Leadbeater*, http://hpb.narod.ru/tph/CWL_KHLE.HTM (accessed July 2018).

ENDNOTES

10 Lutyens, *Awakening*, p. 12.
11 Lutyens, *A Life*, p. 30.
12 Tillett, *Elder Brother*, p. 103.
13 Will of Michael Phillips.
14 *London Evening Standard*, 24 June 1909, p. 5.
15 *Daily Telegraph and Courier*, 1 July 1909, p.4.
16 *Salisbury Times*, 25 June 1909, p. 4.
17 *London Evening Standard*, 24 June 1909, p. 5.
18 Ibid.
19 *Star* (Sydney), 14 Aug 1909, p. 2.
20 *London Evening Standard*, 1 July 1909, p. 11.
21 Ibid.
22 Ibid, 25 June 1909, p. 12.
23 Ibid.
24 Ibid.
25 Ibid.
26 Ibid.
27 Ibid.
28 *Salisbury Times*, 2 July 1909, p. 7.
29 *Evening Journal* (Adelaide), 7 Aug 1909, p. 6.
20 Ibid.
31 *Salisbury Times*, 2 July 1909, p. 7.
32 *Modern Astrology*, September 1909, p. 9.
33 *Evening Journal* (Adelaide), 7 Aug 1909, p. 6.
34 Ibid.
35 *Salisbury Times*, 2 July 1909, p. 7.
36 *Sheffield Evening Telegraph*, 30 June 1909, p. 3.
37 *Theosophist*, July 1909, p. 400.
38 Wood, *Is this Theosophy?* p. 110.
39 Prakasa, *Annie Besant*, p. 70.
40 *Theosophist*, Aug 1909, p. 536b.
41 *Theosophist*, September 1909, p.664.
42 *Theosophist*, October 1909, p. 1.
43 *Occult Review*, October 1909, p. 180.
44 Tillett, *Elder Brother*, p. 111.
45 Ibid, p. 112.
46 Wood, *Is This Theosophy?* p. 135.
47 Brooks, *Esoteric Bogeydom*, p. 283.
48 Besant and Leadbeater, *Man Whence and Whither*, p. 118.

CHAPTER 15
1 Wood, *Is this Theosophy?* p. 107.
2 *Theosophist*, Janu 1910, p. 480.
3 Lutyens, *J. Krishnamurti: A Life*, p. 35.
4 *Register* (Adelaide), 22 February 1911, p. 9.
5 Lutyens, *J. Krishnamurti: A Life*, p. 36.
6 *Theosophist*, July 1927, p. 470.
7 *Bath Chronicle and Weekly Gazette*, 2 June 1910.

ENDNOTES

8 *The Theosophist*, July 1927, p. 472.
9 Leo, *Esoteric Astrology*, preface.
10 *Supplement to The Theosophist*, 1910, p. cxxi.
11 *Astrologers' Magazine*, Aug 1893, p. 16.
12 *Lucifer*, April 1894, p. 164.
13 Bright, *Old Memories and Letters of Annie Besant*, p. 128.
14 Ibid.
15 *Theosophist*, February 1910, p. 554.
16 Nethercot, *Last Four Lives of Annie Besant*, p. 128.
17 Veritas, *Mrs. Besant and the Alcyone Case*, p. 105.
18 *Sphinx*, April 1901, p. 192.
19 *Los Angeles Herald*, 18 October 1909, p. 7.
20 *Theosophist*, March 1910, p. 681.
21 Editor of Justice, *Evolution of Mrs. Besant*, p. 316.
22 *Theosophist*, March 1910, p. 681.
23 *Theosophist*, May 1910, p. 964.
24 White, 'Mrs. Annie Besant vs G. Narayaniah on 29 Oct, 1913.'
25 Brooks, *Neo-Theosophy Exposed*, p. 182.
26 *Modern Astrology*, October 1910, p. 401.
27 Vreede, 'An Attack on Bishop Leadbeater.'

CHAPTER 16

1 Leo, *Life and Work*, p. 134.
2 Leo, *Life and Work*, p. 129.
3 Ibid, p.133.
4 *Hull Daily Mail*, 14 May 1910, p. 5.
5 Horoscope of May Robbins, private papers held by Lucya Szachnowski.
6 Leo, *Key to Your Own Nativity*, p. 285.
7 Ibid, p 287.
8 Leo, *Life and Work*, p. 72.
9 *In Search*, Vol.2, No.2, Spring 1959.
10 *Occult Review*, October 1917, p. 195.
11 Leo, *Key to Your Own Nativity*, p. 17.
12 Alan Leo's lessons. Section 5; series 9; lesson 1, 'Special Instructions in Esoteric Astrology.'
13 Ibid.
14 Leo, *Life and Work*, p. 163.
15 *Chronicle and Weekly Gazette*, 15 September 1910, p. 7.

ENDNOTES

CHAPTER 17

1 Leo, *Esoteric Astrology*, p.v.
2 Hermes Lodge minutes.
3 Summary of talk given by Alan 5 July 1911 on Astrology in India; Hermes Lodge minutes.
4 Raman, *Autobiography*, p. 61.
5 Ibid.
6 Cheiro, *Palmistry for All*, p. 121.
7 *Theosophist*, May 1911, p. 160.
8 Prakasa, *Annie Besant as Woman and Leader*, p. 176.
9 Williams, *Jiddu Jrishnamurti*, p. 42.
10 Prakasa, *Annie Besant as Woman and Leader*, p. 236.
11 Veritas, *Mrs Besant and the Alcyone Case*, p. 35.

CHAPTER 18

1 Gaebelein, *Current Events in the Light of the Bible*, p. 104.
2 Ibid.
3. *Sun* (New York), 24 September 1911, p. 3.
4 Whiting, *Lure of London*, p. 124.
5 *Dundee Courier*, 30 December 1911, p. 5.
6 Leo, *Horary Astrology*, foreword.
7 Hansard.
8 *Astrology Society, Esoteric or Exoteric*, p. 48.
9 *Bedfordshire Mercury*, 11 October 1912, p. 5.
10 *Astrology Society, Esoteric or Exoteric*, p. 58.
11 *Review of Reviews*, May 1911, p. 29.
12 Ibid.
13 *Equinox*, September 1913.

CHAPTER 19

1 Private correspondence from Lucya Szachnowski.
2 *Grenfell Record and Lachlan District Advertiser* (NSW), 11 February 1913, p. 5.
3 *Occult Review*, October 1917, p. 344.
4 Ibid.
5 Ibid, p.345.
6 Ibid.
7 *Modern Astrology*, November 1914, p. 157.
8 Ibid.
9 *Occult Review*, October 1912, p. 187.
10 *Modern Astrology*, November 1914, p. 301.
11 Ibid.
12 *Belfast Telegraph*, 20 May 1914, p. 4.
13 Ibid.
14 Ibid.
15 *Evening Despatch*, 20 Aug 1914, p. 2.
16 *Leeds Mercury*, 21 Aug 1914, p. 5.

CHAPTER 20

1 *Bruce Herald* (New Zealand), 6 May 1915, p. 1.
2 Minutes of the Astrological Lodge of London.
3 *Vahan*, September 1915, p. 21.
4 Minutes of the Hermes Lodge.
5 *Modern Astrology*, September 1917, p. 257.
6 Leo, *Life and Work*, p. 142.
7 *Nottingham Journal*, 10 July 1917, p. 2.
8 Ibid.
9 Ibid.
10 *Times*, 7 May 1917 reported in *Modern Astrology*, September 1917, p. 271.
11 *People*, 22 July 1917, p. 5.
12 *Tewkesbury Register and Agricultural Gazette*, 21 July 1917, p. 2.
13 *Truth*, 25 July 1917 quoted in Modern Astrology, September 1917, p. 259.
14 *Lancashire Evening Post*, 18 July 1917, p. 2.
15 Leo, *Life and Work*, p. 105.
16 Ibid, p. 74.
17 Ibid, p. 76.
18 Ibid.
19 Ibid, p. 77.
20 Ibid, p. 78.
21 Ibid, p. 81.
22 Ibid.

CHAPTER 21

1 Carter, 'Reminiscences of Alan Leo,'
2 Carter, 'Astrological Lodge of the London Theosophical Society.'
3 Carter, 'Reminiscences of Alan Leo.'
4 Minutes of the Astrological Lodge of London.
5 *Modern Astrology,* May 1928, p. 5.
6 Will of Bessie Leo.
7 *Prediction*, 1 May 1936, 162.

BIBLIOGRAPHY

Searches of many occult and spiritual journals were conducted via the International Association for the Preservation of Spiritualist and Occult Periodicals (www.iapsop.com). The *Astrologers' Magazine, Modern Astrology, Old Moore's Monthly Messenger* and the *British Journal of Astrology* form part of my own collection. Other publications were accessed via the British Library.

Much of the background information was gleaned from public records, including:
Census of England and Wales, 1841, 1851, 1861, 1871, 1881, 1891 and 1901.
Scottish Census 1871, 1881 and 1891.
British Phone Books, 1880-1984.
British Army Service Records, 1760-1915.
Birth, marriage and death records.
Electoral registers.
Immigration and travel records.

The primary source for public records was Ancestry (Ancestry.co.uk). Duplicate searches were also conducted on Find my Past (Findmypast.co.uk), the Genealogist (the genealogist,co.uk) and Family Search (family.search.org) where records were available. This helped resolve issues caused by transcription errors and differing treatments of county borders.

BIBLIOGRAPHY

Aberdeen Evening Express, 8 July 1891; 26 January 1917.
Abergavenny Chronicle, 20 January 1888.
Ackerman, Rudolph, *The Microcosm of London or London in Miniature*, Vol III, Methuen and Co, London, 1904.
Age of Uncertainty, 'Victorian Values,' ageofuncertainty.blogspot.co.uk/2010/04/victorian-values_21.html (accessed October 2018).
Aiyar, N Chidambaram, *Brihat Jakata*, Madras, Theosophist Office, 1905.
Aldrich, Robert, *Cultural Encounters and Homoeroticism in Sri Lanka*, Routledge, 2014.
Allen, Paul Marshall and Allen, Joan deRis, *The Time is at Hand!: The Rosicrucian Nature of Goethe's Fairy Tale of the Green Snake and the Beautiful Lily and The Mystery Dramas of Rudolf Steiner*, Steiner Books, 1995.
American Journal of Eugenics, September 1907.
American Phrenological Journal, June 1900; December 1898.
American Theosophist, Sept-Oct. 1988.
Anderson, K, 'The Weather Prophets: Science and Reputation in Victorian Meteorology', *History of Science*, vol. 37, p.179-216, 2005.
—*Predicting the Weather; Victorians and the Scxience of Meteorology*, University of Chicago Press, 2005.
Andrews, Helen, 'Phrenology: bunk Science but it has its Good Points, First Things', www.firstthings.com/blogs/firstthoughts/2012/05/phrenology-bunk-science-but-it-had-its-good-points (accessed October 2018).
Anonymous, 'The Victorian Occult Revival in West Yorkshire, imbolcfire.blogspot.co.uk/2010/06/victorian-occult-revival-in-west.html (accessed August 2018).
ANUBIS: The Occult News and Review, 1902-3.
Aprile, Sylvie & Diaz, Delphine (tr. McNaughton, Kate) 'Europe and its Political Refugees in the 19th Century', *Books and Ideas*, www.booksandideas.net/Europe-and-its-Political-Refugees-in-the-19th-Century.html (2016). (accessed July 2018).
Astrologer, 1887-8.
Astrologers' Magazine, 1890-1895.
Astrological Association Journal, Spring 1976.
Astrological Lodge of London, *Astrology Quarterly*, December 1926; 1928; 1930; 1937; 21:1, 1:66: Summer 1946; 1947; 1943; 39:4, 1965; Summer 1995.
Astrological Lodge of London, Minutes, 1915-1930.
Astrology Society, Transaction 1, *Esoteric or Exoteric, A Symposium*, 1912.
Astrological Society, Transactions, March 1898, April 1898, September 1898, March 1899.
Attractor, 1890.
Auckland Star, 18 October 1886.
Audactor, 'Alan Leo', www.audacter.it/AudAstr1e-P01.html (accessed 31 July 2018).
Aum, April 1896. universaltheosophy.com/pdf-library/theosophy/Theosophy_v11_text.pdf (accesssed 10 October 2018).
Baggs, AP; Bolton, Diane K; Hicks MA; and Pugh, V, 'Finchley: Introduction', in *A History of the County of Middlesex: Volume 6, Friern Barnet, Finchley, Hornsey With Highgate*, ed. T F T Baker and C R Elrington (London, 1980), pp. 38-55. British History Online www.british-history.ac.uk/vch/middx/vol6/pp38-55 (accessed 19 October 2018).
Bailey, E H, (ed.), *Destiny: the magazine of Astrology*, Lincoln, Hadleigh, Thornton Heath, June 1904-October 1905.

BIBLIOGRAPHY

Balfour-Clarke, Russell, *The Boyhood of J. Krishnamurti*, Chetana, 1977.
Banbury Advertiser, 25 July 1895.
Barnes, Henry, *A Life for the Spirit: Rudolf Steiner in the Crosscurrents of Our Time*, Steiner Books, 1997.
Barry Herald, 11 February 1910.
Bath Chronicle and Weekly Gazette, 2 June 1910; 15 September 1910; 27 November 1915.
Beaumont, Matthew 'Influential Force: Shafts and the Diffusion of Knowledge at the Fin de Siècle', *Interdisciplinary Studies in the Long Nineteenth Century*, 19 (3), 2006
Bedfordshire Mercury, 11 October 1912.
Bedfordshire Times and Independent, 13 February 1897.
Belfast Telegraph, 28 June 1909; 11 May 1914.
Belfast Weekly News, 2 April 1908; 30 June 1904.
Bell, Karl, *The Magical Imagination, Magic & Modernity in Modern England, 1780-1914*, Cambridge, 2012.
Besant, Annie and Leadbeater, C W, *Man: Whence, How and Whither. A Record of Clairvoyant Investigation*, Theosophical Publishing House, Adyar, 1913.
Besant, Annie, 'The Object of Co-Masonry', *Theosophic Messenger*, June 1909.
—*An Autobiography*, London: T. Fisher Unwin, 1893.
—'Vegetarianism in the Light of Theosophy, a lecture', 1895.
Beverley and East Riding Recorder, 30 May 1914.
Bibby's Annual, 1914.
Biggs Waller, Sharon (2013). 'Dining Sufragette Style', *Corsets, Cutlasses and Candlesticks*, corsetsandcutlasses.wordpress.com/2013/11/20/dining-suffragette-style (accessed 10 October 2018).
Bland's Astrology, with supplement, no. 1-11, 1889.
Blavatsky News, 'Blavatsky and Astrology, blavatskynews.blogspot.co.uk/2011/07/blavatsky-and-astrology.html (accessed August 2018).
Blavatasky Study Centre, 'Charles Webster Leadbeater', blavatskyarchives.com/leadbeater2.htm#Chronological (accessed 23 October 2018).
—'Charles Webster Leadbeater, His Life, Writings & Theosophical Teachings', www.blavatskyarchives.com/leadbeaterbib.htm (accessed October 2018).
Blavatsky Theosophy Group UK, 'Theosophy on the Sex Problem, web.archive.org/web/20160311114438/https://blavatskytheosophy.com/theosophy-on-the-sex-problem (accessed October 2018).
Blavatsky, H P, 'Theosophy and Sex Problems: Letter of 23 February 1887, The Theosophical Society, International Headquarters, Pasadena, California, www.theosociety.org/pasadena/sunrise/36-86-7/issgdpsx.htm (accessed 6 August 2018).
—*Key to Theosophy*, Theosophical Publishing Company, 1889.
—*Secret Doctrine*, Vol. 2, Theosophical Publishing House, 1971.
—*The Theosophist*, Vol. II, No. 5, February 1881.
—*Isis Unveiled*, Theosophical University Press, 1972.
Blu Buhs, Joshua, 'From an Oblique Angle: Alfred H. Barley as a Fortean.' www.joshuablubuhs.com/blog/alfred-h-barley-as-a-fortean (accessed 23 May 2015).
Bognor Regis Observer, 29 March 1892; 29 June 1892.
Bolton, Carrington H, Relic of Astrology, *Journal of American Folklore*, Vol. 11, No. 41, Apr-Jun 1898.

BIBLIOGRAPHY

Borderland, 1896.
Bournmouth Guardian, 18 February 1893; 9 March 1895; 21 September 1895, 21 July 1900.
Bradford Daily Telegraph, 13 October 1891.
Brand, Paul and Getzler, Joshua, *Judges and Judging in the History of the Common Law and Civil Law*, Cambridge University Press, 2012.
Bright, Esther, *Old Memories and Letters of Annie Besant*, Theosophical Publishing House, London, 1936.
Brighton Gazette, 27 July 1907; 12 September 1907; 21 September 1907; 19 September 1907; 18 July 1907; 21 September 1907.
Bristol Mercury, 28 January 1899.
British Journal of Astrology, 1914-1930.
Brooks, F T, *Neo-Theosophy Exposed*. Vyasashrama Bookshop, Madras, 1914.
—*The Theosophical Society and its Esoteric Bogeydom*, Vyashrama Bookshop, Madras, 1914.
Brubaker, Jason, 'Elizabeth Shutes Relates The Sinking Of The Titanic', *Stories of Survival, heroism & bravery*, survivor-story.com/elizabeth-shutes-relates-the-sinking-of-the-titanic (accessed October 2018).
Burch A and Spark J J, *Marriage a Success. Choice in wedlock, embracing love, courtship, etc.* London: Fowler, 1896.
Calvert, Samantha Jane, 'Eden's Diet: Christianity and Vegetarianism 1809-2009', A thesis submitted to the University of Birmingham for the degree of Doctor of Philosophy, June 2012 web.archive.org/web/20140720205957/http://etheses.bham.ac.uk/4575/1/Calvert13PhD.pdf (accessed July 2018).
Cambrian, 19 March 1897.
Campion Nicholas, *Astrology and Popular Religion in the Modern West*, London, Routledge, 2016.
Carlisle Patriot, 5 August 1895; 9 August 1895.
Carter, Charles, 'Reminiscences of Alan Leo', lecture delivered to the Lodge in March 1965, reprinted in *Astrology Quarterly*, Autumn 1968.
—'The Astrological Lodge of the London Theosophical Society', *In Search*, Vol.2, No.2, Spring 1959.
—*The Classical Astrology Series*, www.digthatcrazyfarout.com/carter/Carter_Leo.htm, 1955. (Acccessed September 2006.)
Chard and Ilminster News, 25 June 1910.
Charubel, *Grimoire Sympathia*, Oxon, IHO Books, 2003.
— *Psychology of Botany*, Tyldesley, R.Welch, 1906.
'Charubel, the Welsh astrologer John Thomas', *History of the Adepts: Spiritual Ancestors of The Church of Light*, www.historyoftheadepts.com/historyoftheadepts/?p=605 (accessed October 2018).
Cheiro, *Palmistry for All*, London, Herbert Jenkins, 1916.
Chelmsford Chronicle, 2 May 1879; 14 December 1883.
Cheltenham Chronicle, 26 November 1835; 30 March 1880; 2 December 1899; 4 April 1908.
Chester Chronicle, 4 June 1853.
Chetty, G Soobiah, *The Purchase of Adyar Headquarters: A Reminiscence of H.P.B.*, Adyar, Madras, India, 1926.
Childs, Gilbert, *Rudolf Steiner: His Life and Work*, Steiner Books, 1996.
Christian Esoteric, December 1938.

BIBLIOGRAPHY

Chronicle (Adelaide), 2 March 1907.
Chronicle and Weekly Gazette, 15 September 1910.
Clark, Linda L, *Women and achievement in Nineteenth-Century Europe*, Cambridge, Cambridge University Press, 2008.
Clarke, Patricia, *Rosa! Rosa!* Melbourne University Press, 1995.
Clements, Diana, 'Its members are of all sorts...', the Male Element of Early Co-freemasonry in England,' *Journal for Research into Freemasonry and Fraternalism*, Vol. 4. NO 1-2 (2013).
Colac Herald (Victoria, Australia), 27 August 1909.
Collins, Mabel, *The Mahatma: A Tale of Modern Theosophy*, London, Downey & Co.1895.
Co-mason, 1909.
Cook, Matt, *London and the Culture of Homosexualty*, Cambridge University Press, 2003.
Cooter, Roger (ed.), *Phrenology in Europe and America*, London, Routledge, 2001.
—*Phrenology in the British Isles*, New York, Scarecrow Press, 1989.
Cornelius, Geoffrey, 'The Astrological Lodge from Alan Leo to the Present Day: An Interpretation of History and Purpose,' *Astrology Quarterly*, Spring 1986.
Cornishman, 31 March 1892.
Cornubian and Redruth Times, 24 June 1898.
Council of the Federation of the European Sections of the Theosophical Society, 'Transactions of the Second Annual Congress of the Federation of European Sections of the Theosophical Society Held in London July 6th, 7th, 8th, 9th and 10th, 1905,' London: Council of the Federation, 1907.'
—'Transactions of the First Annual Congress of the Federation of European Sections of the Theosophical Society Held in Amsterdam June 19th, 20th and 21st, 1904,' Amsterdam: Council of the Federation, 1906. '
Coventry Standard, 5 March 1915.
Cranston, Sylvia, *The Extraordinary Life of Madame Helena Petrovna Blavatsky*, Jeremy P Tarcher, 1994.
Crittal, Elizabeth (Ed.), *A History of the County of Wiltshire*: Volume 6, London, Victoria County History, 1962.
Crofton, Sarah, 'Julia Says: The SpiritWriting and Editorial Mediumship of W T Stead,' www.19.bbk.ac.uk/articles/659/print (accessed October 2018).
Crow, John L , 'Taming the Astral Body: The Theosophical Society's Ongoing Problem of Emotion and Control,' *Journal of the American Academy of Religion*, Volume 80, Issue 3, 1 September 2012.
Croydon Advertiser and East Surrey Reporter, 2 July 1898.
Croysdale, Agnes and Wilde, George, *Your Destiny and the Stars*, Foulsham, 1915.
Cunningham, Peter, *A Handbook for London, Past and Present*, London, John Murray, 1850.
Curry, Patrick, *A Confusion of Prophets: Victorian and Edwardian Astrology*, London, Collins and Brown, 1992.
Daily Express, 17 July 1903.
Daily Mail, 30 June 1909.
Daily News, 27 August 1890.
Daily Telegraph and Courier, 7 January 1895; 17 April 1897;15 September 1897; 10 July 1905; 25 June 1909; 30 June 1909; 1 July 1909.

BIBLIOGRAPHY

Daily Telegraph, 7 May 1914.
Dat, Bernard, *Ritual, Secrecy, and Civil Society*, Volume 1, Number 1, Spring 2013, Policy Studies Organization.
Davies, Nathaniel Newnham, *Gourmet's Guide to London*, London, 1914.
Davies, Owen, *Witchcraft, Magic and Culture*, 1736-1951, Manchester University Press, 1999.
Davis, Sally and Wright, Roger, 'Hemetic Order of the Golden Dawn,' wrightanddavis.co.uk/GD/index.html (accessed October 2018).
de Tollenaere, Herman, A O, *The Politucs of Divine Wisdom: Theosophy and Labour, National, and Women's Movements in Indonesia and South Asia 1875-1947*, Leiden, 1996.
Delap, Lucy; DiCenzo, Maria and Ryan Leila, F*eminism and the Periodical Press*, Taylor and Francis, 2006.
Demerest, Marc, 'Send Stamp to Neptune,' Chasing Down Emma, ehbritten.blogspot.co.uk/2013/04/send-stamp-to-neptune-may-31-1886.html (accessed August 2018)
—'The Mark of Zarah,' *Chasing Down Emma*, ehbritten.blogspot.com/2012/06/mark-of-zarah.html (accessed July 2018).
—'The Society of the Dew and Light,' *Chasing Down Emma*, ehbritten.blogspot.com/2010/02/society-of-dew-and-light.html (accessed July 2018).
—'Thomas Henry Dalton/T H Burgoyne—His Desendents (sic),' *Chasing Down Emma*, ehbritten.blogspot.co.uk/2011/03/thomas-henry-dalton-t-h-burgoyne-his.html (accessed July 2018).
—'W. F. Barrett and Emily Kislingbury on Charles Carleton Massey,' *Chasing Down Emma*, ehbritten.blogspot.com/2013/04/w-f-barrett-on-charles-carleton-massey.html (accessed August 2018)
—'W. F. Barrett and Emily Kislingbury on Charles Carleton Massey'. *Chasing Down Emma*, ehbritten.blogspot.com/2013/04/w-f-barrett-on-charles-carleton-massey.html (accessed July 2018).
—Demerest, Marc, *Back from Jerusalem*, www.ehbritten.org/video/ehb_life_bw_version.pdf (accessed October 2018).
—'Hypotheses on the Orphic Circle, 2011', www.ehbritten.org/papers/hypotheses_on_the_orphic_circle.pdf (accessed July 2018).
Derby Mercury, 19 March 1845.
Dictionary of Canadian Biography www.biographi.ca/en/bio/wilson_edward_arthur_16E.html (accessed 23 May 2015)
'Disclosures in the Fortune Telling World, *The Days' Doings*, 15 July 1871, p. 4.
Dixon, Joy, *Divine Feminine: Theosophy and Feminism in England*, Studies in Historical and Political Science, 119th series, number 1, Baltimore, John Hopkins University Press, 2001.
Dixon, Kevin, 'The Weird Melancholy of Torquay Author Rosa Praed,' wearesouthdevon.com/weird-melancholy-torquay-author-rosa-praed (accessed August 2018)
Dodson J and Ellis, Ida, *Directory of Occult Practitioners*, Blackpool, 1906.
—*Directory of Occult Practitioners*, Halifax, Occult Book Company, 1900.
Dorset Life, 'Continuing the Tradition', August 2011, www.dorsetlife.co.uk/2011/08/continuing-the-tradition (accessed 23 May 2015).
Doughan, David, *Dictionary of British Women's Organisations*, 1825-1960, Woburn Education Series, 2001.

BIBLIOGRAPHY

Dover Express, 18 June 1909; 25 June 1909; 18 December 1914.
Dundee Courier, 24 July 1880; 12 April 1881; 15 May 1909; 30 December 1911; 15 May 1915; 31 December 1915.
Dundee Evening Post, 25 December 1903; 11 March 1904; 2 April 1904.
Dundee Evening Telegraph, 31 December 1898; 24 June 1909.
Earp, Joe, 'Nottingham Street Tales: Drury Hill,' *Nottingham Hidden History Team*, nottinghamhiddenhistoryteam.wordpress.com/2015/02/21/nottingham-street-tales-drury-hill (accessed 28 July 2017).
East and South Devon Advertiser, 27 February 1892; 5 March 1908; 27 February 1908; 12 March 1908.
East London Observer, 19 October 1895; 16 November 1901; 25 April 1896; 16 May 1901; 22 May 1920; 28 May 1927; 18 Jun 1927.
Eastern Evening News, 4 April 1908.
Eastern Order of International Freemasonry, 'Women in Freemasonry,' comasonic.net/#3 (accessed 23 October 2018)
Edinburgh Evening News, 31 May 1886; 8 February 1897; 22 July 1915.
Editor of 'Justice', *Evolution of Mrs. Besant. Being the life and public activities of Mrs. Annie Besant, secularist, socialist, theosophist and politician. With sidelights on the inner workings of the Theosophical Society and the methods by which Mr. Leadbeather arrived at the threshold of divinity by the editor of Justice*, Madras, Justice Printing Works, Madras, 1918.
Elmes, James, *A Topographical Dictionary of London and its Environs*, London, Whittaker, 1831.
Encyclopedia Titanicia, www.encyclopedia-titanica.org (accessed October 2018).
Era, 1 October 1881; 8 June 1895.
Eschener, Kat, 'This Infamous 19th-Century Birth Control Pamphlet Got Its Writer Imprisoned,' Smithsonian.com, www.smithsonianmag.com/smart-news/19th-century-birth-control-pamphlet-got-its-writer-imprisoned-180963140/#xZZQfwY3odOJfAWR.99 (accessed 6 August 2018).
Essex Herald, 4 February 1884; 17 March 1884.
Evening Despatch, 7 May 1914.
Evening Express (Wales), 3 May 1898; 24 June 1909; 1 July 1909.
Evening Herald, 30 July 1896,
Evening Journal (Adelaide), 7 August 1909.
Evening Mail (London), 10 April 1857.
Evening News (Sydney), 9 Dec 1899.
Evening News, Portsmouth, 31 January 1883.
Evening Star, 13 March 1905.
Examiner (London), 8 December 1855.
Exeter and Plymouth Gazette, 23 December 1904; 28 May 1914; 18 February 1915.
Fait, Stefano, A Study in the Anthropology of Science and Social History, Dissertation Submitted to the Department of Social Anthropology University of St. Andrews In Fulfilment of the Requirements for the Ph.D. degree February 18, 2004.
Farnell, Kim, *The Astral Tramp*, Nottingham, Ascella, 1998.
—*Flirting with the Zodiac*, Bournemouth, Wessex Astrologer, 2007.
—*Leo Rising*, London, My Spirit Books, 2015.
—*Mystical Vampire*, Oxford, Mandrake, 2005.

BIBLIOGRAPHY

Farringdon Advertiser and Vale of the White Horse Gazette, 27 July 1895.
Folkestone, Hythe, Sandgate and Cheriton Herald, 19 September 1914.
Forward, Charles W, *Fifty years of food reform: a history of the vegetarian movement in England*, London, Ideal Publishing Union, 1897.
Freemason Information, 'Theosophy and Freemasonry, freemasoninformation.com/2011/04/theosophy-and-freemasonry (accessed August 2018)
Freemasonry and Esoterica, 'Le Droit Humain: History', freemasonryesoterica.tumblr.com/post/164911007962/le-droit-humain-history#.WqP7dvnFInQ (accessed 23 October 2018).
Fulbright, Julia, 'Prof. Hatfield and the Phrenological Assessment of Miss M.J.A. Percival', prezi.com/f1ojyawa_zrt/prof-hatfield-and-the-phrenological-assessment-of-miss-mja-percival (accessed August 2018).
Gaebelein, Arno C, *Current Events in the Light of the Bible*, New York, Our Hope, 1914.
Garcia, Mari & Usher, Joy, 'An Introduction to Charles Carter', *Skyscript*, www.skyscript.co.uk/carter_intro.html (accessed 23 May 2015)
Garrett, Rik, 'Hermetic Brotherhood of Light, the Hermetic Brotherhood of Luxor, the OTO and Chicago.' *Occult Chicago,* occultchicago.blogspot.co.uk/2012/11/hermetic-brotherhood-of-light-hermetic.html (accessed July 2018).
Geelong Advertiser (Victoria), 21 April 1897.
Gen UK, 'Theological Colleges attended by Welsh ministers and priests,' www.genuki.org.uk/big/wal/ChurchHistory/TheoColl, (accessed 20 October 2018).
Gilbert, R A and Armstrong Allan, *Proceedings of the Golden Dawin Conference*, London 1997, Bristol, Privately Printed, 1998.
Gilbert, Robert A, 'The Disappointed Magus: John Thomas and His 'Celestial Brotherhood', *Theosophical History Magazine*, Volume VIII, Issue 3, July 2000.
Globe, 10 June 1837; 20 March 184 5; 7 April 1893; 28 November 1901; 3 October 1904; 6 May 1914.
Gloucester Citizen, 24 January 1852; 16 January 1883; 31 January 1883. 6 December 1892; 5 July 1893; 7 November 1903; 4 April 1908.
Gloucester Journal, 4 April 1908.
Gloucestershire Echo, 11 February 1899; 18 June 1907; 31 March 1908.
Godwin Joscelyn, Chanel, Christian and Deveney, John P, *The Hermetic Brotherhood of Luxor*, Weiser, 1995.
—'A Begimist Circle in Victorian England,' *Hermetic Journal*, alchemyfraternitas.ru/media/libra/kniga/46.pdf (accessed July 2017)
—'The Hidden Hand, Part IV: The Hermetic Brotherhood of Luxor, *Theosophical History*, Volume III, No. 5, January 1991.
— Godwin, Joscelyn, *Theosophical Enlightenment*, SUNY, 1994.
Golden, Catherine, *Posting It: The Victorian Revolution in Letter Writing*, Florida, US, University Press of Florida, 2009.
Grand Lodge of Freemasonry for Men and Women, Great Britain, 'Declaration,' www.grandlodge.org.uk/declaration.html (accessed August 2018)
—web.archive.org/web/20070216102139/http://www.grandlodge.org.uk/index.htm (accessed October 2018).
Gray, Brian, Rudolf Steiner's Planetary Seals, web.archive.org/web/20160819205835/https://wisecosmos.com/wp-content/uploads/Planetary_Seals_Booklet_2015-11-19.pdf (accessed Ocober 2018).

BIBLIOGRAPHY

Green, H S, *The Degrees of the Zodiac Symbolised By Charubel. To which is added, The Theoretical Value of the Degrees of the Zodiac*, London, Nichols & Co., 1898.
Greenock Telegraph and Clyde Shipping Gazette, 9 August 1895; 23 December 1904.
Gregory, James, 'Anna Bonus Kingsford and her Circle,' www.academia.edu/3862213/Anna_Bonus_Kingsford_and_her_Circle (accessed October 2018).
—*Of Victorians and Vegetarians*, London, Tauris Academic Studies, 2007.
Grunow, Dexter C, 'Charubel, the Welsh astrologer John Thomas,' *History of the Adepts: Spritual Ancestors of the Church of Light*, adepts.light.org/2013/03/03/charubel-the-welsh-astrologer-john-thomas (accessed July 2018).
Gula, Josef, The Roman Catholic Church in the History of the Polish Exiled Community in Britain (1939-1950), Thesis, University of London, discovery.ucl.ac.uk/1317997/1/312591.pdf (accessed July 2018).
Hackney and Kingsland Gazette, 9 December 1881; 7 March 1883; 20 April 1883.
Hackwood, Frederick, Staffordshire Worthies, 1891, www.gutenberg.org/files/22200/22200-h/22200-h.htm (accessed 23 May 2015)
Haithi Trust Bulletin, 15-16 19-20.
Halifax Courier, 22 April 1899.
Hampshire Advertiser, 25 April 1877; 26 June 1880; 15 April 1885; 1 March 1890; 11 July 1891; 23 May 1891; 27 May 1891; 30 May 1891; 11 July 1891; 25 July 1891; 26 September 1891; 24 October 1891; 7 November 1891; 5 December 1891; 14 May 1892; 18 January 1893; 27 May 1891; 30 May 1891 ; 5 Dec 1891 6 February 1892; 27 May 1893; 20 March 1897.
Hampstead and Highgate Express, 18 September 1897; 25 September 1897; 3 July 1909; 6 November 1909; 17 September 1910.
HANSARD 1803–2005, ORAL ANSWERS TO QUESTIONS. Palmists. HC Deb 30 October 1912 vol 43 c446, api.parliament.uk/historic-hansard/commons/1912/oct/30/palmists (accessed 9 August 2018).
Hartlepool Northern Daily Mail, 3 August 1895.
Hastings and St Leonards Observer, 22 April 1922.
Hawera and Normanby Star, 16 December 1899.
Heckthorn, Charles William, *The Secret Societies of all Countries and Ages*, London, George Redway, 1887.
Hembry, Phyllis May, *British Spas from 1815 to the Present: A Social History*, Fairleigh Dickinson University Press, 1997.
Hendon and Finchley Times, 27 February 1931; 29 May 1931; 24 July 1931.
Herald of the Golden Age, 1897; January 1913.
Herald of the Star, 1914; 1922; 1927.
Hermes Lodge, Minutes.
Hermetic Library, 'John Yarker,' hermetic.com/sabazius/john-yarker (accessed August 2018).
Hills, John, Pubshistory.com. pubshistory.com/LondonPubs/WestminsterStJohn/AdamEve.shtml (accessed 28 July 2017)
Hine, Phil, "A thousand kisses darling": Sex, scandal and spirituality in the life of Charles Webster Leadbeater —I, enfolding.org, enfolding.org/a-thousand-kisses-darling-sex-scandal-and-spirituality-in-the-life-of-charles-webster-leadbeater-i (accessed August 2018).
Holden, James and Hughes, Robert, *Astrological Pioneers of America*, AFA, 1988.

BIBLIOGRAPHY

Holden, James H, *A History of Horoscopic Astrology*, American Federation of Astrology, Tempe, AZ, 2006.
Horoscope, 1902, April 1904.
House of Commons, 'Report from the Select Committee on the Weymouth & Melcombe Regis Election Petition,' London, Parliamentary Papers Great Britain, H.M. Stationery Office, 1 March 1813.
Howe, Ellic, *Astrology and the Third Reich*, Aquarian Press, 1984.
—*The Alchemist of the Golden Dawn*, Northamptonshire: Aquarian Press, 1985.
—*The Magicians of the Golden Dawn*, Wellingborough, Aquarian Press, 1985.
Hull Daily Mail, 2 November 1893;14 May 1910; 21 August 1914; 25 February 1915.
Humanitarian, March 1897.
Hunt, Bruce, 'London Street Name Changes'. www.maps.thehunthouse.com (accessed 28 July 2017).
Illustrated London News, 25 February 1882; 4 March 1889; 9 July 1892; 25 April 1903.
Inquirer and Commercial News, 24 March 1893.
Inter Ocean from Chicago, Illinois, 18 July 1909.
International Order of Freemasonry for Men and Women—Le Droit Humain, Lodge Hermes No. 20 of The British Federation, www.freemasonryformenandwomen.co.uk/hermes.html (accessed May 2016)
International Order of Freemasonry for Men and Women, Le Droit Humain British Federation, 'Craft Rituals,' www.freemasonryformenandwomen.co.uk/joomla/index.php/craft-rituals (accessed August 2018)
—'Annie Besant Accord,' www.freemasonryformenandwomen.co.uk/joomla/index.php/component/content/article/2-uncategorised/82-annie-besant-accord (accessed October 2018).
International Psychic Gazette, 1912-1917.
International Vegetarian Union, 'History of the International Vegetarian Union, ivu.org/history-legacy-pages.html (accessed July 2018).
Ipswich Journal, 26 May 1900.
Irish Independent, 31 December 1906
Irish Theosophist, Volume III, 1894-5.
Islington Gazette, 12 November 1880; 15 November 1880; 13 July 1881; 20 December 1881; 14 January 1901.
Jackson, Lee, 'The Rookeries of London, by Thomas Beames, 1852,' *Dictionary of Victorian London*, www.victorianlondon.org/publications5/rookeries (accessed 28 July 2017).
Janik, Erica, 'The Shape of Your Head and the Shape of Your Mind,' *The Atlantic*, www.theatlantic.com/health/archive/2014/01/the-shape-of-your-head-and-the-shape-of-your-mind/282578 (accessed October 2018).
Jarrow Express, 9 Jun 1905.
Jewish Chronicle, 9 December 1927.
Jewish Chronicle, Report of the Conference of Jewish Women: held at Portman Rooms, Baker Street, London, on 13th and 14th May, 1902.

BIBLIOGRAPHY

Jinarajadasa, C, *Clairvoyant Investigations by C W Leadbeater and 'The Lives of Alcyone,'* Privately Published, 1947.
—*Letters From the Masters of the Wisdom*, Chicago, Theosophical Press, 1926.
—'K.H. Letters to Leadbeater: C W Leadbeater in London,' kg.vkk.nl/english/organizations/lcc.gb/lcis/scriptures/liberal/leadbeater/jina.html (accessed July 2018)
—*Golden Book of the Theosophical Society*, Adyar, India, Theosophical Publishing House, 1925.
—*Occult Investigations: A Description of the Work of Annie Besant and C. W. Leadbeater*, Adyar, India, Theosophical Publishing House, 1938.
Journal for Psychical Research, 1903–1904, November 1909, 1911.
Journal of the Astrological Society, March 1898.
Judge, William Quan, *The Writings of William Quan Judge, Echoes of the Orient*: Volume 2, www.theosociety.org/pasadena/wqj-echoes/EchoesOrient2-WQJ.pdf (accessed October 2018)
Kaczynski, Richard, 'John Yarker.' Ordo Templi Orientis USA, oto-usa.org/usgl/lion-eagle/john-yarker (accessed July 2018).
—*Perdurabo, Revised and Expanded Edition: The Life of Aleister Crowley*, North Atlantic Books, 2012.
Kent and Sussex Courier, 2 November 1917.
Keswick, John Barton and Mrs J B Kewsick, *How to Remember: Embracing the Natural and Physiological Improvement of Memory*, Broughton House, South Cliff, Scarborough, 1895.
Keswick, John Barton, *Life and Living*, Carlisle : W. Etchells, 1895.
— Keswick, John Barton, *Man and His Sexual Relations*, South Cliff, Scarborough, Broughton House, 1890.
—*Sexual Physiology*, Carlisle, W. Etchells, 1891.
—*The Herbal Family Guide*, Wigton, 1930.
—*Woman, her Physical Culture*, Fowler, 1895.
Kidd Hewitt, David, 'Looking into Futurity,' davidkiddhewitt.wordpress.com/2017/05/18/looking-into-futurity, (accessed August 2018).
Kingsford, Anna Bonus, *Dreams and Dream Stories*, London, George Redway, 1888.
Kneph, December 1883.
Knight, Gareth, 'An Anthology of Occult Wisdom', garethknight.blogspot.co.uk/2010/05/anthology-of-occult-wisdom.html (Accessed 23 May 2015)
Lacey, F W, 'Alan Leo', *Astrologers' Magazine*, September 1893.
Laite, Julia, 'Paying the price again: prostitution policy in historical perspective,' *History and Policy*, httpwww.historyandpolicy.org/policy-papers/papers/paying-the-price-again-prostitution-policy-in-historical-perspective (accessed October 2018).
Lamar, Cecil, 'Albert Ballin: Business and Politics in Imperial Germany, 1888–1918,' Princeton, NJ: Princeton University. OCLC 900428, 1967, digitalcollections.smu.edu/cdm/singleitem/collection/eaa/id/224/rec/2 (accessed October 2018).
Lancashire Evening Post, 5 April 1893; 22 January 1903.
Law Reform Commission, 'The Law Reform Commission Report on Vagrancy and Related Offences, Ireland,' www.lawreform.ie/_fileupload/Reports/rVagrancy.htm (accessed June 2018.

BIBLIOGRAPHY

Leadbeater, C W, *The Hidden Life in Freemasonry*, Adyar, Theosophical Publishing House, 1926.
—*The Soul's Growth Through Reincarnation*, Adyar, India, Theosophical Publishing House, 1949.
Leeds Mercury, 10 January 1883; 6 September 1902; 13 January 1903; 24 January 1903; 25 June 1904; 1 March 1916.
Leeds Times, 18 August 1888; 29 September 1888.
Leicester Journal, 4 January 1861.
Leicestershire Mercury, 20 June 1846.
Leneman, Leah, 'The Awakened Instinct: Vegetarianism and the Women's Suffrage Movement in Britain', *Women's History Review*, 6:2, 271-287, 1997.
Leo, Alan, 'The Purification of Astrology', *Lucifer*, The Theosophical Society, April 1894.
—*Art of Synthesis*, London, Modern Astrology, 1912.
—*Art of Synthesis*, Modern Astrology, 1893.
—*Astrology and the War*, Modern Astrology, 1915.
—*Esoteric Astrology*, London: Modern Astrology, 1913.
—*Everybody's Astrology*, Modern Astrology, 1909.
—*Horary Astrology*, 1909.
—*The Astrologer and His Work: With Some Remarkable Short Stories*, London, Fowler, 1911.
—*The Progressed Horoscope*, London, Modern Astrology, 1906
Leo, Bessie, *Romance of the Stars*, London, Modern Astrology, 1914.
—*The Life and Work of Alan Leo*, London, Fowler, 1919.
—'How I became a theosophist,' *The Theosophist*, January 1928.
Levack, Brian P, *New Perspectives on Witchcraft*, Taylor and Francis, 2001.
—*Witchcraft in the Modern World*, Routledge. 2002.
Levine, Nick, The Dignity of an Exact Science: Evangeline Adams, Astrology, and the Professions of the Probable, 1890-1940, Senior Thesis, History of Science, April 2014, hshm.yale.edu/sites/default/files/files/2014-levine.pdf (accessed July 2018).
Liberal Catholic Church in the British Isles, Newsletter no. 8, https://kg.vkk.nl/gb/ukniewsletter/8.pdf (accessed July 2018).
Library and Museum of Freemasonry, 'Grand Lodge of Druids, late 18th Century,' freemasonry.london.museum/showcase/grand-lodge-of-druids-late-18th-century (accessed 23 October 2018).
—'The Druid Orders', freemasonry.london.museum/it/wp-content/uploads/2011/05/The-Druid-Orders.pdf (accessed 23 October 2018).
Light, 9 December 1883; 5 June 1886; 1 December 1888; 11 March 1893; July 1891; January 1892; January 1896; April 1899; 20 May 1899; December 1899; 18 August 1900; 9 June 1900; February 1901.
Livingstone, David, 'The Salafi,' Conspiracy School, www.conspiracyschool.com/salafi (accessed July 2018).
London Daily News, 4 October 1893; 4 July 1898; 06 October 1904; 24 September 1904; 25 June 1913; 26 June 1913.
London Evening News and Evening Mail, 4 October 1904.
London Evening News, 4 January 1899; 29 24, June 1909. 25 June 1909; 29 June 1909; 30 June 1909; 1 July 1909.

BIBLIOGRAPHY

London Evening Standard, 28 March 1896; 24 June 1909; 25 June 1909; 30 June 1909; 1 July 1909.
London Gazette, 23 May 1899; 7 July 1899; 4 June 1910; 7 January 1916; 13 February 1925.
London Observer, 24 February 1899.
London Standard, 30 June 1909; 1 July 1909; 7 May 1914.
London Vegetarian Society, londonvegansocieties.com/tag/victorian (accessed 23 May 2015).
Los Angeles Herald, 12 February 1897; 18 October 1909.
Lucifer, September 1889; February 1891; June 1891; August 1891; October 1891; February 1892; March 1893; September 1893; December 1894.
Lutyens, Mary, *Krishnamurti: His Life and Death*, New York, St. Martin's Press, 1991.
—*Krishnamurti: A Life*, India, Penguin Books, 2005.
—*Krishnamurti: The Years of Awakening*, London, John Murray, 1975.
Madras High Court, 'Mrs. Annie Besant vs G. Narayaniah on 29 October, 1913', indiankanoon.org/doc/1214788 (accessed July 2018)
Maitland, Edward, *The Story of Anna Kingsford and Edward Maitland and the New Gospel of Interpretation*, Birmingham, Ruskin Press, 1905, p. 29.
Manchester Courier and Lancashire General Advertiser, 26 November 1842; 13 January 1888.
Manchester Courier, 1 December 1899; 10 January 1901.
Manchester Evening News, 1 March 1915.
Manchester Times, 24 May 1890.
Marinacci, Michael, 'The Esoteric Fraternity'. *Califia's Children*, califias.blogspot.co.uk/2014/12/the-esoteric-fraternity.html (accessed July 2018).
Marks, Lara V, *Model Mothers: Jewish Mothers and Maternity Provision in East London 1870-1939*, Clarendon Press, 1994.
Marylebone Mercury, 24 June 1871.
Mate, H Chas and Riddle, Chas, *Bournemouth: 1810-1910, the history of a modern health and pleasure resort*, Bournmouth, W Mate and Sons, 1910.
McIntosh, Christopher, *Astrologers and Their Creed*, Praeger, 1969.
McKelvie, BA, 'Magic, Murder and Mystery, 1966', www.fadedpage.com/books/20140421/20140421.html (accessed 23 May 2015)
Meade, Marion, *Madame Blavatsky: The Woman Behind the Myth*, Putnam, 1980.
Medium and Daybreak, 8 December 1876; 18 April 1879.
Mercury (Hobart), 11 December 1909.
Messenger, Nicholas, 'P & O's India Mail Service', *The Old Peninuslar and Oriental Steam Navigation Company*, www.pandosnco.co.uk/indianmail.html (accessed October 2018).
Meyer, T H, *D.N. Dunlop, A Man of Our Time*, Temple Lodge Publishing, 2014.
Mid Sussex Times, 27 December 1904.
Middlesex and Surrey Express, 19 January 1901.
Mitchell, C Everard, *Foretold by the Stars*, Published by the author, Halifax, 1936.
Modern Astrology, 1895-1931.
Moreas, Frank, *Jawaharlal Nehru A Biography*, Asia Publishing, Bombay, 1956.
Morning Bulletin (Rockhampton, Qld), 27 April 1897.
Morning Post, 19 January 1883; 7 December 1901; 25 June 1909.

BIBLIOGRAPHY

Mortimer, DIC, 'Arcade Serenade'. *DIC Mortimer's Blog,* dicmortimer.com/2011/08/24/arcade-serenade (accessed July 2018).
Most Rev. Alan R. Kemp, D.Min. 'A Brief History of Independent Catholicism in North America', www.cosmas.cnc.net/indcath.htm (accessed 23 May 2015).
Motherwell Times, 3 May 1910.
Mullumbimby Star, 23 September 1909.
Murdie, Alan, 'The History of the Vagrancy Act 1824', www.thepavement.org.uk/stories.php?story=1029 (accessed February 2017).
Murray, David Christie, *Recollections,* archive.org/stream/cu31924013350438/cu31924013350438_djvu.txt (accessed 23 May 2015).
Naylor, PIH, *Astrology: A Fascinating History,* North Hollywood, California, Wilshire Book Company, 1970.
Nethercot, Arthur Hobart, *The Last Four Lives of Annie Besant,* Chicago, US, University of Chicago Press, 1963.
Newman, Aubrey. 'Southampton Jewry in Victorian Britain', *Jewish Communities and Records,* www.jewishgen.org/jcr-uk/Community/southampton_articles/southampton-vic.htm (accessed July 2018).
Nichols, Kimberly, 'Mysteries of the Hermetic Brotherhood of Luxor', *Newtopia Magazine,* newtopiamagazine.wordpress.com/2013/08/15/mysteries-of-the-hermetic-brotherhood-of-luxor/(accessed July 2018).
Niemand, Jasper, *Letters That Have Helped Me: William Q Judge,* Pasadena, California, Theosophical University Press, 1981.
North Devon Gazette, 19 May 1891.
North Wales Weekly News, 2 April 1909.
Northern Daily Telegraph, 8 November 1889; 5 October 1904; 24 June 1909.
Northern Heights Vegetarian Society, 'Annual Report', 1897.
— 'Report and Balance Sheet', 1889.
Notes and Queries, Manchester, S C and L M Gould, Vol. XV, 1897.
Nottingham Evening Post, 10 September 1890; 11 September 1890; 28 December 1891; 19 April 1892; 18 February 1893; 26 October, 1899.
Nottingham Journal, 19 January 1883; 20 September 1898; 10 July 1917.
Nottinghamshire History, 'Drury Hill, nottshistory.org.uk/whatnall1928/drury_hill.htm (accessed 28 July 2017).
Novella, Stephen, 'Phrenology—History of a Science and Pseudoscience', theness.com/neurologicablog/index.php/phrenology-history-of-a-science-and-pseudoscience (accessed July 2018).
NZ Truth, 'Loathsome Leadbeater', 17 July 1909, paperspast.natlib.govt.nz/newspapers/NZTR19090717.2.27 (accessed October 2018).
Oamuru Mail, 17 April 1897.
Observer, 10 February 1907; 7 January 1909.
Occult Magazine, 1885; 1886.
Occult Review, October 1909; October 1912; October 1917; December 1917; June 1923.
Old Moore's Monthly Messenger, 1905; 1907; 1912-1913; February 1914.

BIBLIOGRAPHY

Old, Walter, 'My Unremembered Self: The Experience of an Astral Tramp', *Lucifer*, October 1891.
—*In Memory of Helena Petrovna Blavatsky by Some of Her Pupils*, London, Theosophical Publishing Society, 1890.
Oliphant, John, 'Brother XII', www.brotherxii.com (accessed 23 May 2015).
'Our Solar System Real and Imaginary,' www.quadibloc.com/other/as02.htm (accessed October 2018).
Owen, Alex, *The Darkened Room: Women, Power and Spiritualism in late Victorian England*, University of Chicago Press, 1989.
—*The Place of Enchantment: British Occultism and the Culture of the Modern*, University of Chicago Press, 2004.
Paijmans, Theo, *Free Energy Pioneer: John Worrell Keely*, Adventures Unlimited Press, 2004.
Pall Mall Gazette, 15 January, 1883; 23 April 1887; 30 June 1896; 24 August 1897; 3 December 1914.
Path, 'Brixton Lodge of London held Meeting to listen to Annie Besant', 12 June 1891.
—New York, April 1890; July 1891; February 1895; April 1895, September 1895.
Path-Finder, December 1902.
Pelletier, Ernest E, *The Judge Case: A Conspiracy that Ruined the Theosophical Cause*, Edmonton, Canada, Edmonton Theosophical Society, 2004.
People, 22 July 1917.
Petherbridge, Edward, 'Olympic Resonances,' petherbridgesweeklypost.blogspot.co.uk/2012/07 (accessed 23 October 2018).
Phoenix Masonry Inc., 'Ancient Order of Druids,' www.phoenixmasonry.org/masonicmuseum/fraternalism/druids.htm (accessed October 2018).
Phrenological Magazine, 1889.
Phrenological Review, vol. 2, no. 16-vol. 3, no. 27.
Pilcher-Dayton, Ann Jessica, Women Freemasons and Feminist causes 1908-1935: The Case of the Honourable Fraternity of Antient Masonry, Thesis submitted to the Department of History, University of Sheffield for the degree of Doctor of Philosophy, 2011, etheses.whiterose.ac.uk/15012/1/575742.pdf (accessed October 2018).
—*The Open Door: The Order of Women Freemasons 1908-2009*, London, 2008.
Pontypridd Chronicle and Workman's News, 28 March 1890; 4 April 1890; 11 April 1890.
Popular Phenologist, March 1896; 1899-1901; 1902.
Portsmouth Evening News, 25 June 1909; 7 May 1914.
Praed, Mrs Campbell, 'Alan Leo: An Appreciation', *Occult Review*, December 1917.
Prakasa, Sri, *Annie Besant as Woman and Leader*, Adyar, India, Theosophical Publishing House, 1941.
Prediction, May 1936.
Preece, Rod, *Sins of the Flesh, A History of Ethical Vegetarian Thought*, Vancouver, Toronto, UBC Press, 2008.
Prescott, Andrew, 'Builders of the Temple of the New Civilisation: Annie Besant and Freemasonry,' *Women's Agency and Rituals in Mixed and Female Masonic Orders*. Alexandra Heidle; Jan Snoek (eds.), Leiden, Brill, 2008.
Presidency Magistrate's Court, 'Annie Besant Defamation Case,' www.parascience.org/images/The_Annie_Besant_Defamation_Case.pdf (accessed October 2018).

BIBLIOGRAPHY

Price, Leslie, 'A Martian problem solved?' *Theosophical History*, October 2006.

—'C C Massey. The Man Who Was There,' *Psypioneer Journal* Vol 12 No. 3 May-June 2016 www.iapsop.com/psypioneer/psypioneer_v12_n3_may-jun_2016.pdf (accessed July 2017).

Proceedings of the Old Bailey, 'London 1760-1815,' oldbaileyonline.org/static/London-lifelate18th.jsp (accessed July 2018).

—1674-1913, www.oldbaileyonline.org/ (accessed October 2018).

Psypioneer Volume 5, No 7: July 2009, www.woodlandway.org/PDF/PP5.7July09.pdf (accessed July 2018).

Purucker, G De, 'Theosophy and Sex Problems,' www.theosociety.org/pasadena/sunrise/36-86-7/issgdpsx.htm (accessed October 2018).

Raman, B V, *Autobiography of a Vedic Astrologer*, Bangalore, UBS Publishing, 1996.

Rauch, John B, Medical education, medical colleges and the regulation of the practice of medicine in the United States and Canada. 1765-1891. Medical education and the regulation of the practice of medicine in foreign countries. Illinois State Board of Health: 1891. www.archive.org/details/cu31924012274290 (accessed 28 July 2017).

Register (Adelaide), 22 February 1911.

Report from the Select Committee on the Weymouth & Melcombe Regis Election Petition: Together with the Special Report from the Said Committee; and Also the Report from the Committee who Were Appointed to Inspect the Said Special Report. Ordered by the House of Commons to be Printed, 1 March, 1813.

Review of Reviews, May 1909; May 1911.

Rhodes, Mrs, 'The Lodge Map and its Progressions', a lecture delivered by Mrs Rhodes to the Astrological Lodge on January 13th 1930.

Rothschild Archive, 'Testimonial to Lord & Lady Rothschild from the Jewish Association for the Protection of Women and Girls,' www.rothschildarchive.org/exhibitions/faith_charity/testimonial_from_the_jewish_association_for_the_protection_of_women_and_girls (accessed July 2018).

Salisbury and Winchester Journal, 26 September 1803; 7 December 1835; 12 June 1837; 7 August 1837; 27 August 1838; 2 December 1839; 30 December 1839; 10 May 1841; 17 December 1842 ; 10 April 1845; 11 October 1845; 28 March 1846; 24 April 1847; 17 July 1847; 27 July 1850; 21 September 1850; 1 February 1851; 24 December 1852; 27 December 1852; 9 April 1853; 27 December 1856; 28 February 1857; 2 May 1857; 27 February 1858; 9 July 1859; 6 October 1860; 20 July 1861; 16 August 1862; 15 November 1862; 15 November 1862; 11 July 1863; 9 January 1864; 21 January 1865; 13 April 1867; 23 January 1869; 15 October 1870; 4 May 1872; 13 September 1890; 25 June 1909; 26 June 1909.

Salisbury Times, 9 July 1859; 13 September 1884; 18 January 1890; 20 January 1893; 13 April 1894; 29 September 1899; 10 April 1908; 25 June 1909; 2 July 1909.

Sanat, Aryel, *The Inner Life of Krishnamurti: Private Passion and Perennial Wisdom*, Quest, 2013.

Santucci, James, 'The Aquarian Foundation', 1989, www.theohistory.org/aquarian_foundation.pdf (accessed 23 May 2015).

Saunders, W, *The Stranger's Guide in Brighton; being a complete companion to that fashionable place, and the rides and drives in its vicinity*, 1852.

BIBLIOGRAPHY

Scarborough News, 'Green Gables: We're Just Testing the Waters,' www.thescarboroughnews.co.uk/news/green-gables-we-re-just-testing-the-waters-1-6671261 1.2 (accessed July 2018).
Schuller, Govert, 'Krishnamurti and the World Teacher Project: *Some Theoretical Perceptions,' Theosophical History Occasional Papers*, Volume V Theosophical History, Fullerton, Ca, 1997.
Sease, Virginia (author) and Miller Marguerite and Miller, Doug (translators), *Rudolf Steiner's Endowment: Centenary Reflections on His Attempt for a Theosophical Art and Way of Life*, 15 December 1911, Temple Lodge Publishing, 2012.
Sepharial, *Coming Events*, 1900.
—*Fate and Fortune*, July 1890; October 1890.
—*The Degrees of the Zodiac Symbolised by Charubel, to which is added a translation of a similar series found in "La Volasfera* (translation and additional notes by Sepharial), London: Modern Astrology, 1907.
—*The Forecast*: a popular journal of scientific prediction, 1906.
Sevenoaks Chronicle and Kentish Advertiser, 23 December 1904.
Shafts, 1892.
Shapira, Michal, 'Indecently Exposed: The Male Body and Vagrancy in Metropolitan London before the Fin de Siecle,' *Gender & History*, Vol.30 No.1 March 2018, pp. 52–69.
Shaw's Academical Dress of Great Britain and Ireland. Vol 2.
Sheffield Daily Telegraph, 4 May 1882; 3 August 1895;13 January 1903; 11 March 1903; 24 June 1909; 29 June 1909; 30 June 1909; 28 May 1914.
Shoreditch Observer, 9 July 1881.
Simon, Matt, 'Fantastically Wrong: The Time People Thought a Comet Would Gas Us All to Death,' Wired, www.wired.com/2015/01/fantastically-wrong-halleys-comet (accessed October 2018).
Sinnett, A J P, *Autobiography of Alfred Percy Sinnett*, London, Theosophical History Centre, 1986.
Smith, Leslie, 'Sex on the Brain,' Group.bmj.com, srh.bmj.com/content/familyplanning/39/2/142.full.pdf (accessed October 2018).
Social Democracy for the 21st Century, 'Karl Marx's Life,' socialdemocracy21stcentury.blogspot.co.uk/2015/04/karl-marxs-life-18501860.html (accessed 23 October 2018).
—'A Realist Alternative to the Modern Left,' 25 April 2015, socialdemocracy21stcentury.blogspot.co.uk/2015/04/karl-marxs-life-18501860.html, (accessed 6 August 2018).
Sohrab, Ahmed, 'Abdu'l-Baha in Britain, 1913,' www.hestories.info/abdul-baha-in-britain-1913.html?page=23 (accessed October 2018).
South London Press, 5 February 1880; 22 May 1880; 6 May 1882; 31 January 1885; 10 December 1887; 20 October 1888; 16 April 1898; 3 September 1898; 5 January 1901.
South Shields Gazette, 18 January 1897.
South Wales Echo, 8th February 1890; 14th February 1890; 17 February 1890; 20th February 1890; 10 March 1890; 16 April 1890; 7 July 1890; 20 November 1891; 5 July 1898.
South West Daily News, 10 April 1899.

BIBLIOGRAPHY

Southampton City Council, 'Alphabetical list of Householders and Residents in Southampton and Neighbourhood'. Local History and Digital City Archive, www.plimsoll.org/images/06%20List%20of%20Householders%20and%20Residents_A_tcm4-173753.pdf (accessed July 2018).
Southern Echo, 21 December 1891;14 June 1892; 30 August 1892; 1 October 1892;19 January 1893; 24 May 1893; 19 February 1897; 24 June 1909; 29 June 1909; 12 July 1909.
Spark, J J, *Confessions of a Phrenologist*, London, Fowler, 1891.
—*Scientific and Intuitional Palmistry*, Roxburghe Press, 1900.
—*The Human Face Divine, and how to read it*, London, Fowler, 1891.
Sphinx, October 1899; 1901.
St James Gazette, 11 October 1886; 24 December 1903; 6 February 1904; 24 June 1904; 27 January 1905; 24 June 1904.
Staffordshire Advertiser, 28 October 1899.
Stage, 1 March 1894; 28 Jun 1895;7 July 1898.
Stamford Mercury, 19 March 1897.
Standard, 30 June 1909, 1 July 1909.
Star (London), 6 September 1888.
Star (Sydney), 14 August 1909.
Starlore, October 1897.
Stead, W T, 'Julia's Bureau: An Attempt to Bridge the Grave,' *Review of Reviews*, vol. XXXIX, May, 1909.
Steiner, Rudolf, *Approaching the Mystery of Golgotha*, Steiner Books, 2006.
—*Rosicrucianism Renewed*, Steiner Books, 2006.
—*Spiritualism, Madame Blavatsky & Theosophy*, Steiner Books, 2002.
—*The Anthroposophic Movement: Eight Lectures Given in Dornach, 10-17 June 1923*, Rudlf Steiner Press, 1993.
—*The Story of my Life*, Anthroposophical Publishing Limited, London, 1928.
Stross, Randall. 'The Birth of Cheap Communication,' *New York Times*, 20 February 2010.
Sun (New York), 'A London Club For Ghosts: Accommodations for Spooks at the New Home of the International Club for Psychical Research,' 24 September 1911.
Sunday Times (Sydney), 12 March 1899.
Sunderland Daily Echo and Shipping Gazette, 16 October 1890.
Supplement to the *Theosophist*, 'Financial Statement 1909,' www.iapsop.com/archive/materials/theosophist/theosophist_v31_supplements.pdf (accessed August 2018)
Surrey Comet, 30 June 1909; 14 July 1909.
Surrey Times and General Advertiser, 26 June 1897.
Sutcliffe, George, *Two Undiscovered Planets: Four Lectures Delivered in Oct.-Nov. 1900, at the Blavatsky Lodge*, Theosophical Society, Bombay, 1901.
Swindon Advertiser and North Wiltshire Chronicle, 27 July 1861.
Sydney Morning Herald, 17 Apr 1897.
Taeger, Hans-Hinrich, 150 German Astrologers, astrographer.tripod.com/150_german_astrologers.htm (accessed 23 October 2018).
Talisman (and Occult Review), 1903.
Telegraph, 7 May 1914.
Tenbury Wells Advertiser, 29 August 1905.

BIBLIOGRAPHY

Tewkesbury Register and Agricultural Gazette, 21 July 1917.
Thames, Barbara, 'A History of Women's Masonry,' skirret.com/papers/a_history_of_womens_masonry.html (accessed August 2018).
Thanet Advertiser, 24 September 1898; 6 January 1900.
The Common Cause, 16 September 1909,
The Grand Lodge of Freemasonry for Men and Women, http://www.grandlodge.org.uk/declaration.html (accessed October 2018).
The Occultist, July 1886, p.1.
Theosophic Messenger, December 1909, November 1928.
Theosophic Voice, November 1908-January 1909, Volume 1, no 3.
Theosophical Chronicle, 1900.
Theosophical Forum, Volume 3,no. 2. June 1897.
Theosophical Journal, July/August 1971.
Theosophical Review, August 1902; December 1904; November 1905.
Theosophical Siftings, Vol2,No. 5, 1892.
Theosophical Society General Register, tsmembers.org (accessed August 2018).
Theosophical Society, *Transactions of the First Annual Congress of the Federation of European Sections of the Theosophical Society Held in Amsterdam June 19th, 20th and 21st, 1904*.
Theosophical Society, *Transactions of the Second Annual Congress of the Federation of European Sections of the Theosophical Society Held in London July 6th, 7th, 8th, 9th and 10th, 1905*.
—*Transactions of the Third Annual Congress of the Federation of European Sections of the Theosophical Society held in Paris July 3rd, 4th, and 5th, 1906*.
Theosophist, December 1887; October 1897; December 1897; January 1906; November 1907; March 1909; July 1909; August 1909; September 1909; October 1909; January 1910; February 1910; March 1910; April 1910; May 1910; April 1911; October 1911; April 1912; October 1926-September 1927.
Theosophist, Supplements, 'General report of the Thirty Second Anniversary and Convention,' 1907.
Theosophist, Supplements, 'General report of the Twentieth Anniversary of the Theosophical Society, 1895.
—October 1904.
—Volume 17, Supplements, 1896.
Theosophy, 'The Case against C. W. Leadbeater,' blavatskytheosophy.com/the-case-against-c-w-leadbeater (accessed 31 July 2018).
—'The Unavoidable Facts about C.W. Leadbeater,' blavatskytheosophy.com/the-unavoidable-facts-about-c-w-leadbeater, (accessed 31 July 2018).
Thomas Cook and Son, *India, Burma and Ceylon: Information for Travellers and Residents*, 1912.
Thompson, John, *Man and his Sexual relations: Embracing the Evils and Remedies of a Misguided Youth, Manhood, and Married Life*, Scarborough: J B Keswick, v.1, 1883.
—*Phrenology and its uses: Embracing the Choice of Pursuits, Good Health, How to Save Money, and How to Make Life a Success*, Scarborough: Published by the Author at Broughton House, South Cliff, Scarborough, 1890.
Thornbury, Walter, 'The Royal Exchange' in *Old and New London*, Volume 1, London, Cassell, Petter & Galpin, 1878.
Tiernan, Sonja, *Eva Gore-Booth: An Image of Such Politics*, Manchester University Press, 2013.

BIBLIOGRAPHY

Tillett Gregory John, 'Charles Webster Leadbeater: A Biographical Study: Notes http://leadbeater.org/tillettcwlnotes.htm (accessed 23 May 2015)
—'The (Other) "1908 Committee" Again,' C W Leadbeater 1854-1934, cwleadbeater.wordpress.com/2017/01/02/the-other-1908-committee-again (accessed October 2018).
—'The 1906 Scandal: (i) Allegations,' C W Leadbeater 1854-1934, cwleadbeater.wordpress.com/2016/05/11/the-1906-scandal-i-allegations (accessed October 2018).
—'The 1906 Scandal: (ii) "The Cypher Letter"' C W Leadbeater 1854-1934, cwleadbeater.wordpress.com/2016/05/12/the-1906-scandal-ii-the-cypher-letter (accessed October 2018).
—'In the Lives, In the Lives...' C W Leadbeater 1854-1934, cwleadbeater. wordpress.com/2016/05/16/in-the-lives-in-the-lives (accessed October 2018).
—*C W Leadbeater 1854-1934*, cwleadbeater.wordpress.com (accessed October 2018).
—*Charles Webster Leadbeater 1854-1934: A Biographical Study*, 2008 Online Edition published at Leadbeater.Org, web.archive.org/web/20180130205353/http://leadbeater.org:80/tillettcwlcontents.htm (accessed October 2018).
—*The Elder Brother*, Routledge Kegan and Paul, 1982.
Times, 20 March 1845; 1 July 1909; 7 May 1914; 7 May 1917.
Times of India, 19 April 1911; 13 April 1911; 20 April 1917.
Tipperary Free Press, 2 June 1838.
Tollenaere, Herman de, *The Politics of Divine Wisdom*, 1996, www.pdfarchive.info/pdf/D/De/De_Tollenaere_Herman_A_O_-_The_Politics_of_Divine_Wisdom.pdf (accessed 23 May 2015).
Torquay Times and South Devon Advertiser, 7 December 1900; 22 January 1892; 29 January 1892; 12 February 1892; 26 February 1892; 22 January 1906.
Tower Hamlets Independent and East End Local Advertiser, 3 July 1909.
Trevithick, Alan, 'The Theosophical Society and its Subaltern Acolytes (1880-1986),' *Marburg Journal of Religion*: Volume 13, No. 1, May 2008.
Truth, 14 October 1904.
Two Worlds, 26 May 1888; 8 May 1889.
Unknown World, 1894.
Urania, 1880.
Vagrancy Act 1824, www.legislation.gov.uk/ukpga/Geo4/5/83/wales/enacted and http://www.legislation.gov.uk/ukpga/1824/83/pdfs/ukpga_18240083_en.pdf (accesssed October 2018).
—https://www.legislation.gov.uk/ukpga/Geo4/5/83/section/4 (accessed July 2018)
Vahan, 1895-1907.
van Manen, Johan (ed.), *Transactions of the First Annual Congress of the Federation of European Sections of the Theosophical Society*, Council of the Federation, Amsterdam, 1906.
Vancouver Daily World, 14 October 1909.
Vegetarian, 12 December 1896; 1897.
—(London), September 25th, 1897: The Women's Reception at "Shafts." ivu.org/congress/1897/report2.html; https://ivu.org/congress/1897/report4.html; https://ivu.org/congress/1897/report5.html (accessed July 2017).

BIBLIOGRAPHY

Vegetarian Society, 'The Vegetarian Society UK and IVU 1930s,' www.ivu.org/history/societies/vsuk-1930s.html (accessed 15 May 2015).
Veritas, *Mrs Besant and the Alcyone Case*, Madras, Goodwin and Co,.1913.
Victoria County History, 'Finchley: Introduction', *A History of the County of Middlesex: Volume 6, Friern Barnet, Finchley, Hornsey With Highgate*. Originally published by Victoria County History, London, 1980, www.british-history.ac.uk/vch/middx/vol6/pp38-55 (accessed 23 May 2015).
Victorian Era Exhibition, Earl's Court, London, S.W. daily programme 1897, archive.org/stream/victorianeraexhi00vict/victorianeraexhi00vict_djvu.txt (accessed 28 July 2017).
Victorian Secrets, 'Rosa Praed,' www.victoriansecrets.co.uk/victorian-fiction-research-guides/rosa-praed (accessed August 2018).
Villeneuve, Crispian, *Rudolf Steiner in Britain: A Documentation of His Ten Visits, 1902-25*, Volume 1, Temple Lodge Publishing, 2009.
Vreede Adrian G, 'An Attack on Bishop Leadbeater,' *The Liberal Catholic*, 34.7, February 1964.
Wadia, K J B, *50 years of Theosophy in Bombay*, Bombay, Theosophical Society, 1931.
Waggoner, E J, 'Ellen G. White Writings, Astrologers in Council, The Present Truth,' *Ellen G. White Writings* 13, 5. February 4, 1897 text.egwwritings.org/publication.php?pubtype=Periodical&bookCode=PTUK&year=1897&month=February&day=4 (accessed 23 May 2015).
Walker, Kirsty Stonall, 'Miss Donald the Housekeeper at Cliffe,' *The Kissed Mouth*, fannycornforth.blogspot.com/2015/12/wednesday-2nd-december-miss-donald.html (accessed 23 October 2018).
Walrond, Geo W, *Practical Guide to the Investigation of Spiritualism, Healing and the Occult Sciences*, 1898.
Ware, S, 'The Home of Theosophy, *Register* (Adelaide), 22 February 1911.
Washington Post, 11 June 1911.
Washington, Peter Washington, *Madame Blavatsky's Baboon: A History of the Mystics, Mediums, and Misfits who Brought Spiritualism to America*, New York, Schocken Books, 1995.
Wellington Journal, 21 November 1908.
Wells Journal, 20 April 1893; 19 April 1906.
Wells, Robert Blackley Dodd, *Faces we Meet and How To Read Character*, Observatory Villa, West Bank, Scarborough, 187?.
—*Vital force: or Evils and remedies of perverted sexuality, shewing how the health, strength, energy and beauty of human beings are wasted, and how preserved*, London, Fowler, 1910.
Wessex Astrology Group, 'Charles EO Carter', web.archive.org/web/20070630090804/http://www.charlescarter.co.uk/ (accessed May 2015).
West Gippsland Gazette, Victoria, 6 September 1904.
West London Observer, 23 January 1892; 21 July 1905.
West Somerset Free Press, 16 May 1891; 27 July 1895.
Western Daily Mercury, 27 November 1889; 7 December 1889.
Western Daily Press, 18 April 1903; 28 May 1914; 24 August 1914.
Western Gazette, 2 July 1909.
Western Morning News, 16 May 1874; 18 November 1891;19 November 1891, 21 November 1891.
Western Times, 23 November 1889; 20 May 1891.

BIBLIOGRAPHY

Weston-Super-Mare Gazette and General Advertiser, 11 June 1892.
Whitby Gazette, 24 February 1899; 21 July 1905.
White, A, 'Mrs. Annie Besant vs G. Narayaniah on 29 October, 1913,' Indiankanoon.org, indiankanoon.org/doc/1214788 (accessed 3 August 2018).
White, Jessica, 'Stargazing with Rosa Praed,' *Sydney Review of Books*, sydneyreviewofbooks.com/stargazing-with-rosa-praed (accessed October 2018).
Whiting, Lilian, *The Lure of London*, Boston, Little Brown and Company, 1914.
Whye, John van, 'The History of Phrenology on the Web,' www.historyofphrenology.org.uk/hatfield.html (accessed 6 August 2018)
Wilcox, J H C, *Early History of Hermes Lodge* (unpublished).
Wilde, George, *Antares Almanac for 1913*, Halifax, Rexo Publishing Company, 1912.
Williams, C V, *Jiddu Krishnamurti: World Philosopher (1895-1986): His Life and Thoughts*, Motilal Banarsidass Publ., 2004.
Wiltshire and Swindon Archives, calmview.wiltshire.gov.uk/CalmView/Record.aspx?src=CalmView.Catalog&id=1029%2f1&pos=1(accessed July 2018).
Wiltshire Independent, 17 May 1838; 30 October 1845; 6 May 1847.
Woman and her Sphere, 'WALKS/Suffrage Stories: Suffragettes and Tea Rooms: The Eustace Miles Restaurant—and the Tea Cup Inn,' womanandhersphere.com/2012/09/07/suffrage-stories-suffragettes-and-tea-rooms-the-eustace-miles-restaurant-and-the-tea-cup-inn (accessed October 2018).
Women's Vegetarian Union, First (Third-Sixth) Annual Report, etc. London, 1896.
Wood, Ernest Egerton, *Is This Theosophy?* London, Rider, 1936.
Worthing Gazette, 17 February 1897.
Wright's Directory of Nottingham, 1898-99.
York Herald, 17 April 1899.
Yorkshire Evening Post, 24 July 1893; 4 July 1898; 28 December 1898; 7 April 1899.
Yorkshire Post and Leeds Intelligencer, 21 August 1914.
Young Chronicle, 4 September 1909.
Young, Sue. 'Peter Davidson,' Sue Young Histories, sueyounghistories.com/archives/2009/04/28/peter-davidson-1837-1915 (accessed July 2018).
—'Thomas Henry Burgoyne 1855–1894,' Sue Young Histories, sueyounghistories.com/archives/2009/06/13/thomas-henry-burgoyne-1855-1894 (accessed July 2018).
Zalinski, Countess, *Noted Prophecies Concerning the Great War*, Chicago, Yogi Publishing, 1917.
Zedekiel (A J Pearce), *Star Lore and Future Events*, January 1897.
Zeylmans, Emanuel, *Willem Zeylmans Van Emmichoven: An Inspiration for Anthroposophy, a Biography*, Temple Lodge Publishing, 2002.

INDEX

Adams, Evangeline, 104n
Alger, James, 105
Allan, Caroline (snr) *see* Beresford, Caroline
Allan, Sarah, 69, 78,
Allan, William (snr), 3–7, 77
almanac sales, 13
Ames, Eleanor Maria Easterbrook, 123
Ames, Julia, 180
Arundale, Francesca, 155–158, 160, 236
Arundale, George, 155n, 158, 160, 167, 184n, 209–12
Astrologers' Magazine, 56–64, 67, 72–78, 82–83, 100–1,161n
Astrology for All, 118, 201
Astrology Without Prediction, 240
Astrology
  Age of Aquarius, 193
  Birth data/birth chart
    Blavatsky, H P B, 31; Cross, Robert, 60; Judge, W Q, 31; Krishnamurti, 188; Leo, Alan, 15; Leo, Bessie, 24; 67, 68; Thomas, John, 27, 42
  dark moon, 42
  directions, 82, 125
  Free horoscopes, 59–60, 67
  Groups
    Association for Modern Astronomy and Astrology, 138; Astrological, Cerebral and Mesmeric Society, 79; Astro–Meteorological Society, 80; Astrological Institute, 202, 218–219, 244–246; Astrological Lodge, 236, 243–246; Astrological Society, 79–88, 102, 106, 124–126, 164, 202, 217; Astrological Society of London 106; British Association for the Advancement of Astral Science,106; Hull Astrology Society, 82; London Astrological Society, 79; Mercurii, 79; Society for Astrological Research, 125; Society for Astrological Students, 126; Uranian Society, 126

Halley's comet, 193
heliocentric, 123
hypothetical planets, 191n
Indian: 59, 195, 208
  Astronomical Conference, Kalady, 208; Brihat Samhita of Varaha Mihira, 188; Chitnis, J T, 188; Nadigranthams, 121
  pre-natal epoch, 115n; 117n; 161
  Publications
    Astrologer, Astrology for All, 118, 201; *Astrologers' Magazine*, 56–64, 67, 72–8, 82, 83, 100, 101, 161n, 188; *Astrological Magazine*, 208; Attractor, 56n; *British Journal of Astrology*, 115, 126; *Destiny*, 115; *Fate and Fortune*, 56, 60, 108; *Future*, 63; *Old Moore's Monthly Messenger*, 115; *Primary Directions Made Easy*, 125n; *Sphinx*, 104; *Urania*, 138
  Sun sign astrology, 122–124, 202
Astrological Institute, 202, 218, 219, 244–246
Astrological Lodge, 236, 243–6
Astrological Society, 79–102, 106, 124–126, 164, 202, 217
Ayton, William Alexander, 34

Baddeley, Charles, 13–4
Bailey, E H, 115– 126, 161n
Barley Annie, 64, 198, 206
Barley, Alfred, 77n, 158, 160
Barnard Mr (KC), 171– 172, 177
Bayford, (KC), 171, 175
Becker, Wilhem (Louis), 173–175
Bellamy, George Claxson, 9
Beresford, Caroline, 3–7, 14
Besant, Annie, 39–40, 46, 65–6, 95, 135–39, 142–151, 154–162, 168–171, 178–195, 209–216, 220, 229, 234, 246
Besant Concord, 158
Bibbings, G W, 107n

INDEX

Bigham, Sir John, 171n, 173–177
Birch, A V, 84
Birth control, 46
Bishop-Culpeper, William Alleyne, 84, 86, 87, 107
Blavatsky, Helena Petrovna, 31, 36–40, 48, 66, 74, 85, 110n, 122n, 123, 136, 151n, 167, 184n, 185
Blessington, Countess *see* Gardiner, Marguerite
Boer War, 103
Bolton, H Carrington, 121
Bradlaugh, Charles, 39n, 46, 156
Bradshaw, James, 106
Bright, Charles, 106
Bright, Esther, 156–158, 189, 212
Bright, Ursula, 151n, 156–158, 162
Brooks, Ferdinand T, 194
Brother Twelve *see* Wilson, Edward Arthur
Broughton, Luke, 104n
Broughton House, 50
Brown, Mr F, 125
Bruce the Great American Astrologer *see* Harding, Henry
Bruce, Mrs F J, 93
Bryce, Joan Annan, 216
Bulwer-Lytton, Edward, 80, 125n, 211n
Butler, W E, 84n
Burch, Ann or Murray *see* Lake, Murray
Burch, Samuel, 24, 26
Burgoyne, Thomas *see* Dalton, Thomas
Burrows, Herbert, 40, 149
Butler, Hiram Erastus, 122–123

Carter, Charles, 64, 235, 243, 246
Casael, Edwin, 59, 81
Casting the Horoscope, 201
Castletown, Lady Clare, 177
Celibacy, 47–54, 69, 71, 76
Chariot, King Theebaw of Burma, 99
Charubel *see* Thomas, John
Cheiro *see* Warner, William, John
Chivers Mrs Cedric, 206
Christie-Murray, David, 125
Cobb, Rev. Dr. William Frederick, 160, 161, 162n

Coleman, George, 89, 89n
Collins, Mabel, 41
Conan Doyle, Arthur, 75, 224n
Cooper-Oakley, Isabelle 18n, 157, 184
Cooper-Oakley, A J 184n
Coryn, Herbert, 40, 75
Coulson, William, 106
Crawford, Lady Valancy *see* Skimp, Daisy
Cross, 60, 81–84, 102, 107, 126
Crowley, Aleister, 4n, 184n, 220
Crump, Basil, 40n

Daath, Heinrich, 81
D'Alton, Thomas *see* Dalton, Thomas
Dalton, Thomas, 28–31
Davenport, G H W, 77
Davidson, Peter, 28, 30
de Kelor, W, 216–217
Dennis, Helen, 141, 149
Dennis, Robin, 141–144
Deraismes, Maria, 155–156
Despard, Charlotte, 94–95
Dexter, Sarah, 89, 159
Dodson, Joseph, 107–109

Ebenezer Roberts and Sons, 7, 99–100
Ellerbeck, Alfred, 159
Elliot, Godfrey Turnbull, 125
Esoteric Astrology, 201
Essex Browne, Miss, 84, 86
Everybody's Astrology, 123

Farr, Florence, 141
Faulding, Alfred, 157–160, 162,
Faulding, Florence, 158, 162
Faust Institute of Solar Biology, 121
Foulsham, William, 107
Fowler, Lorenzo Niles, 44, 50n
Fowler, Charlotte, 44
Fowler, Jessie, 44
Fowler, Lydia, 44, 46
Fowler, Orson Squire, 44
Free horoscopes, 60, 67

INDEX

Gardiner, Marguerite, 80
Garnett, Richard, 81
Garrett, Edmund, 74
Ginkel, H J van, 138
Gokuldas, Seth Dharamsey Morarjee, 208
Graham, George, 79
Great emigration, 19
Green, Henry Selby, 15, 28, 33, 61, 66, 71n, 83–87, 93, 104, 122–125, 240, 242
Gritton, Stanley, 235

Harding, Henry, 105
Hamon. Count Louis *see* Warner, William John
Hampstead Lodge 88, 133, 134
Harman, Henry, 128–129, 175
Harman, Maria, 129–130
Hart, Ethel, 241
Hayward, Nancy, 224–226
Hatfield, Charles, 59
Hatfield, William, 45
Hartwell, John, 113–114
Hermes Lodge, 158, 160, 161, 236n, 237, 246
Helios see Martin Ringrose
Herald of the Star, 212
Higgs, Florence, 117, 124, 164, 217, 245
Higgs, Maude Ruth, 159
Higgs, Nellie, 63n
Hills, Arnold, 92
Hoare, Robert, 125
Hodgson-Smith, (Walter) Basil, 151n, 184n
Hoffman Maud, 235
Holmes, Oliver Wendell, 177
Hook, Hubert van, 182, 187
Hook, Anna van, 168, 187
Hook, Hubert van, 168, 180
Hook, Weller van, 149, 168
House of Commons questions, 217
H. S. G. see Green, Henry Selby
Huddleston Gardens, 185
Hume, Allan Octavian, 35n
Humphreys, Travers, 237–238
hydropathy, 50

International Club for Psychical Research 213–221
Irwin, Francis George, 33n
'Isis Very Much Unveiled—The Great Mahatma Hoax,' 74
Iyer, N Chidambaram, 59, 188
Ivy Leaf Society, 96
Iyer, Subramania, 194

Jinarajadasa, Curuppumullage, 141, 151n, 165–167, 184n
Jones, Georgina, 107
Judaism 18–25, 49, 54, 65, 76–77, 152
Bessie adopts Judaism, 176
Judge, William Quan, 31–2, 40, 48, 74, 85
Judge affair, 74n

Keightley, Archibald, 40n
Keightley, Bertram, 139, 146
Keiro *see* Stephenson, Charles and Martha
Kerr, Gertrude, 184
Keswick, Elizabeth, 49
Keswick. John Barton, 49–50, 54
Key to Your Own Nativity, 229
King, Robert, 84– 87, 192, 107, 117, 125, 159, 180, 214
Kingsford, Anna, 35, 94, 95
Kinsgford, Eadith Bonus, 9n
Kirk, Eleanor see Ames, Eleanor Maria Easterbrook
Kollerstrom Oscar, 184n
Knowles George, 214
Knowlton, Charles, 46

Lacey, Frederick William, 8–14, 33, 40, 41, 55, 56, 59–64, 68, 79, 82–84, 88, 104, 117, 154, 158–160, 162n, 188
Lakshman, 194
Lake, Ann see Lake, Murray
Lake, Murray, 17, 21–26, 48
Lake, Murray, marriage, 24
Lauder, Evelyn, 157, 158
Lauder, William, 157, 158
Laws of Population, 46
Leadbeater, C W, 89n, 134–138, 142–151, 158, 162, 165–170, 180–195, 209, 220, 246
Lives 170, 181–182, 189

INDEX

Leo, Alan
  birth chart, 14–15
  books 118, 122, 123, 201, 229
  business, 100, 111–124, 198,
  celibacy, 69
  clients, 198–199
  legal issues, 212, 228–231, 237–240
  name, 14–15
  plagiarism, 122
  predictions, 100, 101, 231, 224
  Sarah Allan, 69
  shilling manuals, 201
  teaching, 117, 204
  test horoscopes, 114, 121
  vegetarianism, 93
  visits astrologers, 61–2, 82
Leo, Bessie
  birth chart, 67–68
  celibacy, 53–54, 71, 76
  family, 22–25
  will case 171–178
  writing, 53, 74
Leo, Alan and Bessie
  Cannes 224–7
  India 183–195, 206–212
  views of Besant, 134
  psychic experiences, 71, 73
Leo, see Green, Henry Selby
Levy, Amelia, 25, 54, 70, 75, 128, 130, 152, 171, 175
Levy, Harris, 25s, 75, 70, 154
Lewton, Annie, 158
Liberal Catholic Church, 84n, 161n
Liebknecht, Wilhelm, 46
Light of Egypt, 31n
Lives, The, 137, 170, 181–182, 189, 209, 212, 226
Lizards on Mars, 180n
Lock, G H, 84
Lund, David, 80, 104, 106
Lutyens, Emily, 211– 212
Lutyens, Mary, 170, 211n

MacBean, Reginald, 184
Mahatma Letters 235n
Maitland, Edward, 95
Major, John, 113

Malcolm, Lady, 85
Mallett, Ethel, 151n, 158
Man: Whence, How and Whither, 137
Manen, Johann van, 168
Markson, Rachel, 128
Martin, Georges, 155
Martin, Maria, 155–157
Marx, Karl, 46
Masonry
  Co-masonry, 155
  Besant Concord, 158
  Besant-Leadbeater ritual 158
  Free Thinkers, 155
  Hermes Lodge, 158, 160, 161, 236n, 237, 246
  Human Duty Lodge, 158, 162
  Lauderdale ritual see Dharma ritual, 158
  Le Droit Humain, 155, 157
  Les Libres Penseurs see Free Thinkers
  Druids, 154
  Freemasonry 34, 51, 152–162, 188
  Lodges
    Athene Lodge, 92n; Bon Accord Mark Masonry Lodge, 40n; Citadel Lodge, 154; Cobb's Craft Council, 162; Emulation Lodge, 162n; Golden Rule Lodge, 158, 162n; Grand Lodge, 155; Grand Lodge of England of the Honourable Order of Antient Masonry, 162n; Grande Loge des Philadelphes, 156; Hengist Masonic Lodge, 67n, 154; Lodges of Adoption, 155; Lodge of Unity, 162n; Lodge Stability, 162n; St Mark's Lodge, 154; United Grand Lodge of England, 162n
  Royal Arch, 154
Massey, Charles Carlton, 11, 11n, 34, 35n
Massingberd, Emily, 91n
Mathers, Samuel Liddell MacGregor, 39, 67n
McLean Hugh, 228–230
McNaughton, Duncan, 247

INDEX

Mead, George Robert Stowe, 37, 41, 89n, 144, 145, 151, 157
Metrovich, Agardi, 31
Minnear, Matilda *see* Robbins, May
Mitchell, Charles, 246
'Maiden Tribute of Modern Babylon,' 36n
Modern Astrology, 64, 84, 85, 100–102, 117–120, 126, 134, 158n, 173–175, 188, 191, 198, 200, 224, 226, 231, 239, 246, 247
Modern Astrology, Dutch version, 138
Moore Charles, 112, 231
Morrison, Richard James, 62–63, 79, 80, 82, 106

Narayaniah, 168, 170 , 180, 188, 193–194, 220
Naylor, Richard Harold, 247
Nelson–Turner, J, 125
Nicholls, Inspector, 237
Nicholls, P, 77
Nityanda, 168 , 187, 193, 209, 194–195, 209, 210, 211n, 220

Occultist's Defence League, 75n, 107, 108, 227
Occult
  Societies
    British and Foreign Society of Occultists, 33; Brotherhood of Luxor, 32, 39; Celestial Brotherhood, 34, 59; Golden Dawn, Hermetic Order of, 34n, 37n, 39; Hermetic Brotherhood of Luxor, 30, 37, 39, 122n; Hermetic Society in Dublin, 37n
  Publications
    Esoteric, 122; *Occultist*, 24, 32, 28; *Occult Review*, 125n, 179; *Psychic Mirror*, 42; *Psychology of Botany*, 42 *Occult Magazine*, 28 *Seer and Celestial Reformer*, 28, 33
Occult Publishing Company, 107
Olcott, Henry Steel, 31–32, 40, 48, 74, 144–147, 168, 185, 186
Old, Bernard, 37, 159, 176
Old, Walter, 11–14, 37, 40, 56, 60, 74, 81– 85, 101–108, 115n, 122–125, 138,

161n, 164, 188, 216, 229
Order of the Golden Age, 91
Oxley, Thomas, 79

Palmer, John, 79
Pearce, A J, 11, 13, 62–63, 81, 125
Penny, R H, 9, 11, 81, 104, 105
Perhouse, Henry (Harry) 13, 117
Perks, Thomas Probert, 107
Petit, Douglas, 142–143
Phillips, Amelia see Levy, Amelia
Phillips, Henry, 22–25
Phillips, Joseph, 22–23
Phillips, Michael, 16– 26, 48–49, 54, 68, 71–77, 128–130, 151, 171–176
Phrenology, 43–54
  American Phrenological Journal and Miscellany, 44
  cranial anthropometry, 44
  British Phrenological Association, 44; Fowler Institute, 44, 48, 89n
Phillips, Solomon, 22–25
Phillips, Sydney, 154
Pin, 13, 83, 86
Pinchin, William, 89
Powell, Arthur, 184
Powell, Hilda, 184
Powley, Philip, 12, 55
Praed Rosa, 224–227
Prakasha Shri, 210–211
Prince, John Thomas, 30–31
psedonyms, 14, 33, 63
Psychism/spiritualism
  Borderland, 179
  Groups
    Delphic Club, 217, 244; International Club for Psychic Research, 180, 214–217; Julia's Bureau, 84n, 179, 180; London Spiritualist Alliance, 214; Society for Psychical Research, 2n, 179; Spiritualist Alliance, 93
  International Psychic Gazette, 216

Quest Society, 27n

Rajagopalacharya Desikacharya, 220, 221
Rao B Suryanarain, 208

INDEX

Raphael's Ephemeris, 60n
Raphael's Guide to Astrology, 12
reincarnation, 35, 188, 221
Richardson, Robert Francke, 1–2
Ringrose, Martin, 81, 87
Robbins, May, 199, 224, 246
Roberts, Ebenezer, 59
Roberts, Janet, 175
Roberts, Leonard Ebenezer, 100
Roberts, Mary, 130
Robinson, Wynter ,235
Robson, Vivian, 246
Ross, Anna see Hartwell, John
Royal Exchange, 19–20
Ruspoli Don Fabrizio, 185
Russell, George W, 37

Sepharial *see* Old, Walter
Shafts, 91
Sharpe, (S) Maude, 158, 237
Shaw, George Bernard, 92n, 214
Shirley, Ralph, 11, 179, 201
Shoesmith, Mary, 130, 173
Shurmer, Margaret, 91
Shutes, Elizabeth Weeds, 159
Sibthorp, Margaret, 91n, 92n
Sievers, Marie, 148
Shearman, Montague, 171–177
Sidley, John William, 88, 89n, 93, 97, 138, 160, 162
Sinnett, Alfred Percy, 35, 36, 42n,134–136, 180; 224n; 229, 235n, 236–237
Skimp, Daisy, 110n
Smith, Robert Cross, 13, 79
Society of Divine Wisdom, 235n
Society of Science, Letters and Art, 51
Spark, Annie, 50, 73
Spark, John Joseph, 50–54, 66, 70–75, 154
Spark, Joseph, 50, 73
Spiritualism see psychism
Stanley, Wilfred E see Bailey, E H
Stead, W T, 2n, 36, 39, 84n, 107n, 179–180, 214–217
Steiner, Rudolph, 139, 147–149, 171, 220
Stephenson, Charles and Martha, 109
Stratchey, Lieutenant Colonel John, 210
Stratton, Harold, 120

Sutcliffe George, 191, 208, 210
Thierens, Adolph (A E), 138
Theobald, William, 94
Theon, Max, 30
Theosophical Society, 74, 133–151
Lodges
Anthroposophical Society, 220; Birmingham Lodge, 133, 133n; Blavatsky Lodge, 92n, 133; Bournemouth Lodge, 61n, 66, 68, 69; British Section, 144; Brixton Lodge, 74; Chiswick Lodge, 133; Croydon Lodge, 133; Esoteric School for Germany and Austria, 148; Esoteric Section, 39, 146, 187; European Section of the Theosophical Society, 85; German Section, 148, 220; Hamburg Lodge, 133; Hampstead Lodge, 88, 133–134; Harrogate Lodge, 151n; London Lodge of the Theosophical Society, 94, 136; Lotus Lodge, 133; Middlesex Lodge, 236; North London Lodge, 133; Philalethian Lodge, 40, 41; Surbiton Lodge, 131; West London Lodge, 133 Ivy Leaf Society, 96
Groups
Order of the Rising Sun, 209, 210; Order of the Servants of the Star, 210; Order of the Star in the East, 210, 212, 220, 246; Order of the Star, 210; Purple Shawl Group, 209; Yellow Shawl Group, 209
Conferences
Annual convention of the British Section 1907, 149; Annual convention 1909, 190; British Convention of the Theosophical Society 1909, 178; British Section Convention1903, 139; European Congress 1903, 138; European Congress 1905, 138–139; European Congress 1906, 147; European Congress 1907, 147; International Congress 1909, 171; International Congress, Theosophical Society, 1909, 171 Theosophical Congress in Munich in 1907, 148

INDEX

Texts
 At the Feet of the Master, 209; *Herald of the Star*, 212; *Occult Chemistry*, 136; *Secret Doctrine*, 35, 36, 39, 234, 236; *Isis Unveiled*, 36, *Rents in the Veil of Time*, 182
Thomas, John, 27–34, 41–42, 60, 144
Thompson, Catherine, 104
Thompson, Hannah, 49, 51, 71
Thompson, John, 46–51, 71
Thompson, Martha Ann, 49
Tingley, Katherine, 40n, 85n
Trent, A G see Garnett, Richard
Turner, Nelson, 125

Vagrancy Act 62, 75n, 104–110, 114, 227–231, 235n, 228, 248
  Astrologers convicted
    Alger, James, 105; Davies, Alexander, 75n; Bradshaw, James, 106; Bright, Charles, 106; Bruce the Great American Astrologer see Harding, Henry; Coulson, William, 106; Harding, Henry, 105; Hartwell, John, 113–114; Major, John, 113; Moore, Charles, 112, 231; Penny, R H, 9, 11, 81, 104, 105; Stephenson, Charles and Martha, 109; Wilson, Frederick, 62, 114
  British Association for the Advancement of Astral Science &c., 106
  House of Commons questions, 217
  repeal, 248
  Occultist's Defence League, 75n, 107, 108, 227
  police action, 13
Varley, John, 79, 80, 136, 137
Veale Helen, 234, 235,
Vegetarianism, 48–49, 81–99
  Societies
    Anti-Vivisection Society, 214; Bread and Food Reform League, 92n; London Food Reform Society, 94; London Vegetarian Society, 92n, 95, 96; National Food Reform Society, 94; Northern Heights Vegetarian Society, 93, 94; Vegetarian Athletic and Cycling Club, 92, 96n; Vegetarian Society, 94, 96; Women's Vegetarian Union, 91, 96
Veigelé, Adrienne, 96
Veigelé, Alexandrine, 96
Vickery Thomas, 229, 230

Wachtmeister, Constance, 40
Wadia, B P, 170
Waite, A E, 36, 37n
Walker, Thomas Maylam, 22
Wallace, William, 105
Ward, Edith, 92n, 144, 145, 158
Warner, William John, 110, 247
Warwick, Daisy, 213, 221
Watson, Annie, 86, 159
Wedgwood, James Ingall, 151n, 184n
Welch, Robert, 42
Wells, Robert Blackley, 50, 53
Wemyss, Maurice see McNaughton, Duncan
West Ham United, 92n
Westcott, William Wynn, 39
Wheeler, Elsie, 61n
Whitting, Charles, 66–67, 154
Whyte, George, 151n, 158
Wilcox, Ella Wheeler, 208
Wild, Ernest, 239
Wilde, Constance, 37
Wilde, George, 61–63, 81, 107, 114
Will 128 129 131
Wilson, Elizabeth, 69–70
Wilson, Edward Arthur, 158n
Wilson, Frederick, 62, 114
Wilson, Thomas, 61
Windsor, Emma, 88–89
Wood, Ernest, 168–170, 181, 184
Wood, Esther, 125
Woodman, Robert, 39
World Teacher, 164–171, 182, 193, 209–210
Wyld, George, 35n

Yarker, John, 33n, 51
Yelverton, Roger Dawson, 108

Zadkiel's Almanac, 63, 81

www.ingramcontent.com/pod-product-compliance
Lightning Source LLC
Chambersburg PA
CBHW070128080526
44586CB00015B/1606